UNEASY ALLIES

Uneasy Allies

*British–German Relations and
European Integration since 1945*

Edited by

KLAUS LARRES

with
ELIZABETH MEEHAN

OXFORD
UNIVERSITY PRESS

OXFORD

UNIVERSITY PRESS

Great Clarendon Street, Oxford OX2 6DP

Oxford University Press is a department of the University of Oxford.
It furthers the University's objective of excellence in research, scholarship,
and education by publishing worldwide in

Oxford New York

Athens Auckland Bangkok Bogotá Buenos Aires Calcutta
Cape Town Chennai Dar es Salaam Delhi Florence Hong Kong Istanbul
Karachi Kuala Lumpur Madrid Melbourne Mexico City Mumbai
Nairobi Paris São Paulo Singapore Taipei Tokyo Toronto Warsaw

and associated companies in Berlin Ibadan

Oxford is a registered trade mark of Oxford University Press
in the UK and certain other countries

Published in the United States
by Oxford University Press Inc., New York

British Library Cataloguing in Publication Data

Data available

Library of Congress Cataloging in Publication Data

Uneasy allies : British-German relations and European integration since 1945 / edited by
Klaus Larres with the help of Elizabeth Meehan.
Includes bibliographical references and index.
1. Germany—Relations—Great Britain. 2. Great Britain—Relations—Germany. 3.
European Union. 4. European Economic Community—Germany. 5. European Economic
Community—Great Britain. 6. Europe—Economic integration. I. Larres, Klaus. II.
Meehan, Elizabeth M.
DD129.G7 U64 2000   337.41043—dc21   99–057192

ISBN 0–19–829383–6

1 3 5 7 9 10 8 6 4 2

Typeset by Graphicraft Limited, Hong Kong
Printed in Great Britain
on acid-free paper by
Biddles Ltd.
Guildford and King's Lynn

In memory of my father
Albert Larres
(1923–1999)

CONTENTS

III. THE POST-COLD WAR RELATIONSHIP: THE ECONOMIC AND SOCIAL DIMENSION SINCE 1990

NOTES ON THE CONTRIBUTORS

IAIN BEGG is Professor of International Economics at South Bank University in London, England. He is joint editor of the *Journal of Common Market Studies* and he acted as an adviser to the House of Lords' European Communities Committee and the Economic and Social Committee. He has published widely on European policy issues including *Paying for Europe*, with N. Grimwade (1998); *Applied Economics and Public Policy*, ed. with S. G. B. Henry (1998); 'Reform of the Structural Funds after 1999', *European Planning Studies* 5 (1997), 677–91; 'Levelling the Playing Field or Changing the Rules of Play? Regulation in the Single Market', *Business Economist* 28 (1997), 14–22.

JIM BULLER is a lecturer in the School of Political Science and International Studies at the University of Birmingham. His research interest focus on British politics in the 1980s and on Britain's relations with the European Union. His publications include *National Statecraft and European Integration: the Conservative Government and the European Union, 1979–97* (forthcoming); *Post-War British Politics in Perspective*, co-authored with D. Marsh *et al.* (1999); 'Civil Service Attitudes towards the European Union', in D. Baker and D. Seawright (eds.), *Britain for and against Europe* (1998), 165–84; and 'Britain as an Awkward Partner: Re-assessing Britain's Relations with the European Union', *Politics* 15/1 (1995), 33–42.

ANNE DEIGHTON is University Lecturer in European International Politics and fellow of Wolfson College, Oxford University. She has published extensively on the cold war, European integration and British foreign policy, including, *The Impossible Peace: Britain, the Division of Germany and the Origins of the cold war, 1945–1947* (1990/1993); *Building Postwar Europe*, ed. (1995); *Western European Union, 1954–1997: Defence, Security, Integration*, ed. (1997); *Widening, Deepening and Acceleration: The European Economic Community, 1958–1963*, ed. with A. S. Milward (1999).

GEOFFREY EDWARDS is Jean Monnet Director of European Studies, Centre of International Studies, University of Cambridge, and Fellow of Pembroke College, Cambridge. His has published widely on European Integration and his recent publications include *The European Commission*, ed. with D. Spence (2nd edn., 1997); *The Politics of European*

Treaty Reform, ed. with A. Pijpers (1997); 'Flexibility and the Treaty of Amsterdam: Europe's New Byzantium', co-authored with E. Philippart (CELS Occasional Paper December 1997).

ROBERT HARMSEN is a lecturer in the Institute of European Studies at the Queen's University of Belfast. He is a co-editor of the *Yearbook of European Studies* (Amsterdam: Rodopi Press). His research interests focus on constitutional and administrative aspects of European integration, with a particular interest in the differing national patterns of institutional adaptation to this process. His publications include 'The Europeanization of National Administrations' *Governance* 12/1 (1999); and 'European Integration and the Adaptation of National Constitutional Orders' *Journal of European Integration* 17/1 (1993). He is currently completing a book on *The Politics of Human Rights in Europe*.

VALUR INGIMUNDARSON teaches modern history at the University of Iceland. He wrote his Ph.D. thesis on 'East Germany, West Germany, and U.S. cold war Strategy, 1950–1954'. Recent publications include ' "Der Chef des Kalten Krieges": C. D. Jackson, psychologische Kriegsführung und die deutsche Frage 1953/54', *Vierteljahrshefte für Zeitgeschichte* (1998); *In the Crossfire: Iceland, the United States, and the cold war* (1996); 'The Eisenhower Administration, the Adenauer Government, and the Political Uses of the East German Uprising in 1953', *Diplomatic History* (1996); 'cold war Misperceptions: The Communist and Western Responses to the East German Refugee Crisis in 1953', *Journal of Contemporary History* (1994).

CHARLIE JEFFERY is Deputy Director of the Institute for German Studies at the University of Birmingham, England. His research interests focus on German Federalism and European Integration. His recent publications include *Recasting German Federalism: the legacies of unification*, ed. (1998); *The Regional Dimension of the European Union*, ed. (1997); *Federalism, Unification and European Integration*, ed. with R. Sturm (1993); *German Federalism Today*, ed. with P. Savigaer (1991).

LOTHAR KETTENACKER is Deputy Director of the German Historical Institute in London and professor of modern history at the University of Frankfurt/Main, Germany. He specializes in the history of the Nazi period and in Anglo-German relations during the Second World War and the post-1945 era. He has published extensively including *Germany since 1945* (1997); *Krieg zur Friedenssicherung. Die Deutschlandplanung der britischen Regierung während des Zweiten Weltkrieges* (1989); *The Race for Modernization: Britain and Germany since the Industrial Revolution*, ed. with A. Birke (1988); *The Fascist Challenge and the Policy of Appeasement*, ed. with W. Mommsen (1983).

EMIL KIRCHNER is Professor of Government and Honorary Jean Monnet Chair at the University of Essex, England. He has published widely on European Integration and German and European security policy. His publications include *Decentralization and Transition in the Visegrad: Poland, Hungary, the Czech Republic and Slovakia*, ed. (1999); *Recasting the European Order: Security Architectures and Economic Co-operation*, with J. Sperling (1997); *The Politics of the Altantic to Urals, New Europe*, with I. Budge, K. Newton *et al.* (1997); *The Future of European Security*, ed. with C. Bluth and J. Sperling (1995); *The Federal Republic of Germany and NATO: 40 years after*, ed. with J. Sperling (1992).

KLAUS LARRES is Reader in Politics at the Queen's University of Belfast. His research interests focus on the cold war, British and American foreign policy, German foreign and domestic policy, Anglo-German and German-American relations. His publications include *Politik der Illusionen: Churchill, Eisenhower und die deutsche Frage, 1945–1955* (1995); *The Federal Republic of Germany since 1949: Politics, Society and Economy before and after Unification*, ed. with P. Panayi (1996); *Deutschland und die USA im 20. Jahrhundert: Geschichte der politischen Beziehungen*, ed. with T. Oppelland (1997); *Germany since Unification: The Domestic and External Consequences*, ed. (1998; 2nd rev. and expanded edn. 2000).

JEREMY LEAMAN is Senior Lecturer in German Studies at Loughborough University (UK) in the Department of European Studies. His research interests focus on the political economy of modern Germany. He is co-editor of *The Journal of European Area Studies* and of *Debatte—Review of Contemporary German Affairs*. He is author of *The Political Economy West Germany* (1988); and co-editor (with A. Hargreaves) of *Racism, Ethnicity and Politics in Contemporary Europe* (1995); and (with D. Eissel and E. Rokicka) *Sustainability: Challenges to the Social Sciences and Local Democracy* (1996). He is currently completing a study of the Bundesbank.

PATRICIA MCCOURT is a Chartered Accountant and a Lecturer in Financial Accounting and Information Technology at the Queen's University of Belfast. Her research interests concentrate on European Accounting, Taxation, and Information Technology in Accounting. Her publications include 'Skills of Newly Qualified Chartered Accountants: A Study of the Training Programme of the Institute of Chartered Accountants in Ireland', *The Irish Accounting Review* 8 (1999); 'A Critical Analysis of Self-Assessed Entry-Level Personal Computer Skills among Newly Qualified Irish Chartered Accountants', *Accounting Education* (1999); 'Taxation and the Choice of Business Medium' (with G. Radcliffe), *Irish*

Journal of Taxation, (March 1996), 32–40; 'Les Relations Fiscalite–Compatibilité in France: A Model for Europe?' (with P. McCourt), *British Tax Review* 5 (1995), 461–83.

ELIZABETH MEEHAN is Professor of Politics at the Queen's University of Belfast. Her research interests cover sex equality, citizenship, European Integration and British-Irish relations in the context of the EU. Her publications include *Citizenship and the European Community* (1993); 'La Cittadinanza Europea delle Donne: Problemi Teoretici e Politici', *Europa-Europe*, VI (1997); 'Member States and the European Union', in R. English and C. Townshend (eds.), *The State: Historical and Political Dimensions* (1998). Currently she is completing a book on *Freedom of Movement: Ireland, Britain and the EU*.

JOHN PINDER teaches at the College of Europe, Bruges. He was Director of the Policy Studies Institute in London, 1964–85. He is Chairman of the Federal Trust and a member of the directorate of the Institut für Europäische Politik in Berlin. He has published widely on European Integration, including *Foundations of Democracy in the European Union: From the Genesis of Parliamentary Democracy to the European Parliament* ed. (1999); *The Building of the European Union* (3rd. edn. 1998); *Altiero Spinelli and the British Federalists: Writings by Beveridge, Robbins and Spinelli, 1937–1943* (1998); *The European Community and Eastern Europe* (1991).

GEORGE RADCLIFFE is a Chartered Accountant and a Barrister at Law. He is a Senior Lecturer in Accountancy in the School of Management of the Queen's University of Belfast. His research focuses on comparative financial reporting and taxation in the European Union. His publications include 'Taxation and the Choice of Business Medium' (with P. McCourt), *Irish Journal of Taxation* (1996), 32–40; 'Les Relations Fiscalite–Compatibilité in France: A Model for Europe?' (with P. McCourt), *British Tax Review* 5 (1995), 461–83; 'The Relationship between Tax Law and Accounting Principles in the United Kingdom and France', *Irish Journal of Taxation* (1993), 1–20; 'Accounting Standards and the Judiciary', *Accounting and Business Research* 20 (1990), 329–36.

NICKOLAS REINHARDT is a Brussels based financial services consultant with Houston Consulting Europe. He is completing a doctorate in the Institute of European Studies at the Queen's University of Belfast. His research interests are concerned with German and United Kingdom membership of the European Union. His doctoral thesis deals with the political debate on EMU in Germany and the United Kingdom. He has written 'A Turning Point in the German EMU Debate: The Baden-Württemberg Regional Elections of March 1996', *German Politics* 6/1

(1997); and 'Monetary Identity and European Integration', in E. Moxon-Browne (ed.), *Who are the Europeans Now?* (2000).

JULIE SMITH is Head of the European Programme, Royal Institute of International Affairs, Teaching Fellow in European Studies, Centre of International Studies, University of Cambridge, and Fellow of Robinson College, Cambridge. She has published extensively on European Integration, including *Europe's Elected Parliament* (1999); *A Sense of Liberty— A Short History of the Liberal International 1947–1997* (1997); *Democracy in the New Europe*, ed. with E. Teague (1999); and *Eminent Europeans*, ed. with M. Bond and W. Wallace (1996).

MICHAEL WOOD is Associate Head of Economics and Senior Lecturer in the Business School at South Bank University in London, England. His research interests are in privatized and regulated industries, British labour markets, and industrial economics, policy, and developments in the UK. Recently he has been involved in a Trans European Policy Studies Association (TEPSA) study of public service regulation in Europe. Among his most recent publications are 'Being a Good European: Britain Leads in Utility Regulation', *New Economy* 5/1 (1998); and 'The Public Service Model of Regulations in the United Kingdom', in Trans European Policy Studies Association, *The Regulations of Public Services in Europe* (1999).

ABBREVIATIONS

AG	Aktiengesellschaften (stock corporations)
ARRC	Allied Rapid Reaction Force
ASB	Accounting Standards Board
ASC	Accounting Standards Committee
BCPIT	British Council for the Promotion of International Trade
BDA	German Employers' Federation
BFH	Bundesfinazhof (Federal Fiscal Court)
BGH	Bundesgerichtshof (Federal Supreme Court)
BRD	Bundesrepublik Deutschland (West Germany and since 1990 united Germany)
CAP	Common Agricultural Policy
CBI	Confederation of British Industry (formerly FBI)
CDU	Christlich Demokratische Union Deutschlands (Christian Democratic Party of Germany)
CEEC	Committee for European Economic Co-operation
CEEP	European Centre for Public Enterprises
CFSP	The EU's Common Foreign and Security Policy
CIS	Commonwealth of Independent States (the loosely organized successor organization of the Soviet Union)
CJTF	Combined Joint Task Forces (e.g. between NATO and WEU)
COCOM	Co-ordinating Committee for East–West Trade Policy
CSCE	Conference on Security and Co-operation in Europe
CSU	Christlich Soziale Union in Bayern (Christian Social Party, only exists in Bavaria)
DDR	Deutsche Demokratische Republik (East Germany)
DGFA	Deutsche Gesellschaft für Auswärtige Politik
DRSC	Deutsches Rechnungslegungs Standard Committee e.V. (German Accounting Standards Committee)
DSR	Deutscher Standardisierungsrat (German Accounting Standards Board)
EC	European Communities (1967–93)
ECB	European Central Bank
ECJ	European Court of Justice
ECS	European Company Statute

ECSC	European Coal and Steel Community
EDC	European Defence Community
EEC	European Economic Community (1958–67)
EFTA	European Free Trade Association
EMI	European Monetary Institute
EMS	European Monetary System
EMU	Economic and Monetary Union
EPC	European Political Co-operation
ERM	Exchange Rate Mechanism
ESDI	European Security and Defence Identity
ETUC	European Trades Union Congress
EU	European Union (since November 1993)
Euro	Common European currency (since Jan. 1999)
FAWEU	Forces Answerable to the WEU
FBI	Federation of British Industry (later CBI)
FDP	Freie Demokratische Partei (Free Democratic Party, Germany's Liberal Party)
FO	Foreign Office
FRG	Federal Republic of Germany
FRRP	Financial Reporting Review Panel
FRS	Financial Reporting Standards
FRUS	Foreign Relations of the United States
GAAP	Generally Accepted Accounting Practice
GDP	Gross Domestic Product
GDR	German Democratic Republic
GNP	Gross National Product
GoB	Grundsätze ordnungsmäßiger Buchführung (principles of regular book-keeping)
IdW	Institut der Wirtschaftsprüfer (Institute of Auditors)
IFOR	Implementation Force
IGC	Intergovernmental Conference
KfA Ltd	Kammer für Außenhandel (East German foreign trade authority)
MLF	Multilateral Force
NATO	North Atlantic Treaty Organization
OECD	Organization for Economic Co-operation and Development
OEEC	Organization for European Economic Co-operation (1948–61), predecessor to the global OECD
OSCE	Organization for Security and Co-operation in Europe
PfP	Partnership for Peace
PHARE	The EU's Economic Regeneration Assistance Programmes for Poland and Hungary

PRO	Public Records Office
RIIA	Royal Institute of International Affairs London (Chatham House)
SACEUR	NATO's Supreme Allied Commander Europe
SDI	Strategic Defense Initiative ('Star Wars')
SEA	Single European Act
SEC	Securities and Exchange Commission
SED	Sozialistische Einheitspartei Deutschlands (the East German Communist Party)
SEM	Single European Market
SFOR	Stabilization Force
SPD	Sozialdemokratische Partei Deutschlands (Social Democratic Party of Germany)
SSAP	Statement of Standard Accounting Practice
TACIS	The EU's Technical Assistance Programmes for the Commonwealth of Independent States
TEPSA	Trans European Policy Studies Association
TUC	Trades Union Congress
UITF	Urgent Issues Task Force
UK	United Kingdom of Great Britain and Northern Ireland
UN	United Nations
UNICE	Union of Industrial and Employers' Confederations of Europe
UNPROFOR	United Nations Peacekeeping Force
US/USA	United States of America
USSR	Union of the Soviet Socialist Republics (the Soviet Union, 1917–91)
WEU	Western European Union

Introduction: Uneasy Allies or Genuine Partners? Britain, Germany, and European Integration

KLAUS LARRES

Throughout the twentieth century British–German relations have been of fundamental importance in shaping the course of European and world history. Often those relations were strained and hostile, no more so than during the Second World War. Having conquered and then governed Germany as one of the four occupation powers between 1945 and 1949, Britain became the FRG's formal ally when West Germany joined NATO in May 1955. However, it was only in the 1970s, when the UK was under great pressure from its increasing economic problems, that London began to view the British–German relationship as a partnership between equals. When Britain became a member of the then European Economic Community (EEC) in 1973, the bilateral British–(West) German relationship gradually intensified. At the same time this relationship began to include an ever greater number of other partners and developed into a truly multinational framework. Although bilateral British–German relations before and after World War II had always been strongly influenced by third parties, with the increasing importance of the European integration factor this tendency intensified. Not least in view of the dramatic redistribution of world power status away from Europe since the end of the Second World War, it made increasingly less sense to focus on bilateral instead of multilateral relations. Moreover, throughout the entire post-1945 era neither London nor Bonn regarded their bilateral relationship as of prime importance; relations with the USA and France appeared to be much more crucial.

Thus, the publication of a book on the strictly bilateral relationship between Britain and Germany may be justified when dealing with the decades prior to 1945 and, perhaps to some degree, even with the 1950s and 1960s. However, when focusing on the years since then such a project no longer seems appropriate. And indeed, during the last few decades international historians and political scientists have recognized that the ongoing rapid development of a complex, increasingly multilateral and interdependent world has made the analysis of bilateral relationships between European states an unsatisfactory option. It may well be true to claim that bilateral relationships will 'continue to be an important part of the complex web which is modern international politics'.[1] However, the multiplicity of internal and external factors of influence which shape the behaviour of contemporary European nations has to be taken into account when considering the nature of the relationships among these highly industrialized and intensively networked countries. This certainly applies to the links between the United Kingdom of Great Britain and Northern Ireland and the Federal Republic of Germany as it developed in the years after the annihilation of Hitler's Reich.[2]

It therefore seems hardly possible to investigate British–German relations since 1945 without acknowledging the crucial influence of European integration on the development of this relationship. In addition great attention must be paid to the decisive role of the United States and France and their 'special relationships' with one or other of the countries under consideration in this book. Furthermore, during the cold war years the perceived threat posed by the Soviet Union and its satellite states had important repercussions on Britain's and Germany's interaction with the outside world. While the role of Russia in international affairs has undergone a dramatic transformation and indeed decline since 1990/1, at the beginning of the twenty-first century the United States and France together with the other EU countries and that diffuse complex of power and influence commonly referred to as 'Brussels' remain of essential importance for Britain's and Germany's external as well as internal policies.

As far as multinational thematic issues are concerned, the consequences of German unification and the end of the cold war, the introduction of the euro, the gradual strengthening of the role of the European Parliament and the real prospect of the eventual realization of a Common European Foreign and Security Policy (CFSP) appear to be of particular importance for British–German relations at the start of the new millenium. The repercussions of the great constitutional changes in

---

[1] C. Hill, 'The United Kingdom and Germany', in B. Heurlin (ed.), *Germany in Europe in the Nineties* (Basingstoke, 1996), 236.

[2] See e.g. the distinction among fourteen possible relationship scenarios in the quadripartite contacts among Britain, Germany, the US, and France, listed in D. C. Watt, *Britain looks to Germany: British Opinion and Policy towards Germany since 1945* (London, 1965), 210–12. For purposes of convenience the UK is often referred to as Britain in this book and it is understood that what came to be called the EU after 1992 with the conclusion of the Maastricht Treaty and the establishment of the Single Market was referred to as European Communities (EC) or European Economic Community (EEC) and Common Market in the decades prior to this date. While Chapter 3 has been dedicated to the relationship between Britain and East Germany (the GDR), all the other chapters refer to either West Germany before October 1990 or united Germany after October 1990.

the UK (above all the devolution of power to the British nations and regions), European monetary union, the increasing harmonization of industrial and financial standards among EU countries as well as the EU's (and NATO's) eastern enlargement and the important role of the inter-governmental conferences and the partially very different industrial and commercial cultures in Britain and Germany as well as the role of the media are other important aspects which will be addressed in this book.

Whilst the strong influence of the United States and France on both Germany and Britain throughout the post-1945 era is reflected in many of the chapters, the volume concentrates above all on highlighting the influence of European integration on the policies of Britain and the FRG towards each other. The scholarly literature has dealt with some of the various bilateral and multilateral relationships referred to above.[3] There are, for example, numerous books (and scholarly articles) dealing with the international history of the cold war[4] and European integration in general.[5] The Anglo-American 'special relationship',[6] German–American[7] as well as Franco-British, Franco-German, and trilateral relations among Britain, France, and Germany have been well covered in

[3] The following literature overview concentrates on studies which cover a large part of the period under consideration. More specialist studies dealing with more minute topics within German–British–European relations or covering a much shorter range of years can be traced by making use of the bibliographies in the listed works and the individual chapters of this book.

[4] See e.g. J. P. D. Dunbabin, *The Cold War: The Great Powers and their Allies* (London, 1994); R. Crockatt, *The Fifty Year War: The United States and the Soviet Union in World Politics, 1941–1991* (London, 1995); W. LaFeber, *America, Russia and the Cold War, 1945–1990*, 8th edn. (New York, 1996); J. L. Gaddis, *We Now Know: Rethinking Cold War History* (Oxford, 1997); G. Lundestad, *East, West, North, South: Major Developments in International Politics, 1945–1996*, 4th edn. (Oslo, 1999); S. J. Ball, *The Cold War: An International History, 1947–91* (London, 1998); M. Trachtenberg, *A Constructed Peace: The Making of the European Settlement, 1945–1963* (Princeton, 1999).

[5] See e.g. J. Pinder, *The Building of the European Union*, 3rd edn. (Oxford, 1998); T. Salmon and W. Nicoll (eds.), *Building European Union: a documentary history and analysis* (Manchester, 1997); P. M. R. Stirk, *A History of European Integration since 1914* (London, 1996); D. W. Urwin, *The Community of Europe: A History of European Integration since 1945*, 2nd edn. (Harlow, 1995); D. Dinan, *Ever Closer Union? An Introduction to the European Community*, 2nd edn. (Basingstoke, 1999); N. Nugent, *The Government and Politics of the European Community*, 4th edn. (Basingstoke, 1999).

[6] See e.g. R. Ovendale, *Anglo-American Relations in the Twentieth Century* (Basingstoke, 1998); C. J. Bartlett, *'The Special Relationship': A Political History of Anglo-American Relations since 1945* (Harlow, 1992); D. Dimbleby and D. Reynolds, *An Ocean Apart: The Relationship between Britain and America in the 20th Century* (London, 1988); W. R. Louis and H. Bull (eds.), *The Special Relationship: Anglo-American Relations since 1945* (Oxford, 1986).

[7] See e.g. K. Larres and T. Oppelland (eds.), *Deutschland und die USA im 20. Jahrhundert: Geschichte der politischen Beziehungen* (Darmstadt, 1997); D. E. Barclay and E. Glaser-Schmidt (eds.), *Transatlantic Images and Perceptions: Germany and America since 1776* (Cambridge, 1997); F. Ninkovich, *Germany and the United States: The Transformation of the German Question since 1945*, updated edn. (New York, 1995); W. R. Smyser, *Germany and America: New Identities, Fateful Rift?* (Boulder, 1994); G. F. Treverton, *America, Germany, and the future of Europe* (Princeton, 1992); W. Hanrieder, *Germany, America, Europe: Forty Years of German Foreign Policy* (New Haven, 1989) [2nd rev. and exp. German edn., Paderborn, 1995].

the literature.[8] A considerable number of books on various aspects of British–European and German–European relations are also available.[9] Several books on the manifold dimensions of the traditional bilateral British–German relationship exist.[10] However, an interdisciplinary volume

[8] See e.g. P. M. H. Bell, *France and Britain, 1940–1994: The Long Separation* (London, 1997); D. Josseline, *Money Politics in the New Europe: Britain, France and the Single Financial Market* (Basingstoke, 1997); F. de La Serre, J. Leruez and H. Wallace (eds.), *French and British Foreign Policies in Transition: The Challenge of Adjustment* (New York, 1990); D. Webber (ed.), *The Franco-German Relationship in the European Union* (London, 1999); C. Mazzucelli, *France and Germany at Maastricht: Politics and Negotiations to Create the European Union* (New York, 1997); G. Ziebura, *Die deutsch-französischen Beziehungen 1945–1995. Mythen und Realitäten* (Stuttgart, 1997); P. McCarthy (ed.), *France-Germany, 1983–93: The Struggle to Cooperate* (New York, 1993); H. Simonian, *The Privileged Partnership: Franco-German Relations in the European Community* (Oxford, 1985); P. H. Gordon, *France, Germany, and the Western Alliance* (Boulder, Colo., 1995); Y. Meny and A. Knapp, *Government and Politics in Western Europe: Britain, France, Italy, Germany*, 3rd edn. (Oxford, 1998); B. Heuser, *Nuclear mentalities? strategies and belief in Britain, France, and the FRG* (New York, 1998); A. C. Lamborn, *The Price of Power: Risk and Foreign Policies in Britain, France, and Germany* (London, 1991); R. Morgan and C. Bray (eds.), *Partners and Rivals in Western Europe: Britain, France, and Germany* (London, 1986).

[9] See e.g. S. George, *An Awkward Partner: Britain in the European Community*, 3rd edn. (Oxford, 1998); H. Young, *This Blessed Plot: Britain and Europe from Churchill to Blair* (London, 1998); D. Baker and D. Seawright (eds.), *Britain for and against Europe: British Politics and the Question of European Integration* (Oxford, 1998); P. Stephens, *Politics and the Pound: The Tories, the Economy and Europe* (London, 1996); J. W. Young, *Britain and European Unity, 1945–92* (Basingstoke, 1993); S. Bulmer, S. George, and A. Scott (eds.), *The United Kingdom and EC Membership Evaluated* (London, 1992); S. George, *Britain and European Integration since 1945* (Oxford, 1991); G. Schmidt (ed.), *Grossbritannien und Europa—Grossbritannien in Europa: Sicherheitsbelange und Wirtschaftsfragen in der britischen Europapolitik nach dem Zweiten Weltkrieg* (Bochum, 1989); A. Volle, *Grossbritannien und der Europäische Einigungsprozess* (Bonn, 1989); see also the still useful book by M. Camps, *Britain and the European Community, 1955–63* (Princeton, 1964); S. Wood, *Germany, Europe and the Persistence of Nations: Transformation, interests and identity, 1989–1996* (Aldershot, 1998); B. Heurlin (ed.), *Germany in Europe in the Nineties* (Basingstoke, 1996); V. Schubert (ed.), *Deutschland in Europa: Wiedervereinigung und Integration* (St. Ottilien, 1996); A. Baring (ed.), *Germany's New Position in Europe: Problems and Perspectives* (Oxford, 1994); P. H. Merkl, *German Unification in the European Context* (University Park, 1993); W. Weidenfeld, *Was ändert die Einheit? Deutschlands Standort in Europa* (Gütersloh, 1993); S. Bulmer and W. Paterson (eds.), *The Federal Republic of Germany and the European Community* (London, 1987).

[10] See e.g. Watt, *Britain looks to Germany*; K. Kaiser and R. Morgan (eds.), *Britain and West Germany: Changing Societies and the Future of Foreign Policy* (London, 1971); A. Volle, *Deutsch-Britische Beziehungen. Eine Untersuchung des bilateralen Verhältnisses* [. . .] (Bonn, 1976); K. Kaiser and J. Roper (eds.), *British–German Defence Co-operation: Partners within the Alliance* (London, 1988); K. Rohe, G. Schmidt, and H. Pogge von Strandmann (eds.), *Deutschland, Großbritannien, Europa. Politische Traditionen, Partnerschaft und Rivalität* (Bochum, 1992); S. Woolcock, M. Hodges, and K. Schreiber, *Britain, Germany and 1992: The Limits of Deregulation* (London, 1990); C. Bluth, *Britain, Germany and Western Nuclear Strategy* (Oxford, 1995); G. Schmidt (ed.), *Zwischen Bündnissicherung und Priviligierter Partnerschaft: die deutsch-britischen Beziehungen und die Vereinigten Staaten von Amerika, 1955–1963* (Bochum, 1955); D. Ebster-Grosz and D. Pugh, *Anglo-German Business Collaboration: Pitfalls and Potentials* (Basingstoke, 1996); E. Foster and P. Schmidt, *Anglo-German Relations in Security and Defence: Taking Stock* (London, 1997). See also the popular book financed by both the British and the German governments (and available in both English and German): T. Kielinger, *Crossroads and Roundabouts: Junctions in German–British Relations* (London and Bonn, 1997). A new book on the bilateral relationship by Sabine Lee and a collection of essays edited by Jeremy Noakes *et al.* are in preparation.

examining the role of European integration on British–German relations, while not neglecting other multilateral influences since the Second World War and integrating historical and contemporary political dimensions, has been missing. This book has been written to close this gap.

Despite the ever increasing influence of multinational interest and pressure groups (for instance transcontinental corporations, agricultural lobbies) as well as regional groupings (for example the German *Länder*), the nation state still plays a central though perhaps declining role within the European Union. It therefore appears justifiable to take the territorially defined traditional nation state as the point of departure for the horizontal and vertical investigations into the various political, security related, economic, financial–monetary, and social policy areas dealt with in this volume. The book recognizes however that in twenty-first-century Europe the boundaries of the EU member states have become rather permeable. After all, the domestic policy (as shaped by the many societal forces which influence a nation's domestic life directly and indirectly) of any given EU country impacts to a considerable degree on the policies of other EU states. Thus, it can be noticed that the foreign policies of many EU countries are directed not only at the decision-making and thus elite level of other EU states but also, to an increasing degree, at the economies and societies of these states and their values, prejudices, memories, images, and other factors which can be influenced from outside. Consequently, the more or less subtle intervention into the domestic affairs of EU countries by their fellow member states is by no means an exception. Indeed, the foreign policies of the EU states are connected by 'a multitude of domestic policies' and seem to be well on the way to developing into what soon might be termed internal European affairs. It has resulted in an ever greater 'intermeshing, varying considerably in intensity, of the political life of the nation-state units' which thus constitute 'one of the basic elements in the interdependence of contemporary international politics'.[11] The EU countries have become deeply penetrated states.[12]

This has certainly been the case with respect to both Britain and Germany. Ever since the British were admitted to membership of the then EEC on 1 January 1973, European integration and the policies of the individual EC member states have become increasingly important factors

[11] K. Kaiser, 'Interdependence and Autonomy: Britain and the Federal Republic in their Multinational Environment', in Kaiser and Morgan (eds.), *Britain and West Germany* (London, 1971), 25.

[12] See the articles by J. N. Rosenau, 'Pre-theories and Theories of Foreign Policy', in R. B. Farrell (ed.), *Approaches to Comparative and International Politics* (Evanston, 1966); 'Foreign Policy as an Issue Area', in J. N. Rosenau (ed.), *Domestic Sources of Foreign Policy* (New York, 1967), 11–50; and 'A Pre-theory Revisited: World Politics in an Era of Cascading Interdependence', *International Studies Quarterly* 28 (1984), 245–305.

in Britain's domestic and foreign policy. Because of its political, geographical, and economic importance the Federal Republic of Germany is a particularly weighty ally. Correspondingly, Britain is one of the most significant EU partners for the Federal Republic. For example, trade between the two countries has traditionally been very healthy. Throughout the 1990s Britain tended to be Germany's third biggest export market and the second biggest within the EU after France; moreover, the UK was the fifth largest supplier of goods to Germany.[13] Yet, due to the many British squabbles over European issues throughout the 1980s and 1990s and such issues as the BSE crisis of the mid- and late 1990s, which was perceived in London as having both integrationist European and traditional power political dimensions, these close and important links between the two countries tended to be overlooked by many people.[14] Thus, throughout the post-war years hardly anyone ever talked about a British–German 'special relationship' on the model of the long-established privileged partnerships between the US and the UK within the Atlantic alliance and France and Germany within the EU (and also possibly between the FRG and the USA within NATO).[15] Instead, the terms 'awkward' or 'semi-detached' partners and, at best, 'silent alliance' dominated the discussion when characterizing the nature of British–German relations in the post-war years.[16]

However, since the late 1990s, when in both countries the long period of Conservative governments led by Helmut Kohl and Margaret Thatcher/John Major came to an end, the importance as well as the improvement of British–German relations has become more obvious. This applies in particular to the successful strengthening of the British–German alliance around the mutual search for a new social-democratic 'third way' which appears to preoccupy both Tony Blair in London and

---

[13] See 'UK–German Trade Figures Soar', Report by the Embassy of the FRG, London, 31/5/1999.

[14] For the causes and implications of the BSE crisis (there is however very little on its impact on British–German relations), see S. C. Ratzan, *The Mad Cow Disease: Health and the Public Good* (London, 1998); R. J. Maxwell, *An Unplayable Hand? BSE, CJD and the British government* (London, 1997); R. Rhodes, *Deadly Feasts: Tracking the Secrets of a Terrifying New Plague* (London, 1997).

[15] Of course throughout the post-1945 era the Franco-German partnership was viewed as particularly important in view of the historical hostility between Germany and France and the potentially dire consequences of a severe breakdown of Franco-German relations for the well-being and indeed peace of the European continent.

[16] See S. George, *An Awkward Partner* (1998); S. George (ed.), *Britain and the European Community: The Politics of Semi-Detachment* (Oxford, 1992); K. Kaiser and J. Roper (eds.), *Die stille Allianz: deutsch-britische Sicherheitskooperation* (Bonn, 1987) [this is the German edn. of the book quoted in note 10 above]; also J. Buller, 'Britain as an Awkward Partner: Reassessing Britain's Relations with the EU', *Politics* 15/1 (1995), 33–42. See also Foster and Schmidt, *Anglo-German Relations*, 4–7. For a more harmonious view of Anglo-German relations, see the interesting article by Wright, 'The Role of Britain in West German Foreign Policy since 1949', *German Politics*, 5/1 (1996), 26–42.

Gerhard Schröder in Berlin.[17] Yet, also with respect to the further evolution of the European Union both governments seem to have moved closer to developing common political goals and pragmatic solutions. At the time of writing only France is still regarded as a more crucial ally for Germany's position within the EU. Still, whether one can already speak of 'a very firm political harmony' in British–German relations and of 'great openness and readiness to act jointly', as German Foreign Minister Joschka Fischer did on the occasion of the 50th anniversary of the British–German Königswinter Conference in March 1999, is somewhat questionable.[18] As far as European integration is concerned, many of the chapters in this book will demonstrate that there are still major differences in outlook and policy between Britain and Germany. With regard to the 'vision thing' both countries still have very different ideas about the future of Europe.[19]

Yet, at the same time, a certain gradual convergence of many practical aspects of Britain's and Germany's European policies can be observed. For instance, past differences about the widening and deepening of Europe have been partially reconciled. Moreover, competing notions as to whether the EU should orientate itself along Germany's traditional social market economy or Anglo-Saxon neo-liberal economic concepts appear to have become much less important. While the Schröder government attempts to move towards a more market orientated approach despite great opposition within the SPD towards this course, the Blair administration is not averse to putting a greater emphasis on the incorporation of social dimensions in its policy than its predecessor. For instance, the Labour government terminated its opt-out from the EU's Social Chapter which John Major negotiated in the course of the Maastricht intergovernmental conference. In mid-May 1999, the *Financial Times* even credited Prime Minister Blair with giving 'the most pro-European speech by a British premier since Sir Edward Heath in the 1970s'. In the speech he made on the occasion of receiving the Charlemagne prize of the German town of Aachen, Blair recognized that 'half-hearted partners are rarely leading partners'. He declared that he had the 'bold aim that over the next few

[17] See e.g. A. Giddens, *The Third Way: The Renewal of Social Democracy* (Oxford, 1998); T. Blair, *The Third Way: New Politics for the New Century* (London, 1998); B. Hombach, *Aufbruch: Die Politik der neuen Mitte* (Düsseldorf, 1998); T. Meyer, *Die Transformation der Sozialdemokratie. Eine Partei auf dem Weg ins 21. Jahrhundert* (Bonn, 1998); F. Unger, A. Wehr, and K. Schönwälder, *New Democrats, New Labour, Neue Sozialdemokraten* (Berlin, 1998); also R. Misik, *Die Suche nach dem Blair-Effekt: Schröder, Klima und Genossen zwischen Tradition und Pragmatismus* (Berlin, 1998).

[18] Report by the German Embassy in London, dated 22 March 1999.

[19] For the German vision, see the interesting article by H. Mayer, 'Early at the Beach and Claiming Territory? The Evolution of German Ideas on a New European Order', *International Affairs*, 73/4 (Oct. 1997), 721–37.

years Britain resolves once and for all its ambivalence towards Europe'. Britain had much to contribute to Europe and that it could only do so 'on the basis of partnership and by playing our part fully'. He envisaged a European Union that would become a global economic and military power with full British involvement.[20] This did indeed sound very different from Winston Churchill's famous phrase which largely can be taken as an apt characterization of Britain's European policy in the twentieth century. Churchill proclaimed as early as 1930 that his country was 'with Europe, but not of it. We are linked but not compromised. We are interested and associated but not absorbed'.[21]

However, times are changing. In the spring of 1999 for the first time since the battle of Waterloo in June 1815, British and German soldiers suddenly became 'comrades-in-arms'. They found themselves fighting on the same side when the western alliance embarked on the war in Kosovo on 24 March 1999. This may have important long-lasting consequences for British–German relations within the European Union. United Germany's almost unilateral action in recognizing Croatia and Slovenia in 1991 led to a severe crisis in the western alliance and the displeasure of Britain and France and other EC countries.[22] But these discords were overcome long before the western world belatedly noticed the development of the Kosovo crisis. The war in Kosovo refocused attention within the EU away from the exaggerated squabbles over budget costs and other material aspects of a misunderstood concept of the 'national interest' towards the basic values underlying European integration: the belief in a liberal-democratic continent and the necessity of preserving peace and political stability in Europe.

Thus, in many EU capitals the war in Europe contributed to a greater understanding of the deeper values of European political co-operation within the framework of European integration.[23] At the same time, dissatisfaction with the American Clinton administration's prevarications, hesitations, and domestic constraints as well as a certain self-righteousness of US leadership and European envy of Washington's overwhelming technological power resulted in greater efforts on the part of France, Britain,

---

[20] For Blair's speech, see the *Financial Times*, 14/5/1999, 1; *The Guardian*, 14/5/1999, 1.

[21] For Churchill and Europe, see K. Larres, 'Integrating Europe or Ending the cold war? Churchill's post-war foreign policy,' *Journal of European Integration History* 2/1 (1996), 15–49.

[22] See M. Libal, *Limits of Persuasion: Germany and the Yugoslav Crisis, 1991–92* (Westport, Conn., 1997).

[23] Moreover, Samuel Huntington's controversial thesis of the clash of civilizations, of a severe rift between the Christian world and the Muslim world, may also have been contradicted for good. After all, the EU did its utmost to protect and materially support the Kosovo Albanian refugees and thereby uphold the human rights of a Muslim people. See the interview with German Foreign Minister Fischer in *Die Zeit*, No. 16 (15 April 1999), 3. For Huntington's thesis see his book, *The Clash of Civilizations and the Reworking of World Order* (New York, 1996); see also his original article 'The Clash of Civilizations?', *Foreign Affairs* 72/3 (1993), 22–49.

Germany, and other EU countries to develop a distinctive European defence structure and identity.[24] This policy was officially confirmed at the EU summit meeting in Cologne in early June 1999. During the meetings in Cologne it was also unanimously decided that Javier Solana, the outgoing Secretary General of NATO, would be put in charge of overseeing the genuine development of a common European Foreign and Security Policy. All fifteen EU members, including Britain, were in agreement that this was a desirable goal. Indirectly, the war in Kosovo has produced greater harmony in British–German relations within the European context than was the case until then.

Yet, during the Kosovo War it also appeared at times that the British government's 'hawkish' attitude to the conflict and the German Red–Green coalition government's much more hesitant attitude would lead to continued friction between the two countries. After all, it was not only the first war conducted by NATO and entirely by means of airpower, it also was the first time since the Second World War that German soldiers were engaged in warfaring activities. The German government's refusal to approve of Britain's advocacy of the deployment of ground troops in Yugoslavia was strongly influenced by the country's much more pacifist and sceptical public opinion. This tendency could not only be noticed among the members of the German Green party but throughout the rank and file of all main parties. The Blair government did not have these problems. British public opinion was solidly behind its government. However, the termination of the conflict on 10 June 1999 before the introduction of allied ground troops and, subsequently, close British–German co-operation in NATO's and the EU's prolonged peacekeeping operation, including the return and resettling of the refugees, had a positive effect on British–German relations. It also seems to have changed Britain's attitude towards European integration in the defence and foreign policy fields to a considerable degree. The Kosovo War demonstrated that the high quality of Britain's professional military offers the country the chance to become a major player in Europe after all. And this appears to be necessary if Britain's uneasy relationships with Europe and its German ally are to be permanently transformed into genuine partnership. The low turn-out and very disappointing results of the European elections in June 1999 for Tony Blair's government only temporarily dampened New Labour's pro-European sentiments.

Moreover, the appointment of British defence secretary George Robinson to succeed Solana as Secretary General of NATO in October 1999 may prove beneficial for the development of a greater British involvement with Europe. Robinson will be responsible for maintaining the

---

[24] See e.g. *Financial Times*, 29–30/5/1999, 2; *The Observer*, 13/6/1999, 18.

coherence of NATO by facilitating the integration of the three new Eastern European NATO members (Poland, Hungary, the Czech Republic) who were admitted in the spring of 1999. He will also have to prepare NATO for the admission of further Eastern European members early in the new century. Above all, the new Secretary General will play a crucial role in managing transatlantic defence relations. The firm intention of the EU members to develop a genuine European foreign and security dimension and to integrate the Western European Union (WEU) fully as its military arm means that Robinson has the task to oversee the structural changes of NATO that are necessary to accommodate the establishment of a European Common Foreign and Security Policy (CFSP). With the establishment of the Combined Joint Task Forces (CJTF) between NATO and WEU, NATO has already accepted the WEU as its European security partner and agreed to provide the resources to enable the EU and the WEU to embark on military activities without American participation. Thus, the EU has the intention to become involved in European security policy with the help of NATO's resources but without having to ask for permission from Washington to do so.[25]

This process is fraught with danger as it may well escalate into transatlantic disagreements and intense strategic and political rivalry. Thus, with Robinson's appointment as NATO's Secretary General, a British politician (the third in NATO's fifty-year history), and therefore indirectly also the British government, has been given crucial responsibility for co-ordinating NATO's role with the European Union and ensuring the smooth functioning of the important transatlantic relationship. It may have had advantages that Washington's initial attempts to persuade Rudolf Scharping, the German defence minister, to become NATO's new Secretary General were not successful. It can be expected that the British government's traditional closeness to the USA will be helpful in convincing the United States to swallow some of the unpalatable aspects of increasing European independence in the security field. At the same time the British government itself may be more prepared to accept and support the development of a European foreign and security dimension as London is crucially involved in this process. Thus, Robinson's important role will give Britain a stake both in the management of transatlantic relations and the development of a common European foreign and security dimension. Robinson's new post will therefore make it much more difficult for the British government to sit on the fence or come down clearly in favour of the USA and in opposition to Germany, France, and other EU countries in any transatlantic clashes as was so often the case in the past. Thus, the appointment of a generally respected British politician as

---

[25] See *Frankfurter Allgemeine Zeitung*, 6/8/1995, 5.

NATO's Secretary General may well further bolster the positive developments in the British–German relationship. This would be very desirable; after all, until very recently British–German relations in the context of European Integration were rather volatile.

Throughout the second half of the twentieth century fundamental differences in values and policy can be discerned in British–German relations. Above all, as the Bonn Republic became one of the six founding nations of the EC fifteen years before Britain managed to join, the Germans were able to obtain certain crucial advantages in practising the habit of being confined to a mere European role in international politics and economics. The dissimilar time factors involved—the one country being present at the creation, the other joining only belatedly and after many frustrating experiences and much heated internal debate—as well as the very diverse motivations for joining the EC are among the main factors which have decisively influenced (and partially explain) the very different German and British approaches to European integration since 1945. Furthermore, both nations identified membership of the EC with contrasting experiences of national well-being. While West Germany's gradual rise to renewed international respectability and economic prosperity was closely related to the country's role within the EC, Britain's road after 1945 was largely littered with financial difficulties and absolute political and relative economic decline. In the main this continued to be the case once the UK had become a member of the EC in 1973. In addition, it has been very difficult for Britain, the victorious member of the 'Big Three' of the Second World War, to overcome its pride and embark on genuine co-operation on a basis of equality with the country it liberated from the Nazis and re-educated afterwards. It is thus no wonder that the collective memories of both nations have retained very different national identities and attitudes towards the European continent and European integration.[26]

British–German relations within the framework of European integration can be divided into three main phases (1945–72, 1973–90, post-1990) and the parts and chapters in this book follow this general division. The first phase lasted from 1945 to the early 1970s. During these years Britain viewed the European integration process with great scepticism, if not hostility, while the West Germans were enthusiastic supporters of it. They realized that EC (as well as NATO) membership was almost the only way open to them to turn their country once again into a respected

---

[26] For a brief general overview, see F. Cameron, 'Britain and Germany as European Partners, 1949–1989', in A. M. Birke and M. L. Recker (eds.), *Upsetting the Balance: German and British Security Interests in the nineteenth and twentieth Century* (Munich, 1999), 177–87. For a still interesting discussion of the spirit of Britain, see R. Dahrendorf, *On Britain* (London, 1982).

member of the international community. From 1958, when the Rome Treaties came into effect, until 1 January 1973 Britain was outside the European Community while West Germany quickly rose to be one of the Community's most important and influential member states. Britain's attempt to develop a less formal alternative to the EEC in the form of the European Free Trade Association (EFTA) was not successful. A decisive turning point in Britain's relations with both the EC and West Germany occurred in the early 1960s. The building of the Berlin Wall and the increasing legitimization of the GDR, as well as the end of the Adenauer era and the beginning of an era of East–West rapprochement, meant that West German decision-makers were faced with the fact that there would be no solution to the German question in the foreseeable future. Britain's temptation to move towards recognizing the GDR in return for a peaceful settlement of the Berlin crisis (1958–62) was only one of the processes which made this clear to the West Germans.[27] Thus, increasingly, West Germany concentrated on developing its place within the western community of nations in general and within the EC in particular. More or less simultaneously Britain arrived at the conclusion that its declining economic and world power position required a rapprochement with the EC, and also that the long-cherished Commonwealth would not be a substitute for EC membership. However, the development of a genuine European frame of mind in Britain took a long time. De Gaulle's two vetoes of London's membership applications in 1963 and 1967 deeply angered the country but the French President's reasoning was not without substance. De Gaulle argued quite convincingly that Britain had not yet been converted to a genuine European commitment and still valued its 'special relationship' with the United States much more than its relationships with France, Germany and the other EC member states.[28]

The British government's conversion into a true believer occurred under the premiership of Edward Heath in the early 1970s. With the support of de Gaulle's successor Pompidou and German Chancellor Willy Brandt it led to British EC membership.[29] This represents the beginning

---

[27] This episode as well as earlier plans by Churchill in 1953/4 and Eden in 1955 to create a reunited but neutral Germany in order to appease the USSR and end the cold war turned the British into very difficult and cumbersome troublemakers; this at least was the perception of the Adenauer government in Bonn. See K. Larres, *Politik der Illusionen: Churchill, Eisenhower und die deutsche Frage, 1945–55* (Göttingen, 1995), 133 ff.

[28] See N. P. Ludlow, *Dealing with Britain: The Six and the First UK Application to the EEC* (Cambridge, 1997); G. Wilkes (ed.), *Britain's Failure to Enter the European Community, 1961–63* [. . .] (Ilford, Essex, 1997).

[29] See E. Heath, *The Course of My Life: Autobiography* (London, 1998), esp. ch. 13; C. Lord, *Britain's Entry into the European Community under the Heath Government of 1970–74* (Aldershot, 1993); U. Kitzinger, *Diplomacy and Persuasion: How Britain Joined the Common Market* (London, 1973).

of the second phase in British–German–European relations (1973–89/90). However, London's conversion to the European vision was rather short-lived. Under the Wilson and Callaghan governments in the 1970s and 1980s Britain first renegotiated the treaty of admission and then continued to be a most awkward ally. In particular, the Common Agricultural Policy (CAP) and the EC budget negotiations proved to remain major obstacles between Britain and its EC partners. Moreover, both Labour Prime Ministers were forced to work with very small parliamentary majorities and Callaghan was indeed dependent on Liberal support for a period of time. Wilson's and Callaghan's freedom of manoeuvre was not only limited by their own half-hearted belief in the value of European integration but also by the Euro-sceptic domestic opinion in the country at large as well as within the Labour Party itself. According to Stephen George the latter explains 'the more nationalistic aspects' which characterized British behaviour towards European institutions including the biased chairing of some of the meetings of the Council of Ministers.[30]

During the 1970s under the firm leadership of Helmut Schmidt West Germany moved to become an ever more influential EC country which weathered comparatively well the economic and financial storms of the decade, which caused so many problems for the British. Schmidt continued to nourish Bonn's close partnership with France and decisively helped to turn the Franco-German axis into the leadership alliance of the EC. Both leaders were for example responsible for the creation of the original European Monetary System and for stabilizing the EC's financial affairs in the wake of the oil crises of the 1970s. In fact the years when Schmidt and French President Giscard d'Estaing were in power (1974–81/2) can be regarded as the 'golden age' of Franco-German relations.[31] However, unlike his predecessor Willy Brandt, who had focused on demonstrating Bonn's undiminished commitment to European integration and the Atlantic alliance in view of West Germany's enthusiastic pursuit of *Ostpolitik*,[32] Chancellor Schmidt began to emphasize German economic and political self-interests. Although during the Schmidt era West Germany remained prepared to be the paymaster of Europe, the beginning of a certain new German firmness and self-confidence could be observed which in general did not endear the Germans to their British allies. Despite the good personal rapport between Callaghan and Schmidt,

---

[30] George, *An Awkward Partner*, 135.

[31] Quoted in Bulmer and Paterson, *The FRG and the EC*, 226. For an excellent analysis, see above all Simonian, *The Privileged Partnership*, chs. 10 and 11.

[32] See e.g. K. Larres, 'Germany and the West: the "Rapallo Factor" in German Foreign Policy from the 1950s to the 1990s', in K. Larres and P. Panayi (eds.), *The Federal Republic of Germany since 1949: Politics, Society and Economy before and after Unification* (London, 1996), 301–19.

as far as European issues were concerned, British–German relations remained distanced.[33]

This situation continued and even worsened once Margaret Thatcher had become British Prime Minister in 1979. She embarked on a crusade to reassert Britain's global influence in ever closer co-operation with the Reagan administration in Washington. Her contempt, disguised only with great difficulty, for the squabbling European Community and its supposedly provincial and small-minded leaders was all too obvious. Moreover, the manner of Thatcher's fight for a rebate of Britain's EC contributions (otherwise the UK would have been paying almost 1 per cent of GDP as net contribution) and her insistence on obtaining 'opt out' clauses from various EC agreements made things worse. In addition, her personal relationship with Chancellor Kohl was very cool indeed. Fundamentally, Thatcher continued to believe in the classical realist 'balance-of-power' concept and thus preferred to concentrate on bilateral relations as well as on the world beyond Europe. Thatcher's strong and publicly voiced opposition to German unification did not improve matters. In contrast to Kohl and indeed the vast majority of politicians in West Germany, Thatcher was deeply convinced of the value of national sovereignty and independence. She believed that European integration ought to be about the improvement of intra-European free trade opportunities and not about the introduction of supranational schemes leading towards a federal Europe.[34] Fundamentally, this attitude did not even allow her to approve of the further deepening of European integration as a reaction to the establishment of a large united German state. However, Kohl and French President Mitterrand were agreed that further European integration was necessary to complement the new European order brought about by unification. Embedding the united country within European structures even more tightly than hitherto was meant to reassure Germany's neighbours. Moreover, Mitterrand wished to use the opportunity to end Germany's and the *Bundesbank's* monetary dominance in Europe by means of European Monetary Union and the introduction of a common currency. Yet, Thatcher continued to downgrade the European Community in favour of the Atlantic alliance. She was unable to see beyond Lord Ismay's

[33] See H. Schmidt, *Die Deutschen und ihre Nachbarn*, paperback edn. (Berlin, 1992), 132–4, 153–64; for a general account of the economic difficulties of the 1970s, see G. Ambrosius, *Wirtschaftsraum Europa: Vom Ende der Nationalökonomie* (Frankfurt/M., 1996), 123 ff.

[34] See M. Thatcher, *The Downing Street Years*, paperback edn. (London, 1995), 790–1, 792 ff.; H. J. Küsters and D. Hofmann (eds.), *Deutsche Einheit: Sonderedition aus den Akten des Bundeskanzleramtes 1989/90* (Munich, 1998), e.g. 546–7, 574–7, 719–20; K. Diekmann and R. G. Reuth, *Helmut Kohl: Ich wollte Deutschlands Einheit*, 3rd edn. (Berlin, 1996), 138, 149–50, 184, 196, 306, 340–3. For an overview of the 'illusion of national autonomy' in Britain, see e.g. W. Wallace, 'What Price Independence? Sovereignty and Interdependence in British Politics', *International Affairs* 62/3 (1986), 367–89.

famous dictum of the early 1950s that NATO was supposed to keep the Americans in, the Russians out, and the Germans down.[35]

The third phase in British–German relations within the context of European integration commenced in late 1990 after German unification and the end of the cold war. Initially, under Thatcher's successor John Major, who was faced with a largely Euro-sceptic cabinet and an out-right Euro-hostile popular press, British–German and British–European relations remained severely strained. Above all, monetary issues and for example the BSE crisis proved to be very contentious. However, most contributors to this book conclude that with the change of government in the late 1990s in Britain (May 1997) and Germany (October 1998) both countries developed a much more constructive policy towards each other. Britain also began to engage much more actively with the further development of the European Union.

The chapters in this book attempt to offer interesting and challenging insights with regard to the evolution of British–German relations within the context of European integration in the last half of the twentieth century. Most articles in the book look at the issues under consideration from both a British and a German point of view; yet it has not always been possible to arrive at an absolutely balanced account. The British point of view predominates in some of the chapters. However, in view of the fact that compared to the European policy of Germany and France, the strategy of the British government towards and within the European Union is often expressed and understood much less well and tends to be under-represented in the scholarly literature,[36] this does not seem to be a disadvantage. The present book is a substantial and interdisciplinary attempt to analyse British–German relations within the framework of European integration and without overlooking multilateral influences. It is therefore hoped that this volume will stimulate further research.

The first part of the book is dedicated to the British–German cold war relationship; it consists of four chapters covering the years 1945–1990. In the first chapter of this part Ann Deighton investigates the period from the end of the Second World War to the early 1970s when European integration played a relatively unimportant role in British–German relations. After all, these were the years when the world was dominated by the height

[35] Quoted in M. Mandelbaum, *The Dawn of Peace in Europe* (New York, 1996), 12. The author is convinced that this dictum (in particular its German dimension) still guides the policy of the western alliance in the 1990s.

[36] See e.g. G. Niedhart, D. Junker, and M. Richter (eds.), *Deutschland in Europa. Nationale Interessen und internationale Ordnung im 20. Jahrhundert* (Mannheim, 1997); also Bulmer and Paterson (eds.), *The FRG and the EC*. In both books (as in many others) France is given much greater attention than Britain; substantial chapters on Britain's role in Europe and the country's relationship with the FRG are missing.

of the East–West conflict. Thus, to some extent Bitish-German relations during this time span resemble the traditional bilateral relationship between states characteristic of the late nineteenth and first half of the twentieth century. Deighton attempts to discern continuities in the British–German relationship in the context of European integration and looks above all at the different approaches to power politics. She concludes that Britain was still trapped by assumptions about its global status and the import-ance of the sterling area. While rejecting all proposals for becoming involved in the European integration movement, the UK played a decisive role in the creation of a western, American-led security framework. West Germany was liberated by the defeat in the Second World War but its freedom of manoeuvre was severely limited by the country's integration with the West. Thus, the Federal Republic was keen on playing a role within the framework of European integration. Although there was great general distrust of the German people in Britain, Deighton explains that polit-ical tension which did arise on occasion between the two governments in London and Bonn seldom operated on the bilateral level. These diffi-culties had more to do with British–American and German–American economic and strategic problems than with British–German issues as such.

Chapter 2 by Julie Smith and Geoffrey Edwards deals with the years from 1973, when Britain joined the EC, to the end of the cold war in 1989/90. The authors conclude that neither Britain nor West Germany viewed the bilateral British–German relationship as of primary signific-ance. Instead, Britain considered its relations with the United States as overwhelmingly important while West Germany looked above all to France, without neglecting its links to Washington. Moreover, the cold war and the strategic balance between Washington and Moscow con-tinued to frame the parameters of the relationship. Naturally, in the course of the 1970s and 1980s British–German relations underwent certain changes. Smith and Edwards conclude that domestic political factors in both countries as well as international strategic and economic events were mostly responsible for this. While in foreign and defence affairs Britain and West Germany had much in common during these years, this was not the case as far as the European Community was concerned. In par-ticular, Britain was strongly opposed to the vision of a federal Europe that predominated in German political circles. In general the UK remained a difficult partner and uneasy ally for the Federal Republic and the other EC countries. Despite a certain improvement of the British–German bilateral relationship during these years, the multilateral European frame-work was dominated by problems and complications caused by Britain's lukewarm attitude to the EC.

Chapter 3 consists of a study of Britain's relationship with the GDR between 1949 and 1989. Klaus Larres argues that in contrast to

British–West German divergences over European issues, the UK fully supported the Federal Republic's non-recognition of the East German government until 1973 when *Ostpolitik* led to the international acceptance of the existence of a second German state. However, in view of Britain's increasingly difficult economic situation, the authorities in London were often tempted to greatly expand trade contacts with East Germany. Yet, in the last resort Britain always realized that its relationships with West Germany, the United States, and indeed the entire NATO alliance were much more important than any advantageous export deals with the GDR which would have antagonized Britain's allies. The GDR's own problems in establishing satisfactory trade links with Britain also contributed to this insight. In this context, the Macmillan government's readiness to extend *de facto* recognition to the East German Ulbricht regime in the course of the long Berlin Crisis of 1958–62 appears to be an exception rather than the rule. However, most British decision-makers did not strongly object to the continued division of Germany and they were convinced that the GDR would survive much longer than the West was prepared to admit officially. Still, together with the United States London was prepared to take Bonn's great sensibilities regarding any violation of its increasingly outdated Hallstein Doctrine into consideration. It is much less clear whether the West German authorities always fully realized Britain's endeavours in this regard. On the whole both Bonn and East Berlin appear to have remained convinced that Britain was the weak link in the West's non-recognition strategy. Yet, this view does not seem to have done justice to Britain's fairly consistent adherence to the non-recognition of the GDR prior to 1973. Once the international recognition of the GDR had occurred, Britain's links with the GDR remained formally correct though still fairly distanced. Moreover, trade relations did not develop as much as had been promised by the East German government. Britain's increasing trade with the EC countries in the 1970s and 1980s made London much less keen on developing its links with East Germany. Thus Britain continued to remain on the right side of the West Germans.

Chapter 4, the last in the cold war section of the book, deals with Britain and the process of German unification in 1989/90 and takes all the primary sources into account which have become available recently. Lothar Kettenacker embarks on an overview of Britain and the German Question prior to 1989 before investigating, above all, the role of Margaret Thatcher during the momentous events which led to both German unification and the end of the cold war. He concludes that with the exception of some sections of the British press, it was primarily the British Prime Minister herself who resisted the process leading towards unification as long as possible. Wrongly anticipating the support of both Soviet leader Gorbachev and French President Mitterrand for her strategy, Thatcher even attempted to preserve the GDR as an independent democratic state in its own right. Yet, despite her strong belief in the Anglo-American 'special relationship' she did not even obtain the support of the American Bush administration for her increasingly idiosyncratic policy. Thatcher's reasons for her political course in 1989/90 can largely be found in her very subjective reading of recent European history which resulted in deep personal mistrust of the Germans and their unreformed 'national character', exemplified in the notorious Chequers Seminar in March 1990. Thatcher was also strongly opposed to the deepening of European integration as advocated by Mitterrand and even by Chancellor Kohl himself in order to embed a united Germany more securely in the international community. The British Foreign Office under Douglas Hurd however was much less opposed to the unfolding events and made increasing efforts to counter Thatcher's emotional policy with constructive counter proposals. Yet, not surprisingly, the Prime Minister's attempts to undermine and redirect the process of German unification led to severe difficulties with the Kohl government in Bonn and did not endear her to Washington either. Thatcher's policy and her deep suspicion of both Germany and European integration were to ensure that British–German and British–European relations in the post-cold war era were handicapped by a bad start.

Parts II and III of this volume deal with the post-cold war years. Part II looks at issues of politics and security since 1990; it consists of four chapters. In Chapter 5 Jim Buller and Charlie Jeffery examine the transition to the post-cold war world and consider the role of domestic norms and institutions in British–German relations with reference to the deepening of Europe. The authors argue that German unification reinforced the basic philosophy underlying European integration, namely that Germany had to be firmly tied into multilateral European structures. This belief resulted in the convening of the Maastricht Conference of December 1991 and the drawing up of plans for the creation of European monetary and political union. Buller and Jeffery examine and explain the different British and German reactions to the acceleration of the deepening of European integration in the early 1990s. They conclude that domestic politics were largely responsible for British–German difficulties. Domestic political norms and institutions played a predominant role in influencing the decision-making procedures of policy-makers in both countries. This also helps to explain the ease with which German delegates were able to adapt to the co-operative decision-making within the EU; British representatives found this much more difficult. Moreover, during the Major government a certain revival of anti-German sentiments could be observed in Britain. The authors also examine the developments in the decision-making process of the Blair government and assess whether or not it is likely that the traditional patterns of European policy-making will change towards a 'more German' way of getting things done. They view such a development with scepticism.

Chapter 6 considers British–German relations and the eastern enlargement of the EU. John Pinder argues that eventually the adherence of a number of Eastern European states to the EU will add to the security and perhaps prosperity of the Union. However there has been much divergence among the present member states on the changes necessary to enable the EU to cope with the influx of new members. Reform of the Common Agricultural Policy (CAP), the structural funds and various EU institutions is essential. Pinder investigates the differing reactions from Germany (as well as its main partner, France) and Britain to these changes. Until very recently the UK appears to have favoured the eastern enlargement of the EU in order not only to stabilize the East but at the same time to dilute the further deepening of the European integration process. Germany, on the other hand, was (and still is) in favour of both widening and deepening the Community and saw no contradiction between these two aims. Instead, the Germans believed that acting on one policy while ignoring the other would have a disintegrative effect, so that enlargement must be accompanied by deepening. Yet, the author concludes that despite the traditional divergence between the British and the German (and indeed the French) standpoint on widening and deepening which was particularly obvious towards the end of the Major government, this has been changing. Since the election of the Blair government in May 1997 and of Gerhard Schröder as Chancellor in October 1998, there has been considerable convergence of British–German views on the enlargement of the EU. The author demonstrates this by investigating in what way the different British and German stances interacted with each other from the late 1980s to the late 1990s. Although strong British–German differences of view regarding institutional reform, a Common Foreign and Security Policy (CFSP), Justice and Home Affairs, and the euro can still be observed, there does indeed seem to have developed a new British approach to Europe as far as most of these dimensions are concerned. Moreover, the Berlin European Council in March 1999 showed a remarkable convergence between the two governments with respect to the agricultural policy as well as the structural funds. On the whole, the author is hopeful that there might well be a 'happy ending' with regard to British–German approaches not only to these policy changes but also to the deepening of the EU.

Chapter 7 consists of an analysis of the importance of the American Dimension in British–German relations in the 1990s. Valur Ingimundarson argues that discussion in the United States throughout the 1970s and 1980s was dominated by assumptions about American economic and political 'decline'. Even by the early 1990s the United States still appeared to be a reluctant world power (with the exception of the Gulf War and Washington's activities in the process of German unification). However, towards the end of the 1990s (and in the course of the war in Kosovo) the United States consolidated its international leadership position and reasserted its political and military hegemony in Europe. Ingimundarson argues that the active contribution of the US and its interaction with Britain and Germany decisively helped to shape the developments within the EU during the 1990s. In view of Britain's and Germany's differing vision regarding European integration this was a highly volatile process. However, both Bonn and London were (and still are) united in their resolve to maintain a strong American presence in Europe despite the absence of a Soviet threat. Both countries thus demonstrated that they had remained Washington's most loyal European partners. Ingimundarson illuminates the interaction between the debate over deeper and wider European integration and the wish to continue tying the US to Europe by looking at four different policy areas: the general European integration process in the 1990s, the discussions over a European defence identity, NATO's Eastern expansion, and the prolonged crises and wars in the former Yugoslavia. He concludes that in all of these areas the European vision of the United States and its continued willingness to be involved in European security issues were of crucial importance in preventing the development of a genuine European security identity.

The final chapter in Part II (Chapter 8) also deals with transatlantic security concerns. Emil J. Kirchner considers the role of both NATO and the Western European Union (WEU) as reflected in the policy preferences in Britain and Germany. After giving a brief overview of the complex NATO–WEU relationship since 1990, the author discusses issues which are of crucial importance for both military organizations and their member states: threat perception, the leadership question, and cost considerations including American-European economic competition. Moreover, Kirchner examines instances of burden sharing and successful co-operation between NATO and the WEU with respect to ethnic conflicts and the democratization processes in Central and Eastern Europe. He also considers the issue of NATO enlargement and the implications for British–German security policies. The author concludes that compared with the difficult development of the WEU and an EU defence policy, NATO seems to hold all 'the trump cards'. Above all, not only the United States but also an increasing number of EU member states, in particular Britain and Germany, appear to be convinced that NATO ought to be the main European security provider and should feel responsible for supporting the development of a non-competitive European security pillar closely intertwined with the Atlantic alliance. However, the 1999 war in Kosovo greatly strengthened the resolve of France, Britain, Germany, and other EU countries to develop a much more coherent and effective European defence identity and common European foreign policy than was the case until then.

Finally, Part III of this book consists of five chapters dealing with the economic and social dimension of the British–German post-cold war relationship. In Chapter 9 Jeremy Leaman analyses the industrial and commercial cultures in Britain and Germany. He argues that the traditional picture of Germany as an economic giant and a political dwarf with a deep commitment to multilateralism has been upset by the events in 1989/90 to some degree. In the 1990s the German economy underperformed considerably and not only for reasons of unification. Structural economic difficulties led to an intensive debate within and outside Germany about the country's appeal as an attractive location for economic investment. Moreover, the advantages of the Anglo-American neo-liberal economic model were intensively discussed. Yet, at the same time the liberation of Central Europe from communist rule has turned Germany into the central power on the continent. This has given the country an even more influential role in European politics and it is clear that many of the Eastern European countries are looking to united Germany for economic and financial leadership. Leaman examines British–German economic relations both in the context of the cold war and in the much less secure environment of the post-1990 era. He attempts to compare the economic culture in the two countries, examines their pursuit of neo-liberalism since the early 1980s and finally looks at Germany's economic crisis. He argues that the competition between the Anglo-Saxon and German model can only be understood within the framework of global economic conflicts. As neo-liberalism and the strengthening of the power of the transnational corporation is still the flavour of the month it appears that in the short term the British economic model would be more flexible and adaptable to a constantly changing international economic environment. However, Leaman concludes that despite all necessary reforms of united Germany's economic structure, in the medium and long run the more inclusive German economic model will have certain institutional and cultural advantages and may well prove successful again.

In Chapter 10 Elizabeth Meehan deals with the German and British perspectives of industrial democracy within the context of general European social policy. She argues that among EU countries the co-ordination of social security arrangements for migrant workers, the equality of the sexes, and occupational health and safety regulations have been very successful. However, as far as industrial citizenship is concerned, a major controversy has occurred. Meehan therefore begins her article by examining the reasons for the generally held view that industrial and social rights are a necessary component of equal citizenship. She then analyses the role of industrial and social rights in the German-'Rhenish' and 'Anglo-Saxon' models of capitalism. Subsequently, the author looks at developments in EU industrial citizenship and social policy during the 1990s. Meehan concludes that the hybrid model of welfare rights and industrial rights has not been displaced; neither the British nor the German model has triumphed at the expense of the other country's preferred concept. While the German approach has not disappeared, the author regards it as unlikely that the UK will have to adopt a 'Europeanized' version of German industrial rights. Perhaps, she concludes, a Europe specific 'third way' needs to be developed.

Chapter 11 analyses the creation of the Single Market. Within the framework of British and German views on European integration Iain Begg and Michael Wood review the process which led to the creation of the Single Market and analyse the events resulting in the Major government's dramatic withdrawal from the European Monetary System (EMS) in 1992. Subsequently the authors discuss the regulatory and monetary developments since this turning point in Britain's relations with the EU which led to the establishment of EMU and the introduction of the euro on 1 January 1999. The authors argue that in contrast to the supranational EMU which appears to be strongly influenced by Germany's political priority of stabilizing Eastern Europe through prosperity and democracy, Britain could identify much more readily with the Single European Market project. This project appealed to Britain's newly reformed market-orientated economy and its belief in free, efficient, and largely unregulated markets. Begg and Wood draw the conclusion that it is likely that Britain will soon fully join EMU. Moreover, it appears that European integration has led to a certain convergence of British and German economic philosophies. For example, on the one hand, German ideas about stability and independence for the European central bank and the central banks of the EU member states have been largely accepted in London; on the other hand, Germany has moved towards liberalization and deregulation and other Anglo-Saxon economic characteristics without however entirely abandoning its social welfare model.

Chapter 12 describes progress in harmonizing accounting practice in the European Union and its effects on financial reporting in Germany and the UK. Patricia McCourt and George Radcliffe point out that the financial statements of large corporations are important determinants of corporate tax liabilities and future levels of investment. The authors argue that large differences in national accounting practices significantly affect investment decisions and may lead to distortion in capital flows between Britain and Germany and within the European Union in general. Moreover differences in accounting practices have also resulted in very different systems of business taxation in individual EU countries. Only the harmonization of accounting practices can lead to a fair harmonization of corporate tax rates across the European Union. Attempts to harmonize accounting practices have been made with the help of the EU's Fourth and Seventh Company Law Directives. McCourt and Radcliffe conclude that although these Directives have been implemented into national law, the flexibility still permitted under the principle of subsidiarity has resulted in the continued existence of very different financial reporting systems in both Germany and Britain. The elimination of unfair tax competition through harmonization of corporate tax rates is unlikely to succeed without simultaneous harmonization of tax bases through standardization of European accounting rules.

Finally, Chapter 13 deals in detail with the negotiations and the results of the EU's intergovernmental conferences leading to the Maastricht (1991/3) and Amsterdam (1997/9) treaties. Robert Harmsen and Nickolas Reinhardt analyse the progress towards economic and monetary union as well as political union during these two conferences convened to make changes to the existing EU treaties. They also discuss the developments since the conclusion of the Amsterdam treaty in June 1997. Harmsen and Reinhardt analyse the strategies of the British and German governments during the Maastricht and Amsterdam negotiations within the complex framework of an institutionalized multilateral EU bargaining procedure with its important emphasis on coalition-building, compromise and package deals. In the past Britain and Germany displayed very different capabilities in influencing this process and its results; the authors argue that this was also the case with regard to the Maastricht and Amsterdam negotiations. In close co-operation with France, the Germans once again proved to be much more successful in adapting to the required negotiating procedures. The British appeared to remain the outsiders condemned to reacting to Franco–German initiatives. Harmsen and Reinhardt conclude that both the Maastricht and Amsterdam treaties demonstrated that France and Germany were still the 'motor' of the process of European integration. Unification does not seem to have changed Germany's enthusiasm for European integration. With respect to the UK's engagement with European integration in the 1990s the authors detect a 'dreary consistency'. While recognizing that the Blair government appears to have embarked on a pro-European policy course, the authors are sceptical that in view of reticent public opinion a genuine conversion in favour of a greater commitment to European integration has already occurred in Whitehall. Yet, regarding the medium to longer term the authors see indications that there might be a cultural change in the UK as far as a more intensive British engagement with the European Union and Britain's EU allies are concerned.

Most of the contributors to this book agree that throughout the second half of the twentieth century and within the context of European integration the UK and Germany were indeed uneasy allies. However, at the beginning of the twenty-first century this appears to be changing. There are clear indications of the development of a more constructive and less problem-ridden British–German partnership within the framework of the European Union. Perhaps a 'golden age' in British–German–European relations is just round the corner. Unless the conflicts in the Balkans and elsewhere lead to further unexpected developments and controversial western reactions which may cause serious political divergences among the EU states (and the NATO members), it appears to be quite possible that Britain and Germany can soon be characterized as genuine partners rather than merely as uneasy allies.

At the end of writing the introduction and editing this book it gives me great pleasure to thank the nineteen authors represented in this volume for their willingness to participate in this project and enthusiasm in writing their contributions. Above all, I wish to express my sincere gratitude to Dominic Byatt, OUP's commissioning editor, for his much-needed support and advice with which he accompanied the realization of this volume. I would also like to thank Amanda Watkins and Tom Chandler from OUP as well as Professor Robert Eccleshall, Head of the School of Politics of The Queen's University Belfast, for their support which was very much appreciated.

PART I

The Cold War Relationship

1

British–West German Relations, 1945–1972

ANNE DEIGHTON

The rhythms of the histories of West Germany and Britain between 1945 and 1972 have been strikingly different, and the day-to-day pattern of their relations over this period has been uneven. It is hard to analyse a bilateral relationship that developed during a rapidly changing period of history, but it is possible to discern threads of continuity in Anglo-German relations in the context of European integration. The continuities can be best understood first in the context of the different approaches to power politics adopted in Britain and West Germany, and second, through the wider pattern of interstate relations as they developed in this period. After a brief account of the changes in the fortunes of the two countries between 1945 and 1972, these two themes will be developed, followed by snapshots of Anglo-German relations at two critical junctures, 1954–5 and 1958–63. If the story is one of success for the Federal Republic, the opposite is true for Britain.

GERMANY, 1945–1972

In May 1945, Germany surrendered unconditionally, the Second World War in Europe ended, Hitler committed suicide, and the whole Nazi edifice collapsed. By 1972, however, two German states were firmly embedded in the international system. With a population of much the same size as that of Britain, West Germany now had the fastest growth rate and the highest GDP of any country in Western Europe.[1] A provisional democratic constitution, the Basic Law, had been agreed in 1949, which organized life in the new West Germany.[2] The shadow of Germany's past was a force for regret, for change, and for re-evaluation.

---

[1] See P. Ludlow, 'Constancy and Flirtation: Germany, Britain and the EEC, 1956–1972' (paper presented at Exeter University, March 1998).

[2] S. Padgett (ed.), *Adenauer to Kohl: The Development of the German Chancellorship* (London, 1994). The prized constitution gave latitude to allow for legal re-evaluation when necessary. On the 'provisionality' of the new state, see W. Hanrieder, *Germany, America, Europe: Forty Years of German Foreign Policy* (New Haven, 1989), 145.

The new Chancellor, the Christian Democrat Konrad Adenauer (1949–63) established foreign policy priorities that were, by and large, to sustain the broad sweep of German foreign policy throughout the cold war. First, West Germany was a country that was deeply committed to the western camp, and, for twenty years, to the so-called Hallstein Doctrine which was intended to isolate the GDR diplomatically.[3] After 1955, West Germany became a key member of NATO, not least because its borders touched those of the Warsaw Pact, and foreign troops and weaponry, including nuclear weaponry, were based on German soil. This policy was developed although weaving West Germany so firmly into the western camp seemed to contradict views that, one day, Germany should be unified once again.[4] Second, Adenauer committed West Germany to a process of European supranational integration. It was a founder member of the European Coal and Steel Community (ECSC, 1952), and the European Economic Community (EEC, 1958). The latter had an ultimate aim that was hazy, but which nevertheless provided an effective framework for German political rehabilitation as well as for economic regeneration and growth. Third, a sometimes troubled, but effective and dynamic and very public special relationship was formed with France, historically Germany's most fearful neighbour. This operated both bilaterally and within the context of international institutions.

Foreign policy—and particularly the priority and strategy given to possible reunification—was, in West Germany, a deeply contested area. The SPD was committed to German unification as a primary objective, and was initially hostile to NATO. In 1959, it published its so-called 'German Plan', which proposed unification in the context of a European-wide security pact, although, after the Bad Godesberg programme and then the construction of the Berlin Wall in 1961, the SPD moved more openly into acceptance of the *status quo* of West Germany.[5] The foreign policy position of the CDU was not entirely consistent either, as divisions of opinion developed over this period. Indeed, as we shall see, Adenauer himself shifted towards a 'Gaullist', as opposed to 'Atlanticist' view in the autumn of 1962. The nuclear and MLF debates in the 1950s and early 1960s also revealed continuing tensions about West Germany's foreign policy role.[6]

[3] For a summary of the doctrine, see D. L. Bark and D. R. Gress, *A History of West Germany*, vol. 1, 2nd edn. (Oxford, 1993), 374. The doctrine was effectively abandoned between 1970 and 1972, with the Brandt government's change of course to 'one nation and two states'. See H. J. Küsters, 'West Germany's Foreign Policy in Western Europe, 1949–58: The Art of the Possible' (Oxford, 1955), and Gustav Schmidt, ' "Tying" (West) Germany into the West—But to What? NATO? WEU? The European Community?', in C. Wurm (ed.), *Western Europe and Germany: The Beginnings of European Integration, 1945–1960* (Oxford, 1995), 55–85 and 137–74 respectively.
[4] A. J. Nicholls, *The Bonn Republic: West German Democracy, 1945–1990* (London, 1997), 128, 147, 153–8. [5] Bark and Gress, *History of West Germany*, 442.
[6] B. Heuser, *NATO, Britain, France and the FRG: Nuclear Strategies and Forces for Europe, 1949–2000* (London, 1997), esp. ch. 6. M. Trachtenberg, *A Constructed Peace: The Making of the European Settlement, 1945–1963* (Princeton, 1999).

In the mid-1960s, shifts in the balance of priorities of West German foreign policy became more apparent, as *Ostpolitik* emerged as a complex but potent policy through which West Germany could build a safer security regime with the active co-operation of the Soviet Union, East Germany, and Eastern Europe, whilst leaving open the possibility of a fundamental change in German–German relations: unifying the two Germanys was thus never taken off the agenda of German foreign policy, but *Ostpolitik* sought in the short term to bring an 'easement' to West Germany's relations with countries in the Soviet bloc, and with the Soviet Union itself. This was pursued in the context of a strong *Westpolitik* —continued NATO membership, and support of further European integration, including both widening—to include the UK, and deepening— with proposals for monetary union. However, relations with Britain were not a central plank of German foreign policy.

Between 1945 and 1972 there had emerged a strong desire in West Germany to learn from the lessons of the past and a willingness to pay the price of its earlier history, yet to look forward with the intention of re-building Germany with a different kind of foreign policy.

BRITAIN, 1945–1972

As the war ended, Britain was generally acknowledged as the major West European power, as well as a major global power. Not only had Britain retained its existing constitution during the war, it had also successfully resisted invasion and had engaged in combat with the Axis powers in every major arena of conflict. Prime Minister Winston Churchill was a key player at the numerous conferences held by the Allies to devise their military strategy, and to plan for the post-war world. Britain was one of four occupying powers, with responsibilities for deciding the territorial and political future of Germany.

The broad priorities of successive British governments over this period were to manage their existing resources and assets, and to continue to project Britain's power globally, in contrast to the massive exercise of state-building and reconstruction that characterized the German experience. In 1945 the Empire/Commonwealth was the primary source of British energy and commitment, pride and national loyalty. However the erosion of imperial cohesion that had manifested itself after the First World War, and which surfaced again, meant that 'decolonization' was to become a leitmotif of British imperial policy. In spite of this process, attachment to Empire/Commonwealth remained very high in the public imagination.[7]

---

[7] A. Orde, *The Eclipse of Great Britain: the United States and British Imperial Decline, 1895–1956* (London, 1996), esp. chs. 3 and 6; P. Unwin, *Hearts, Minds and Interests: Britain's Place in the World* (London, 1998), 192–3.

The Germans could not draw upon the immediate past for positive images of their role in the international system, but the British were, in contrast, preoccupied by the past. Victory in war, a stable constitution, empire and the sterling area, their capacity to project power beyond the shores of the island, all created an image of greatness and easy superiority which successive governments always tried to sustain.[8] Integration of government functions with Continental countries was completely out of the question: 'The United Kingdom, [it was concluded in 1951], cannot seriously contemplate joining in European integration . . . we cannot consider submitting our political and economic system to supra-national institutions. Moreover, if these institutions did not prove workable, their dissolution would not be serious for the individual European countries . . . it would be another matter for the United Kingdom which would have to break its Commonwealth and sterling area connections to join them . . . it is not in the true interests of the continent that we should sacrifice our present unattached position, which enables us, together with the United States, to give a lead to the free world.'[9] However, this image, driven by perceptions of the past, was to be increasingly at odds with reality: the need for a special relationship showed that Britain could only be 'great' in partnership with the US.

It was clear to the first post-war British Labour government that the British project to sustain its role as a leading power required American support. This realization resulted in the manufacture of the seductive image of the 'Special Relationship' between the United States and Britain. This was built upon a common language, common traditions of Anglo-Saxon culture and mores, and was inspired by the wartime experience and close personal relationships at head of state level. Intelligence, access for the US to military bases in the empire and on the British mainland, and the Anglo-American nuclear partnership gave the special relationship a real bite, and was to sustain it, especially in moments of crisis.[10]

During the first few years after the war, the US also looked to the UK as a leader of the Europeans. The British played a key role, both in ensuring the delivery of vast amounts of aid from the US for reconstruction, including the reconstruction of the West German zones through the Marshall Plan of 1948; and in the creation of NATO in 1949. As Philip Bell has written, in the 'sense of taking the lead in establishing the

---

[8] P. H. M. Bell, 'A Historical Cast of Mind: Some Eminent English Historians and Attitudes to Continental Europe in the Middle of the Twentieth Century', *Jornal of European Integration History* 2/2 (1996), 5–19.

[9] Quoted in A. Deighton, 'Britain and the Three Interlocking Circles', in A. Varsori (ed.), *Europe, 1945–1990s: The End of an Era?* (London, 1995), 155–69.

[10] See D. Reynolds, 'A "Special Relationship": America, Britain and the International Order since the Second World War', *International Affairs* 62/1 (1985/6), 1–20; A. Danchev, 'On Specialness', *International Affairs* 72/4 (1996), 737–50.

political and military security of Europe, they [the British] grasped the opportunity with both hands'.[11] However, although continuing to respect the British connection within NATO, by the 1950s the Americans came increasingly to support supranational, as opposed to intergovernmental modes of co-operation within Western Europe, and supported Franco-German efforts to create the ECSC and then the EEC. The US favoured a more tightly knit Europe for a variety of reasons that included idealism (federalism would stop war) and a desire for control over the western project. That Britain could not generate American backing for its inter-governmental approach to European policy was to dog policy-makers throughout this period.[12] 1950 marked a critical moment for Anglo-German relations, as the Franco-German foreign policy project became viable, and the European dimension of the Anglo-American special rela-tionship started to look ragged.[13] Anglo-German relations were hence-forth doomed to play a less important role. The creation of the ECSC thus set a pattern of cautious relations in European integration that were to continue until 1972, and the question has been raised as to whether it was in part because of reluctant British policy up to 1949, that the West Germans then turned to France.[14]

British moves towards membership of the EEC/EC, as exemplified by the diplomacy of 1961–3, 1967, and 1969–72, were conducted under both Conservative and Labour governments. 'Europe' was a cross-cutting issue *par excellence* in Britain, with differences between and within both the major parties.[15] By the same token, NATO membership had solid and continual support from both parties, and was an issue upon which there was so much consensus that, during these years, it never became a deeply contested issue in political life.

Meanwhile, every British government tried, but without resounding success, to grapple with the twin problems of sterling, and the failure of the British economy to grow and modernize as fast as its European coun-terparts. In 1945, Britain was bankrupt. The costs of the war had put an extraordinary strain upon the British economy, and wartime debts forced

[11] P. H. M. Bell, *France and Britain 1940–1994: The Long Separation* (London, 1997), 104.

[12] The diplomacy surrounding the Council of Europe, and the OEEC, established to admin-ister Marshall Aid, convinced the Americans that the British were not committed to co-operation beyond intergovernmentalism. On the USA and European Integration, see G. Lundestad, *'Empire' by Integration: The United States and European Integration, 1945–1997* (Oxford, 1998); K. Larres, 'Torn between Idealism and Egotism: The United States and European Integration, 1945–1990', *Irish Journal of American Studies* 8 (1999); see also the article by Valur Ingimundarson in this book.

[13] J. Gillingham, *Coal, Steel and the Re-Birth of Europe, 1945–1955* (Cambridge, 1991), ch. 3.

[14] See H. P. Schwarz, 'Germany's National and European Interests', in A. Baring (ed.), *Germany's New Position in Europe: Problems and Perspectives* (Oxford, 1994), 118.

[15] Labour officially opposed the application when it finally went to the House of Commons in 1971, though it was a Labour government who had initiated it.

the Labour government to approach the Americans for a massive loan. Although British GDP was higher than that of the Continent in 1945, and the economy did continue to grow throughout the period, by the 1950s, the rate of growth was lower than that of France and West Germany. However, sterling was seen not only as a mechanism for the management of the UK's global economy, but was also a symbol of global status. Successive sterling crises after 1947 did not alter this conviction, so, by 1972, when sterling's role as a world currency was under severe threat, the impact of this was both economic and psychological. It is thus clear that the configuration of the global balance of power had been transformed irredeemably by the war and then the post-war settlement; further competition from other powers for markets and political influence spelt the inevitability of a profoundly changed role for the UK.

POWER AND PRIORITIES

Given these two very different 'streams' of development, how did Anglo-German relations develop until 1972? The period between 1945 and 1949 was, of course, exceptional. Strictly speaking, there were no formal Anglo-German relations, as no German government existed. The British played a key role in the division of Germany, and the rehabilitation of the western part of the country, although the British 'model' of democracy was not exported wholesale into the occupied zones. The administration of the zonal division of Germany that was agreed as the war ended required large amounts of money (the British zone cost the taxpayer roughly £70m. a year), and a very high level of diplomatic skill that was directed towards building a West Germany which would be both democratic and westward-looking.[16] When the Federal Republic of Germany came into existence in 1949, the relationship remained a curious one, as Britain was still an occupying power, with a direct interest in West Berlin. This hangover from the post-war settlement remained an important feature of Anglo-German relations, particularly as *Ostpolitik* took shape in the late 1960s.

It is possible to discern two features that account for the uneven development of Anglo-German relations in Europe. The first concerns the different nature of power relations in Europe that were entertained by the British and the Germans; and the second was the different ordering of the priorities of their bilateral relations.

---

[16] See e.g. I. D. Turner (ed.), *Reconstruction in Postwar Germany: British Occupation policy and the Western Zones, 1945–1955* (Oxford, 1989); N. Annan, *Changing Enemies: the Defeat and Regeneration of Germany* (London, 1995).

The British concept of its power relations with the Continent was essentially based upon a hard power, strategic view of its security in the developing cold war world. This view was largely determined by Britain's position in the world after 1945—relations with Germany were conceived within the wider framework of Britain's own need to try to manage the changes in the international system, and to secure a continuing role for itself. The British wished to create and be part of a framework of democratic Continental countries that would, with the US, be stronger and more capable of standing up to the double menace of communism and of the Soviet Union's emerging European empire. It was plain that, alone, Britain and the Continental powers would not be a match for the Soviet Union. As Prime Minister Clement Attlee graphically expressed it: 'what was left of Europe was not strong enough to stand up to Russia by itself. You had to have a world force because you were up against a world force. Without the stopping power of the Americans, the Russians might easily have tried sweeping right forward.'[17] France had collapsed in the face of German aggression in 1940, and the post-war Fourth Republic was not bringing any guarantee of political stability to a country in which the communists were registering as much as 30 per cent of voter support.

And what about Germany? There remained, in the UK, a residual antipathy, if not hostility, towards Germans and Germany, even though the defence of Berlin during the blockade of 1948–49 had the effect of reducing British antagonisms.[18] Yet, strategically, West Germany was essential to a western defence posture. It was this dilemma that lay at the heart of British thinking about West Germany's role in cold war Europe. On the one hand, there quite naturally still existed a traditional suspicion and distrust that had characterized Anglo-German relations since the beginning of the century and which had been marked by Germany's leading role as an economic power on the Continent, and a rival to Britain overseas, and which had been intensified by the two wars. Further, the consequences of the awkward period of appeasement in the inter-war period now led British policy-makers instinctively to resent rapprochement with the Germans. On the other, a reconstructed West Germany was the *sine qua non* both for an economically regenerated Europe and a strong defence posture against the Soviet bloc. This had been made clear as the Marshall Plan was set in place: aid to participating German zones lay at

[17] Quoted in F. Williams, *A Prime Minister Remembers: The Pre-War and Post-War Memoirs of the Rt Hon Earl of Attlee* (London, 1961), 171.

[18] Lack of space prevents any attempt to address the complex nature of the mutual perceptions of Britain and West Germany, as viewed through the press, and in wider public opinion, which naturally extends well beyond the period under consideration. Two key moments in Anglo-German relations were, in one popular view, the victory in 1945, and 1966, when Britain defeated Germany in the World Cup football series. See *The Guardian*, 4 July 1998. See also Ch. 5 by J. Buller and C. Jeffery in this book.

the centre of the CEEC report of 1947. In strategic terms, it was almost inconceivable that Europe could be defended against the East if an independent, neutral West Germany existed, capable perhaps of alliance building with the Soviet Union in the expectation of its future unifica- tion.[19] Thus, throughout this period there existed on the one hand, an acceptance that a strong western bloc could not be constructed without West Germany, and on the other, a sense that integration with Germany was politically unacceptable, and, further, that supranational integration would not of itself tie West Germany down. It is fair to say that, not only did the British fail to build a deep relationship with West Germany, they did not want to do this, particularly if it would involve participation in the integration process. Hard power considerations based on control, dom- inance, and alliance diplomacy dominated perceptions of their relations with West Germany.

Power perceptions in West Germany were rather different. The Ger- man project was to fashion for itself a new role in a new system: West Germany had a major role to play, but the constraints of its history, and of its particular legal position in the international system gave rise to very different sets of priorities. Adenauer's *Westpolitik* was to rebuild relations with the West to ensure eventual equality for West Germany in the inter- national and West European system. This was to be done through a more imaginative, and indeed courageous, process of political and economic integration, and by soft power mechanisms. By agreeing to bind the West German state to supranational functional organizations which would limit the freedom of action of all member states, Adenauer's approach was to build confidence, to merge centres of power, and, ironically, to agree to a process of reducing German national independence to secure its important national interests, its equality and its international acceptability. That is, German national interests would actually be enhanced by sharing power. The British appeared content that West Germany should take this path, and this view was expressed publicly many times by leaders from both parties. However, this difference of approach to the ordering of power politics remained one of the most intractable areas of contention between the two when practical issues concerning European integration were addressed.

If differing views of power politics developed in both countries, so also did different sets of priorities for the ordering of their bilateral relations with respect to European integration. It is not possible to understand Anglo-German relations in the context of European integration without

---

[19] See A. Deighton, *The Impossible Peace: Britain, the Division of Germany, and the Origins of the Cold War, 1945–1947* (Oxford, 1990/1993); R. Steininger, 'Germany after 1945: Divided and Integrated or United and Neutral?', *German History* 7 (1989), 5 ff.

reference to these other relationships, which were themselves changing over the period under consideration. The relationship of both powers with the United States is central to this. The US provided the security and defence framework for West Europe through its championing of the Atlantic Alliance and NATO. In this respect, the US was itself a European power, and in spite of the tensions between Britain and West Germany over European integration, there remained a firm substrata of common security interests between them. In the British case, the US had to be the major partner in Europe, and this relationship was intended to be one, if not of equals, then of co-players. The continuing presence of the US in Europe as an occupying power with a direct political and military interest in the future of West Germany, and as the key western protagonist in the cold war was always the touchstone of Britain's European politics. Thus often contentious questions with an Anglo-German dimension, such as Berlin, the presence of British military forces in Germany and their costs, and burden-sharing, were shaped in Britain by the role of the US. For the Germans, their security relations with the US was one of security dependence. West Germany was an artificial state, created almost *faute de mieux* after the war, and the US was the ultimate guarantor, both of the *status quo*, and of its role as a western player after 1955. West Germany had agreed both to abstain from becoming a nuclear power, and to have Alliance troops on its soil. Its primary security relationship within NATO was with the US, not the UK.

It is a truism that the Franco-German partnership was the most trumpeted European bilateral relationship in this period. It stemmed in part from West Germany's need for a partner in its project of rehabilitation. A brave and imaginative shift was made by both countries, given the historical context, although on the commercial level and in the areas of, for example, industrial cartels, the two countries had always had more closely interwoven histories than either cared publicly to admit in the 1950s.[20] This partnership posed a problem for Britain. Whilst the British did not seek to disrupt permanently the Franco-German partnership, they were nevertheless left without a major partner on the Continent. It was only when relations between France and West Germany worsened—as in 1954, and again when France withdrew from the NATO military command structure in 1966, that relations between Britain and West Germany were more constructive.[21]

---

[20] G. H. Soutou, *L'Alliance incertaine: les rapports politico-stratégiques Franco-Allemands, 1954–1996* (Paris, 1996), esp. chs. 6–8. The contrast with Franco-German relations in the early interwar period is, of course, striking.

[21] H. Haftendorn, *Nato and the Nuclear Revolution: A Crisis of Credibility, 1966–1967* (Oxford, 1996), esp. 396. Haftendorn emphasizes the importance of American diplomatic mediation between the British, the West Germans and the French.

DEFINING MOMENTS: 1954–1955

There were two moments at which Anglo-German relations were particularly important. The first occurred between 1954 and 1955. When NATO was created in 1949, West Germany had not formally come into existence. However, by 1950, the Americans were pushing for German admission to NATO, particularly after the Korean War began. But this idea was anathema to the French, who instead, and on the advice of Jean Monnet, proposed the Pleven Plan, which would have allowed the West Germans to contribute to the defence of the West without joining NATO as full members.[22] The tortuous negotiations that followed lasted until 1954. Adenauer was initially sceptical about the EDC proposal, but, as it became increasingly linked to West Germany's own emergence as a virtually sovereign power through the Contractual Agreements, he came around to this solution. Although the British never wished to be part of the EDC they, and the Americans, were prepared to back the idea, and to give guarantees to protect the French if it ever became clear that the Germans would exploit their new-found military role in ways that threatened France. Then, in the summer of 1954, the whole plan collapsed when it failed to be ratified by the French National Assembly. This had been widely anticipated since 1952, but left an enormous policy vacuum. Adenauer was furious with the French, not simply because he had staked much domestic political prestige on the project, but because its collapse also threatened the Contractual Agreements, which had linked EDC and the restoration of German sovereignty.

Between August and October 1954, the British worked extremely hard to secure an alternative arrangement. They, like the Americans, saw that West Germany had to be incorporated in the western defence system, and that Adenauer had now found himself in a position from which he could not extricate himself without British help. The Western European Union (WEU) solution represented a moment of maximum influence for the British, as, through it, the West Germans were admitted in NATO while securing the Contractual Agreements and achieving quasi-sovereignty. During these months there emerged a clear convergence of British and German interests, and the resulting settlement seemed to fit well with Britain's own perceived interests of providing a strong Atlantic security setting, but one in which West Germany was still militarily constrained through the self-denying ordinance over atomic, biological, and chemical weapons, and the renunciation of the use of force to alter borders. Further, WEU lacked

---

[22] On the EDC, see E. Fursdon, *The European Defence Community: A History* (London, 1980), 86–92; R. Dwan, 'An Uncommon Community: France and the European Defence Community, 1950–1954' (D. Phil. thesis, University of Oxford, 1996).

the supranational elements which the British abhorred, but was instead based upon the intergovernmental Brussels Treaty. WEU created, as the EDC proposal had also done, a major debate within Britain about West Germany's role in Europe, and there was strong opposition to German re-armament within both political parties, which well reflected fears about German military power that were still strong in the country.

By the end of 1954, the British thought that they had drawn a line under further supranational integration, and indeed had managed to show both that British leadership in Europe was not a spent force, and that the strategic interests of the country had been preserved without having to make concessions on the sovereignty question. Adenauer was also pleased by the results, as direct entry to NATO was a preferable solution to the fuzzy position in which the West Germans would have been left in the proposed EDC structure. Thus the WEU episode was a clear example of the way in which diplomacy backed by the hard power considerations of Britain created an Atlantic framework that included the weight of West Germany. However, any British hopes that this diplomatic solution would end attempts at supranational integration were to be sadly misplaced. Although subsequent developments proved that, in the arena of defence, the British position was in fact that which held sway—through the cold war and beyond—the outcome was, ironically, more beneficial to the integrative impulses in German foreign policy. For even as the EDC/WEU episode was being resolved, talks on economic integration were con-tinuing, but without Britain. Within a year, proposals for the EEC were under way. The British, while securing their perceived national interests in the short term, actually helped to create an environment of Atlantic security within which French dominated supranational integration, which Adenauer favoured, could then move forward. The creation of WEU reflects well the argument that Anglo-German relations can only be fully under-stood in their multilateral context, that there existed very deep common security interests, that Anglo-German relations over Europe improved when Franco-German relations were under threat, and that supportive relations were only possible when British and German approaches towards integ-ration in Europe were not at stake.[23]

DEFINING MOMENTS: 1958–1963

Between 1958 and 1963, Anglo-German relations suffered a severe set back, one that is well marked by the fact that when Frank Roberts was sent to

[23] A. Deighton (ed.), *Western European Union 1954–1997, Defence, Security, Integration* (Oxford, 1997), ch. 1; also A. Deighton, 'The Last Piece of the Jigsaw: Britain and the Creation of Western European Union, 1954', *Contemporary European History* 7/2 (1998), 181–96.

Bonn as the British Ambassador in 1963, he did not at first establish personal contacts with Adenauer.[24] This period was important because of the second Berlin crisis of 1958 to 1961; for the proposals for political co-operation between the six members of the ECSC and EEC; and because, in 1961, the British applied for membership of the EEC. But what lay beneath this turbulent phase of bilateral relations was a marked shift in West German policy towards France, with its resulting impact upon Anglo-German relations. In each of the three diplomatic episodes mentioned above, Adenauer, when encouraged by the US to choose between Britain and France, chose France, as long as West Germany's place in the Atlantic Alliance was not obviously permanently jeopardized. For their part, the British did not opt for closer relations with West Germany as a means to move towards conflict resolution.

When the Soviet leader Khrushchev threatened the West with a unilateral proposal to change the agreements over Berlin in favour of the German Democratic Republic (GDR), a bitter struggle broke out, not only in the context of East–West relations, but also between the Americans and the British on the one hand, and the French and the Germans on the other.[25] Adenauer's attacks upon the tempered response to the crisis by the Anglo-Saxon powers increased when the British Prime Minister, Harold Macmillan visited Moscow in 1959. The crisis, muted by the building of the Berlin Wall in 1961, however revealed important aspects of Anglo-German relations. Perhaps the most important of these was that for neither country was the other the key player. Macmillan was first and foremost concerned to keep close to the Americans, then to try and extract maximum benefit to the UK's prestige as a great power by working for a summit of the Potsdam powers. Adenauer's main concern was the threat of escalation, and the possibility that the FRG might become a battlefield once more. Thus, his diplomacy with the US was far more important than that with the British. Further, the support that the French President, General Charles de Gaulle gave him, reinforced the Franco-German relationship, and the talks on political co-operation between the Six took place in the context of the Berlin crisis. When they broke down in great acrimony after the Dutch refused to countenance any measures that might undermine the primacy of the Community system, or to allow multilateral talks to develop before the UK joined the Community, the notion of a bilateral Franco-German treaty was hatched. This proposal itself feeds into the last aspect of the crisis years of 1958–63, Britain's application to the EEC.[26]

[24] F. Roberts, *Dealing with Dictators: the Destruction and Revival of Europe, 1930–70* (London, 1991), 236.

[25] Gearson, *Harold Macmillan and the Berlin Wall Crisis, 1958–1962* (London, 1998).

[26] See the articles by W. Loth, 'Franco-German Relations and European Security, 1957–1963', and G.H. Soutou, 'Le General de Gaulle et le Plan Fouchet d'Union Politique Europeenne:

Britain's decision to apply for membership of the EEC was taken, somewhat hesitatingly, in July 1961, after nearly two years of intensive domestic and international talks.[27] The British decided that France held the key to the success of the application.[28] In one respect, they were absolutely right to make this assumption. It was widely known that de Gaulle was at best lukewarm about British membership; he had proved this by vetoing the British free trade area proposal in 1958, and he was quite content to snub the British publicly if he felt it was in France's national interests so to do.[29] But the corollary to Britain's assumption about France was that the other five members of the Community could be relied upon to support the British application as a foreign policy priority. And this is where the British misjudged the situation. The British records of the negotiations reveal an overemphasis upon the importance of Ludwig Erhard, who supported British ideas about a relatively open trading system. The British projected the EEC as a forum of European negotiation, and as a trading system with unfortunate but inescapable, supranational over-tones, and they assumed that their application would have the uncritical support of the whole German foreign policy establishment, including the Chancellor himself, as well as of the other Community members.[30]

The crisis of January 1963, when de Gaulle vetoed the British applica-tion, also created a crisis in Anglo-German relations. The shifts in Adenauer's priorities towards Franco-German relations that had emerged during the Berlin crisis and the Fouchet Plan talks were finally exposed when, only days after de Gaulle's infamous press conference, Adenauer travelled to Paris—against the advice of nearly all his staff—and signed the bilateral Elysée Treaty. It took some very tough negotiation under-taken by the Americans in the context of rumours about plots to over-throw Adenauer, to secure a preamble to the Treaty which upheld the principles of the Atlantic Alliance, and which thereby undermined the 'Gaullist' tenor to which Adenauer had agreed.

From the German perspective, the two events—the veto, and the signature of the Elysée Treaty—raise some serious questions about Adenauer's competence and consistency. Although there is evidence that

un Projet Strategique', in A. Deighton and A.S Milward (eds), *Widening, Deepening, Accelera-tion: The European Economic Community, 1957–1963* (Bonn, 1998).

[27] N. P. Ludlow, *Dealing with Britain: The Six and the First UK Application to the EEC* (Cam-bridge, 1997).

[28] A. Deighton and P. Ludlow, '"A Conditional Application": British Management of the First Attempt to seek Membership of the EEC, 1961–63', in A. Deighton (ed.), *Building Postwar Europe: national decision-makers and European institutions* (London, 1995), 107–13.

[29] A. Deighton, 'La Grande-Bretagne et la Communauté européenne, 1958–1963', *Histoire, Economie, et Société* 13/1 (1994), 113–30.

[30] H. Mayer, 'Germany's Role in the Fouchet Negotiations', *Journal of European Integration History* 2/2 (1996), 39–95, emphasises the commitment of the Dutch, first to UK membership, but, more important, to the EEC.

the old Chancellor had swung away from support for British membership of the EEC after the summer of 1962,[31] he faced intense opposition
from across the political spectrum in West Germany. Perhaps he had been
'seduced' by de Gaulle; perhaps his judgement had left him over both
the content and the execution of policy.[32] Whatever the reasoning, the effect
was to crush any goodwill in Anglo-German relations until the British
decided that, once again, an application would be made for membership.

But the episode also raises questions about the wisdom of Britain's
application, and the manner in which the application bid was pursued.
The foreign-policy aspects of the decision to apply was driven in part
by American dislike of the European Free Trade Association (EFTA).
The timing was predicated very largely upon British domestic interests,
and its conditionality—acceptable solutions for Commonwealth, for
British agricultural interests, and for EFTA—gave an added air both of
noblesse oblige, and of a real ambivalence about Community membership. Further, Macmillan's decision to deal directly with de Gaulle and
Adenauer as heads of state during the negotiations was another blunder:
not only did he overestimate his own capacity to convince de Gaulle,
but the Adenauer/Macmillan relationship was not a good one either,
and Macmillan only saw Adenauer once during the negotiations, whilst
having three meetings with de Gaulle.[33]

1963 revealed that, unlike the period of the early 1950s, when
Adenauer tried hard to engage the British in continental European projects, he was not now prepared to threaten Franco-German relations in
the interests of the British.[34] Whilst there was, of course, no line of defence
against an unexpected unilateral veto, the British failed to construct
arguments and strategies for their entry into the Community which
could have made the idea of such a veto effectively impossible. For, not
only did Adenauer continue with the Elysée Treaty, the other four EEC
members, while shocked, were not prepared to sacrifice what they had
achieved collectively, in the interests of Britain. The adverse effects of British
post-war arrogance were now all too apparent, not only in its relations
with West Germany, but across the Continent. Thus the fiasco of January
1963 provides a sharp snapshot of the weaknesses of Anglo-German relations. On the one hand, British foreign policy priorities had not genuinely
shifted since the end of the war: the conditions surrounding the application, lukewarm public opinion polls, and the splits in both parties were

---

[31] Archiv Stiftung Bundeskanzler-Adenauer-Haus, Rhöndorf, 12/63.1, 13.08.62; S. Lee, 'Germany and the First British Application', in Deighton and Milward (eds.), *Widening, Deepening,
Acceleration*.   [32] Deighton and Ludlow, 'A conditional application', 113–17.
[33] A. Horne, *Macmillan, 1957–1986, Vol. 2* (London, 1989), 32–4. By 1959, Macmillan was
recording in his diary that 'De Gaulle and Adenauer are just hopeless. Adenauer because he is
a false and cantankerous old man . . . half crazy'. Ibid., 134.
[34] Ludlow, *Dealing with Britain*, 237.

evidence that the image remained of Britain as a world power and a balancer of powers, for whom integration would represent a loss and not an upgrading of national interests. There was not a good working relationship with the Germans, but rather a residual sense of British superiority, coupled with insecurity given Germany's strong economic performance. That this cut across party divides was typified by Harold Wilson's tactless reference in the House of Commons to the 'German finger on the trigger' in relation to the 1964 MLF debate.[35] The Berlin crisis and the Fouchet Plan talks had strengthened Franco-German relations, while Britain remained trapped in the conservatism of its immediate post-war foreign policy. For West Germany, the period between 1958 and 1963 witnessed a strengthening of trends established since 1950, and these trends did not include a decisive mutual partnership with the UK: in Europe, France was the key partner; and in the security sphere, despite the very difficult period in 1963, the US remained the key alliance partner.

OSTPOLITIK AND ENLARGEMENT

If the years 1958–63 mark the lowest moment of Anglo-German relations in this period, the period from 1967 to 1972 were years in which a shift and an easing of relations became possible. The decision to follow a policy of *Ostpolitik* was yet more evidence of the ability of the West Germans increasingly to set the pattern of post-war European history. *Ostpolitik* was both about policy content and about policy style, and the way to effect changes in German–German relations, East–West European relations, and relations with the Soviet Union. As such, it promised not only easement of existing tensions, but also the prospect of fundamental changes in East–West relations.[36] It started to change the nature of German policy after the arrival in power of the Grand Coalition in 1966, and was intensified, and became epitomized by the Chancellorship of Willy Brandt after 1969. To be successful, *Ostpolitik* could not be conducted without French support; and further, the Germans did not see *Ostpolitik* as an alternative to a continuing commitment to the EEC/EC. The possible contradictions of this policy were to remain near the surface, while de Gaulle remained in power.[37]

[35] J. C. R. Wright, 'The role of Britain in West German Foreign Policy since 1949', *German Politics* 5/1 (1996), 26–42.
[36] The complexities and ambiguities of *Ostpolitik* are outside the remit of this chapter, but see T. Garton Ash, *In Europe's Name: Germany and the Divided Continent* (London, 1993), esp. chs. 1–5.
[37] After the Luxembourg crisis and the difficulties with NATO, the West Germans were worried about the capacity of the EC to weather the storms. They feared that the Franco-German duet might turn into a fatal duel. See Public Record Office, London (hereafter: PRO): EW 5/8, Roberts to FO, No. 95, 2/5/1966.

Also in 1966, the British decided to renew their EEC membership bid, although the tone of the first application: conditionality, and a desire to reformulate a Europe in British interests remained.[38] The main thrust of British policy towards West Germany under Labour was to try and mend fences with the Germans, not least because Adenauer had now left politics, and Chancellor Kiesinger's team (1966–9) was considered to be more sympathetic to British membership, and more prepared to stand up to the French.[39] For this reason the British were thus generally supportive of Germany's *Ostpolitik*, although their support was to be considered somewhat muted.[40] However, the timing of the new EEC application was not auspicious, although an Anglo-German working group was established to look at the economic issues, and the Germans suggested that de Gaulle should be forced to clarify his position on British entry early on. When de Gaulle once again indicated that the British were not ready for membership, the Germans failed to stop him, although they engaged the French in talks to keep the enlargement issue open until the applicants were in a position to 'enter effectively, or . . . link themselves with them in another form'.[41] It was only after the retirement of de Gaulle that the British application, for which formal negotiations had not even begun in 1966–7, was successful. By 1972, the British were finally accepted in the European Community after more than ten years of painful negotiations and two rejections of their application for membership. West Germany's role had been supportive but in no way decisive: Community enlargement, it can only be concluded, was never an issue over which successive German Chancellors were prepared to sacrifice other policies, whether with regard to France, or to *Ostpolitik* (although, de Gaulle's departure from power meant the latter was not tested). But, ironically, the timing of Britain's entry could now hardly have been worse. Continental images of Britain's attitude to European integration became frozen as the Community itself struggled to find ways to operate in a far less auspicious international climate, as the post-war years of economic growth came to an end.

[38] Willy Brandt recalls that, 'The British were not especially adroit. When I met George Brown [the British Foreign Secretary] . . . he told me, "Willy, you must get us in, so we can take the lead".' W. Brandt, *My Life in Politics* (London, 1992), 420. The Soames affair was another example of the capacity of the British to continue offending the West Germans. See U. Kitzinger, *Diplomacy and Persuasion: How Britain Joined the Common Market* (London, 1973), 45 ff.

[39] PRO: CAB129/122, C119, 5/8/1965. Roberts pointed out early on that preventing the break-up of the EC was a more important objective for the Germans than British membership. See also PRO: EW 5/8, Roberts to O'Neill, 27/6/1966.

[40] D. C. Watt, 'Anglo-German relations today and tomorrow', in K. Kaiser and R. Morgan (eds.), *Britain and West Germany: Changing Societies and the Future of Foreign Policy* (London, 1971). See also *Documents on British Policy Overseas*, Series III, Vol. I, 111/1, Nos. 36, 60 (London, 1997).

[41] *Keesing's Contemporary Archives* 16 (1967–68), 23175: 16/2/1968, re Franco-German talks; see also 23172: 1–8/2/1969, re Kiesinger's visit to London, 23–25/10/1967.

CONCLUSION

In 1945, Britain was trapped by victory in war. Positive images of the past cast forward shadows over the future, and the British became victims of assumptions about their global status, the importance of the sterling area, and a resistance to suggestions for change that emanated from the Continent, particularly over supranational integration. However, Britain did have very real obligations to fulfil, not least in the formulation of a viable peace settlement. With regard to Germany, then an object of foreign policy and not yet a player, there were obligations here too, and in these, the British played a serious and constructive role, first in dividing Germany in the perceived interests of the West, and then in the creation of democracy, the rehabilitation of civilian life, and the delivery of Marshall Aid to its western zones.

In 1949, on the other hand, West Germany was in effect liberated by defeat, and was then able to follow policies that would allow for reconstruction, reconciliation, and the pursuit of its national interests. This was despite the fact that the international system was now constructed in such a way that West Germany's freedom of manoeuvre was severely constricted by the Iron Curtain, by its membership of the ECSC, the EEC/EC, by the conditions surrounding its membership of WEU and NATO, and by the residual direct controls exercised over it by the allied powers. These constraints help to explain the subtle and low-key approach to both the methods and the long-term aims of *Ostpolitik*, and the only cautiously positive response to *Ostpolitik* that its partners gave.

In the context of western security, it has been argued that Britain played a positive part in creating a hard security framework, which was a *sine qua non* for economic and political integration, and moreover, favoured giving West Germany a strong role to allow it to contribute to the defence and the security of the West. This was despite a deep-seated and persistent ambivalence in Britain about Germany and the Germans, and a fear of German revanchism. Although there were bitter disputes about occupation costs, about Western policy towards Germany and Berlin, particularly in 1958–61, and within NATO, West German and British policy converged over the fundamental need to secure the status quo in the cold war structures that had been secured by 1955. Tensions that arose in this arena, were, moreover intimately linked to the course of Anglo-American and German–American relations, rather than operating at a purely bilateral level.

In the years leading up to Britain's accession to the EC, Anglo-German relations failed to escape from the pattern described above. For neither country was the other the most important, nor yet so unimportant as to be safely ignored. Their past histories and different geo-strategic priorities and positions in the international system led them to a relationship of common interests in the hard security field, but different paths over integrative policies. This uncomfortable position formed the bilateral context of Britain's role in the European Community after 1973.

2

British–West German Relations, 1973–1989

JULIE SMITH AND GEOFFREY EDWARDS

Britain's accession to the European Community on 1 January 1973 altered the context of British–West German relations, but it did not fundamentally alter the nature of the relationship. Neither country saw their bilateral relations as its first priority. For much of the period from 1973 to 1989 Britain continued to perceive its ties with the United States as more important, despite difficult moments during the 1970s and growing tensions in the 1980s that the close personal relationship between Mrs Thatcher and President Reagan only partially masked. Germany, despite its support for British membership of the EC, continued to look to France as its primary partner. Yet it, too, remained preoccupied with its relationship with the United States over issues of security and détente.[1] Nevertheless, for most of the time between Britain's accession to the European Community and the end of the cold war, Britain and Germany typically worked well together, albeit with little warmth, differing priorities, and, perhaps, a latent suspicion of each other's motives. While the Franco-German relationship continued to be central to the development of the Community during the period, relations between Britain and German were typically more low-key, often producing positive results, but with rather less drama than sometimes surrounded Franco-German co-operation.[2]

Within the framework of the European Community, the basic conditions of British membership had been set out at the Hague Summit in 1969 and longer term goals at the summits of 1972 and 1974.[3] France's President Pompidou had very largely determined the conditions. While he recognized the desirability of enlargement to include the British, Pompidou explicitly linked it to the completion and deepening of the Community.[4]

[1] On the influence of the US, see Ch. 7 by V. Ingimundarson.
[2] W. Wallace, *Britain's Bilateral Links Within Western Europe* (London, 1984), 29.
[3] For a useful assessment of the implications of the Hague Summit, see C. Franck, 'New Ambitions from the Hague to Paris Summits (1969–72)', in R. Pryce (ed.), *The Dynamics of European Union* (London, 1987).
[4] See H. Young, *This Blessed Plot: Britain and Europe From Churchill to Blair* (London, 1998), 234–5; and H. Simonian, *The Privileged Partnership: Franco-German Relations in the European Community* (Oxford, 1985), 78 ff.

This meant that a number of policies were to be finalized before the British arrived, notably the Community's budgetary arrangements and issues relating to the Common Agricultural Policy (CAP). The results were terms of entry that were less than favourable to Britain and which sowed the seeds of the so-called 'British Budgetary Question' that was to over-shadow the first eleven years of British membership. It was only with the resolution of the problem in 1984 that the British adopted a more positive stance, especially on completing the internal market and on for-eign policy co-operation. The change was welcomed by the Germans but without any enthusiasm for improving the bilateral relationship. This was partly because, for Germany, the French remained the primary focus of attention, especially after the Mitterrand experiment of 'Keynesianism in one country' ended in 1983. Britain was isolated on measures going beyond mere deregulation in a single market. Thus provisions for a single currency and other 'flanking' policies such as social, environmental, and industrial policy, eventually adopted in the Single European Act (SEA) of 1986, created difficulties for the British. The Franco-German tandem, by contrast, though sometimes uncomfortable was ultimately still roadworthy. In addition, despite the growing complexities of the secur-ity and defence relationship with the United States, the British were simply unwilling to follow the Germans and the French towards a more significant European defence identity.

As this chapter demonstrates, the nature of the British–German rela-tionship inevitably changed over time. It depended primarily on domestic political considerations in both countries—including which political parties and leaders were in office—but also on international and global events; especially important was the strategic balance between the United States and the Soviet Union.

DIVERGING ATTITUDES TOWARDS EUROPEAN INTEGRATION

West Germany's attitude towards European integration, as the Intro-duction and Chapter 1 have indicated, was coloured by the division of Germany and by a continued sensitivity to public opinion outside as well as inside Germany towards its *Deutschlandpolitik*.[5] Thus West Germany

---

[5] *Deutschlandpolitik* refers to the idea of the unity of the German nation and was closely linked to the concept of *Ostpolitik*: West Germany's policy towards the East. The Christian Democrats pursued a policy of non-recognition of the German Democratic Republic and its associates (the so-called 'Hallstein Doctrine'). When Brandt came into office in 1969 his *Ostpolitik* recognized the reality of a divided German nation and began to co-operate with East Germany. For a discussion of these policies and an overview of their competing demands

sought a balance between its *Deutschlandpolitik* and its *Ostpolitik* on the one hand and a *Westpolitik* that allowed for a constructive, active role in both the process of European integration and within the Atlantic Alliance on the other. Since all these factors sometimes pulled in different directions, it is perhaps not surprising that the British were occasionally baffled by German positions. It was often assumed that Germany was keen to be 'a good European', hence its willingness to bear the financial costs of being the largest and economically strongest member state. Yet German motives were continuously debated: for some, it was a way for West Germany to appease the past; for others, it was seen as a means for the Bonn Republic to consolidate its position as an international actor. The latter view was strongly represented in the Thatcher governments, as became clear during the process of German reunification. Moreover, successive British governments seemed unwilling or unable to appreciate the demands placed on German leaders by both the federal system and coalition government. These constraints were reflected, for example, by the fact that chancellors and finance ministers urged budgetary prudence and agricultural reform while their agricultural ministers worked effectively against any change.[6] The highly centralized British system of government rarely seemed to allow for the lack of any strong co-ordinating power in the West German system.

In contrast to West Germany's European credentials, Britain's approach to the European Community both before and after accession has frequently been portrayed as one of semi-detachment.[7] British pretensions to being a world power—a junior but privileged partner alongside the United States—remained. However, poor economic performance and a growing fear of being left behind meant that the UK entered the Community as a *demandeur*. In 1972–3 the West German Foreign Office formulated a set of four possible scenarios concerning the potential impact of Britain's membership of the EC: (1) Britain would act as a leader in the integration process; (2) Britain would become a normal member of the Community; (3) Britain would adopt a 'minimalist' approach, doing enough to remain in the EC but attempting to slow down the process; (4) Britain

see Michael Stürmer, '*Deutschlandpolitik, Ostpolitik* and the Western Alliance: German Perspectives on Détente', in K. Dyson (ed.), *European Détente* (London, 1986); E. Bahr, *Zu meiner Zeit* (Munich, 1996), 268 ff., 381 ff.

[6] The situation reached a point in 1984 when, despite Chancellor Kohl's calls for financial stringency, his Bavarian Agriculture Minister, Ignaz Kiechle, used his veto in the Agricultural Council to prevent a cut in cereal prices. See C. Tugendhat, *Making Sense of Europe* (Harmondsworth, 1987), 46–7.

[7] S. George (ed.), *Britain and the European Community: The Politics of Semi-Detachment* (Oxford, 1992). See also R. Jenkins, 'Britain and Europe: Ten Years of Community Membership', *International Affairs* 59/2 (Spring 1983), 147.

would use membership as a way to 'torpedo' the process from within.[8] The British invariably tended, rhetorically at least, towards the first as reflected in the remark of the then Foreign Secretary, George Brown, to Willy Brandt, 'Willy, you must get us in, so we can take the lead.'[9] The preferred German outcome would, presumably, have fallen somewhere between the first and second scenarios, with Britain playing a constructive role, perhaps taking a lead alongside France and Germany. The reality was somewhat different, at least once Edward Heath was ousted from office in 1974.[10]

British–German differences over European issues were clear at the party political level as well. The major German parties were in favour of European integration, albeit with some variations. The Christian Democrats, whether under Adenauer, Erhard, or Kohl were intimately associated with the creation and deepening of the integration process. The Social Democrats had initially been far less certain about the integration process, but by the time Britain joined the Community were clearly in favour of it, although they became rather more pragmatic during Helmut Schmidt's chancellorship. In marked contrast, both main political parties in Britain suffered deep divisions over questions of European integration, which weakened (and continue to weaken) their ability to 'take the lead' in Europe. Edward Heath, the only post-war Prime Minister to put European considerations ahead of Atlanticist ones, led his party and country into the European Community.[11] Yet many in the Conservative Party, including his successor as party leader, Margaret Thatcher, remained at best uncertain about the European ideal, at worst sceptical.

The rifts in the Labour Party went even deeper and contributed to a deterioration in British–German relations.[12] Although the Labour Party under Harold Wilson had initiated the second British application in 1967, by the time Heath had negotiated accession, the party was hopelessly divided. To resolve the issue, the minority Labour Government which took office in February 1974 undertook a renegotiation of the terms of the Treaty of Accession and, at a second general election in October 1974, pledged to hold a referendum after the renegotiation to allow the public to express their views.[13] Although the outcome of the June 1975

[8] A. Watson, 'Thatcher and Kohl—Old Rivalries Revisited', in M. Bond *et al.* (eds.), *Eminent Europeans—Personalities who Shaped Contemporary Europe* (London, 1996), 267.

[9] W. Brandt, *My Life in Politics* (Harmondsworth, 1992), 420.

[10] Indeed, as Hugo Young points out, even Heath was preoccupied by domestic issues once he had negotiated entry. *This Blessed Plot*, 306.

[11] Heath's European credentials went back a long way: he made his maiden speech to the House of Commons in the debate on the Schuman Plan in June 1950. E. Heath, *The Course of My Life—My Autobiography* (London, 1998), 147.

[12] See J. Young, *Britain and European Unity, 1945–1992* (London, 1993); and H. Young, *This Blessed Plot*, ch. 8.

[13] See H. Young's discussion of Wilson's decision to hold a referendum: *This Blessed Plot*, 283; and J. Smith, 'The 1975 Referendum', *Journal of European Integration History* 5 (1999).

referendum was positive, the whole episode coloured Britain's relations with its Community colleagues. Nor did the referendum finally put an end to the question of Britain's continuing membership. In 1981 many of the party's Europeanists broke away to form the Social Democratic Party (SDP). This left Labour to campaign on a platform of withdrawing from the Community in the 1983 general election.

The divisions within the parties and pragmatic if not sceptical leadership meant that successive British governments were drawn only reluctantly towards further deepening of the integration process. This was in marked contrast to the usually enthusiastic support that governments gave to EC enlargement, the belief being that a wider Europe inevitably meant a looser Europe. Germany, on the other hand, while generally in favour of enlargement was equally determined to ensure that this should not hinder the process of European integration. Differences can also be seen in British and German attitudes towards the European Parliament and direct elections and towards the Council and to qualified majority voting. During the negotiations that eventually led to the Single European Act, the British, despite the government's keenness to expedite the completion of the internal market, held that a 'Gentleman's Agreement' on not using the veto in the Council would suffice. Fewer differences, at least during the 1970s, were discernible in attitudes towards the Commission, Helmut Schmidt tending to share the British scepticism over its role. Matters changed during the 1980s, however, with the advent of Helmut Kohl as German Chancellor and Jacques Delors as Commission President. Delors's clear and effective leadership in favour of deepening the integration process inevitably aroused growing opposition in the UK to the President, his institution, and to further integration.

THE PROBLEM OF THE BUDGET

However, in 1974 the incoming Labour government had turned first to Germany to discuss the proposed renegotiation. The Social Democrats were fellow members of the Socialist International and relations between the two parties were generally good. The Foreign Secretary, James Callaghan, charged with the task of undertaking the renegotiation, found Chancellor Brandt reluctant to engage in detailed discussion—the reason for which became apparent just a few weeks later when Brandt resigned in the wake of a spy scandal. Callaghan immediately established a good relationship with Brandt's successor as Chancellor, Helmut Schmidt, both in personal terms and in their common belief in the Atlantic Alliance.[14] Schmidt's more pragmatic approach found a ready welcome, Callaghan

---

[14] J. Callaghan, *Time and Chance* (London, 1988), 301, 307.

noting in his memoirs that this 'new spirit influenced me to move more towards support for Britain's continued membership, always provided we could broadly satisfy our negotiating objectives'.[15] Yet, if the change in leadership helped foster Europeanism within the British elite, the renegotiation did little to endear the British to the Germans.

The key problem for Britain was the level of net contributions to the Community budget.[16] The budgetary arrangements finalized at the Hague Summit put Britain at a disadvantage: its VAT receipts were high and continued heavy trading with Commonwealth countries meant Britain collected significant amounts of import duty.[17] These payments were not offset by transfers from the Community budget, 80 per cent of which went to fund the Common Agricultural Policy. Thus in the early 1970s Britain's contribution to the Community budget was around 10 to 12 per cent, while her receipts were only 8 per cent, and it was clear that the situation would only get worse over time. The British government estimated that by 1980 Britain's net contribution would be 24 per cent compared with a Gross National Product (GNP) of only 14 per cent of the Community total.[18] Although this problem had been foreseen during the accession negotiations, Edward Heath had accepted the terms, partly because of his own commitment to the European ideal, partly because he believed that there would be a shift in Community expenditure away from agriculture towards regional and social policy.[19] British–German bilateral negotiations suggested that an arrangement could be reached based on Germany's interest in social policy and Britain's desire for a regional policy. As Heath notes in his autobiography, he and Brandt 'agreed that Germany and the UK would meet Pompidou's wish to underline progress towards monetary integration, provided that the French accepted our wish to give priority to regional and social policy'.[20]

The outcome was rather different, however. In his memoirs Brandt says that he had been in favour of a regional fund, but that pressure from the Finance Ministry and the Bundesbank had meant that he could not make heavy commitments on Germany's behalf.[21] Thus, the plans for a Regional Development Fund put forward at the 1972 Paris Summit offered the British considerably less than they might have hoped for— or expected—and even then Brandt was rather reluctant to endorse a

[15] Ibid. 306.

[16] Foreign and Commonwealth Office, 'Britain in the European Community—The Budget Problem', September 1982, reprinted in T. Salmon and W. Nicoll (eds.), *Building European Union— A Documentary History and Analysis* (Manchester, 1997), 182–8.

[17] Hugo Young offers a useful account of various aspects of the original budgetary issues. *This Blessed Plot*, 227–33.   [18] Callaghan, *Time and Chance*, 307.

[19] For an overview of the problems faced by Heath in pursuit of the Regional Fund, see J. Campbell, *Edward Heath* (London, 1994), 559–61.

[20] Heath, *The Course of My Life*, 389.   [21] Brandt, *My Life in Politics*, 423–4.

policy that seemed to be more 'an exercise in old-fashioned, pork-barrel politics rather than a political instrument for the unification of Europe'.[22] Only with Brandt's replacement by Schmidt in 1974 was agreement finally reached, in large part because Schmidt recognized the need to help the Labour government in its renegotiation and in the referendum on continued membership that was to follow it. Yet even with Schmidt as Chancellor, German support for the British position was muted.[23] The German Finance Ministry created a solution accepted by Prime Minister Harold Wilson that met the political needs of the moment rather than settling any basic issues relating to the budget. The result was that the budget became an even bigger issue under the government of Mrs Thatcher.[24]

The advent of Mrs Thatcher put the question of the budget firmly back on the European agenda for nearly five years. Despite her own claims to be pro-European, Mrs Thatcher was determined to get the best possible deal for Britain from the Community with little regard for the niceties of European protocol.[25] She appeared to have taken to heart the advice Christopher Soames had proffered her, 'to the effect that the Community had never been renowned for taking unpleasant decisions without long wrangling and that I should not worry too much, because a major country like Britain could disrupt the Community quite effectively if it chose'.[26] This was, indeed, what Mrs Thatcher chose, leading to very difficult relations with all her European Council colleagues and stagnation of the integration process, about which she appeared little concerned. British–German relations suffered even further with the replacement of the generally pro-British, if clearly irritated Helmut Schmidt by the very much more federalist Helmut Kohl. In 1985, for example, Helmut Kohl declared that, 'Being the driving force behind European unification is one of the Federal Republic's reasons for existence.'[27] Such a statement is indicative both of the differences between British and German attitudes to their national roles and identities and of the clear differences between Kohl and Thatcher as individual politicians and leaders. Moreover, personal relations between Thatcher and Kohl were fairly cool: both

---

[22] W. Feld, *West Germany and the EC: Changing Interests and Competing Policy Options* (New York, 1981), 67, cited in D. Dinan, *Ever Closer Union? An Introduction to the European Community* (London, 1999), 82.

[23] As Schmidt was to recall twenty years later, the renegotiation was essentially perceived by the other Europeans as window-dressing. However, 'If, from British hindsight, it worked as a cosmetic operation, then the rest of the members were successful.' Schmidt speaking on *The Last Europeans*, 3 Dec. 1995, cited in H. Young, *This Blessed Plot*, 283.

[24] See D. Allen, 'British Foreign Policy and West European Co-operation', in P. Byrd (ed.), *British Foreign Policy Under Thatcher* (Oxford, 1988), 38.

[25] M. Thatcher, *The Downing Street Years* (New York, 1993), 537.   [26] Ibid. 79.

[27] Helmut Kohl addressing the Davos Management Forum, cited in Tugendhat, *Making Sense of Europe*, 99.

found French President Mitterrand a more charismatic colleague and Thatcher's relationship with President Reagan was considerably warmer.[28]

Despite advice to 'woo her colleagues', Margaret Thatcher continued to press her case for a budgetary rebate in combative fashion.[29] The approach had not worked particularly well in the early years of her premiership. Sir Michael Butler, Britain's Permanent Representative to the EC, noted in regard to the Dublin Summit of December 1979, 'Chancellor Schmidt and President Giscard seemed to have agreed that they would do all they could to discourage her from pressing the issue.'[30] Nor did Kohl's arrival on the scene alter matters much. Differences could be discerned within the German position, however, as a result of the coalition government. Foreign Secretary Geoffrey Howe felt that during the Greek Presidency of the Council in the second half of 1983, 'Only the Germans, generally in the person of Hans-Dietrich Genscher [the Free Democrat Foreign Minister], were our regular allies in the overall search for budgetary and fiscal restraint.'[31] Helmut Kohl, was less sympathetic to the British case and did little to broker a solution to the question during the German Presidency of the Council, leaving it to the French, in the form of President Mitterrand and his Finance Minister, Jacques Delors, to ensure a positive outcome at the Fontainebleau Summit in June 1984.

The British Budgetary Question was finally resolved not by any bilateral British–German or British–French co-operation, but as a result of the growing awareness that the Community was facing a budgetary crisis. Mrs Thatcher successfully used this as a way to secure her own ends. Some member states favoured raising the budgetary ceiling from 1 per cent to 1.4 per cent of Community VAT receipts.[32] Such a solution required a unanimous vote in the Council. Thus the British had an ideal bargaining chip: they would only agree to raise the ceiling if this was linked to 'reform of the CAP, budgetary discipline and a permanent formula for resolving the problem of budget imbalances'.[33] The urgency of the situation meant that the French became determined to end the problem during their Presidency in the first half of 1984. Yet there was also a problem of how the imbalance should be calculated. Britain was concerned

---

[28] See e.g. G. Smith, *Reagan and Thatcher* (New York, 1991), 23 ff.

[29] Geoffrey Howe recalls an incident at the Williamsburg Economic Summit in 1983, when Helmut Kohl suggested that Howe should try to persuade Thatcher to 'woo her colleagues', pointing out that 'People like François [Mitterrand] would be much more likely to respond to that kind of approach than the argumentative one. And she is certainly well able to do it that way, if she wants to.' G. Howe, *Conflict of Loyalty* (London, 1994), 293.

[30] M. Butler, *More than a Continent* (London, 1986), 95–6 and 104–9, reprinted in A. G. Harryvan and J. van der Harst, *Documents on European Union* (London, 1997), 218.

[31] Howe, *Conflict of Loyalty*, 307.   [32] Dinan, *Ever Closer Union?*, 115.

[33] Allen, 'British Foreign Policy and West European Co-operation', 40.

with the fairness and the size of net contributions (while France rejected any idea of *juste retour*), claiming that Britain's relatively low receipts from the Community budget were the key issue to tackle.[34] In late 1983, Sir Michael Butler suggested a compromise solution to Hans Tietmeyer, State Secretary in the German Finance Ministry. The Germans subsequently adopted this VAT-share/expenditure-share gap solution and persuaded their European colleagues to do likewise. However, the solution favoured by Kohl offered a rebate of only 50 per cent, whereas Mrs Thatcher had hopes of 70 per cent or more. Eventually the Germans, under French pressure, upped their offer to 60 per cent and finally to the 66 per cent the British demanded. The Germans also secured a rebate for themselves: they were granted a two-thirds rebate on the additional costs to the Community arising from Britain's rebate.[35] The crucial point, however, was that the Community log-jam had finally been broken.

Yet, although the budgetary question had been solved at least in the medium term, the question of the CAP remained unanswered.[36] From the outset, the British had found the Common Agricultural Policy particularly difficult to tolerate. It clearly favoured the French and also the Danes and Irish, who joined the Community alongside Britain, but offered few benefits to Britain with its very limited agricultural sector. Moreover, the British frequently assumed that the system did not serve German interests, and that Germany would therefore prove an ally in calls for its reform.[37] Callaghan rapidly discovered during the renegotiation, however, the situation was not so straightforward: Hans Apel made it clear that the principles of the CAP could not be changed; for Germany the CAP was accepted as part of the implicit European bargain.[38] As former European Commissioner Christopher (now Lord) Tugendhat noted, 'the Federal Republic receives enormous non-budgetary benefits from the Community, including a special trading relationship with East Germany, and was itself responsible for many of the absurdities of the Common Agricultural Policy that lay at the root of the British problem.'[39] More importantly it also favoured Bavarian farmers, who represented a significant lobby the government had no wish to ignore. The situation altered little in the course of the 1980s.

[34] This paragraph draws heavily on Butler, *More than a Continent*, reprinted in A. G. Harryvan and J. van der Harst, *Documents on European Union*, 217–23.

[35] For further discussion of the parallel German issue see Butler, ibid. 222.

[36] The question of budgetary contributions resurfaced in the late 1990s when several former net beneficiary states became net contributors. A partial solution was brokered at the Berlin Council meeting in March 1999, but the question seemed set to rumble on—as does the question of reforming the CAP.

[37] As Christopher Tugendhat noted, 'Many people are surprised to learn that the lion's share of these [CAP] surpluses are now held in Germany.' Quoted in Y. Hu, *Europe Under Stress* (London, 1981), 41.　　　　　　　　　　　　　　　　[38] Callaghan, *Time and Chance*, 301.

[39] Tugendhat, *Making Sense of Europe*, 97.

SINGLE MARKET, SINGLE CURRENCY, AND SINGLE EUROPEAN ACT

By contrast, the solution to the *impasse* brokered at the Fontainebleau Summit enabled the 'great leap forward' that was to become the Single European Act, with Britain playing an active role. In many ways the SEA seemed to show a convergence of British, German and French preferences, yet the period leading up to the signing of the Act was characterized by sharp differences between all the larger member states, particularly over the desired end state of the process.[40] For Mrs Thatcher the completion of the internal market was as far as the integration process should or needed to go. She was opposed to adding monetary provisions to treaty reform and to any European level social policy; she was even more implacably opposed to the still-undefined European Union and institutional reforms favoured by the German government. Moreover, while the market liberalization measures introduced by the SEA might appear the logical outcome of right-of-centre co-operation between the British Conservatives and the German Christian Democrats, this was far from the case. The Germans, with their more regulatory, even corporatist, philosophy were in fact closer to the French Socialists than to the Conservatives.

German enthusiasm for the completion of the single market was therefore sometimes tempered by an awareness that even if there were no additional financial costs, deregulation was not always easy. The landmark *Cassis de Dijon* ruling of the European Court of Justice had, after all, been against German regulations.[41] One of the reasons that led Mrs Thatcher to accept more qualified majority voting was 'because things which we wanted were being stopped by others using a single vote. For instance, we have not yet got insurance freely in Germany as we wished'.[42] Differences arising from rival corporate models of ownership and control, the role of banks, and so on inevitably affected attitudes towards liberalization and deregulation. But there were issues on which

[40] Thomas Pedersen argues that the French and Germans did co-operate very closely in the early stages of the SEA. In particular the shift from Schmidt to Kohl saw a decline in German willingness to try to placate the British. T. Pedersen, *Germany, France and the Integration of Europe—A Realist Interpretation* (London: 1998), 112. On the creation of the single market, see also Ch. 11 by I. Begg and M. Wood in this book.

[41] The plaintiff in the *Cassis de Dijon* case wanted to import a consignment of the said liqueur from France to sell in Germany. The German *Bundesmonopolverwaltung* claimed that the alcohol content was too low for the drink to be marketed in Germany. The European Court of Justice took this to be a barrier to trade. Its ruling paved the way for the principle of mutual recognition of goods and hence the completion of the internal market.

[42] Cited in R. O. Keohane and S. Hoffmann, 'Institutional Change in Europe in the 1980s', in R. O. Keohane and S. Hoffmann (eds.), *The New European Community: Decison-Making and Institutional Change* (Oxford, 1991), 17.

Britain and Germany co-operated easily, such as ensuring that completing the single market did not lead to a 'fortress Europe', since both were heavily dependent on trade beyond the Community. One area where the German government went significantly further than that of Mrs Thatcher was on deregulating the movement of people and eliminating other border controls. In that instance the Germans looked towards France and the other original members of the EEC; the British Government standing resolutely aside from anything that might allow rabid animals, drug-traffickers, and terrorists easier access to the UK.[43]

The Thatcher government was reluctant to envisage the sort of institutional reforms Kohl supported, such as increasing the powers of the European Parliament or 'European Assembly' as Mrs Thatcher insisted on calling it until its name was formally changed by the Single European Act. The Parliament was granted new powers of assent and co-operation in the SEA, but only after Britain had voiced its objections to such reforms in a series of footnotes in the Dooge Report, which helped set the agenda for the SEA.[44] Similarly, while Germany was an active proponent of increased qualified majority voting, Britain accepted it only reluctantly, as a way of ensuring other objectives.

The social dimension of the internal market clearly highlighted other differences between the British (Conservative) and German attitudes. It was one of the policy areas advocated by the President of the Commission, Jacques Delors, who argued that it was a necessary corollary to economic integration. The other member states accepted the logic of this argument and later signed up to the Social Charter. By contrast, the idea of raising social and other interventionist and regulatory policies to the European level was anathema to Mrs Thatcher (as was the role of the Commission President in pushing them), and contributed markedly to her Eurosceptic Bruges speech of September 1988.[45] According to the

[43] More rapid movement towards a 'borderless' Europe was thus made by a few core countries outside the Community framework on the basis of the Schengen Agreement of 1985 and its Convention of 1990. Britain was to remain isolated as its opt-outs from the 'Communitarization' of Schengen provisions of the 1997 Amsterdam Treaty indicated. See also Ch. 13 by R. Harmsen and N. Reinhardt in this book.

[44] The Dooge Report emanated from the Committee set up in the wake of the Fontainebleau Summit to 'make suggestions for the improvement of the operation of European cooperation in both the Community field and that of political and other cooperation.' See P. Keatinge and A. Murphy, 'The European Council's Ad Hoc Committee on Institutional Affairs (1984–85)', in R. Pryce (ed.), *The Dynamics of European Union*, 217–37.

[45] Mrs Thatcher's attitudes towards Europe gradually shifted from support for economic aspects to hostility. As she herself noted, 'It seemed to me then [in the 1970s and through most of the 1980s] that the economic benefits of a real common market still outweighed the political problems that would arise if Europe gave institutional flesh to the skeletal concept of "ever closer union". However, by the late 1980s I had become convinced that a reassertion of national rights and interests was overdue—hence the Bruges speech.' M. Thatcher, 'When Powell was right', *The Daily Telegraph*, 23/11/1998.

journalist Thomas Kielinger, after this speech the German government felt that 'Britain could not be trusted on Europe'.[46] From this point on, Britain's and Germany's positions on the future of European integration were only too publicly at odds: Britain sought to preserve the status quo of the SEA; Germany wanted to move towards a more federal entity, as events over the next decade would show.

The idea of economic and monetary union (EMU) had first been put on the Community agenda at the Hague Summit in 1969, given flesh in the Werner Plan of 1970 and formal status as a Community objective at the 1972 Conference of Heads of State or Government meeting in Paris.[47] It was regarded with little more than horror by all the British governments that succeeded Edward Heath's. Throughout the following two decades the issue remained on the Community agenda, even if it sometimes looked unlikely that it could ever be achieved. Member states were divided on the desirability of EMU; the French were its most consistently enthusiastic advocates since, in effect, they were in a Deutschmark zone and saw EMU as a way of regaining some control over monetary affairs. The Germans were less keen since the strength of their currency was a visible symbol of post-war economic success. They were thus determined to ensure that economic union should precede monetary union so that the stability of the *Deutschmark* would not be threatened. (The French consistently argued for the opposite strategy of introducing monetary union prior to economic union.) Britain's attitude throughout was more hostile, although a growing number of Mrs Thatcher's ministers, including her Chancellor of the Exchequer, Foreign Secretary, and Home Secretary were determined to take Britain into the European Monetary System (EMS). Indeed, her Chancellor, Nigel Lawson, had pursued a strategy of shadowing the DM; in the last year of her government the first stage of EMU was agreed.

The experience of the Heath Government in taking sterling into the 'snake in the tunnel', the forerunner of the EMS, and rapidly out again coloured the attitudes of successive British governments towards EMU. The exercise, during the period of 'dirty floating' after the US dollar was taken off the gold standard, was frequently held to have been a mistake which had then been seriously compounded by the consequences of the quadrupling of oil prices and stagflation. Thereafter, Britain's unique position within the EC of being an oil producer only reinforced other, more politically related concerns about different business cycles and, above

[46] Cited in Watson, 'Thatcher and Kohl', 267.
[47] On the evolution towards EMU, see B. Tew, 'Onwards to EMU', in D. Swann (ed.), *The Single European Market and Beyond: A Study of the Wider Implications of the Single European Act* (London, 1992), 193–213.

all, fears over the loss of sovereignty entailed by membership of the Exchange Rate Mechanism (ERM). In that sense Mrs Thatcher's government merely continued the position set out first by James Callaghan of, at best, ignoring plans for further economic integration and, at worst, attempting (signally unsuccessfully) to scupper them.

By contrast, in the post-Gaullist Community, Germany had readily agreed to the French taking part in the 'snake' in the early 1970s, and then playing a leading role in the creation of the EMS. The EMS resulted in part from an idea launched by then President of the Commission, the British Labour (later Social Democrat and finally Liberal Democrat) politician Roy Jenkins in 1977, but also from the close collaboration of two former Finance Ministers, Helmut Schmidt and Giscard d'Estaing. The aim might well have been to create a zone of monetary stability in Europe, rather than fulfil any integration blueprint but it was still too much for a third former Finance Minister—James Callaghan—by then British Prime Minister. The EMS's gradual success in stabilizing exchange rates, together with the success of the internal market programme (and the energetic lobbying of the French whose clear aim was to 'Europeanize' the Bundesbank) meant the German government increasingly accepted the logic of a single currency. But it took some time for the British to appreciate the change in Germany's position. At the Luxembourg Council of 1985, which led to the signing of the SEA, Britain remained opposed to any moves towards economic and monetary union and assumed Germany to be an ally: Nigel Lawson having reminded Thatcher that Kohl had said that the Germans 'like us, were totally opposed to any amendments to the monetary provisions of the Treaty of Rome'.[48] At the Council meeting Kohl declared himself willing to bring monetary matters into the Community framework, much to Thatcher's dismay. A brief discussion with Kohl enabled Thatcher to limit the Treaty amendment to 'co-operation in economic and monetary union' but the episode once again suggested to the British Prime Minister that Britain could not assume the support of Germany in European affairs.[49]

EUROPEAN POLITICAL CO-OPERATION

The very different conceptions of their international roles inevitably meant that Britain and Germany approached foreign policy co-operation from profoundly different angles. The British, rather like the French, tended to see the potential of European Political Co-operation (EPC), the extra-Community intergovernmental framework for foreign policy co-operation,

---

[48] Thatcher, *The Downing Street Years*, 554.   [49] Ibid. 444.

as a supplement to national foreign policy, supportive of continued aspirations to a global role.[50] For the Germans, EPC was more a vehicle, sometimes even a substitute, for a national policy. Yet there were also points of convergence: neither country espoused the anti-Americanism of the French since they were both keen to foster their respective relationships with the United States. The British typically claimed a 'special relationship' with the US, albeit with a brief interruption under Heath during the 1973 Arab–Israeli War and the so-called 'Year of Europe' of 1973–4.[51] Germany, too, had its own customized relationship with the US. This latter relationship became increasingly complex with the decline in the German consensus on defence in response to NATO's double track policy of renewing intermediate nuclear weapons at the same time as pursuing dialogue with the Russians on arms control and strong US pressure to reflate the economy.[52] Genscher's long period as Foreign Minister, however, did ensure considerable continuity.[53]

British–German differences were visible in their divergent approaches to détente and to the Conference on Security and Co-operation in Europe (CSCE) and its follow-up meetings. The British tended to keep a fairly low profile on détente during the 1970s, adopting a view more akin to that of the United States. After the Soviet invasion of Afghanistan in 1979, for example, Britain and the US agreed on the impossibility of doing 'business as usual' with the Soviets. It was only when American claims to extra-territoriality in the aftermath of the declaration of martial law in Poland in 1980 threatened to disrupt UK trade, that Mrs Thatcher sought an alternative path.[54] It was a path that the Germans had been keen to see adopted. Throughout the 1970s, Germany had worked for a relaxation of East–West tension. It viewed the embryonic EPC, for example, as an ideal vehicle to exert pressure on the East during the CSCE process, first in Helsinki, and later in Belgrade and even Madrid in 1980. The American position after Afghanistan, that détente was indivisible, was regarded with distinct unease. As Theo Sommer pointed out, the flip-side of the indivisibility of détente was the indivisibility of tension.[55] Schmidt and others argued strongly that conflicts in the Third World should not be allowed to undermine the relative stability that existed in Europe.[56]

[50] S. Nuttall, *European Political Cooperation* (Oxford 1992).

[51] G. Edwards, 'National Approaches to the Arab-Israeli Conflict: the UK', in D. Allen and A. Pijpers (eds.), *European Foreign-Policy Making and the Arab–Israeli Conflict* (Dordrecht 1984), 47–59.

[52] See K. Larres, 'Torn between Idealism and Egotism: The United States and European Integration, 1945–1990,' *Irish Journal of American Studies* 8 (1999).

[53] See H.-D. Genscher, *Erinnerungen* (Berlin, 1995), chs. 8, 10 and 11.

[54] See e.g. Byrd, *British Foreign Policy under Thatcher*.

[55] T. Sommer, 'Europe and the American Connection', *Foreign Affairs* 58/3 (1980), 622–36.

[56] Ibid. 633–4.

US sanctions against the Soviet Union gave a possibly artificial impression of a convergence of British and German positions, though it was reinforced by the alarm created by President Reagan's Strategic Defence (or 'Star Wars') Initiative (SDI) of 1983, which threatened to decouple the US from Europe's defence. But while the SDI led to agreement on a revival of the Western European Union (WEU), it did not lead immediately to any significant shifts towards the codification of EPC or any greater European security identity.[57] There was no question for the British that defence remained a matter for NATO, even if for Germany there appeared to be merit in steps towards a 'European' force that were being proposed initially on a bilateral basis by the French, first in the Franco-German Brigade and later the Eurocorps. For the British, wider issues of security were to be dealt with only cautiously and on a pragmatic basis, when the member states were able to agree unanimously on closer co-operation and with the United States closely associated.

Both Douglas Hurd, when Minister of State in the Foreign and Commonwealth Office, and Geoffrey Howe when Foreign Secretary were enthusiastic in their support for greater co-operation on foreign policy within the EPC framework—as, indeed, Lord Carrington had been before them. In their declarations on EPC, all three pointed to its usefulness in regional disputes, not least in the Middle East with, for example, the Venice Declaration of 1980, or in support of the UK at the United Nations after the Argentine invasion of the Falkland Islands in 1982. As Mr Hurd put it, EPC had 'come a long way in ten years . . . though there is certainly still room for improvement'.[58] But while the British may have established the first EPC archives, Lord Carrington was prepared to take only limited measures relating to more efficient decision making—such as crisis management measures—in the London Report of 1981. Certainly he and his successors, Francis Pym and Geoffrey Howe, preferred co-operation to either a treaty-based common policy or closer relations between EPC and the European Community. These alternatives were both subjects of Hans-Dietrich Genscher's proposals in what began as the Genscher-Colombo Initiative (Emilio Colombo being the Italian Foreign Minister) of 1981, and which ended as the Solemn Declaration on European Union agreed at the Stuttgart European Council of 1983.

That the Germans should appear to adopt such a positive approach was largely a reflection of anxieties in the German Foreign Ministry that there was an unpalatable gap between Europe's 'potential role and her

---

[57] See W. Wallace, 'European Defence Cooperation: The Reopening Debate', *Survival* 26/6 (1984), 251–61.

[58] D. Hurd, 'Political Cooperation', *International Affairs* 57/3 (1981), 387. See also M. Stuart, *Douglas Hurd The Public Servant: an Authorised Biography* (Edinburgh, 1998).

actual influence'.[59] They felt that an excessive amount of time was being devoted to the British budgetary question and agricultural issues, which *inter alia* risked undermining public support for the Community.[60] Following their initiative with the Italians, the Germans turned again to the French, despite overtures from the British. Indeed, much to the indignation of the British, the French and Germans came up with proposals for strengthening EPC that the British had already discussed bilaterally with the Germans. Geoffrey Howe had been keen to see progress in the area of foreign policy and had drafted a paper proposing what the government had previously rejected: the codification of existing practice. He persuaded Mrs Thatcher that it should be the British who floated the proposal at the European level. Hoping that she would actually 'woo people', Howe suggested that it would be even better to have Helmut Kohl as a co-sponsor of the scheme. Kohl was duly invited to Chequers, where the British Prime Minister made a clear offer, 'I am putting it to you personally like this, Helmut, because I want it to be a genuinely joint endeavour, between the two of us. It will be a useful partnership—and anyway, it's a good idea.'[61] Taking Kohl's response to be positive Mrs Thatcher then sent a copy of the paper to France. Her overture appeared to have failed, when no clear response came from Germany. The reality was even worse: shortly before the Milan Summit a Franco-German proposal for a Treaty on European Union appeared. It contained a section on political co-operation. No reference was made to the British, but Howe and Thatcher found the section disconcertingly similar to the paper they had given Kohl. The attempt to improve British–German relations had backfired, leaving the situation worse rather than better.[62]

Codification of EPC in the SEA of 1986 did not entail any significant additional commitments, although the establishment of a Secretariat promised greater efficiency. Thus, as Françoise de la Serre has argued, 'Although group diplomacy has become more difficult to orchestrate with twelve countries now involved, its advantages are not counterbalanced by any unacceptable constraints upon national policies.'[63] As such, EPC allowed the British under Mrs Thatcher to remain Atlanticist, sometimes pursuing policies with little recourse to EPC and the other member states, even if increasingly in unison with them on most issues. At the same time it enabled Germany's Chancellor Kohl to pursue his *Deutschlandpolitik*. German policy, however, increasingly reinforced Britain's

[59] P. Neville-Jones, 'The Genscher/Colombo Proposals on European Union', *Common Market Law Review* 20 (1983), 658.

[60] Significantly, the Stuttgart Council, which saw agreement on the Solemn Declaration, failed to reach an outcome on the budgetary question.   [61] Howe, *Conflict of Loyalty*, 408.

[62] Ibid. 408–9 and 455; Thatcher, *The Downing Street Years*, 549.

[63] F. de la Serre, 'The Scope of National Adaptation to EPC', in A. Pijpers *et al.* (eds.), *European Political Cooperation in the 1980s* (Dordrecht, 1988), 207.

need for EPC, in that it provided an important additional means to pursue a policy that for the Conservative Government above all carried the weight of the past with it. As Nicholas Ridley put it in 1990, 'We've always played the balance of power in Europe. It has always been Britain's role to keep these various powers balanced, and never has it been more necessary than now, with Germany so uppity.'[64]

CONCLUSION

Despite radically altered circumstances, the post-war period up to 1989 can be seen as one of *'plus ça change, plus c'est la même chose'* in British–German relations. The pattern of bilateral activity intensified within the Community framework, but the relationship continued to ebb and flow, rather than simply deepen. Indeed, Britain's membership of the Community proved an additional complication to a relationship that was bound by mutual support and membership of so many organizations. But it meant disappointment for many in Germany and elsewhere who had expected Britain to offer a measure of leadership within the Community and serve as a counterweight to an exclusively Franco-German axis that had tended to dominate the integration process since the 1950s.[65] Britain, for its part, tended to look to Germany to support its 'lead', even when it was unable to provide one, and despite a residual suspicion and a certain envy of Germany and its economic success.[66]

None the less, in the early 1970s, Britain and Germany appeared to have much in common, at least in terms of attitudes towards economic affairs and foreign and defence policy. This was not, however, mirrored by the emergence of a British–German axis within the European Community. Germany favoured a much more federal Europe, while the British approach was considerably more pragmatic. These attitudes to the integration process thus served both to reinforce British–German relations on some issues, but also to highlight fundamental differences between the two states on others, with the result that despite increased bilateralism within the multilateral framework, there were uncertainties and complications in the relationship. Moreover, British–German relations were deeply affected by

[64] *The Spectator*, 14/7/1990.
[65] In 1972 Theo Sommer wrote an editorial in the German weekly *Die Zeit* as an open letter to a British MP, calling on him to support EC membership in the vote in the House of Commons. One of the reasons was that 'Only if Britain became a member would the Community be saved from permanent Franco-German confrontation'. Eleven years later he questioned Germany's eagerness to see Britain as part of the EC. Theo Sommer, 'Britain and the European Community: A German View', *The World Today* (April 1983), 130.
[66] Hans Apel argued, 'The problem is that the Germans are simply too good. The permanent good example makes the others ill.' *Financial Times*, 18/10/1976.

the relationships between the political leaders and their attitudes towards Europe.

Britain did not go so far as to 'torpedo' the Community from within once it had finally joined. Yet it rarely took the lead either and on many occasions seemed unnecessarily bellicose, in marked contrast to the Germans, whose behaviour was almost always irreproachably pro-European. Britain neither sought to play a leading role in the integration process nor did she accept readily the existing Community *acquis*. In part this was the result of differing national traditions of decision-making—where Germany was used to consensus politics and coalition government, Britain was accustomed to confrontational politics and many British politicians had great difficulty coming to terms with the negotiating practices required to reach agreement within the European Community.[67]

Only once the budgetary problem had been resolved was the British government prepared to take a more positive role. But the cost of resolving the issue was expensive in bilateral terms. While Britain and Germany did co-operate on some issues, their relationship during the latter part of the cold war was characterized by missed opportunities and misunderstandings as well. On balance, the relationship was positive but relatively undramatic prior to 1989, in marked contrast to Margaret Thatcher's hostile attitude towards German reunification typified by the Chequers seminar of 1990, which was subsequently to cast a shadow over British–German relations.

[67] H. Wallace, 'The British Presidency of the EC Council of Ministers: The Opportunity to Persuade' *International Affairs* 62/4 (Autumn 1986), 585.

3

Britain and the GDR: Political and Economic Relations, 1949–1989

KLAUS LARRES

Official political and economic relations between Britain and the German Democratic Republic (GDR) were only established in early 1973—almost twenty-five years after the founding of the East German state in October 1949. However, due to Britain's important and jealously guarded position as one of the four occupation powers in Berlin, London never ignored the developments in the eastern zone of Germany. Both before and after 1973, British governments of all persuasions remained deeply distrustful of the unelected East German government and opposed to its authoritarian and undemocratic political system. In particular, during the 1950s very little contact existed between Britain and the GDR. In April 1954, after the Soviet Union had declared the GDR a sovereign country, Britain, France, and the United States felt the necessity to publicly reiterate the western world's strategy towards the GDR. They announced that they would 'continue to regard the Soviet Union as the responsible Power for the Soviet Zone of Germany' and were thus not prepared to 'recognise the sovereignty of the East German regime which is not based on free elections'. The three allied powers did 'not intend to deal with it as a Government'. Moreover, they were convinced that this view would 'be shared by other states who, like themselves, will continue to recognise the Government of the Federal Republic as the only freely elected and legally constituted government in Germany . . .'.[1]

However, in practice British–East German relations changed somewhat towards the end of the 1950s. This was mainly due to the Berlin crisis (1958–62) and then, in the 1960s, to an improving international climate brought about by the beginning of the era of détente. Increasing pressure on policy-makers from Labour and Conservative backbenchers who favoured exploiting trade opportunities with East Germany also played an important role. At the same time the GDR regime was waging an active

---

[1] Joint Declaration by the three western Allied High Commissioners on 8 April 1954. Quoted in Public Record Office, London (hereafter, PRO): FO 371/189 154/RG 1011/4, 17/2/1966.

and on occasion successful campaign to enter into closer contact with western countries, including Britain. East Berlin even believed at times that due to the UK's increasing economic problems the country was the weak point where a breakthrough could be achieved regarding the GDR's recognition by one of the leading western nations.

Yet, despite the fact that for several months during the momentous events in 1989/90 British Prime Minister Thatcher was one of the very few western politicians who strongly advocated the continued existence of the second German state, British–East German relations were never particularly close, neither before nor after recognition in 1973. One of the main reasons for the caution with which policy-makers in London approached relations with East Berlin appears to have been Britain's much more important relationship with West Germany. Until Willy Brandt's *Ostpolitik* in the early 1970s the Federal Republic of Germany (FRG) insisted on a policy of non-recognition of the GDR and, on the whole, Britain firmly supported West Germany's strongly defended claim to be the only legal and moral representative of the entire German nation.

Even after 1973 the Federal Republic's views on East Germany were always taken into consideration as far as Britain's relations with the GDR were concerned. Throughout the cold war it therefore appeared to many contemporaries that Britain's relationship with East Germany was to a large extent dominated by the wishes of a foreign, albeit allied, state. Indeed some British industrialists believed that the British government was in Bonn's pocket and that undue West German influence on the country's relations with the GDR was harmful to Britain's economic self-interest.[2] Whether or not this was a justified interpretation of the UK's relationship with the GDR in the cold war world will be analysed in this essay.

This article will therefore concentrate on the issues which clearly dominated British–East German relations: politics and trade.[3] Britain's

---

[2] See PRO: FO 371/183 049/RG 1054/21, 17/5/1965.

[3] See in general A. Bachmann, 'Die Beziehungen der DDR zu den angelsächsischen Ländern', in H.-J. Veen and P. R. Weilemann (eds.), *Die Westpolitik der DDR. Beziehungen der DDR zu ausgewählten westlichen Industrieländern in den 70er und 80er Jahren* (Melle, 1989), 125–9. The comparatively unimportant (though not always unsuccessful) attempts by the ruling East German Communist Party (SED) to enter into contact with British parties, trade unions, churches and other organisations have been neglected. Although the GDR made some effort to establish British–East German cultural links (the twinning of towns, e.g. between Dresden and Coventry, the staging of artistic exhibitions, etc.), they never made any deep impact on neither the UK government nor the British people. Moreover, all British governments were aware that the GDR only tended to be concerned about establishing cultural links with Britain and other western countries when all other points of contact in the political and economic sphere had failed. For the town twinning programme see F. Eymelt, *Die Tätigkeit der DDR in den nichtkommunistischen Ländern, V. Grossbritannien* (Bonn, 1970), 30–36. For an overview on the cultural links, see B. Becker, *Die DDR und Großbritannien 1945/49 bis 1973. Politische, wirtschaftliche und kulturelle Kontakte im Zeichen der Nichtanerkennungspolitik* (Bochum, 1991), 236 ff.

unusual political and economic relations with the East German regime will be assessed in four phases. First, the years 1949–61 reveal the beginning of private British–East German trade contacts. Moreover, during the Berlin crisis the Macmillan government seemed to be increasingly willing to accept the *de facto* sovereignty of the regime in East Berlin. Second, the 1960s saw the development of ever more intensive trade relations between London and East Berlin while political relations remained strained. Third, the year 1973 witnessed the international recognition of the GDR once West Germany's *Ostpolitik* had been successfully concluded. Finally, the period beginning with the recognition of the GDR and ending with the fall of the Berlin Wall and German unification in 1989/90 showed the establishment of diplomatically correct though still fairly cool relations between the two countries.[4] As will be seen, European integration, both before and after Britain became a member of the EEC in 1973, had a rather limited influence on British–East German relations.

THE POLITICS OF STRICT NON-RECOGNITION
(1949–1961)

During the first (1949–1961) and indeed during the second phase (1962–1972) of British–East German relations the nature of the GDR's policies towards London and the western world as a whole can be characterized as the search for political recognition. At the same time Britain's and the western world's strategy may be termed the politics of non-recognition. Indeed, no sooner had the GDR been established in October 1949 than the new state was dismissed as an 'artificial creation' by the western occupation powers.[5]

Britain (but also other western countries like France and the US) realized immediately that any recognition of the undemocratic and illegal regime in East Berlin would give GDR leader Walter Ulbricht enormous prestige. It would also undermine the spirit of resistance towards the regime

[4] Due to the availability of primary sources covering the 1950s and 1960s, the article concentrates mainly on these decades. At the time of writing most British and East German documents until 1968 were available for research purposes. However, in the scholarly literature British–East German relations have attracted very little attention. There are only two book-length detailed assessments of the relationship up to 1973 (both are important studies) and none dealing with the time after recognition. See Becker, *DDR und Großbritannien*; and M. Bell, 'Britain and East Germany: The Politics of Non-Recognition' (unpub. M. Phil. thesis, University of Nottingham, 1977). Henning Hoff is completing a doctoral thesis on British–East German relations in the 1960s at the University of Cologne. For an overview on the post-1973 period see Bachmann, 'Die Beziehungen der DDR', 72–111.

[5] See Foreign Relations of the United States (hereafter: FRUS), 1949, vol. 3, 532. See also H.-J. Rupieper, 'Die Reaktionen der USA auf die Gründung der DDR', in E. Scherstjanoi (ed.), *'Provisorium für längstens ein Jahr': Die Gründung der DDR* (Berlin, 1993), 59–66.

within Berlin and East Germany. In addition it could be expected that once the UK, at the time the most important and influential western European state, recognized the GDR many other countries 'would follow suit'. The idea that there might be 'an exchange of ministers with the Communist Government of the Soviet zone' was regarded as 'repugnant'. The recognition of the GDR would also undermine the western claim that the FRG was the only legal German government. It could be expected that this would greatly demoralize and 'dishearten' the West and East German people as well as the population of Berlin.[6] After all, the British assumed that the Ulbricht regime would gain 'no popular backing whatever' and would 'be hated and despised throughout the length and breadth of Germany'.[7] Moreover, the majority of West Germans seemed to be convinced that the West's strategy of containment and policy of strength towards the Soviet Union would lead to reunification in a fairly short period of time. West German Chancellor Konrad Adenauer's 'magnet theory' was given great credibility by his voters. This was the thesis that once the Bonn Republic had been integrated with the democratic West and begun to flourish economically, the East Germans would be so attracted to the western way of life that the GDR would collapse from within.[8] Thus, any official recognition of the GDR would undermine the West German population's belief in the western world's ability to bring about unification. It was therefore out of the question. After all, it was crucial that the West German people maintained their faith in the western powers and continued supporting Adenauer's *Westpolitik*. The dreaded vision of the emergence of a neutral reunified Germany swinging freely between East and West strongly influenced the western allies' policy towards both the GDR and the FRG.[9] Furthermore, in late 1949 some officials in London were still worried that the East might become 'a magnet for the West'. Instead, the British wished to 'make ourselves attractive' and solve the German question by pulling 'the Soviet zone into the Western orbit'. The policy 'to win over the whole of Germany to

6   PRO: FO 371/76 617/C 8047, 11/10/1949; also C 7898, C 7896, both 13/10/1949.
7   PRO: FO 371/76 617/C 8047, undated, c.18/10/1949.
8   For Adenauer's political thinking, see for example N. Altmann, *Konrad Adenauer im Kalten Krieg: Wahrnehmungen und Politik, 1945–1956* (Mannheim, 1993), 43 ff., 76 ff.; also my article 'Konrad Adenauer (1874–1967)', in T. Oppelland (ed.), *Portraits der deutschen Politik 1949–1969*, vol. 1 (Darmstadt, 1999), 13–24.
9   After all, this was the solution to the German question which was favoured by the opposition SPD at the time and which Stalin was to propose in his 1952 note. See K. Larres, *Politik der Illusionen: Churchill, Eisenhower und die deutsche Frage 1945–1955* (Göttingen, 1995), 94–101. For the Stalin note see R. Steininger, *The German Question: The Stalin Note of 1952 and the problem of reunification* (New York, 1990); G. Wettig, 'Stalin and German Reunification: Archival Evidence on Soviet Foreign Policy in Spring 1952,' *Historical J.* 37/2 (1994), 411–19; G. Wettig, *Bereitschaft zu Einheit in Freiheit? Die sowjetische Deutschland-Politik 1945–1955* (Munich, 1999), 205 ff.

the Western cause' made any recognition of the GDR and thus of the long-term division of Germany inconceivable.[10]

The Foreign Office realized however that there were also a number of disadvantages to not recognizing the GDR. The diplomats worried, for example, about the fate of the recently concluded interzonal trade agreement between the western zones and the Soviet zone of Germany which regulated the exchange of goods between the western and eastern zones on the basis of fixed clearing rates. However, on balance it seemed 'clear that the disadvantages of de jure recognition far out-weigh those of non-recognition, despite the practical difficulties involved in the latter'.[11] Already in October 1949 it was decided in London to encourage verbal attacks on the new government in East Berlin by pointing out publicly that the regime was a foreign imposed body totally unrepresentative of the Soviet zone and Germany as a whole and completely under Stalin's control.[12] London felt uneasy about the Soviet Union's determination to give the GDR 'rights and powers' which were 'going beyond those enjoyed by the Federal Republic' and were thus causing 'some jealousy' in Bonn. Although it was abundantly clear that the nominal 'freedoms granted to the Eastern Government are bogus', it could be expected that Chancellor Adenauer would put pressure on the Allied High Commission to extend the authority of the West German government.[13] It appears that the conclusion of the Petersberg Agreement between the western allies and the Bonn government on 24 November 1949 was to some extent influenced by the establishment of the GDR. It resulted in the termination of the allied dismantlements in West Germany which, according to British officials, 'markedly increased' Adenauer's prestige. Subsequently they observed with great relief that the GDR's national front propaganda was an 'almost total flop' as far as its impact on the West German population was concerned.[14]

In November/December 1949, in the course of lengthy negotiations which were concluded on 15 December, the western foreign ministers and the Permanent Commission of the Brussels Treaty Powers agreed upon an official strategy of non-recognition of the GDR.[15] This policy included

---

[10] Quotes: PRO: FO 371/76 615/C 6615, 20/8/1949; 76 617/C 8047, undated, c.18/10/1949.

[11] PRO: FO 371/76 617/C 8047, 11/10/1949. For a discussion on the limited practical differences between *de jure* and *de facto* recognition, see ibid., undated, c.18/10/1949.

[12] PRO: FO 371/76 617/C 8047, 13/10 and 14/10/1949, and undated, c.18/10/1949. For the internal discussions of how to refer to the East Berlin government, see FO 371/76 617/C 8082, 7/10/1949 (one suggestion was 'Ozonia', see FO 371/76 619/C 9990, 22/12/1949).

[13] PRO: FO 371/76 617/C 7898, 13/10/1949; also 76 618/C 8452, 29/11/1949.

[14] PRO: FO 371/76 618/C 8452, 29/11/1949.

[15] In fact, on British Foreign Secretary Ernest Bevin's suggestion, the Permanent Commission of the Brussels Treaty Powers in London was used to work out 'a concerted policy' to 'avoid independent action' by western countries. It was also agreed to use this forum to clarify the western attitude regarding the conclusion of trade agreements with East Berlin. See PRO: FO 371/76 619/C 9680, 8/11/1949.

governmental trade relations. It was feared that entering into official trade relations could easily be misinterpreted as the *de facto* if not *de jure* recognition of the GDR. The decision was also taken that the Soviet Union would continue to be viewed as being responsible for the eastern zone. Moreover, the western powers expressed their opposition to the participation of the GDR in any international bodies.[16]

At this stage it appears that it was not so much the United States but Britain who took the leading role in preventing the recognition of the GDR by western governments. There was however hardly any difference in substance between the UK and the USA in this question.[17] Throughout the early 1950s the British government attempted to co-ordinate the non-recognition policy among the western states, particularly within NATO, as well as among the Commonwealth countries and, in co-operation with Washington, amongst the South American and non-aligned states. However, this was not easy. Due to expected trade opportunities and other commercial interests some countries were quite open-minded regarding contact with the communists in East Berlin. It was especially tiresome to ensure the reliability of several Latin American and some Scandinavian countries (above all Sweden and Finland). However, Switzerland and the Benelux countries, in particular the Netherlands, also proved to be very difficult cases.[18]

It was clear that by early 1950 political reality had intruded upon the West's non-recognition doctrine. Indeed, already in a minute dated 11 October 1949 the Foreign Office had been realistic enough to realize that 'we cannot pretend indefinitely that the Government in the Soviet Zone does not exist'.[19] Particularly, as far as interzonal trade, interzonal communications, and similar matters were concerned, it appeared to be 'very difficult to avoid some form of de facto recognition, or at any rate a certain degree of de facto co-operation'.[20] It was however assumed that the allied powers and the West Germans would not take any initiative themselves 'which would involve de facto recognition'. The experts in the Foreign Office concluded that 'In view of the need of the Eastern zone

---

[16] PRO: FO 371/76 619/C 9776, 15/12/1949 (= Document No.A/561, Final Version); also e.g. in FO 371/109 504/CS 1017/25(2); and in FRUS 1950, vol. 4, 942–3. See also FO 371/76 618/C 8905, 27/10/1949; 76 619/C 9680, 8/11/1949, 13/15/10/1949; C 9501, 7/12/1949.

[17] For an overview regarding Washington's policy towards the GDR, see C. Ostermann, 'Im Schatten der Bundesrepublik. Die DDR im Kalkül der amerikanischen Deutschlandpolitik (1949–1989/90)', in K. Larres and T. Oppelland (eds.), *Deutschland und die USA im 20. Jahrhundert: Geschichte der politischen Beziehungen* (Darmstadt, 1997), 230–55; also B.C. Gaida, *USA–DDR. Politische, kulturelle und wirtschaftliche Beziehungen seit 1974* (Bochum, 1989).

[18] See e.g. PRO: FO 371/76 617/C 7879, 10/10/1949; /C 8047, undated, *c.* Oct. 1949; /C 8127, 22/10/1949; FO 371/76 619/C 9501, 8/12/1949; FO 371/85 122, 1949–50 (Switzerland); also Becker, *DDR und Großbritannien*, 74–82.   [19] PRO: FO 371/76 617/C 8047, 11/10/1949.

[20] PRO: FO 371/76 617/C 7929, 19/10/1949.

for trade with the West, it seems probable that we could afford to wait for an approach from the Government in the Soviet Zone.'[21]

Thus, almost from the founding of the GDR in October 1949 the British government was torn between its principled standpoint of not recognising and basically ignoring the GDR (and remaining faithful to the support of the Bonn government) and the practical difficulties of doing so. In addition, a certain temptation to trade with the East could already be observed.

Developments in Britain's Non-recognition Policy in the 1950s

Between Stalin's death in March 1953 and the building of the Berlin Wall in August 1961 a certain weakening of Britain's loyalty to West Germany could be noticed. Although this was not motivated by a development of greater sympathy for the GDR's political system, in effect it worked to the long-term advantage of the East German regime. To some extent it appeared in the course of the 1950s as if the GDR was gradually, though very slowly, able to overcome its international *pariah* role.

Initially however, the crushing of the popular uprising in the GDR on 17 June 1953 by Soviet tanks and East German police forces confirmed the Foreign Office's assessment of the undemocratic nature and the deep unpopularity of the Ulbricht regime with the East German people. Prime Minister Churchill's belief after Stalin's death that new Soviet Prime Minister Malenkov and his Security Minister Beria were genuinely considering agreeing to the establishment of a neutral reunited Germany and sacrificing the GDR as an independent state to arrive at a less expensive and less dangerous *modus vivendi* with the West had been proved incorrect.[22] In May 1953 Churchill had publicly suggested the convening of an informal 'Big Three' summit conference to discuss and overcome all outstanding cold war problems. Furthermore, in several secret memoranda and minutes the British Prime Minister had expressed the notion that a reunited and neutral Germany and the sacrifice of the Federal Republic's rearmament and integration with the West by way of the

---

[21] PRO: FO 371/76 617/C 8047, 11/10/1949.

[22] PRO: FO 371/103 660/C 1016/32 (19/5/1953), 33 (29/5/1953), 34 (1/6/1953); also: FO 371/103 704/C 1073/1–10 (May–July 1953); for the considerations of the new Soviet leaders regarding the German question, see E. Scherstjanoi, ' "In 14 Tagen werden Sie vielleicht keinen Staat mehr haben". Vladimir Semenov und der 17. Juni 1953', *Deutschland-Archiv* 31/6 (1998), 907–37; also my articles 'Preserving Law and Order: Britain, the United States and the East German Uprising of 1953', *Twentieth Century British History* 5/3 (1994), 320–50; and 'Großbritannien und der 17. Juni 1953: 'Die deutsche Frage und das Scheitern von Churchills Entspannungspolitik', in C. Kleßmann and B. Stöver (eds.), *1953-Krisenjahr des Kalten Krieges in Europa* (Cologne, 1999), 155–79; and G. Wettig, *Bereitschaft zu Einheit in Freiheit?*, 235 ff.

envisaged European Defence Community (EDC) might prove a suitable price to pay for an end of the cold war.[23] Not surprisingly, Churchill's ideas were strongly opposed by the American Eisenhower administration, Chancellor Adenauer in Bonn, and even by his own Foreign Office including Foreign Secretary Anthony Eden. Thus merely the Prime Minister himself—not the British establishment as such—was challenging the cold war status quo. Indeed, the experts in London, Washington, and Bonn noted with great satisfaction that the uprising in the GDR on 17 June 1953 undermined the credibility of Churchill's plans decisively. After all, how could one possibly start negotiating with the politicians in the Kremlin who had just given their approval to the invasion of the GDR and the brutal crushing of the uprising? Moreover, it could be expected that the weakened Soviet Union would hardly be interested in participating in Churchill's conference at present or in giving up the GDR. The latter might well lead to a general protest movement against Soviet rule in the whole of eastern Europe. Thus, the western powers were convinced that the integration of the FRG with the West and the continued division of Germany were 'the key to the peace in Europe'.[24]

After the uprising in the GDR and the subsequent arrest and execution of Beria, the chief proponent within the Kremlin of sacrificing the GDR as an independent state, Moscow remodelled its German policy. Once again the Kremlin began to return to its strong support of the GDR regime and it aided Ulbricht in consolidating his power against his internal opponents within the GDR party hierarchy.[25] Moreover, from now on Moscow began to push hard to obtain at least the *de facto* acceptance of the existence of the East German state by the western world. In late March 1954 the Soviet Union declared the GDR a sovereign state and on 20 September 1955—after the Bonn Republic had become a member of NATO and a semi-sovereign state in May—a formal Soviet–East German treaty of sovereignty was signed. It gave the GDR responsibility for its own foreign policy.[26] The western allies refused to recognize this treaty and were moreover not prepared to allow the Soviet Union, in its capacity as one of the four occupation powers, to transfer its responsibilities for the eastern zone to the internationally unrecognized GDR

[23] See Churchill's parliamentary speech, *House of Commons, Parliamentary Debates, 5th series* (hereafter: *H.C. Deb.*), vol. 515, 883–98 (11/5/1953); and PRO: FO 371/103 660/C 1016/32, 19/5/1953.
[24] PRO: PREM 11/673, PM/MS/53/254, 22/6/1953; also Larres, *Politik der Illusionen*, 175–81; see also the articles mentioned in n. 22.
[25] See H. Weber, *Geschichte der DDR*, 2nd edn. (Munich, 1986), 249–51; also the account of a contemporary, K. Schirdewan, *Aufstand gegen Ulbricht. Im Kampf um politische Kurskorrektur, gegen stalinistische, dogmatische Politik* (Berlin, 1994).   [26] Weber, ibid. 255–9.

regime. Adenauer received several private and public western assurances that no recognition of the GDR was contemplated.[27]

This did not prevent Moscow from developing the so-called 'two-state theory' in the course of 1955. Although Ulbricht continued thinking about the reunification of a socialist Germany, the Kremlin appeared to have given up any attempt to realize German reunification.[28] After the 1953 uprising Moscow had become aware that overcoming the division of Germany, even on a neutral basis as suggested by Stalin in early 1952 and by Churchill in 1953, might well lead to the integration of the whole of Germany with the West in the long run. The Soviet Union now intended to maintain the post-war status quo and therefore the continuation of Soviet influence over at least one part of the German nation. Thus, West Germany's western integration did not lead to further tension between East and West as had been gloomily anticipated by many in the West. On the contrary, it actually helped to ease cold war tension by demarcating clear spheres of influence between East and West—a lesson which was lost on neither the western allies nor on the men in the Kremlin.

Although Britain, the other western powers and the West German government remained unimpressed by Soviet efforts to grant more independence to the GDR, great fears were harboured that the Russians might complicate western access to Berlin. Already after the not entirely unexpected Soviet declaration of sovereignty for the GDR on 25 March 1954 anxiety had been expressed in Bonn and London that it 'might not be possible to continue to keep the Pankow regime at quite such an arm's length'.[29] Indeed, the British embassy in Bonn reported that even Adenauer appeared to have realized that despite the continuation of non-recognition, 'it might be necessary for reasons of practical convenience and in the interests of the Germans themselves, to be less rigid or to have rather more extensive day-to-day dealings on technical matters with the East German authorities'.[30]

This assessment was certainly justified as far as the situation from 1955 onwards was concerned. After all, in September Adenauer had agreed to

[27] E.g. on 8 April 1954 (Allied High Commissioners), 23 April 1954 (NATO foreign ministers), and on 3 Oct. 1954 (Three-Power Declaration by the western allies). Adenauer was particularly worried that some neutral countries like Sweden would be tempted to recognize the GDR. See e.g. PRO: FO 371/109 504/CS 1017/14, 2/4/1954; CS 1071/25, 9/4/1954.

[28] Weber, *Geschichte der DDR*, 257–58; also B. Meissner, 'Die deutsch-sowjetischen Beziehungen seit dem Zweiten Weltkrieg', *Osteuropa* (1985), 631–52.

[29] PRO: FO 371/109 504, CS 1017/14, 2/4/1954; CS 1017/31, 8/4/1954; see also the memorandum and the minutes in CS 1017/20, 26/3/1954 regarding the repercussions on the EDC.

[30] PRO: FO 371/109 504/CS 1017/14, 5/4/1954. As the British authorities always believed that any initiative for dealings with the East Germans initially 'should come from the Federal Government and not from the Western Powers', this was a welcome development. See ibid. 4/4/1954.

enter into diplomatic relations with the Soviet Union during his visit to Moscow in order to obtain the release of all remaining German prisoners of war.[31] Yet, embarking upon official relations with the Kremlin threatened to undermine West Germany's non-recognition strategy as Bonn had now taken up diplomatic relations with a state which recognized the GDR. The Adenauer government realized that it was very doubtful that the letter on German unity which the Chancellor handed to the Soviet head of state, Nikolai Bulganin, would be given much attention in the world at large. The letter pointed out that it was Bonn's understanding that the Federal Republic was still the sole legitimate representative of the whole of Germany and that the FRG neither recognized the legitimacy of the GDR nor the Oder-Neisse line as Germany's eastern border; Bonn insisted on Germany's 1937 borders.[32] Thus, the West German government announced that the Soviet Union, as one of the four occupation powers was a special case. Therefore, the recognition of the East Berlin regime by any other country would be regarded as an unfriendly act to be followed by appropriate action. Bonn had invented the 'Hallstein Doctrine'.[33]

As events would show, after 1955—in particular during the 1960s—it would prove ever more difficult to insist on the international non-recognition of the GDR. Consequently, the Bonn government became increasingly sensitive about any signs that the united western front regarding the non-recognition of the GDR was weakening. The Foreign Office realized this and concluded in early October 1955 that it was particularly important 'that we should not give the Federal Government any opportunity to be suspicious of us'.[34] British officials were however fairly certain that the Adenauer government would have to modify its policy towards the GDR over time 'though of course this may never go so far as to involve actual recognition'. Decision-makers in London agreed that as far as the strict non-recognition of the GDR was concerned 'we should . . . march in step with the Federal Government, and only reconsider this question

---

[31] See K. Larres, 'Germany and the West: the "Rapallo Factor" in German Foreign Policy from the 1950s to the 1990s', in K. Larres and P. Panayi (eds.), *The Federal Republic of Germany since 1949* (London, 1996), 288–301.

[32] K. Adenauer, *Erinnerungen, vol. 2: 1953–1955* (Stuttgart, 1966), 547–51; PRO: FO 371/118 181/WG 10338/107, 14/9/1955. On the legal implications of the establishment of diplomatic relations from the British point of view, see the memorandum in FO 371/118 181/WG 10338/143, 15/9/1955. See also PRO: FO 371/118 181/WG 10339/109, 14/9/1955; FRUS, 1955–7, vol. 5, 580, 13/9/1955; S. Talbott (ed.), *Khrushchev Remembers: The Last Testament* (London, 1974), 359–60.

[33] See D. Kosthorst, *Brentano und die deutsche Einheit. Die Deutschland- und Ostpolitik des Außenministers im Kabinett Adenauer 1955–1961* (Melle, 1993), 88–93; R. Booz, *Hallsteinzeit: deutsche Außenpolitik 1955–1972* (Bonn, 1995); W. Grewe, *Rückblenden, 1951–76* (Frankfurt, 1979), 251–62.   [34] PRO: FO 371/109 514, CS 1051/2, 6/10/1955.

if the West German attitude warrants it'.[35] Prime Minister Eden's disengagement proposal during the Geneva Four Power Summit Conference in July 1955 had already caused suspicion in Bonn that London was prepared to recognize the existence of two German states. After all, the new British Prime Minister had suggested the creation of a neutral zone in the middle of Europe along the German–German border to de-escalate East–West tension, thus indirectly acknowledging the division of Germany and the existence of the GDR.[36] Indeed, internally the Foreign Office had come to the conclusion that 'we are in for a long period of living with the DDR . . .'.[37]

Trade Opportunities with the GDR in the 1950s

During the 1950s British–East German trade relations were mostly limited to so-called compensation deals and barter agreements for a limited range of goods (mostly chemicals, particularly fertilizers, potash, timber, and machinery) which required import or export licences.[38] According to the western non-recognition agreement of 15 December 1949, trade relations with the GDR ought to be 'conducted solely through the intermediary of private organisations, such as Chambers of Commerce'. It was assumed that the 'fact that such private organisations on our side may deal with "official" organisations on the other side is of no significance with regard of (sic!) recognition'.[39] Only in highly exceptional cases should governmental contact take place with East Berlin but at 'as low and "technical" a level as possible'. In such a case the GDR trade

[35] PRO: FO 371/109 514, CS 1051/2, 6/10/1955. Already in January 1955 the FO had come to the conclusion: 'Should the Federal Government one day establish some kind of working relations with the East German Authorities, then we could follow suit. We have indeed drawn up plans for this in case . . . the Russians refuse to have dealings with the East German Authorities while still not recognising them. But in the meanwhile we should not go ahead of the West Germans in showing any courtesies to the East Germans.' PRO: FO 371/109 514, CS 105/2, 10/1/1955.

[36] See A. Eden, *Full Circle* (London, 1960), 292–4, 298–9, 302–5. Although the implementation of the Eden Plan was not even considered during the subsequent Geneva foreign ministers' conference in Oct./Nov. 1955, the Plan led indirectly to the development of various similar disengagement plans between 1956 and 1958 (including the Rapacki Plan; there were even similar top secret considerations in Bonn). See Kosthorst, *Brentano*, 118 ff.

[37] PRO: FO 371/109 514/CS 1051/2, 27/10/1954.

[38] For a detailed list of traded goods for the year 1963, see e.g. PRO: FO 371/172 171/RG 1154/5, dated 2/11/1963.

[39] PRO: FO 371/76 619/C 9776, 15/12/1949 (Document No.A/561, Final Version). After the establishement of the GDR it was the Norwegian government which first renewed their trade agreement with Eastern Germany on this basis. In full compliance with the non-recognition agreement Norway rejected dealing with the Soviet Zone 'Government' as suggested by the Soviet authorities. Instead an association of private Norwegian exporters and the German Foreign Trade Organization which was subordinate to East Berlin's Ministry for Foreign Trade began their negotiations in early 1950. PRO: FO 371/76 619/C 9776, 20 Dec. 1949.

representatives would be regarded as acting as agents of the responsible Soviet occupation authorities.[40]

Almost immediately after the founding of the GDR the Ulbricht regime began to lure western countries, and in particular the United Kingdom, into trade relations. East Berlin indicated that 'those countries which got in first would doubtless secure . . . trade agreements . . . on very advantageous terms' while those who delayed recognition would 'find themselves in a less favourable position over economic negotiations'. Moreover, the UK's apparent economic problems and the country's 'consequent need to find new markets and trading partners' encouraged the GDR authorities to point out that the Bonn Republic's economy was deteriorating while 'East Germany offered useful prospects in the field of trade relations'.[41] However, this had little effect. It was only after the end of the Korean War in mid-1953 and the beginning of a recession in the West that Western European firms became keener on developing trade contacts with Eastern Europe including the GDR. At first the relatively few British companies who tried to concentrate on developing such links with the GDR were organized in the British Council for the Promotion of International Trade (BCPIT) or, to a lesser extent, in the London Export Corporation. In particular the former was regarded as a communist front organization and the British government was strongly opposed to supporting the trading endeavours of the firms organized in this umbrella organization. London believed in fact that it was 'most unfortunate' that trade relations with East Berlin were largely 'in the hands of spivs and crooks who are doing this country no good'.[42]

While the GDR managed to exploit the post-Korea recession to some extent and, during 1953/4, concluded various trading agreements with the Benelux countries, Austria, Turkey, and some Scandinavian nations, no treaty with Britain could be signed. The Foreign Office continued to believe that entering into official trade negotiations with the GDR was not advisable, both for reasons of principle and in view of West German objections.[43] However, the East German authorities used the services of British businessmen like R. Sternberg of the company British Propane Ltd., for example, and Members of Parliament, like Conservative MP Burnaby Drayson, to further their cause. In the course of 1953 and 1954 both men made numerous (unsuccessful) attempts to convince the British authorities to enter into semi-official trade negotiations with

[40] PRO: FO 371/76 619/C 9776, 15/12/1949 (Document No.A/561, Final Version).
[41] PRO: FO 371/76 618/C 8496, 4/11/1949 (article in the magazine *Neue Zeit*).
[42] PRO: FO 371/109 537/CS 1151/7, 2/12/1954; also CS 1111/11, 14/10/1953; on the London Export Corporation, see CS 1151/8, 9/12/1954. See also Becker, *DDR und Großbritannien*, 201 ff.; FO 371/124 599/WG 1152/9, 25/2/1956.
[43] PRO: FO 371/103 857/CS 1111/5(1), 12/6/1953.

GDR representatives and to open an official GDR account with the Bank of England.[44] It was alleged that the latter would reduce 'Soviet control over the economic life of the East Germans' which in view of the June uprising in 1953 might be very advantageous.[45] Yet London was not convinced. Apart from Britain's obligations to West Germany and the government's readiness to adhere to the non-recognition doctrine, in the early 1950s it also appeared important to be able to use trade as a cold war weapon. After all, in case of another Berlin crisis or Soviet pressure on West Germany, Britain's 'only effective weapon of retaliation' short of military action was 'to cut off East Germany's trade with the West'. It was concluded that 'We must therefore leave our hands free to do this and we cannot therefore enter into any trade agreements.'[46]

Yet, since 1949 Sternberg's Propane Company Ltd. had already conducted considerable business, on the basis of barter deals, with the East German DIA authority (Deutscher Innen- und Aussenhandel). In fact, Sternberg was acting as the DIA's and thus as the GDR government's UK agent.[47] However, the first major deal of a British company which was not largely serving East German interests was negotiated in the course of the Leipzig trade fair in autumn 1953. In early September Burnaby Drayson MP managed to conclude a deal on behalf of the British company Dominions Export Ltd. The GDR purchased raw coffee and cocoa beans to the value of 1.5 million dollars from the company. This proved to be the effective beginning of private British–East German trade relations.[48]

Not only did it make much sense for the GDR to conclude trade deals with western countries in view of the severe economic difficulties in East Germany but East Berlin also hoped to make progress towards political recognition.[49] However, the British Foreign Office and the Board of Trade still insisted that official trade contacts could not be entered into. With the exception of goods whose export had been declared forbidden by the allied COCOM-lists for trade with Eastern Europe, there were

---

[44] See above all the detailed documents in PRO: FO 371/103 857 (1953).

[45] PRO: FO 371/103 857/CS 1111/7, 22/6/1953.

[46] PRO: FO 371/103 857/CS 1111/5, 12/6/1953.

[47] See PRO: FO 371/103 857/CS 1111/6, 17/6/1953.

[48] However, Drayson had a substantial private interest in the company. The British authorities concluded that there were neither any political nor other objections to the contract. 'Indeed the proposal is in accordance with our policy of encouraging legitimate East/West trade . . .'. PRO: FO 371/103 857/CS 1111/13, 13/11 and 19/11/1953. The contract is in PRO: FO 371/103 857/CS 1111/11, 29/10 and 2/9/1953. See also Bell, *Britain and East Germany*, 136; Becker, *DDR und Großbritannien*, 193–4.

[49] For the GDR's internal developments and its successive economic crises, see J. Kopstein, *The Politics of Economic Decline in East Germany, 1945–1989* (Chapel Hill, 1997); also U. Mählert, *Kleine Geschichte der DDR* (Munich, 1998); D. Staritz, *Geschichte der DDR 1949–1990*, expanded edn. (Darmstadt, 1996).

however no objections to trade contacts of a private nature, such as these between individual companies or preferably the Federation of British Industry (FBI) and an East German body.[50] The model here seemed to be the French–East German agreement concluded in December 1953 between the Banque de France and the GDR authorities which was even signed by a French diplomat.[51] It was considered that it might be advantageous to the government if a member of the Board of Trade was on the negotiating team of the FBI, though this would not be disclosed to the East Germans.[52] Towards the end of 1954 London gave its agreement to the commencement of somewhat more generous private trade links 'by reputable British exporters' with the GDR in order to increase the UK's trade 'with the Eastern Zone of Germany'.[53] On the whole, however, the UK government remained extremely cautious as far as any economic or indeed political relations with the GDR were concerned. The Foreign Office spelled out clearly that it was mainly interested in ensuring 'that we should take no action which could be interpreted as recognition of the so-called East German Government'.[54] The Federation of British Industry was also most hesitant to start negotiating with the GDR in earnest. The prospects for UK trade with East Germany appeared to be so small that it did not seem worth the effort and expenditure to promote it.[55]

Soon, however, this attitude began to change. After 1955 and in particular from 1957/8 East German trade links with Western European countries intensified as the GDR made an ever greater effort to establish such relations. Moreover, Britain's generally unsatisfactory export figures induced the government to be more flexible. In April 1955 the East German 'Leipzig Fair Agency' was set up in London to facilitate better trade contacts between the two countries and eventually in 1959 a GDR office in the name of KfA Ltd. was founded. The KfA Ltd. was an agency of the Department for Foreign Trade (Kammer für Außenhandel) of the GDR government's Ministry of Foreign Affairs.[56] London's permission

---

[50] See PRO: FO 371/109 537/CS 1151/2, 14/10/1954; FO 371/169 263/RE 1154/6 (CRE 10912/62), 19/2/1963. For the severe Anglo-American differences regarding the CoCom list, see Ian Jackson, *Co-operation and Constraint: Britain's Influence on American Economic Warfare Policy in CoCom, 1948–1954* (Ph.D. thesis, Queen's University of Belfast, 1997).

[51] The agreement was signed by the French Commerical Attache accredited to West Germany. For two good analyses, see PRO: FO 371/109 537/CS 1151/2, 14/10/1954; CS 1151/3, 25/10/1954; also CS 1151/6, 18/11/1954.

[52] Ibid.; also FO 371/163 702/CG 1861/18, 22/2/1962; FO 371/189 308/RG 1861/9, 18/8/1966.

[53] PRO: FO 371/109 537/CS 1151/5, undated, *c*.25 or 26/10/1954; also CS 1151/8, 4/12 and 9/12/1954; also FO 137 462/WG 1152/1, 10/2/1958.

[54] PRO: FO 371/109 537/CS 1151/8, 9/12/1954.

[55] PRO: FO 371/109 537/CS 1151/7, 2/12/1954; see also Becker, *DDR und Großbritannien*, 209, 212.

[56] On the KfA Ltd., see Eymelt, *Die Tätigkeit der DDR*, 15–19; Bell, *Britain and East Germany*, 147 ff.; M. Howarth, 'KfA Ltd und Berolina Travel Ltd. Die DDR-Präsenz in

to allow the East Germans to set up the KfA Ltd. as well as the FBI's willingness to act as its British contact partner were primarily a result of the pressure of private British business interests on both the Eden and the succeeding Macmillan government.

While other countries including the FRG appeared to be busy developing profitable trade relations with the GDR, the British government's extremely strict adherence to the principle of non-recognition in its widest sense was causing much dissatisfaction among British businessmen. It appeared unacceptable that in view of the UK's unsatisfactory level of exports the government had called for a general export drive but declared that the GDR was considered to be an exception to the rule. The Foreign Office, however, was not easily moved by economic concerns. Its prime aim continued to be, as was expressed in a memorandum in March 1958, 'that the purity of the non-recognition doctrine is preserved'.[57] Yet, there was mounting pressure on the government to adopt a more liberal trading relationship with the GDR. At one stage more than twenty MPs were put under much pressure in their constituencies to lobby the government on behalf of an alternative policy. Once again Burnaby Drayson but also Arthur Lewis, Ian Mikardo, and some other MPs with business interests in the GDR were particularly active. It was argued that even West Germany seemed to have embarked on more extensive trade relations with the GDR, despite its insistence on western non-recognition of the East Berlin government. It appeared that 'in practice' trade between Bonn and East Berlin was 'completely inter-governmental'. Moreover, it was clear that the West German civil servant in charge of Bonn's Inter-Zonal Trade Office for trade with the GDR (a Dr Leopold) had actually met with Heinrich Rau, the East German Minister for Foreign Trade, in early March 1958.[58] Bonn kept saying that its trade links with the GDR would make East Germany more dependent on the FRG and thus destabilize the Ulbricht regime in the long run. However, this cut little ice with Britain's business community and the parliamentarians sympathetic to the GDR.[59] Many of these MPs regularly travelled to the important trade fairs in Leipzig in spring and autumn of each year where they frequently met influential GDR politicians. Thus they often mixed business with ideological convictions and strong anti-West German sentiments.[60] They

Großbritannien vor und nach der diplomatischen Anerkennung', *Deutschland-Archiv* 32/4 (1999), 591–600.

[57] PRO: FO 371/371/137 462/WG 1152/7, 12/3/1958.

[58] See PRO: FO 371/137 462/WG 1152/16(A), 18/4/1958; also WG 1152/1, 2, 5 (Jan.–March 1958).

[59] See e.g. PRO: FO 371/177 920, 16/10/1964; FO 371/189 250/RG 1154/10, 9/2/1966; FO 371/177 963/RG 1154/42, 29/12/1964; also FO 371/169 263/CG 1154/8, 6, 8/3 and 19/3/1963.

[60] See e.g. the Foreign Office memorandum in PRO: FO 371/163 695/WG 1052/17, 17/11/1960.

often suspected the West German Adenauer government of neo-fascist tendencies and of attempting to benefit from international trade at the expense of Britain. The backbenchers were also motivated by certain feelings of sympathy for the GDR as an international 'underdog' and were often flattered by the attention given to them by the GDR government. While it is difficult to assess the real influence of those business minded MPs, and it does not seem to be justified to overrate it, on occasion they were able to make life awkward for the government of the day.[61]

By early 1958 Prime Minister Macmillan had had enough. He was clearly influenced by the increasingly loud public debate which was taking place in Britain's press and in the House of Commons about whether or not to trade with East Germany. Moreover, Macmillan was particularly suspicious of West Germany's ever closer trade links with the GDR. On 15 April 1958 the Prime Minister wrote in a secret memorandum:

There is a good deal of trade I think to be done with East Germany. Since we do not recognise the East German Government diplomatically, we are very much at a disadvantage. A slight absurdity of this situation is that we do not recognise the East German Government in order to please the Government of Western Germany. But of course the Federal Government of Western Germany do in effect recognise them, have continual diplomatic and trade relations with them and do a very large business. Other countries, through various Consular and other devices, do the same. We leave it for the F.B.I. to deal with Eastern Germany and the F.B.I. are not a very good body for this purpose. . . . I think this question of trade with Eastern Germany ought to be looked at.[62]

Indeed, from now on the development of British–East German trade relations was speeded up. While many Foreign Office officials continued to believe that 'West Germany has a legitimate special relationship with the DDR and that we should not cave in to pressure from a handful of M.P.s', an increasing number of officials disagreed. They had come to the conclusion that 'we have bent over backwards for too long in trying to be nice to the West Germans'.[63] In October 1958 negotiations between the KfA and the FBI were resumed in London. In late January 1959 the talks were successfully concluded with a one-year trade agreement to the value of £7 million and the permission for the KfA to establish a London office which was opened in May 1959. One of the KfA's major

---

[61] Ibid.; also D. Childs, 'British Labour and Ulbricht's State. The Fight for Recognition', in A. M. Birke and G. Heydemann (eds.), *Britain and East Germany since 1918* (Munich, 1992), 100–4. Childs implies however that mostly only Labour backbenchers were active on behalf of the GDR. This is incorrect though as Bell states 'these Conservative MPs . . . were out of step with their own party' (p. 214). See Bell, *Britain and East Germany*, 135–47, 213 ff.; also Becker, *DDR und Großbritannien*, 210–18; U. Brochhagen, *Nach Nürnberg: Vergangenheitsbewältigung und Westintegration in der Ära Adenauer* (Hamburg, 1994), 259 ff.

[62] PRO: FO 371/137 462/WG 1152/16, 15/4/1958; also quoted in Becker, ibid. 218–19.

[63] PRO: FO 371/137 462/WG 1152/16(A), 18/4/1958.

tasks was annually to renegotiate the volume of trade and the list of goods to be traded between the two partners. The trade agreement led to a 10 per cent increase of British–East German trade and it turned Britain into the GDR's second largest trading partner in western Europe after West Germany. However, on average, only 1 per cent of all British exports were to go to the GDR.[64] The East Germans were aware of the FBI's close co-operation with the Board of Trade and this of course increased the political value of the agreement for East Berlin.[65] However, in international law the agreement between the KfA and the FBI was a treaty between private partners, it was not a treaty between governments. Despite Macmillan's personal views, on the whole the British Foreign Office was careful to ensure that such an agreement would not be concluded until 1973. Thus, the KfA did not have diplomatic or consular status and did not manage to establish direct links with the Board of Trade or other governmental agencies.

The Berlin Crisis and East German Sovereignty: British–West German Discords

On 10 November 1958 Soviet leader Nikita Khrushchev announced that he was considering ending the four-power agreement regarding the occupation of Germany within six months. He intended to hand over the Soviet Union's occupation rights in Berlin to the GDR government and give the Ulbricht regime political and legal responsibility for the routes leading to West Berlin.[66] The implication of this seemed to be that, in future, access to the whole of the divided city would require the western powers to deal directly and officially with the East German government thus giving the GDR *de facto* recognition. Apart from forcing the western powers to recognize the GDR government Khrushchev also wished to eliminate the attraction of West Berlin to the East German population[67] and to stabilize the status quo of a divided Germany. Another main reason for the Berlin Crisis was Khrushchev's intention to prevent the FRG's

---

[64] See Becker, *DDR und Großbritannien*, 219; Bell, *Britain and East Germany*, 38–9.

[65] For the FBI's close links with the Board of Trade, see e.g. PRO: FO 371/137 462/WG 1152/16(A), 18/4/1958; FO 371/169 263/CG 1154/6, 19/3/1963; FO 371/163 702/CG 1861/18, 21/2/1962.

[66] On the Berlin crisis and the change in the West's view of the German question, see above all J. P. S. Gearson, *Harold Macmillan and the Berlin Wall Crisis, 1958–62: The Limits of Interests and Force* (Basingstoke, 1998); J. Arenth, *'Der Westen tut nichts' Transatlantische Kooperation während der zweiten Berlin-Krise (1958–1962) im Spiegel neuer amerikanischer Quellen* (Frankfurt/M., 1993).

[67] Many young and talented East Germans were emigrating to West Berlin before moving to the FRG. Soviet Foreign Minister Gromyko later said that 'West Berlin was a cancer which must be removed'. PRO: PREM 11/3805/IAD 410/614, 29/3/1962. The elimination of west Berlin as a major western centre of espionage was another soviet objective.

development of nuclear arms as well as the equipment of West German forces with nuclear weapons as was the ambition of both Adenauer and American President Eisenhower. Thus, it may well have been the German nuclear question which was essential for Moscow's policy during the Berlin Crisis.[68]

Giving in to Khrushchev would have meant a serious blow to western and particularly to American prestige. After all the United States were the major western guarantor of West Berlin's independence and well-being. Thus, such a course of action might well have led to the disintegration of the western alliance and, in its wake, possibly to a dangerous *rapprochement* between Bonn and Moscow.[69] Prime Minister Macmillan realized how dangerous the situation was and how easily the western allies could be divided by Moscow on the matter; he thus began to look for a compromise solution. He was most worried about Washington's belligerent stand as the Americans seemed to be prepared to open the motorway to West Berlin by force if the Soviets imposed another blockade on the city. Moreover, the United States did not seem to be averse to using the 'ultimate threat' of nuclear war. Acting Secretary of State Christian Herter told the Senate Foreign Relations Committee during a secret session in March 1959, 'I cannot visualise . . . fighting this out in the middle of Europe in a limited war.'[70] This appeared to be highly unreasonable. After all, according to Macmillan, the crisis which could well lead to a major war, if not a nuclear war, was all about minor matters. To the British government the non-recognition of the GDR did not seem to be all that important anymore; it certainly did not justify the outbreak of war:

What is the row all about? . . . As I understand the Russian move, it is just to go away and leave us to make our own arrangements with the DDR. We say, and rightly, that this is a breach of an understanding which the Russians cannot do unilaterally. . . . If that is so, I do not see how we can have a world war or take action which endangers peace on a point of this kind.[71]

---

[68] See the convincing arguments in M. Trachtenberg, *A Constructed Peace: The Making of the European Settlement, 1945–1963* (Princeton, 1998), 251–351. Khrushchev also called on the West to declare West Berlin a 'demilitarised free city'. For the entire Berlin crisis see in particular the detailed documentation in FRUS 1958–1960, vols. 8 and 9; FRUS 1961–1963, vols. 14 and 15. See also the extensive documentation: W. Burr (ed.), *The Berlin Crisis, 1958–1962* (Alexandria, Va.: National Security Archive, 1991).

[69] See W. Burr, 'Avoiding the Slippery Slope: The Eisenhower Administration and Berlin', *Diplomatic History* 18 (1994), 177–205; V.M. Zubok, 'Khrushchev and the Berlin Crisis (1958–1962)', *Cold War International History Project*, Working Paper No. 6 (1993). Eisenhower did not hesitate to tell his British ally that 'it would be a serious blow to the entire western position if we showed ourselves to be weak in Germany'. FRUS 1958–60, vol. 9, 240.

[70] Quoted in Burr, ibid. 178.

[71] PRO: PREM 2715, Dec. 1959; also quoted more fully in R. Lamb, *The Macmillan Years, 1957–1963: The Emerging Truth* (London, 1995), 323–4; see also Burr, ibid. 187–8; and Gearson, *Macmillan*, 33 ff.

Not surprisingly, Macmillan soon found himself at loggerheads with both Bonn and Washington. President Eisenhower and particularly ever suspicious West German Chancellor Adenauer, whom Macmillan regarded as 'a false and cantankerous old man',[72] suspected him of being only too ready to appease the Kremlin in order to obtain a quick resolution of the situation.[73] Khrushchev's suggestion in early January 1959 for a four-power summit conference to discuss the problem was viewed favourably in London but much less so in Washington and Bonn. Macmillan pressed Eisenhower to agree to such a meeting but Washington was not interested.[74] As a result the Prime Minister decided to take up the Soviet invitation issued to Anthony Eden in 1956 to negotiate with Khrushchev in Moscow.[75]

On 5 February 1959, after consultation with only a few members of his Cabinet, Macmillan declared his intention to visit Moscow to a surprised House of Commons. However, he stressed cautiously to both the Commons and a Cabinet meeting that he intended to embark on 'a reconnaissance not a negotiation'.[76] The American administration was unenthusiastic. Washington even believed that such an initiative was 'dangerous' in the present crisis situation. However, the US would not object to Macmillan's journey if he made it clear that he was just speaking for himself and not on behalf of the entire western alliance.[77] Adenauer was deeply annoyed and feared that Macmillan might make some unrealistic promises to Khrushchev over Berlin. The Chancellor believed that Macmillan did not understand the crucial importance of remaining tough on the issue of uninhibited access to West Berlin, on western responsibility for the city and the whole of Germany as well as on the non-recognition of the GDR.[78] Furthermore, British ideas about the

---

[72] Quoted in R. Aldous, 'A Family Affair: The Art of Personal Diplomacy', 10, in R. Aldous and S. Lee (eds.), *Harold Macmillan and Britain's World Role* (Basingstoke, 1996).

[73] See H. Köhler, *Adenauer: Eine Politische Biographie* (Frankfurt/M., 1994), 1013 ff.; V. Mauer, 'Macmillan und die Berlinkrise, 1958–59', *Vierteljahrshefte für Zeitgeschichte* 44 (1996), 229–56; Gearson, *Macmillan*, 39 ff. Moreover, severe Anglo-American dissention continued over military contingency planning in case Khrushchev started to impose another Berlin blockade. Macmillan regarded the American plans as much too aggressive and dangerous. See Burr, 'Slippery Slope', 178 ff.; Gearson, 48 ff.

[74] For summit diplomacy and the Berlin crisis, see M. Jochum, *Eisenhower und Chruschtschow. Gipfeldiplomatie im Kalten Krieg, 1955–60* (Paderborn, 1996).

[75] See Aldous, 'Family Affair', pp. 19–20; I. Warner, 'The Foreign Office View of Macmillan's Visit to Moscow', in *Foreign and Commonwealth Office, Historical Branch, Occasional Papers*, No. 7 (London, 1993), 24–5; H. Macmillan, *Riding the Storm, 1956–59* (London, 1971), 557–9.

[76] See Gearson, *Macmillan*, 59.

[77] Washington was convinced that the main reason for the Prime Minister's proposal to visit Moscow was the forthcoming general election in Britain. PRO: PREM 11/2775 and CAB 21/3233, 20/1/1959; R. Aldous, 'Family Affair', 18–19.

[78] Above all he also suspected that in order to obtain short-term electoral advantages Macmillan would be inclined to appease Khrushchev and achieve a quick settlement of the

disengagement and thinning out of western and Soviet forces in Germany through the creation of neutral zones on West and East German territory (the so-called Macmillan Plan) found little favour in Washington and infuriated Adenauer.[79] After Churchill's enthusiasm for German neutralization in 1953 and Eden's disengagement plan of 1955, Macmillan appeared to be the third British Prime Minister who was prepared to question the status quo in the German question to pacify Moscow.

Thus, throughout the Berlin crisis Britain appeared to be the country most inclined to 'deal with the East German puppet government' and eventually even prepared, as Foreign Secretary Selwyn Lloyd expressed it, 'to recognise it, rather than expose Berlin to the danger of a blockade'.[80] The GDR recognition question and Macmillan's journey to Moscow in February 1959 led to what probably amounted to the most serious West German-British crisis ever.[81] Indeed it appeared that when Khrushchev snubbed the Prime Minister by making a speech strongly attacking Eisenhower and Adenauer during Macmillan's visit and subsequently proclaiming that he would not accompany Macmillan to visit Kiev as he had a 'terrible toothache', the British gave in to prevent the failure of the visit. Selwyn Lloyd's hint that recognizing the GDR might be the solution to overcoming the Berlin crisis persuaded Khrushchev to overcome his toothache and continue his talks with the British delegation.[82] On his return to London Macmillan was able to declare his visit a huge success for the preservation of world peace and he decisively won the British general election later in the year. However, American President Eisenhower and not least the British Foreign Office successfully prevented any recognition of the GDR from being seriously contemplated in London once Macmillan had returned from Moscow.[83]

crisis at the expense of the West German position. See S. Lee, 'Perception and Reality: Anglo-German Relations during the Berlin Crisis 1958–59', in *German History* 13 (1995), 47–69; B. Leupold, '*Weder anglophil noch anglophob.*' *Großbritannien im politischen Denken Konrad Adenauers* (Frankfurt/M., 1997), 266–76; Gearson, *Macmillan*, 63–6.

[79] See A. Horne, *Macmillan, 1957–1986*: vol. 2 (London, 1989), 129–30; E. Hinterhoff, *Disengagement* (London, 1959), 306–7, 319, 349; FRUS 1958–60, vol. 7, part 2, 842–3; Gearson, ibid. 60–3.

[80] See Dwight D. Eisenhower, *The White House Years*, vol. 2: *Waging Peace, 1956–1961* (New York, 1965), 333.

[81] For Macmillan's journey to Moscow see the convincing analysis in Gearson, *Macmillan*, 56–78.

[82] For the discussions during the Moscow visit, see in detail PRO: CAB 133/293, including Top Secret annex; also PREM 11/2690, 11/2716; FO 371/143433–40 and 143686–8; CAB 21/3233; FRUS 1958–1960, vol. 7, part 2, 837–41; Macmillan, *Riding the Storm*, 592–634; and for the British Ambassador's (Sir Patrick Reilly) analysis of the visit see PRO: FO 371/143 439/NS 1053/179, 9/3/1959. See also Gearson, ibid. 70–5.

[83] See Gearson, ibid. 78 ff. This was not unlike the situation in 1953/54 when both Washington and the FO undermined Churchill's initiative.

Still it became increasingly clear that Khrushchev's strategy of using a crisis over Berlin to gain international recognition of the GDR was not entirely without success. After all, on Soviet insistence delegations from both German states were allowed to attend the four power foreign ministers' conference in Geneva in May/June 1959 as advisers. The western foreign ministers did not hesitate to point out that the presence of the GDR delegation under Foreign Minister Lothar Bolz in Geneva was not identical to the diplomatic recognition of the GDR. Moscow however regarded the attendance of both a West German and an East German delegation as the international *de facto* recognition of Ulbricht's state.[84]

The 1959 Geneva conference, President John F. Kennedy's formulation of the 'three essentials' in 1961 for violation of which Washington would consider going to war,[85] and also the western world's weak response to the building of the Wall in August 1961 indicated that Adenauer's German policy no longer had the support of the western allies.[86] In particular it seemed as if the British government was increasingly ready to acknowledge that there was a second German state. During the Berlin Crisis this had done great damage to Anglo-West German relations. In fact, it had made Adenauer quite unwilling to persuade French President Charles De Gaulle to give his agreement to Macmillan's application to join the European Community.[87] However, the tendency in British politics to consider recognizing the GDR was strongly influenced by Macmillan's personal and well-known dislike of the West German Chancellor and his general suspicion of the German people. After Macmillan's resignation, Britain would once again become much more careful about taking West Germany's views into consideration as far as the GDR was concerned. Despite Foreign Secretary Alec Douglas Home's confidential utterances about East German sovereignty in 1962,[88] when he succeeded Macmillan in October 1963 and became Prime Minister himself, he was much more circumspect. Douglas Home was much more inclined than Macmillan to do his utmost to keep on good terms with the West German government.

---

[84] See Becker, *DDR und Großbritannien*, 133–34.

[85] They consisted of the following points: the military and economic security of West Berlin; the protection of the western allied troops in Berlin; the guarantee of western allied access to Berlin. The realization of German unification was not included. See Ostermann, 'Im Schatten der Bundesrepublik', 241.

[86] See J. Arenth, 'Die Bewährungsprobe der Special Relationship: Washington und Bonn (1961–1969)', in K. Larres and T. Oppelland (eds.), *Deutschland und die USA im 20. Jahrhundert*, 151–77.

[87] See Gearson, *Macmillan*, 201; also N. P. Ludlow, *Dealing with Britain: The Six and the First UK Application to the EEC* (Cambridge, 1997); G. Wilkes (ed.), *Britain's Failure to Enter the European Community, 1961–63* (Ilford, Essex, 1997).

[88] PRO: PREM 11/3805/IAD 410/614, 29/3/1962.

THE POLITICS OF RAPPROCHEMENT: THE 1960S

During the 1960s both the political repercussions of the Berlin crisis and increasing trade contacts were slowly but steadily undermining the Foreign Office's policy of strict non-recognition of the GDR. Even the building of the Berlin Wall in August 1961, and the negative propaganda in the West which resulted from it, did not strengthen the non-recognition policy in the long run. Instead, the Ulbricht regime went on the offensive to overcome its credibility gap; East Berlin even pointed to the Berlin Wall separating the two Germanys to prove the GDR's claim of being an independent state.[89] By the early 1960s it seemed to be only a matter of time before London would enter into at least semi-official relations with East Germany and recognize the state *de facto*. However, both the practical impossibility of Britain breaking ranks with its allies in a question of vital importance for western unity and London's desire to ensure that the rapidly changing cold war environment would not lead to another serious rift with the FRG were important reasons for the British government to avoid such a strategy. Thus, on the whole throughout the 1960s Britain continued to adhere to the 'Hallstein Doctrine'.

Still, times were certainly changing. In the aftermath of the Berlin Crisis, the building of the Wall and the 1962 Cuban Missile Crisis American President John F. Kennedy was intent on embarking upon a general era of East–West détente. As the world had been on the brink of nuclear war during the Cuban Missile Crisis, Washington decided that nothing was important enough to stand in the way of a rapprochement between East and West to create a safer world. Thus, the old linkage which made a fruitful climate of détente dependent on progress in the German question was given up. While the West's rhetoric still expressed strong support for unification, in practice from the early 1960s onwards, the western world (as well as the Soviet Union) was much more interested in East–West détente than in the German question.[90] Although the West continued its policy of non-recognition towards the GDR for the time

[89] For a brief overview of the GDR's activities, see Becker, *DDR und Großbritannien*, 139–42. For a more detailed account of British–East German relations in the 1960s, see my contribution in J. Noakes *et al.* (eds.), *Britain and Germany, 1949–90* (Oxford, 2000) [forthcoming]; also M. Lemke, 'Kampagnen gegen Bonn. Die Systemkrise der DDR und die West-Propaganda der SED, 1960–1963', *Vierteljahrshefte für Zeitgeschichte* 41 (1993), 151–74.

[90] See J. C. Ausland, *Kennedy, Khrushchev, and the Berlin-Cuba Crisis, 1961–64* (Oslo, 1996); A. Wenger, 'Kennedy, Chruschtschow und das gemeinsame Interesse der Supermächte am Status quo in Europa', *Vierteljahrshefte für Zeitgeschichte* 46 (1998), 69–99. Indeed, already from the mid-1950s a severe crisis in West German-American relations could be noticed. See K. Larres, 'Eisenhower, Dulles und Adenauer: Bündnis des Vertrauens oder Allianz des Mißtrauens? (1953–61)', in K. Larres and T. Oppelland (eds.), *Deutschland und die USA im 20. Jahrhundert*, 136–40.

being (not least in order to avoid difficulties with Bonn), much to the delight of Moscow and East Berlin the western alliance's new priorities became increasingly clear. Speaking at the Free University of Berlin in the summer of 1963, Kennedy even advised the West German government not to hesitate in entering into closer trade relations with the GDR and to intensify all other possibilities of contact with the GDR, a proposal which official Bonn politely declined.[91]

Kennedy's less dogmatic attitude towards the GDR was continued by the succeeding Johnson administration. As early as May 1964 Johnson spoke of the need for 'building bridges' between West and East and he soon mentioned the necessity of engaging peacefully with the countries of the eastern bloc. The Harmel Report, approved by the NATO member states in December 1967, also explicitly mentioned the western alliance's aim 'to further a détente in East–West relations'.[92] Moreover, in 1964/5 French President Charles de Gaulle had embarked on his own *Ostpolitik*. Although he did not make any serious attempt to recognize the GDR, the threat to do so was always on the horizon if the government in Bonn should consider frustrating de Gaulle's desire to make France the undisputed leader of the European Community.[93]

On the whole it seemed that the United States as well as Britain and France were increasingly ready to accept the existence of the GDR although they were not yet prepared to recognize this state officially. In this respect they were waiting for a more realistic view emanating from Bonn. But during Adenauer's last years and also largely during the reign of Ludwig Erhard who succeeded Adenauer in October 1963, Bonn attempted to cling to the political concepts developed in the 1950s. It thus felt on the defensive and deserted by its allies. However, Erhard's Foreign Minister Gerhard Schröder began embarking on a cautious 'policy of motion' which was greatly welcomed by the British Foreign Office. It seemed to indicate a more 'pragmatic view of German relations with Eastern Europe' and thus the beginning of West Germany's normalization of its

---

[91] Becker, *DDR und Großbritannien*, 137; for Kennedy's détente strategy see R.W. Stevenson, *The Rise and Fall of Detente, 1953–1984* (Basingstoke, 1985), 103 ff.; A. W. Schertz, *Die Deutschlandpolitik Kennedys und Johnsons* (Cologne, 1992), 51 ff.; T. A. Schwartz, 'Victories and Defeats in the Long Twilight Struggle: The United States and Western Europe in the 1960s', in D. Kunz (ed.), *The Diplomacy of the Crucial Decade: American Foreign Policy in the 1960s* (New York, 1994), 115–48, esp. 125–7.

[92] See R. L. Garthoff, *Détente and Confrontation: American-Soviet Relations from Nixon to Reagan* (Washington, 1994), 123–4, 127–8; Schertz, ibid. 253 ff.

[93] PRO: FO 371/177 922/RG 104 117/1, 21/1, 30/1/1964. On de Gaulle's Ostpolitik, see F. Bozo, 'A French View', in R. Davy (ed.), *European Détente: A Reappraisal* (London, 1992), 54–85; D. Buda, *Ostpolitik á la Française: Frankreichs Verhältnis zur UdSSR von de Gaulle bis Mitterrand* (Marburg, 1990); K. Linsel, *Charles de Gaulle und Deutschland* (Sigmaringen, 1998).

relationships with the Warsaw Pact countries. It might even lead to the termination of the outdated Hallstein Doctrine.[94]

In the course of the gradually developing era of détente the 'creeping' world-wide acceptance of the second German state could be noticed. The GDR was able to score several important international victories which further undermined both the credibility of the West's non-recognition strategy and the West German Hallstein Doctrine.

A case in point was the American–Soviet–British Test Ban Treaty which was signed on 5 August 1963 in the last months of both Macmillan's and Adenauer's terms in office. The treaty was open to any other state who wished to join and it emphasized the equality of all the signatory states. The Soviet Union demanded that the GDR was allowed to sign the treaty. While this was vehemently opposed by the Federal Republic, Kennedy as well as Macmillan were not prepared to endanger the treaty because of this complication. Instead of full-heartedly backing Bonn's position— as both countries would have been much more likely to do prior to 1958/9— they found a compromise solution with the Soviet Union. The western states declared that they still did not recognize the GDR but internation- ally unrecognized states would be permitted to sign. In such a case, the document should be handed to one of the original signatories of the treaty. Lord Hood, a Foreign Office minister, wrote that the 'West Germans are making a ridiculous fuss about this—but we must go as far as we can to satisfy them'.[95] Thus, Foreign Secretary Alec Douglas-Home explained to his West German Counterpart Gerhard Schröder that the East German signature of the Test Ban Treaty would not change the nature of the relationship between the UK and East Germany. Bonn was not terribly reassured but was in no position to prevent the GDR from signing the treaty.[96] The FRG however managed to ensure that negotiations about a non-aggression pact between NATO and the Warsaw Pact, which indirectly would also have strengthened the GDR's position, were not entered into.[97]

On 8 October 1965 the International Olympic Committee announced that from 1968 two German teams were allowed to participate in the Olympic Games. This success may have encouraged Ulbricht to apply

[94] PRO: FO 371/169 215/CG 1081/4, 4/4/1963; FO 371/172 132/RG 1071/8, 23/9, 3/10, 4/10/1963. For the limits of Schröder's 'wind of change'-policy and the strong desire in Bonn to continue thinking within the old non-recognition framework, see e.g. FO 371/163 559/CG 1051/5, 12/3/1962; also Schertz, *Deutschlandpolitik*, 258–64.

[95] PRO: FO 371/162 212/RG 1075/8, 1/8/1963.

[96] PRO: FO 371/162 212/RG 1075/8, late July/early August 1963; FO 371/172 132/RG 1071/8, 25/9/1963.

[97] See e.g. PRO: FO 371/163 559/CG 10151/5, 11/3/1962; Schertz, *Deutschlandpolitik*, 225–6. Bonn signed the treaty on 19 August 1963.

for membership of the United Nations in late February 1966 which was, however, turned down.[98] Not surprisingly, both the Soviet Union and the GDR regarded the East German signature under the international test ban treaty and the IOC's decision to let two German teams compete at the Olympic Games as the *de facto* recognition of the existence of the GDR. Both seemed to signal a new attitude towards East Germany within the West which was not lost on the politicians in Moscow and East Berlin.[99]

Undoubtedly, East Berlin had hoped that the election victory of Harold Wilson's Labour Party in October 1964 would inaugurate a new phase in Britain's policy towards the GDR. After all, the Labour Party had already called for the recognition of the GDR during its party conference in 1961. Moreover, in February 1963, after the end of the Berlin crisis when Wilson had been elected leader of the Labour opposition, he declared that in return for a satisfactory solution of the Berlin problem the West should be prepared to both recognize the GDR *de facto* and to accept the Oder–Neisse line as the German–Polish border. However, he did not repeat such sentiments after he had become Prime Minister. During a visit to West Berlin in early 1965 Wilson confirmed that he was convinced that the FRG was the only German government legally entitled to speak for the whole of the German nation.[100]

The GDR's participation in the invasion of Czechoslovakia in August 1968 once again led to a crisis in East Germany's and indeed the Soviet Union's relations with the western world. Prime Minister Wilson firmly condemned the invasion. He dramatically recalled Parliament from its summer vacation but he was careful not to endanger Britain's bilateral relations with Moscow too much.[101] Moreover, by mid-1969 the Soviet Union had embarked upon a renewed détente initiative and as the West was deeply interested in improving East–West relations, the crisis was soon overcome. In September 1969 Britain and the Soviet Union signed a long-term trade agreement. The non-recognition policy towards the GDR however continued. It also remained the policy of the British government when Edward Heath became Prime Minister in 1970.

[98] See PRO: FO 371/183 165/RG 1801/7 (April 1965), 13 (June 1965), 20, 21 (Oct. 1965), and 10 (May 1965), 14, 15 (July 1965), 24 (Nov. 1965); also Becker, *DDR und Großbritannien*, 140–1.

[99] See PRO: FO 371/172 139/RG 1076/3, 20/11/1963 (speech by Bolz as published on 12 Nov. 1963); see also M. H. Geyer, 'Der Kampf um die nationale Repräsentation. Deutsch-deutsche Sportbeziehungen und die Hallstein-Doktrin', *Vierteljahrshefte für Zeitgeschichte* 44 (1996), 55–86.

[100] Becker, *DDR und Großbritannien*, 143–44; also P. Ziegler, *Wilson: The Authorised Life of Lord Wilson of Rievaulx* (London, 1993), 149–50. Wilson's own account reveals little, see his *The Labour Government, 1964–70: A Personal Record* (London, 1971), 81–2.

[101] See *The Guardian*, 1 Jan. 1999, 5; Wilson, ibid. 551–4; also PRO: FCO 28/47–55; Bell, *Britain and East Germany*, 41–2.

Trade Relations in the 1960s

In the 1960s, as before, progress towards a closer understanding between London and East Berlin was achieved through unofficial trade relations rather than on a political level. Despite the successful beginning of intensified private trade contacts in 1959, initially the Board of Trade proved to be inflexible as far as exports to the GDR were concerned. A major steel export deal to the value of £40m. pounds was not approved as the Board refused to give a credit guarantee which would have gone beyond the KfA-FBI agreement of 1959. It also might have been disapproved of by West Germany.[102] There was much public criticism of this inflexibility and exaggerated willingness to consider West Germany's wishes. Soon the 'All-Party East–West Trade Group' within the House of Commons, originally founded in the early 1950s, was reactivated. Parliamentarians like Burnaby Drayson and Lord Boothby used this group to boost economic relations with East Berlin and promote the recognition of the GDR.[103] However, the building of the Berlin Wall in August 1961 caused a crisis in the GDR's economic relations with the West. Yet, it did not prove to be of a lasting nature. Western states merely advised their business communities not to attend the Leipzig autumn fair to avoid giving the impression that they approved of the building of the Wall.[104] This strategy only led to a temporary decline in the number of foreign businessmen visiting the GDR. In 1964 Britain was the second largest exhibitor after France with 228 companies and 936 British citizens attending the Leipzig spring fair.[105]

Despite considerable improvements in private British–East German economic relations, throughout the 1960s the FBI (renamed Confederation of British Industry—CBI) and the Board of Trade were rarely satisfied with the development of the export trade with East Germany. While the GDR was keen on sending its own products to Britain and, in 1963/4, had begun with a new initiative to improve its trade with the western world, East Berlin often proved to be unable (or unwilling) to fulfil its quotas of purchasing British goods.[106] In particular, such crises occurred in early 1962 and in 1964/5. It led to the temporary cancellation of the KfA's import licences and to a considerable reduction in the export quotas originally agreed with the KfA. Moreover, the annual trade agreement with the KfA was only extended for a few months and not for

---

[102] This led to much public criticism. See Becker, *DDR und Großbritannien*, 222.

[103] Becker, ibid. 223–4; Bell, *Britain and East Germany*, 144.

[104] PRO: FO 371/163 702/CG 1861/1, 3/1, 16/1, 18/1, 19/1, 2/2 and 12/2/1962.

[105] Becker, *DDR und Großbritannien*, 225–6.

[106] PRO: FO 371/172 171/RG 1154/5, 2/11/1963; FO 371/163 649/CG 1154/11, 6/4/1962; FO 371/163 650/CG 1154/25 (C), 3/12/1962. See also Bell, *Britain and East Germany*, 165 ff., who states quite rightly that trade 'volumes fluctuated wildly during the 1960s' (p.165).

the entire year as was common practice. The GDR's wish to sign three-year or longer trade agreements was not even seriously considered by the CBI/Board of Trade.[107] But the situation improved in the latter part of the 1960s. In the first nine months of 1966 trade increased by an impressive 164 per cent and in early 1968 the CBI and the KfA negotiated an annual agreement to the value of £18.25 million. Yet, once again the GDR did not honour this arrangement. The Board of Trade cancelled it and replaced it with a six-month agreement. These economic difficulties as well as the GDR's participation in the invasion of Czechoslovakia in late 1968 caused British businessmen to boycott the 1969 Leipzig spring fair.[108]

Soon, however, the economic difficulties in British–East German relations were overcome again. Thus, East Berlin continued to call for the conclusion of long-term trade agreements with western countries including Britain and spoke of a potential trade volume of approximately £100m. which could well be achieved within two to three years, particularly if the GDR's statehood was fully recognized. However, the British Foreign Office was much more realistic. On the whole it did not believe that there was as much potential to expand trade with the GDR as was claimed by East Berlin and some British business interests. The Foreign Office view was largely based on the GDR's weak economy, its concentration on trade with the FRG and on past experience. Moreover, London still hesitated to enter into any long-term agreements for fear that this would undermine the policy of western non-recognition. Other countries, like France, the Netherlands, and Denmark were however much less cautious and had already concluded five-year trade agreements with the GDR.

Encouraged by new West German Chancellor Willy Brandt's more flexible policy towards the East (*Ostpolitik*), in November 1969 Britain also entered into a long-term three-year trade agreement between the CBI and the KfA Ltd. A general improvement of British–East German trade relations could soon be noticed.[109] In the summer of 1970 the new developments in East–West relations also led to the creation of a 'UK Section' within the KfA in East Berlin (which represented more than 100 firms) and to the establishment of so-called 'GDR Committees' within the CBI and the London Chamber of Commerce. These Committees soon

[107] PRO: FO 371/163 650/CG 1154/25 (B) (C), 30/11/1962, 3/12/1962; FO 371/163 649/CG 1154/3, /5, /15, Jan., Feb., and June 1962.

[108] Becker, *DDR und Großbritannien*, 145, 226–7.

[109] See Bell, *Britain and East Germany*, 42–5. Moreover, the role of the Allied Travel Office, which was responsible for issuing TTDs (Temporary Travel Documents) to East Germans visiting the West, became increasingly obsolete. On this practice see PRO: FO 371/177 987, 25/2/1964.

represented more than 400 British companies. A year later the first official CBI office was opened in East Berlin. Surprisingly, the British government had not objected to this joint CBI/KfA initiative. However, when the GDR tried to insist on a governmental declaration as the basis for this agreement the project was delayed as Downing Street adamantly refused to involve the British government in any such deal. Treating the GDR as an official partner was still unacceptable.[110] Thus, despite all trade temptations, on the whole, the East German government did not succeed in undermining Britain's adherence to the western world's non-recognition policy during the 1960s. Consequently, Britain would only grant 'most favoured nation' status to the GDR after recognition.[111]

RECOGNITION

The non-recognition of the GDR remained official British policy until Chancellor Brandt successfully concluded his *Ostpolitik*. Brandt's treaty negotiations with the GDR in 1970 and, more successfully, in 1972 would lead to West Germany's *de facto* recognition of East Berlin in the Basic Treaty paraphrased and signed in November/December 1972. The treaty institutionalized the status quo of a divided Germany. West Germany now accepted that the GDR was a sovereign and independent state. Bonn attempted however to keep alive the notion that the GDR did not represent foreign territory and that the German nation as a whole continued to exist ('one nation, two states'). The Basic Treaty, therefore, did not deal with the question of citizenship; for Bonn, the recognition of a separate GDR citizenship was unacceptable. Still, the Brandt government agreed to give up West Germany's claim to be the sole representative of the German people.[112]

Throughout the negotiations the governments of both Harold Wilson and Edward Heath strongly supported the West German strategy—despite some initial fears that a new Rapallo policy might be developing.[113]

---

[110] See Becker, *DDR und Großbritannien*, 226–32; also Bell, ibid. 47.

[111] See U. Dietsch, *Aussenwirtschaftliche Aktivitäten der DDR gegenüber den Mitgliedsländern der Europäischen Gemeinschaft* (Hamburg, 1976), 247.

[112] See e.g. P. Bender, *Die Neue Ostpolitik und ihre Folgen. Vom Mauerbau bis zur Vereinigung*, 4th edn. (Munich, 1996) (the text of the Basic Treaty is published on pp. 309–12).

[113] See K. Larres, 'Germany and the West: the "Rapallo Factor" in German Foreign Policy from the 1950s to the 1990s', 301–18. Denis Healey even writes in his memoirs that 'Brandt's Ostpolitik had made him one of the Labur Party's heroes'. See his *The Time of My Life*, paperback edn. (London, 1990), 359. See also H. Wilson, *Labour Government*, 765; J. Campbell, *Edward Heath: A Biography* (London, 1993), 346; A. Douglas-Home (Lord Home of the Hirsel), *The Way the Wind Blows: Memoirs* (London, 1976), 250–1; also R. Morgan, 'The British View', in E. Moreton (ed.), *Germany between East and West* (Cambridge, 1987), 90; E. Heath, *The Course of My Life: My Autobiography* (London, 1998), 606, 608.

London did not feel encouraged to enter into official bilateral relations with the GDR before Bonn and East Berlin had arrived at an agreement. Despite the pressure from many backbenchers to recognize the GDR government for reasons of trade as soon as possible,[114] the Heath government was convinced that 'it would be inappropriate for Her Majesty's Government to take any steps which might enhance the status of the GDR and prejudice the success of the [German–German] negotiations'.[115]

Only after the signing of the Basic Treaty did Britain, in close co-operation with France, allow official governmental contacts with the GDR. On 22 December Prime Minister Edward Heath's Foreign Secretary Alec Douglas-Home sent a telegram to his East German colleague Otto Winzer and suggested talks between the two foreign ministries. The negotiations began on 23 January 1973 in London and it was jointly announced on 8 February that diplomatic relations would be entered into and ambassadors would be exchanged. The British Embassy in East Berlin was opened in April 1973 and Ambassador Curtis Keeble was accredited in January 1974. The first East German representative to the Court of St James had already taken up residence in March 1973.[116] Furthermore, on 18 December 1973 official ten-year agreements were concluded regarding economic, industrial, scientific, and technological co-operation between London and East Berlin. Within a few years this was followed by agreements regarding co-operation between both country's health systems and with respect to legal procedures in civil cases.[117]

THE GDR, BRITAIN, AND THE EUROPEAN COMMUNITY

As Britain only became a member of the EEC in 1973 (confirmed by a referendum in 1975), European integration did not play a distinctive role in British–East German relations during the first half of the cold war. However, as was the case with other bilateral relationships in the post-war era, European integration did have an indirect impact on East Berlin's and London's dealings with each other. Throughout the 1960s the GDR viewed the EEC as a neo-colonial and neo-capitalist instrument with which the old European imperial powers wished to bolster their waning international influence. East Berlin also believed that the United

[114] See *H.C. Deb.*, 5th ser., vol. 847, 880 (Renee Short), 4/12/1972.
[115] See ibid., vol. 843, 775, 23/10/1972; also e.g. vol. 847, 880, 4/12/1972; vol. 838, 17, 5/6/1972; vol. 837, 423–24, 24/5/1972; also quoted in Becker, *DDR und Großbritannien*, 149.
[116] C. Munro, 'The Acceptance of a Second German State', in Birke and Heydemann, *Britain and East Germany*, 112; see also Bell, *Britain and East Germany*, 53–56.
[117] Bachmann, 'Die Beziehungen der DDR', 117.

States only supported the EEC in order to strengthen NATO. Moreover, the GDR leaders regularly accused West German politicians of harbouring ambitions to embark on the reconquest of the lost eastern territories with the help of its EEC allies. Thus, the Ulbricht regime used its opposition to the EEC to demonstrate the GDR's ideological convictions to the world. At the same time it never tired of accusing the West of intensifying and prolonging the division of Europe and Germany by attempting to make further progress with the integration of western Europe.

In fact, however, ever since the establishment of the EEC, the GDR had gained substantial advantages from it. On the insistence of West Germany a clause had been added to the 1957 Rome Treaties that trade between the two German states (and with Berlin) was to be regarded as internal German trade and thus exempt from the EEC's external tariffs. With the acceptance of this clause all present and future EEC members acknowledged the principle of non-recognition of the GDR as a separate state; Germany was to be regarded as one entity. Although the legal and political implications of this proviso were much resented by East Berlin, in financial and economic terms, the GDR benefited considerably from its quasi-association with the EEC which the Bonn government had insisted upon.[118]

Nevertheless, during the 1960s the GDR continued to expect the imminent collapse of the EEC due to its inherent capitalist contradictions and power political rivalries, as perceived in East Berlin. It was however clear that the attacks on the EEC were primarily aimed at one of its foremost countries and the GDR's main political and economic rival, the Federal Republic.[119] As far as Britain's ambition to join the EEC in the 1960s was concerned, London's relations with the GDR played hardly any role. In general the repercussions of the severe clash of opinion between the West Germans and the British during the Berlin crisis led to greater caution in London. However, in connection with Britain's second attempt to join the EEC, it appeared temporarily as if this had been forgotten again. Much to Ulbricht's delight, in October 1967 Lord Chalfont, Minister of State at the Foreign Office, told western journalists 'off the record' that Britain might well reconsider her non-recognition policy towards East Berlin if Bonn was not helpful in enabling Britain to join the Common Market.[120]

---

[118] See H. D. Genscher, *Erinnerungen* (Berlin, 1995), 391–92; D. Gielisch, *Die ehemalige DDR und das Projekt 'Europäischer Binnenmarkt'. Versuch einer Bestandsaufnahme und Analyse ihrer Wirtschaftsbeziehungen zur Europäischen Gemeinschaft* (Münster, 1992), 105 ff.; Dietsch, *Aussenwirtschaftliche Aktivitäten*, 47 ff.; also A. James McAdams, *Germany Divided: From the Wall to Reunification* (Princeton: Princeton University Press, 1993), 105.

[119] See K. P. Schmidt, *Die Europäische Gemeinschaft aus der Sicht der DDR, 1957–1989*, 2nd edn. (Hamburg, 1995), 101–238, 405–8.

[120] See PRO: PREM 13/1468, 1498; Bell, *Britain and East Germany*, 36.

Britain's membership of the EEC after 1973 would actually be detrimental to the GDR's interest. From the mid to late 1970s it became ever clearer that Britain's main export markets in the foreseeable future were the countries of the Common Market. This development gradually undermined not only the importance of the old colonial and Commonwealth connections but also trade with eastern Europe. At the same time, the GDR became increasingly dependent on closer economic contacts with the members of the European Community. In fact, in the early 1970s East Germany's trade with the Soviet Union declined while its trade with the West expanded considerably.[121] Therefore, in the 1970s and particularly in the 1980s the GDR embarked upon a different policy towards the EC and its member countries. A certain toning down of the importance of ideology in East Germany's policies under Erich Honecker also led to a different analysis of the nature of the European Community. It was moreover recognized that a collapse of the EC could hardly be expected after the Community had weathered the oil crises and the difficult economic times of the 1970s. Above all, in view of East Germany's serious economic problems, the GDR had no choice but to intensify its trade with the countries of the European Community.[122]

THE POLITICS OF UNEASINESS: ECONOMIC AND POLITICAL RELATIONS, 1973–1990

Even after recognition in 1973 Britain's relations with the GDR remained relatively cool; they never resembled that state of 'normalcy' which London's dealings with West Germany had gradually assumed after the Second World War. British governments of all persuasions were not prepared to overlook entirely the GDR's dictatorial system. New East German leader Erich Honecker (since May 1971) continued East Berlin's efforts to pretend that the GDR was just another sovereign state with great independence from Moscow.[123] However, he had little success. After all, during the various cold war crises of the 1980s, from the Afghanistan invasion to the Polish crisis and the many disputes over disarmament and rearmament issues, East Berlin always firmly supported the Soviet

---

[121] See McAdams, *Germany Divided*, 104; see also P. Plötz and K. Bolz, *Westhandel der DDR: Eine vergleichende Betrachtung* [. . .] (Hamburg, 1987), 35 ff.

[122] See Schmidt, *Die Europäische Gemeinschaft*, 239 ff., 410–13.

[123] On the enforced change-over from Ulbricht to Honecker, see M. Kaiser, *Machtwechsel von Ulbricht zu Honecker: Funktionsmechanismen der SED-Diktatur in Konfliktsituationen 1962 bis 1972* (Berlin, 1997); J. Stelkens, 'Machtwechsel in Ost-Berlin. Der Sturz Walter Ulbrichts', *Vierteljahrshefte für Zeitgeschichte* 45 (1997), 503–33; also G. Naumann and E. Trümpler, *Von Ulbricht zu Honecker: 1970—ein Krisenjahr der DDR* (Berlin, 1990).

Union.[124] Furthermore, in the years after the Helsinki conference of 1975 the forceful suppression of the ever increasing number of political dissidents and protest movements in the GDR ensured that western governments were constantly reminded of the illiberal nature of the East German system.[125] Thus, Britain's relations with the GDR in the 1970s and 1980s continued to be characterized by a certain uneasiness. London intended to steer a careful course between its continued (though somewhat muted) interest in expanding trade with the GDR and West German political sensibilities as well as more general cold war considerations.

Trade between Britain and the GDR did not substantially increase in 1970–2. With the exception of the year 1973/4, during which trade doubled, this also applied to the period of time after the recognition of the GDR. Neither East Germany's old promises that the GDR would consider paying compensation for the loss of British property in Eastern Germany during the Nazi period nor a considerable long-term increase of British exports to the GDR materialized.[126] East Germany's claim that it intended to scale down its emphasis on intra-German trade in favour of trading with other western states was never realized.[127] Despite efforts to make British products more attractive for the East German government, most western goods imported by East Berlin continued to come from countries other than Britain, above all from West Germany.

On the whole, while the GDR increased its exports to the UK substantially in the 1970s and 1980s, Britain's trade with the GDR almost stagnated (except for the years 1970, 1979/80 and 1981). Therefore, the country's trade deficit with the GDR continued to show a disturbing increase. The establishment of a governmental commission which met alternately once a year in London and East Berlin to discuss bilateral trade matters did not reverse this general trend.[128] The first major East German contract was only awarded to a British company as late as 1977.[129]

[124] This only gradually changed after Gorbachev's rise to power in 1985. In the second half of the 1980s the GDR adhered to a much more hard-line and orthodox communist course than the Soviet Union under Gorbachev's policies of *Perestroika* and *Glasnost*. However, initially, when Moscow embarked on a renewed hard-line course after the collapse of détente in 1979/80, Honecker favoured the continuation of negotiations, German-German détente and damage limitation. He also opposed the deployment of new nuclear weapons on East German soil. See K. Larres, 'Germany in 1989: the Development of a Revolution', in K. Larres (ed.), *Germany since Unification: The Domestic and External Consequences* (Basingstoke, 1998), 38–39; H.-J. Spanger, *The GDR in East–West Relations* (London, 1989), 3–4, 19-ff.; Mählert, *Kleine Geschichte der DDR*, 146 ff.

[125] M. Fulbrook, *Anatomy of a Dictatorship: Inside the GDR, 1949–1989* (Oxford, 1995), 201 ff.　　　　　　　　　　　　　　　[126] See e.g. PRO: FO 371/172 188/RG 1462/1, 5/11/1963.

[127] PRO: FO 371/163 650/CG 1154/25, 20/11/1962.

[128] See the table in Bachmann, 'Die Beziehungen der DDR', 121, 124.

[129] Munro, 'The Acceptance of a Second German State', 124. French and Japanese industries proved to be much more successful in attracting East German projects. See H. J. Fink, 'Westeuropa: Übrige Westeuropäische Länder. Großbritannien', in H. A. Jacobson *et al.* (eds.), *Drei Jahrzehnte Außenpolitik der DDR. Bestimmungsfaktoren, Instrumente, Aktionsfelder* (Munich, 1979), 514–15.

In the same year an office of the East German Bank for Foreign Trade was opened in London.[130] The reluctance of the East German authorities to purchase a greater volume of British goods often led to unpleasant comments about the GDR's trade habits in the British media. A particular large drop in British exports (particularly in agricultural goods) occurred in 1985.[131]

The unsatisfactory British trade relationship with the GDR in the decades after recognition indicate that the policy of non-recognition had not been the main reason why British–East German trade relations had not been more fruitful prior to 1973. The increasing global uncompetitiveness of British goods in the 1960s and 1970s which lingered on into the 1980s inhibited Britain's export drive. Furthermore, the GDR's rigid economic system, its technological backwardness and latent economic and financial difficulties including its lack of hard currency also played a decisive role. Above all, East Berlin's concentration on trade with Eastern Europe and on intra-German trade relations contributed decisively to this situation.[132] Thus, the Foreign Office's old scepticism regarding claims that trade with the GDR could be massively expanded once recognition had occurred proved to have been fully justified.

After recognition, political relations between Britain and East Germany also remained fairly poor. In the summer of 1974 both the GDR's disruption of the motorway traffic to Berlin in reaction to the establishment of the West German Authority for the Protection of the Environment in West Berlin (which the GDR regarded as illegal) and the arrest of two British citizens for helping GDR citizens to escape to the West led to expressions of British dismay. Prime Minister Wilson decided not to accept a visit to East Berlin which GDR Foreign Minister Oskar Fischer had extended to him during the meeting of the UN general assembly in late 1974 when both German states became UN members.[133] However, on 4 May 1976 Britain and the GDR signed a consular agreement which East Berlin regarded as highly important. After all, for the first time one of the three western occupation powers appeared to have accepted GDR citizenship. Although the Foreign Office explained to West German Foreign Minister Hans-Dietrich Genscher that the 1956 consular treaty between Britain and the FRG, which was based on the underlying assumption of the existence of only one German citizenship, was not affected, this appeared to be doubtful.[134]

---

[130] Bachmann, 'Die Beziehungen der DDR', 124.   [131] Bachmann, ibid. 120–3.
[132] Bachmann, ibid. 123; Kopstein, *Politics of Economic Decline*, 73 ff.
[133] Fink, 'Westeuropa', 515–16; Bell, *Britain and East Germany*, 296–7.
[134] For example, any visitor from the GDR was now free to contact either the West German or the East German embassy in London. See Fink, ibid. 516; Bachmann, 'Die Beziehungen der DDR', 116–17.

In the following years London made it clear that unless trade relations improved considerably, the GDR could not expect any more concessions as far as East Berlin's international standing and the political dialogue with Britain were concerned. That trade was indeed still the most important aspect of British–East German relations from London's point of view becomes clear when reviewing the subsequent political contacts between the two countries. During GDR Foreign Minister Oskar Fischer's one-day visit to London in September 1976 to exchange the ratification documents for the consular agreement he was reminded that Britain was mainly interested in flourishing trade relations with the GDR. Similar statements were made when Edmund Dell, the Secretary of State for Trade, visited East Berlin in February 1977.[135] Soon more junior British ministers and their East German counterparts visited each other's capitals, mainly to review trade links. However, humanitarian issues were also often mentioned.

The Afghanistan invasion in December 1979 led to a certain decline in British–East German relations. Moreover, new Conservative Prime Minister Margaret Thatcher began differentiating between eastern bloc countries which were loyal followers of Moscow like East Berlin and more independent and allegedly more liberal countries like Romania under its dictator Nicolae Ceausescu.[136] Still, in 1981 Hermann Axen, responsible for foreign policy in the East German Politburo, was received by Thatcher and Foreign Secretary Lord Carrington although the West German government had asked London to refrain from paying Axen too much attention. His meeting with the Prime Minister was therefore regarded as a major East German diplomatic success and a snub to Bonn.[137]

Throughout the 1970s and 1980s, GDR leader Honecker had been hoping that he would eventually be able to pay an official state visit to London. Foreign Secretary Geoffrey's Howe's journey to East Berlin in 1985 as well as Oskar Fischer's return visit a year later were regarded as steps in the right direction to bring this about but it would never happen. Despite Honecker's official 1987 visit to Chancellor Helmut Kohl in Bonn, the GDR leader's obvious lack of enthusiasm for Gorbachev's reform policies and the difficulties created for his regime by the ever more outspoken East German opposition movements made this unlikely. Above all, in 1989 the opening of the Hungarian–Austrian border, the

[135] Bachmann, ibid. 113. During an interview on 3 Feb. 1999 in London, Edmund Dell confirmed this. However, he emphasized that at the same time the Labour government was always aware of the limited potential for increasing the volume of trade with the GDR.

[136] Munro, 'The Acceptance of a Second German State', 124; M. Thatcher, *The Downing Street Years*, paperback edn. (London, 1995), 87–8.

[137] Bachmann, 'Die Beziehungen der DDR', 113.

flight of East Germans to the West German embassies in Prague, Warsaw, and Budapest, and the dramatic mass demonstrations in the GDR intervened before Honecker could realize his dream of being received by the Queen. On 18 October 1989 Honecker's colleagues in the East German Politburo forced him to tender his resignation. Three weeks later the Berlin Wall was breached and on 28 November West German Chancellor Kohl announced his ten-point plan outlining the road to German unification.[138]

After much hesitation and counteraction by the Prime Minister, eventually, on 6 February 1990 Foreign Secretary Douglas Hurd officially confirmed Britain's support for the unification of the two German states.[139] By the time the merging of the East and West German state occurred in October 1990 the GDR had ceased to be a factor in British politics. However, Mrs Thatcher's support for the continued existence of the GDR in late 1989/early 1990 and the ensuing accusations with regard to her growing political eccentricity which appeared to be harming her country internationally contributed to the Prime Minister's rapidly increasing lack of popularity and eventual downfall in late 1990.[140] In this way the GDR made a final splash on the world scene after it had already disappeared for good on 3 October 1990.

CONCLUSION

Despite some willingness in British governmental circles to diverge from West Germany's (and Washington's) preferred policy towards the East German state, on the whole it is clear that Britain remained loyal to the western non-recognition of the GDR until 1973, when East Germany was eventually recognized by the western world. Moreover, despite being occasionally tempted by the promise of closer trade links with East Berlin, improvements in economic relations with the GDR were almost always viewed in London as much less desirable than keeping on good terms with the economically and politically much more important government in Bonn. Britain's increasing trade with the countries of the European Community after 1973 also helped to undermine the GDR's efforts to lure London with promises of greater exports into a closer economic and political relationship with East Berlin. Throughout the cold war British governments of all political persuasions were neither in

---

[138] For an overview of these dramatic events, see Larres, 'Germany in 1989', 43–52.

[139] See also Hurd's speech in Parliament, *H.C. Deb.*, 6th ser., vol. 166, 1088–90 (22 Feb. 1990); also M. Stuart, *Douglas Hurd the Public Servant: an authorised biography* (Edinburgh, 1998), 233–50.

[140] For Mrs Thatcher and German unification, see Ch. 4 by L. Kettenacker in this book.

the pockets of the UK's West German ally nor of Britain's own business community. While London was able to pursue a fairly independent policy, most of the time it also managed successfully to adhere to the western world's agreed strategy towards the GDR and thus maintain its friendly relations with the Federal Republic.

4

Britain and German Unification, 1989/90

LOTHAR KETTENACKER

The final verdict on Britain's stance towards German unification will have to wait at least another twenty years until the release of HM official documents. However, this does not mean that until then we are reduced to making more or less intelligent guesses. For once the diplomatic process and the decisive position taken by the American Bush administration have been studied in detail by two aides of the president's national security advisers.[1] Their study will be unsurpassed for some time to come, not least because they draw on a vast array and variety of official documents, including Russian records. It is most telling that the only superpower left should also have been the first to direct our understanding of the momentous historical events of 1989/90. In addition, a great number of the German Chancellery's documents pertaining to unification have already been published in one massive volume which constitutes an important source.[2] It was, after all, the Chancellery, not the German Foreign Office, that was in charge of German–German affairs. One name which crops up again and again as the author of important minutes and memoranda is Horst Teltschik, Chancellor Helmut Kohl's trusted civil servant and witness to most of his confidential talks. There is general agreement amongst historians that his diaries are the most candid and reliable source of information about the day-to-day business.[3] He was behind all moves to accelerate the process of unification which so worried the British and German Foreign Ministries. Moreover, the memoirs of at least three of the major actors have now been published, those of Margaret

---

[1] See P. Zelikow and C. Rice, *Germany Unified and Europe Transformed: A Study in Statecraft* (Cambridge, Mass., 1995). See also H. Bortfeldt, 'Die Vereinigten Staaten und die deutsche Einheit', in K. Larres and T. Oppelland (eds.), *Deutschland und die USA im 20. Jahrhundert. Geschichte der politischen Beziehungen* (Darmstadt, 1997), 256–73. The best German account by a participant is R. Kiessler and F. Elbe, *Ein runder Tisch mit scharfen Ecken. Der diplomatische Weg zur Wiedervereinigung* (Baden-Baden, 1986). Elbe was Genscher's *chef de cabinet* between 1987 and 1992.

[2] H. J. Küsters and D. Hofmann (eds.), *Deutsche Einheit. Sonderedition aus den Akten des Bundeskanzleramtes 1989/90* (Munich, 1998).

[3] H. Teltschik, *329 Tage. Innenansichten der Einigung* (Berlin, 1991). For an assessment: A. Röder, 'Staatskunst statt Kriegshandwerk. Probleme der deutschen Vereinigung von 1990 in internationaler Perspektive', *Historisches Jahrbuch* 118 (1998), 227–9.

Thatcher, Helmut Kohl, and Hans-Dietrich Genscher.[4] Thatcher's memoirs in particular are so candid that one is reminded of James Byrnes, Truman's first Secretary of State who published his reminiscences under the title *Speaking Frankly*.[5] However, the memoirs of someone as prominent and opinionated as Margaret Thatcher confront the historian immediately with one big problem: the picture of Britain's attitude towards Germany when it matters most since 1949 might be, as it were, over-exposed.

There is one method that might help to throw some light on how the Foreign Office, after all the government's collective body of advisers, interpreted Britain's national interests in 1989/90, and that is the past record of Britain's dealing with the German question. The 'official mind' is by its nature never quite as prejudiced as that of the individual decision-maker and in a way should therefore be given more credit by historians. For example, an institution like the Foreign Office would always feel more bound by previous commitments to Britain's allies than any one Foreign Secretary.

BRITAIN AND THE GERMAN QUESTION

The historical approach to the German question reveals, on close inspection, that there were always two different routes: the short-cut preferred by politicians and journalists and a somewhat more long-winded road which is often overlooked. The short-cut route was first signposted by Disraeli, and latterly by Margaret Thatcher: a united Germany is bound to destroy the balance of power in Europe and is therefore bad for Britain.[6] A more thorough-going historical analysis, however, is more likely to lead us to the attitude eventually taken by the Foreign Office.

Recent research on Britain's relations with Prussia on the eve of German unification 'Mark I' (1870/1) shows that the policy of non-intervention on the Continent was by no means a symptom of British weakness or decline, but the result of a sober calculation of her true national interests.[7] Nor was there any genuine opposition in Britain to national

---

[4] M. Thatcher, *The Downing Street Years*, paperback edn. (London, 1995); H. Kohl, *Ich wollte Deutschlands Einheit*, ed. K. Diekmann and R. G. Reuth (Berlin, 1996); H.K.-D. Genscher, *Erinnerungen* (Berlin, 1995). There are also three memoirs that shed light on the Soviet government's point of view: E. Schevardnadze, *The Future Belongs to Freedom* (London, 1991); V. Falin, *Politische Erinnerungen* (Munich, 1993); J. Kwizinskij, *Vor dem Sturm. Erinnerungen eines Diplomaten* (Berlin, 1993). In these memoirs the British Prime Minister hardly figures at all.

[5] J. F. Byrnes, *Speaking Frankly* (London, 1947).

[6] See his speech in the House of Commons on 9 Feb. 1871, in *Parliamentary Debates, House of Commons*, Fifth Series (hereafter: *H.C. Deb.*), vol. 204, 81, and Thatcher's *Downing Street Years* (pp. 790–1) regarding 'The German problem and the Balance of Power'.

[7] See K. Hildebrand, *No Intervention. Die Pax Britannica und Preußen 1865/66–1868/70. Eine Untersuchung zur englischen Weltpolitik im 19. Jahrhundert* (Munich, 1997).

unity amongst the Germans. One was not called upon to intervene in what was regarded as a natural, and to some extent inevitable process. It was only after the event that certain reservations began to surface concerning the manner in which unification had actually been brought about: the proclamation of the new empire on the battlefield, the fateful message that military might mattered most. The lesson to be drawn from the calamities of the ensuing seventy-five years concerned the modus of German unification rather than its essence.

At the end of this period, in May 1945, the Germans had paid a bitter price for their belief that war would be profitable. Their country was now totally occupied by foreign troops. However, dismemberment of the Reich, though advocated in certain quarters, was never an official British war-aim. The most persuasive arguments put forward at the time against such a draconian policy of deliberately undoing Bismarck's achievement should also prove to be the most relevant to an understanding of the Foreign Office attitude in 1989/90: first, dismemberment was historically retrograde. Since it could not, in the long-run, be enforced against the will of the German people it would not be backed up by public opinion at home. On the whole it was a recipe for rekindling German nationalism. Second, joint responsibility by the four powers for Germany as a whole would be undermined by a break-up of the country into its component parts.[8] Therefore, the experts at the Foreign Office came to the conclusion that rather than dismembering the Reich it made more sense to decentralize its power structure by partitioning Prussia, then viewed as the core of German militarism. As a matter of fact, the zoning of Germany for the purpose of occupation had already resulted in the break-up of Prussia. However, it is important to stress that the subsequent division of Germany along the western boundaries of the Soviet zone was the outcome of the cold war or, in other words, the failure of the allies to agree on a common policy for all zones.[9] Had it not been for Berlin, four-power control would probably not have stood the test of time throughout the years of the cold war.

A separate zone for the Reich's capital, to be occupied jointly by the major Allies, was the brainchild of British advisers, who conceived this idea as early as spring 1943. A joint zone, though not split up into various sectors, would accommodate an inter-allied Control Commission with

---

[8] For the internal decision-making on dismemberment: L. Kettenacker, *Krieg zur Friedenssicherung. Die Deutschlandplanung der britischen Regierung während des Zweiten Weltkrieges* (Göttingen, 1989), 479–502; as to the public debate: H. Fromm, *Deutschland in der öffentlichen Kriegszieldiskussion Großbritanniens 1939–1945* (Frankfurt/M., 1982), 180–96. All the quality newspapers voiced their objections to any dismemberment plans.

[9] V. Rothwell, *Britain and the Cold War 1941–1947* (London, 1982), 291–352; also H. Graml, *Die Alliierten und die Teilung Deutschlands. Konflikte und Entscheidungen 1941–1948* (Frankfurt/M., 1985).

the task of supervising a German government, or at least central authorities, which would ensure that the country as a whole would be admin-
istered in this way, regardless of the division into zones of occupation.
Berlin was supposed to furnish the model for the application of indirect
rule which had served Britain well in colonial days. However, this was
not to be because there was no administrative machine left to speak of
by the end of the war. Nor were the allies sufficiently determined to set
up central departments as agreed at Potsdam.[10] Berlin was meant to hold
Germany together and also maintain the unity of the allied powers, the
receivers, who now controlled the bankrupt country. Thanks to Berlin
the principle of four-power control survived, despite all crises, up to the
crucial moment of 1990.

From this short historical synopsis it seems likely that as far as the
Foreign Office's professional advice was concerned there was no tradition of objecting in principle to German self-determination up to the point
of restoring national unity. Moreover, as one of the three occupation
powers, Britain was committed to 'the achievement through peaceful means
of a fully free and unified Germany' as 'a fundamental goal of their
policy'.[11] Many similar pronouncements were to follow this declaration
made in the course of the Paris Conference of October 1954. In essence,
it was the essential allied pledge for the Federal Republic's throwing in
its lot with the West. What mattered crucially was the modus of how
this would be achieved. In the circumstances of 1989/90 this meant that
the four allies, still in control of Berlin, also remained responsible for
Germany as a whole. Germany could neither be allowed to unite of its
own accord nor was Germany's fate in the hands of one power, namely
Soviet Russia. The terms of reference would decide what kind of
Germany was to emerge from the turmoil of 1989/90. Of all the four
powers Britain was most concerned about the principle of four-power
control and, in a way, the one power most reluctant to relinquish that
control at short notice. Washington, Paris, and Moscow had other
priorities like adherence to NATO, further European integration and
a neutral status for a united Germany. More than any other nation, Britain was aware that the new Germany could only be contained in co-
operation with those powers that had brought down Hitler's Reich in
1945. The war, rather than the post-war era, moulded Britain's thinking on

---

[10] What was probably the last chance to prevent division has been analysed by E. Kraus,
*Ministerien für das ganze Deutschland? Der Alliierte Kontrollrat und die Frage gesamtdeutscher
Zentralverwaltungen* (Munich, 1990).

[11] Royal Institute for International Affairs (ed.), *British Foreign Policy: Some Relevant
Documents (January 1950–April 1955)* (London, 1955), 105. Bush reminded the Allies on 4 Dec.
1989 at a NATO council meeting in Brussels that they had, after all, been pledged to support
unification 'for decades' (Kiessler and Elbe, *Ein runder Tisch*, 56). See also Zelikow and Rice,
Germany Unified, 131–4.

Germany, as though by assembling the various parts which had drifted in different directions after 1945 the old Germany would be reconstituted. The emphasis on four-power control was legitimate, but also vindictive if overplayed. No doubt there was a greater inclination in London to reach decisions about, rather than with, Germany, just as in 1945. This was well known in allied councils and explains why Mrs Thatcher had preferred the formula 'Four plus two', rather than 'Two plus four'.[12]

Saying that the Foreign Office would not oppose unification does not mean that such a development was welcome. Nor did Germany's political class expect Britain to embrace this prospect. Indeed, among the western allies the level of support for German unification was lowest in Britain (45 per cent). No less than 53 per cent of Britons feared a return of 'German fascism'.[13] Allied support was no more than a treaty obligation in the sense that the question of German unification remained open, only to be settled in some distant future. Former Prime Minister Edward Heath expressed the view of many of his generation when he said: 'Naturally we expressed our support for German unification because we knew it would never happen.'[14] British expectations about the process towards unification had been influenced by the steady course of German Ostpolitik, unaffected by a change of government in Bonn, and by the acceleration of détente as a result of Gorbachev's new departure. In other words, as in 1871, the assumption was that reunification could only come from above, the product of a new détente between Germany and Russia. But this was not anticipated in the near future. There was a 'firm assumption', as Sir Julian Bullard recalls, 'supported by a lot of respectable evidence, that the Soviet national interest required in 1988 as in 1948 the division of Germany and the inclusion of the GDR in the Soviet defence and industrial system'.[15]

A popular movement towards reunification was discounted as either unlikely or too dangerous to be contemplated. After all, the East Germans had learned their lesson since June 1953 and the failure of the Prague Uprising in 1968. French President François Mitterrand confided to George Bush in May 1989 that he could visualize only two causes of war in Europe: the West Germans acquiring an independent nuclear *force*

---

[12] Thatcher, *Downing Street Years*, 799. According to Kiessler and Elbe, ibid. 88, Douglas Hurd suggested (no doubt with the Prime Minister's backing) during a visit to Washington at the end of January, 'Four plus zero', i.e. leaving the Germans out altogether.

[13] According to an opinion poll by the *Los Angeles Times/Economist* (compared to 61 per cent in America and France). See P. Merkl, *German Unification in the European Context* (University Park, Pa., 1993), 315.

[14] Quoted in *Der Spiegel*, No. 39, 25 Sept. 1989, 16–17.

[15] See the contribution by Sir Julian Bullard (based on a paper at a conference in Exeter in March 1998) in J. Noakes *et al.* (eds.), *Britain and Germany in Europe, 1949–1990* (Oxford/GHI, 2000 [forthcoming]).

de frappe, and a popular movement towards unification.[16] The latter scenario also horrified the political establishment in both German states. Consequently nobody was prepared for what was to come: a tidal wave which took them all by surprise. In the end unification was only possible as the result of crisis management. The process was also helped by the clever double-act performed by Chancellor Kohl and his Foreign Minister Hans-Dietrich Genscher who gave different signals to different people: Kohl encouraging the East Germans in the streets, whereas Genscher kept his foot on the brakes, thus reassuring Germany's neighbours.

THE IMPENDING END OF THE COLD WAR

In the spring and early summer of 1989 Anglo-German relations were completely overshadowed by the unnecessary dispute over the modernization of short-range nuclear missiles. The British quality newspapers were united in their frantic condemnation of German defeatism, only because Bonn was concerned about missiles targeted at East German cities and preferred NATO to sound out the Soviet government before any rash decisions were taken. One paper, generally friendly towards Germany, wrote: 'The seduction of West Germany by Mr Gorbachev proceeds apace.'[17] Only the Labour Party remained clear-headed and supportive of Chancellor Kohl's preference for talks. For Margaret Thatcher this was an occasion to live up to her reputation as the Iron Lady and the most loyal of American allies. In her memoirs she admits to having had 'acrimonious discussions with Chancellor Kohl behind the stage-managed friendliness of our meeting at Deidesheim'.[18] Clearly the first sightings of the end of the cold war left the British government frightened and confused, not least because this development was bound to enhance Germany's position as a bridge-builder and raised the spectre of German unification. However, the Bush administration was more concerned about German than British sensibilities in this matter. The President's advisers did not wish to supply the SPD with ammunition, a party 'that, as currently constituted, has too little regard either for nuclear deterrence

---

[16] See J. Attali, *Verbatim*, vol. 3 (Paris, 1995), 241 (19 May 1989).

[17] *Independent*, 24 April 1989. For Labour see the paper's report of 26 April: 'Thatcher clashes with Kinnock on NATO Strategy'. According to the Labour leader, Kohl was 'absolutely right' to press for early talks between America and the Soviet Union when two-thirds of the Germans opposed modernization of short-range missiles.

[18] Thatcher, *Downing Street Years*, 786. Elsewhere she says: 'I took him to task on this' (p. 747).

or for conventional defence'.[19] Bush and his Foreign Secretary James Baker changed track and opted for talks on the reduction of conventional forces, much to the frustration of Margaret Thatcher who was left in the lurch as the last cold war warrior. More upsetting still was the fall-out from Bush's visit to the Federal Republic where he welcomed the Germans as 'partners in leadership' and called for the Iron Curtain to come down: 'Let Berlin be next.'[20] The end of the cold war also seemed to signal the end of the 'special relationship' between the two Anglo-Saxon powers, quite apart from the fact that the new American president was less charmed by Mrs Thatcher than his predecessor.

The American administration realized, no less than the British media, that overcoming the division of Europe and that of Germany were inseparable, and Washington welcomed this process without reservation. On the whole American decision-makers were less dominated by the past and more forward-looking than their British counterparts. The prospect of German unification did not worry them, on the contrary, it seemed to be the key to making Europe 'whole and free'.[21] Germany's European allies were not really looking forward to the end of the cold war, which in a way provided stability under the umbrella of mutual superpower deterrence. Yet they were committed to the Helsinki process and the application of political self-determination in eastern Europe. In a situation of fermentation and uncertainty all kinds of potential developments are projected into the future, more often than not based on the worst-case scenario. British common-sense in particular, deeply affected by the experience of imperial decline, was prone to such thinking. The most powerful assumption was that under the guise of détente Germany would drift out of the western and into the Soviet orbit, in order to achieve national reunification.

A strong pointer in this direction, already marked by Bonn's refusal to welcome the modernization of short-range missiles, was Gorbachev's enthusiastic reception in the Federal Republic in June 1989. The ground had been well prepared. Gorbachev let it be known that a thousand tanks were to be sent out of East Germany by the end of 1990. Shortly afterwards he announced the unilateral cut of 500 warheads of short-range nuclear missiles, coupled with an offer to renegotiate radical reductions in conventional weapons.[22] On the eve of his visit various of his advisers were quoted in the British press as saying that Moscow would not rule

---

[19] Quoted in Zelikow and Rice, *Germany Unified*, 28.
[20] Bush's address in Mainz on 31 May 1989, quoted in ibid. 31. Following Washington's defusion of the missile crisis, the *Financial Times* reported on 23/5/1989: 'Britain concerned about weakening of "special relationship"'. [21] Ibid.
[22] *The Times*, 6/5/1989; *Guardian*, 13/5/1989.

out unification on certain conditions.[23] Faced with the 'Gorbymania' that gripped Germany the British media felt decidedly uncomfortable. For the *Daily Express* it was 'patently obvious' that Gorbachev's 'wooing' of the West Germans was 'part of the Soviet design to divide NATO and uncouple the United States from Europe'.[24] By uniting the two Germanys the Soviet leader could 'destroy NATO at a stroke'.[25] There was a widespread belief in Britain that the Germans' changing mood could not be trusted: yesterday fiercely anti-communist, today trusting Gorbachev more than their own politicians and growing more pacifist by the day. Would a democratically elected government not have to take these swings into account? It is worth mentioning in this context that Margaret Thatcher's generation of Britons had been brought up on A. J. P. Taylor's 'Course of German History', which opens with the following sentences: 'The history of the Germans is a history of extremes. It contains everything except moderation . . .'.[26] Perhaps it was not sufficiently realized abroad that in post-1949 Germany when it comes to fundamental decisions, like continued membership of NATO or European monetary union for that matter, German democracy is, for good reasons, less at the mercy of opinion-polls than is the case in Anglo-Saxon countries. A sigh of relief went through the British press when it turned out that the joint declaration at the end of Gorbachev's ominous visit contained 'nothing particularly startling'.[27] The German vessel did not cause havoc by breaking loose from its moorings. Unjustified as these anxieties may have been, for the subsequent process of decision-making it was important that they were expressed and then properly addressed by German diplomacy.

THE COLLAPSE OF THE GDR AND
THE FUTURE OF NATO

Nobody in the West expected a sudden collapse of the GDR, brought about by a flood of refugees that threatened to burst the river-banks of a controlled development, except for one person, the new American Ambassador in Bonn, Vernon Walters, who had a strong feeling that German unification was in the offing.[28] Nobody took him seriously,

---

[23] See, e.g., *Independent*, 13/5/1989 ('One Germany wouldn't worry Moscow') and 7/6/1989 ('Gorbachev's advisors see "open" Germany'). Also, later, the *Daily Mail*, 3/7/1989: 'Soviets "won't stop a united Germany"', reporting on Enoch Powell's interview with a Soviet general.
[24] *Daily Express*, 14/6/1989.　　　　[25] *Sunday Times*, 11/6/1989.
[26] A. J. P. Taylor, *The Course of German History* (London, 1962). First published in 1945, this popular textbook was reprinted five times.　　　　[27] *The Times* (leader), 16/6/1989.
[28] See V. A. Walters, *Die Vereinigung war voraussehbar: Hinter den Kulissen eines entscheidenden Jahres* (Berlin, 1994).

though later on his encouragement to press on proved to be an important signal to the German government. Among the Warsaw Pact countries the East German state seemed to be least affected by the virus of reformist ideas. The near-perfect State Security surveillance system made sure that the population was kept in check, while incorrigible nonconformists were expelled to West Germany. Yet the apparent stability of the GDR was a sham: months before the Wall came down it had already, though almost imperceptibly, begun to crack when, on 2 May, Hungary started to dismantle the barbed-wire along its border with Austria. At first it was but a trickle of East Germans escaping across the border. With the start of the holiday season the numbers swelled. By the end of July the *Guardian* referred to 'hordes of East Germans being sent back by the Hungarian border guards'.[29] Only a week later the same paper reported that between forty and fifty East Germans were daily queuing for passports at Vienna's West German embassy.[30] From 25 August British papers were full of reports about thousands of East Germans trying to escape to the promised land of West Germany. But the regime was not yet thought to be under threat from within. On 22 August the journalist Patricia Clough wrote: 'There is virtually no active internal opposition.'[31] She dismissed the 'handful of tiny protest groups' sheltered by the Protestant church. The judicial perception of German discipline preventing all pressure for change still prevailed. However, the haemorrhage continued unabated. Only a week later *The Times* wrote, under the headline 'Voting with their Feet': 'There is no greater indictment of a government than when large numbers of its brightest and most ambitious young people seek their future elsewhere.'[32] Again, a few days later in early September, the *Sunday Times* reported on the flood of refugees under the headline 'Regime Crumbles Round Dying Honecker'.[33]

During that most crucial period the East German leadership, with their chief not at the helm but in hospital, maintained an icy silence. When Hungary fully opened its borders on 10 September it looked like the floodgates had been stormed. Although the first demonstrations in Leipzig on 4 September were not yet noticed by the British media, the East German regime was already written off: 'a state which has lost its meaning'.[34] Did this mean that the German question was now back 'on the agenda

---

[29] *Guardian*, 26/7/1989.

[30] Ibid. 8/8/1989. A week later (15 Aug.) the East German writer Stefan Heym warned in the same paper: 'Exodus threatens to destroy GDR', pointing out that the majority of refugees were younger people and that 1.5m. East Germans had chosen the legal path by submitting applications to leave.　　　　　　　　　　　　　　　　　　　　[31] *Guardian*, 22/8/1989.

[32] *The Times*, 28/8/1989.　　　　[33] *Sunday Times*, 3/9/1989.

[34] *Independent* (leader), 12/9/1989. As to the term 'agenda', see *The Sunday Times*, 10/9/1989. A dissenting voice was Neal Ascherson in the *Observer* of the same day: 'But reunification isn't on anybody's agenda'.

of world politics'? All of a sudden this phrase turned out to be highly controversial: yes, said the media; no, said the Prime Minister. The official position was that what was at issue was not reunification but the liberalization of the existing system in accordance with the wishes of East German dissidents. The British press, too, pinned great hopes on the East German opposition.[35] Independent minds like former Foreign Secretary David Owen and eminent journalist Peter Jenkins turned out to be more generous and far-sighted than the Conservative establishment round the Prime Minister. David Owen foresaw that a united Germany could well 'remain committed to the defence of the West' since it would, no doubt, have its centre of gravity in Western Europe.[36] Peter Jenkins warned his country's political class 'not to be governed by old prejudices and out-of-date assumptions'.[37] What mattered was to think 'not of ways of preventing German unification but of ways of bringing it about peaceably'. This proved to be the position soon adopted by both the Labour and the Liberal Democratic parties. Not so by the Prime Minister and her still considerable following. They now pinned their hopes, though expressed as fears, on the Soviet Union. 'The vacuum created [by a sudden collapse of the GDR] in the centre of Europe', wrote the *Financial Times*, 'and the ensuing instability would risk provoking a Soviet military intervention and thus constitutes a serious menace to world peace.'[38] Another more likely scenario depicted by *The Times* was no less threatening: a majority of Germans in both East and West opting for the proposal of the Social Democrats that Germany should not be attached to any single alliance, but be part of a European security system.[39] This might have meant the demise of NATO. No doubt Kohl knew how to play upon such anxieties to his own advantage. Better unification on his terms than on those of his opponents who would benefit from any evidence of deliberate delay on the part of Germany's allies.

As we know, Gorbachev, having abandoned the Brezhnev Doctrine, had no intention of intervening in what was first seen as a push for internal reforms. On her way back from an international conference in Tokyo (19–22 September) Mrs Thatcher had arranged for a stop-over in Moscow. She is quite candid in her memoirs that her main concern was Germany: 'Although NATO had traditionally made statements', she explained to Gorbachev, 'supporting Germany's aspiration to be reunited, in practice we were rather apprehensive.'[40] The Soviet leader assured her that his

---

[35] See I. Lehmann, *Die deutsche Einigung von außen gesehen. Angst, Bedenken und Erwartungen in der ausländischen Presse* (Frankfurt/M., 1996), vol. I, 208.
[36] *Independent* (leader), 13/9/1989.   [37] *Daily Express*, 12/9/1989.
[38] *Financial Times*, 12/9/1989.   [39] See Lehmann, *Die deutsche Einigung*, 420.
[40] Thatcher, *The Downing Street Years*, 792.

government did not want German reunification either. 'This reinforced me in my resolve to slow up the already heady pace of the development,' she wrote. In this she utterly failed because she might have controlled her cabinet but was unable to influence events on the streets of Leipzig. Over the next couple of months she did, however, manage to antagonize the political class in Germany, all the more so since any reference to 'Wiedervereinigung' was still a taboo until the fall of the Wall. From now on Margaret Thatcher, once the cold war warrior personified, posed as Gorbachev's champion in western councils. A key word was 'destabiliza- tion' which implied a weakening of Gorbachev's position within the Soviet Union, with unforeseeable consequences.

However, similar to Gorbachev's considerations, wishful thinking got the better of the Prime Minister: she believed it possible to split political self-determination, i.e. to separate democratic reform in East Germany, from the demand for unification. This was, incidentally, also the mistaken belief of the *avant-garde* of reformers in East Germany who in these days were gathering strength and helped to bring down the Honecker regime. The Monday demonstrations in Leipzig were only really discovered by the British media after 9 October,[41] which proved to be the decisive event, historically more important than the fall of the Wall a month later. On that day the regime had gathered itself up for a final showdown. However, the demonstrators, no more than approximately 70,000, would not be intimidated. They remained peaceful and defiant, and as a con- sequence brought down the hated regime. Honecker resigned on 18 October; he was replaced by Egon Krenz's short-lived leadership.[42]

A week later several British journalists were invited to Bonn to address an audience of some 200 VIPs on the German question. Oddly enough, the latter seemed 'somewhat taken aback that instead of expressing *angst*, we each of us, in our different ways looked forward to a united Germany'.[43] The standard phrase which these journalists encountered in their conversations was that unification 'won't happen in our lifetime'. Hans-Dietrich Genscher avoided the word altogether and propagated his idea of a confederation, subsumed within some pan-European order.[44] Not only was this meeting a great boost to German morale, it also showed that viewed from abroad and by independent minds, not shackled by official

[41] See e.g. the *Daily Telegraph* and the *Independent* of 10/11/1989. For the significance of the Leipzig demonstrations see the observations of the 'historian on the spot', H. Zwahr, *Ende einer Selbstzerstörung: Leipzig und die Revolution in der DDR* (Göttingen, 1993).

[42] For an overview of these events, see e.g. K. Larres, 'Germany in 1989: the Development of a Revolution', in K. Larres, *Germany since Unification: The Domestic and External Con- sequences* (Basingstoke, 1998), 33–59.

[43] Peregrine Worsthorne in the *Daily Telegraph* (25 Oct.) and Peter Jenkins in the *Independ- ent* of the same day.

[44] Ibid. See also Genscher's memoirs (*Erinnerungen*), 652–61.

briefings, German unification appeared to be much more natural than in the eyes of the over-anxious West Germans. It is a strange and sad reflection on the make-up of human nature: the closer one lives to something as depraved and unnatural as the fortified inner-German border, the more one gets used to it. Whatever governments said in public, Germany's neighbours could not quite reconcile themselves to the state of affairs in the middle of Europe. In this respect the British were no different from others, except that they were more worried about the return of fascism as a result of German reunification.

For Mrs Thatcher, the critical voices in the media and among members of the opposition were of no importance. What carried weight were the views of her supposed allies amongst the heads of state. These provided no comfort: President Bush let it be known that he was relaxed about German unification,[45] and on 4 November the British press reported that Mitterrand, too, was not alarmed by this idea.[46] Even though the French president felt equally uneasy about this prospect, he was prudent enough not to say so in public. This was also the position taken by the Foreign Office, which advised that it was best not to risk alienating the Germans by openly discouraging reunification. A separate state like Austria, democratic but independent, was thought to be a feasible alternative.[47]

The Prime Minister lived up to the occasion when the Berlin Wall was breached. Briefing the press outside 10 Downing Street on 9 November she said that this was a great day for freedom and now the Wall had to be fully dismantled. Her response was well received in Bonn.[48] Consensus between London and Bonn remained intact for another fortnight. The Chancellery fully concurred with the contents of a letter the Prime Minister had sent to Gorbachev: stability was at stake and had to be safeguarded. The best way to achieve this was through far-reaching reforms in the GDR, such as free elections, a multi-party system, free movement etc. No one in the West wished to meddle in the internal affairs of the GDR or endanger its security.[49] Apparently, Thatcher saw no contradiction between these two sets of propositions. Nevertheless, after the fall of the Wall it did not escape political commentators in London that the government remained silent on what had been the most momentous event in 1989. According to an internal assessment in Bonn the Americans were most favourably disposed towards unification, the French were more reserved, but agreed that this was a legitimate goal, whereas the British

[45] *Financial Times*, 20/10/1989. See also *The New York Times*, 25 Oct. 1989: 'Possibility of a Reunited Germany is No Cause for Alarm, Bush Says'.

[46] *Daily Telegraph* (4/11/1989) reporting on the Franco-German summit in Bonn.

[47] See the Foreign Office paper 'The German Question', quoted in Zelikow and Rice, *Germany Unified*, 97.   [48] See Teltschik, *329 Tage*, 21 (10/11/1989).

[49] Ibid., 34 (16/11/1989).

were pressing for 'self-determination' in terms of reforming the GDR.[50] Commentators in London were agreed that 'the crumbling of the Wall marked the end of the post-war order in Europe', and urged the government to take a more active role in creating a new order.[51] Instead the British cultivated East German dissidents and the Prime Minister sent a message to President Bush reiterating her view 'that the priority should be to see genuine democracy established in East Germany and that German reunification was not something to be addressed at the moment'.[52] Shortly afterwards, at a special meeting of EC heads of government in Paris, she insisted that the Helsinki Final Act must apply: no question of changing borders. Gorbachev should not be inconvenienced by rash talk about German reunification. She even pleaded for the Warsaw Pact to remain intact, 'to create a background of stability'.[53]

While Genscher kept on appeasing his French and British colleagues, Chancellor Kohl would not be intimidated and went on to the offensive. In a speech to the Bundestag on 28 November he submitted, without further consultation, a Ten-Point Plan, with the aim of creating 'confederate structures' as a step towards eventual unification.[54] Now the German question was indeed officially on the agenda, however much Mrs Thatcher had tried to prevent it. To Genscher she complained on 30 November that the firm foundations laid in Paris were suddenly giving way.[55] A recent trip to Washington had not been reassuring. President Bush listened politely to her admonitions, but remained non-committal.[56] When Kohl met Bush for dinner in Brussels on 3 December he explained that Britain's reaction to his Ten-Point Plan had been somewhat reserved. The President replied that this was 'the understatement of the year'.[57]

Bush had by now reasserted his leadership role and followed the advice given by his chief adviser Brent Scowcroft that 'we are prepared to honor the German people's choices about their future—including a choice

[50] Memorandum by Teltschik for Kohl, 17/11/1989, pub. in H. J. Küsters and D. Hofmann (eds.), *Deutsche Einheit*, Doc. 94B, 546–7.   [51] Denis Healey in the *Observer*, 12/11/1989.
[52] Thatcher, *Downing Street Years*, 793.
[53] Ibid., 794. See also Kohl, *Ich wollte Deutschlands Einheit*, 149–50: 'Margaret Thatcher fordert am nachdrücklichsten die Beibehaltung des Status quo: Die Frage der Grenzen stehe nicht auf der Tagesordnung.' Kohl commented: she meant the inner-German border, not the Oder-Neiße line.
[54] *The Times* (leader), 29/11/1989. As to the exposition of the 'ten points' see Kohl, ibid., 157–77. The Prime Minister forcefully voiced her preconditions (such as free elections and rule of law all over Eastern Europe and Russia) on television (Panorama), which occasioned the *Guardian's* comment (29/11/1989): 'This is procrastination to the nth degree.'
[55] H. J. Küsters and D. Hofmann (eds.), *Deutsche Einheit*, Doc. 102, 575.
[56] Thatcher, *Downing Street Years*, 794.
[57] H. J. Küsters and D. Hofmann (eds.), *Deutsche Einheit*, Doc. 109, 600. See also Teltschik, *329 Tage*, 64.

for reunification; that we are committed to peaceful change in a stable way'.[58] Henceforth this was to become the official western response to how the German question ought to be handled. British diplomats were worried that NATO had not been mentioned anywhere in Kohl's Ten Points. However, decision-makers in Washington had reached the conclusion that moving fast was the best way of securing a united Germany's membership of NATO. Downing Street's advice to go slowly was ignored. American Foreign Secretary Baker spelt out the most important principles at a press conference: first, self-determination 'without prejudice to its outcome'; second, Germany to remain in NATO (Thatcher: 'with which I heartily agreed'), and to be part of an increasingly integrated Europe (Thatcher: 'with which I did not').[59] Because of Mrs Thatcher's reservations about Europe, all her subsequent efforts to forge an *entente cordiale* with President Mitterrand to abort, or at least delay German unification came to nothing. In her memoirs she accuses Mitterrand, who sympathized with the British Prime Minister in private, but not in public, of 'a tendency to schizophrenia'. When he observed, in a philosophical manner, that the Germans were a people in constant movement and flux, Mrs Thatcher produced a map from her famous handbag 'showing the various configurations of Germany in the past which were not altogether reassuring about the future'.[60] According to Jacques Attali, one of Mitterrand's closest advisers, she pointed to Silesia, Pomerania, and East Prussia and said: 'They'll take all that and Czechoslovakia.'[61] When they met again at the Elysée Palace on 20 January, the French President and the British Prime Minister were at a loss as to how to slow down the German 'juggernaut'. 'The trouble was that in reality there was no force in Europe which could stop reunification happening.'[62] Nor could they agree about the best way of containing the new Germany. Mitterrand opted for further European integration instead of the Palmerstonian concept of constantly changing alliances and alignments in the pursuit of national interests. In her memoirs Mrs Thatcher states categorically: 'He made the wrong decision for France.'[63] She firmly believed that 'a reunited Germany' was 'simply too big and powerful to be just another player within Europe', and that the country was 'by its very nature a destabilising rather than a stabilising force in Europe'.[64] This fear was widespread in Britain and expressed succinctly by the *Economist*: a stronger

---

[58] Quoted in Zelikow and Rice, *Germany Unified*, 115.
[59] Thatcher, *Memoirs*, 795.   [60] Ibid., 796.
[61] Attali, *Verbatim*, vol. 3, 369 (8/12/1989). Thatcher told Mitterrand that the United States would not hinder German unification: 'Il y a un fort lobby pro-allemand en Amérique.'
[62] Thatcher, *Downing Street Years*, 797.   [63] Ibid., 798.
[64] Ibid., 791. This is the crucial page in her memoirs regarding her views on the 'German problem'.

European Union would not restrain Germany but be dominated by it.[65] However, the French approach was forward-looking, rather than inspired by the past, and, moreover, was backed by Chancellor Kohl as well as President Bush. Once again Margaret Thatcher was out of tune in the concert of the West.

There is no doubt that the British Prime Minister felt the German question to be primarily the responsibility of the four victorious powers now that the cold war had come to an end. She was only too eager to comply with the request of the Soviet government to convene a meeting of the four ambassadors in the building of the former Control Council, with a view to discussing the potentially explosive situation in Berlin. However, Baker and Genscher were agreed 'to resist Soviet calls for four-power intervention in German politics'.[66] The US ambassador made sure that the discussion would be confined to practical matters concerning Berlin. It was the French ambassador, Serge Boidevaix, who then went out of his way to inform Bonn about the details of the negotiations. At the next NATO Council meeting Genscher made it plain that this four-power *rendezvous*, including a photo-call, was incompatible with Germany's membership of the Atlantic Alliance and the EC.[67] Under pressure from the German Foreign Office no further meeting of this kind, reminiscent of post-war conferences, was convened. Incidents like these caused Kohl to remark to Hans Modrow, who had become the GDR's last communist Prime Minister on 13 November 1989, that should a solution with the four powers be found 'they must not regard us as a protectorate'. Apparently, he added, the British Prime Minister had not grasped this. Mitterrand was different because he had told him: 'Eighty million Germans are a reality and France accepts realities.'[68]

Relations between London and Bonn reached their lowest point when the Prime Minister expressed her views in the *Wall Street Journal* on 25 January 1990. The long-term interests of Europe, she exclaimed, were more important than Kohl's and Genscher's narrow nationalistic aspirations. This had to be drummed into their heads. German unity would only upset the economic balance of Europe. Evaluating her position, Teltschik stressed Thatcher's adherence to outdated British traditions of the nineteenth century. Moreover, she hoped to pose as Gorbachev's true friend. The Chancellor was advised not to engage in a public debate but to impress upon British Foreign Secretary Douglas Hurd that the Prime Minister's

[65] See Lehmann, *Die deutsche Einigung*, 422. See also the article by L. Kettenacker, 'Zwangläufige deutsche Dominanz? Über Konstanten britischer Europaperzeptionen', *Tel Aviver Jahrbuch für deutsche Geschichte* 26 (1997), 235–49.

[66] Zelikow and Rice, *Germany Unified*, 155.   [67] Genscher, *Erinnerungen*, 695–96.

[68] Meeting in Davos, Switzerland, 3/2/1990, in H. J. Küsters and D. Hofmann (eds.), *Deutsche Einheit*, Doc. 158, 756.

comments were inappropriate in view of Kohl's determination to achieve unification within the European process. No doubt the Foreign Office was thought to be a more suitable channel of communication than Downing Street.[69] Kohl never tired of pointing out in private, especially to President Bush, that Margaret Thatcher was greatly influenced by the last war and was out of step with the spirit of modern times which transcended the narrow confines of the nation state.

THE FAST-TRACK SOLUTION TO UNIFICATION

Some framework had to be devised to deal with the external aspects of German unification which had gained momentum due to the rapid deterioration of the political and economic order in East Germany. In late November 1989 Gorbachev had proposed a 'Helsinki II summit' to deal with Germany. Initially, both London and Paris backed the suggestion and saw it as a clever device for slowing down the pace towards unification, i.e. dragging the German Question to the Helsinki forum and consulting each and every one of the thirty-five European states, regardless of the special rights of the four powers. Not so Washington. Bush opted for a fast-track solution, because his primary concern was the future of NATO and the continued presence of US troops in Europe. It was obvious that Russian anxieties had to be addressed. The 'two plus four' mechanism which would be acceptable to all participants was devised by two of James Baker's close advisers: 'If the Germans work out unification with the Soviets', they argued, 'NATO will be dumped and will become the obstacle.'[70] Kohl was the first to be taken into their confidence and proved to be 'completely supportive'. Now Margaret Thatcher was also brought back on board, since she was anxious to involve the Soviet Union in any arrangement. The irony was, however, that the new mechanism helped to smooth German unification, not to delay it as she had hoped. Still, on 6 February she admitted for the first time in parliament that German unification was on the cards.[71] Only a few days later probability turned into certainty. In his talks with Chancellor Kohl Gorbachev consented to the principle of German self-determination and also approved of the 'two plus four' mechanism for overcoming all

---

[69] Memorandum by Teltschik, 25 January 1990, in ibid., Doc. 148, 719. See also M. Stuart, *Douglas Hurd the Public Servant: An Authorised Biography* (Edinburgh, 1998), 233–50.

[70] Quoted in Zelikow and Rice, *Germany Unified*, 168.

[71] See *H.C. Deb.*, vol. 166, 757 (6/2/1990) and 1005–06 (8/2/1990). Afterwards Charles Powell contacted Teltschik, his opposite number in Bonn, in order to calm the Prime Minister's uneasy feelings about the prospect of a greater and stronger Germany. She belonged to a different generation and her attitude had been moulded at a time when the 'cultural gap' between the two countries was still considerable (Teltschik, *329 Tage*, 134, 9 Feb. 1990).

outstanding problems.[72] The magic formula was announced at the open-sky conference in Ottawa on 13 February, the first and only meeting of NATO and Warsaw Pact foreign ministers. Even before the first talks began Britain and France had accepted in principle—due to American diplomatic pressure—that they would be willing to renounce their rights in Germany as laid down by the post-war settlement.

By the second half of February it was clear that the time-span for unification had contracted considerably. The momentum was unstoppable now that the 'two plus four' mechanism had been put in place and that the East German elections had been brought forward to 18 March. All attempts by the British Prime Minister to slow down this process in one way or another proved to be futile. One of her favourite arguments had been that democracy had to be implemented all over Eastern Europe before German unification could be considered in earnest. Although the Foreign Office briefings are not yet available there are unmistakable indications that Whitehall was growing increasingly nervous about the impression created by Mrs Thatcher's policy of procrastination over Germany. Douglas Hurd therefore felt the need for an official explanation in parliament regarding the Ottawa agreement, which served at the same time as a kind of diplomatic damage limitation exercise.

Hurd's speech on 22 February gave rise to the only extensive debate on this issue in the House of Commons. He now claimed that the government was 'glad that the years of painful division are coming to an end'.[73] Unification was now likely to happen 'sooner rather than later', due to the political momentum generated by the continuing flow of people from the East. He put a diplomatic gloss on Britain's recent policy:

Our message was not one of obstruction but that we risked muddle and instability if the issues were not addressed in some orderly way. Many felt those anxieties and told us about them, and we were probably foremost in spelling them out. Because of that a notion grew up, particularly in parts of the German press, that we were in some way going back on our traditional support for the principle of unification. I hope that that notion has now been dispelled to the comfort of all of us.

Douglas Hurd was pleading for united Germany to remain a member of NATO, and not least for 'American and other foreign troops and their nuclear weapons' to remain in Germany 'in significant numbers as a stabilizing element in European security'. Nor did he have any problems with 'perhaps the continued presence of Soviet troops for a transitional period'. On the same day the Prime Minister had a long telephone

---

[72] See Kohl, *Ich wollte Deutschlands Einheit*, 253–82 ('Grünes Licht aus Moskau, aber . . .'), as well as Teltschik, ibid., 137–46.   [73] *H.C. Deb.*, vol. 166, 1088–90 (22/2/1990).

conversation with President Bush. She tried to persuade him to suggest 'that Soviet troops be allowed to stay on indefinitely in a united Germany'.[74] Hurd was however more concerned about Germany being locked into NATO and, in his speech in parliament, he expressed his belief that the Soviet Union would come 'to accept that its own interest in stability will be served by having Germany as a member of the defensive Western alliance'.[75] One can well imagine what kind of arguments were put forward by British diplomats behind the scenes to persuade Moscow that these troops had at best a dual purpose. After all, the division of Germany which was to come to an end was not only a result of the cold war but, prior to that, a means of implementing total occupation. On 12 March 1990 the German Chancellor ventured the guess that the Soviets would also wish Germany to remain firmly anchored in NATO. Their motives, he told Douglas Hurd, might not be altogether friendly but he did not mind. It was up to the British Foreign Secretary to conclude that Kohl knew perfectly well that British reasons were not entirely dissimilar.[76]

It is a sign of political maturity that nobody in Germany latched on to the secret agenda of four-power diplomacy in 1990. No German government in the inter-war years would have allowed its sovereignty to be infringed by the indefinite presence of foreign troops.[77] However, since this had never been an issue since World War II, it was unlikely to become one now that the matter was raised by the Soviet Union. NATO membership has always been associated with the presence of allied armies, which were referred to as *Schutzmächte* (protecting powers). It was only neutral status that was seen as incompatible with foreign bases. 'We believe', said Hurd, 'that the Federal Government was right to reject that option.' What he meant was, of course, that the British government was greatly relieved at Kohl's repeated assurances that Germany was committed to remaining a trustworthy member of NATO and the EC come what may.

The parliamentary debate on 22 February had been the first proper opportunity for the Labour opposition to voice its criticism of the Prime Minister's handling of the German question. Denis Healey's remarks were most revealing on two counts. He referred to the Germany of today as being 'by far the least nationalistic of all the larger European powers', only to point out: 'The one thing that could revive nationalism in Germany today would be an attempt by the former occupying powers to

---

[74] See Zelikow and Rice, *Germany Unified*, 207. See also Thatcher, *The Downing Street Years*, 798–9: 'I thought it best to allow some to stay for a transitional period without any specific terminal date.'   [75] See n. 73.

[76] H. J. Küsters and D. Hofmann (eds.), *Deutsche Einheit*, Doc. 214, 933.

[77] For the very different attitudes to Allied occupation after the First World War, see D. G. Williamson, *The British in Germany 1918–1931. The Reluctant Occupiers* (Oxford, 1991).

continue acting as occupying powers. That is the danger that the Prime Minister's recent behaviour has aroused.'[78] He was explicitly expressing the anxieties felt by German public opinion about Britain, known to be psychologically shackled to the memory of the Second World War. More important still is the revelation that the Foreign Office was deeply unhappy about Mrs Thatcher's ungracious views on Germany at a crucial juncture in Anglo-German relations. 'I know', Healey said, 'that the Foreign Secretary agrees with me, because he has tried his best to soften the asperities of some of the nonsense that she has talked.' The former Labour Chancellor then went on to complain about the British tabloids following her lead.[79]

Mrs Thatcher had always been a staunch supporter of liberalization in Eastern Europe. If the principle of political self-determination applied to all Warsaw Pact countries, the GDR could not be an exception. The first free elections in the GDR on 18 March 1990 were fought by those who rallied around Chancellor Kohl's battalions under the banner 'Allianz für Deutschland', i.e. for speedy unification. The landslide victory by the 'Alliance' and its significance were given due credit by all the major British papers. For example, the *Guardian* wrote on 19 March: 'Country's First Free Election Endorses Rapid Unification'.[80] Mrs Thatcher hailed the new beginning as 'a great day for Europe'.[81] According to the *Daily Telegraph* she now accepted the inevitability of the two Germanys coming together 'despite her earlier anxieties about the speed of the unity process'. The Prime Minister abandoned her crusade to modernize NATO's short-range nuclear missiles (Lance) and realized that these weapons should be phased out. The challenge was now to synchronize Germany's internal development towards merger with international efforts 'to reconcile unity with the two Germanys' membership of NATO and the Warsaw Pact'.[82] This was no easy task, as the *Financial Times* pointed out. Chancellor Kohl issued a warning by employing a powerful image to illustrate the force of the historical momentum: 'I was born along the Rhine. Nobody can stop its flow. But if people try to it will burst its banks and destroy everything. The current is accelerating and nobody can stop it.'[83] As the *Daily Express* put it on 24 March: 'You Can't Stop Unity—Kohl Warns Thatcher'. According to Valentin Falin, one of Gorbachev's close advisers and a former Soviet Ambassador in Bonn, Gorbachev was seized by a similar sense of history as an independent agent. He referred, though not in public, to the image of a train that had already left the station.[84]

---

[78] *H.C. Deb.*, vol. 166, 1110.   [79] Ibid.
[80] *Guardian*, 19/3/1990. The *Daily Express* of the same day announced: 'Germans Stampede to Unity'.   [81] *Daily Telegraph*, 20/3/1990.
[82] *Financial Times*, 19/3/1990.   [83] *Daily Express*, 24/3/1990.
[84] Falin, *Politische Erinnerungen*, 492.

Apart from the main problem of how to overcome Soviet opposition to Germany's continued membership of NATO, a further issue to be addressed was that of Poland's western border. Since no peace treaty would be concluded, this question had to be settled with the united Germany now, once and for all, even though the two German states had already recognized the Oder-Neiße border long ago. All four allies were agreed that Polish anxieties in this respect ought to be relieved. Thus they all put pressure on Chancellor Kohl to come clean. According to Bonn's interpretation of international law, it required the successful completion of the unification process and an all-German government to reach a final settlement. Then there was the question of reparations. In view of the enormous financial commitments vis-à-vis the Soviet Union, this Pandora's Box had to be kept shut tight in order to ease the transition. It was difficult enough for Kohl to persuade his party, which included a strong right-wing element of former refugees from the East, to cede a quarter of Germany's pre-war territory. Again Bush was more sympathetic to Kohl's worries and tactical considerations than either Mrs Thatcher or Mitterrand. He knew that the Chancellor would never question the existing border.[85] The issue was soon to be settled when the West German *Bundestag* and the East German *Volkskammer* passed identical resolutions according to which united Germany would conclude a treaty with Poland according to the Helsinki principles.[86] Although Mitterrand was the most adamant advocate of Polish interests, it was Anglo-German relations that were most afflicted by the fall-out from this problem. In a *Spiegel* interview Mrs Thatcher maintained that she had heard Kohl exclaim in Strasbourg: 'No, I guarantee nothing, I do not recognise the present borders.'[87]

The German government was most upset and claimed that Kohl had been misquoted. The quote attributed to the Chancellor, spokesman Hans Klein said, was 'neither literally correct nor did it reflect the sense of what he said'.[88] All this did not help to improve the atmosphere. Clearly, Kohl did not feel at ease with Margaret Thatcher. When she welcomed him at Cambridge airport at the end of March he refused to share an official car with her on the way to the Königswinter Conference at

[85] Zelikow and Rice, *Germany Unified*, 217–22.
[86] Kiessler and Elbe, *Ein runder Tisch*, 113–18. Apparently Kohl was so upset about opposition from his own ranks that he contemplated resignation over this issue.
[87] *Der Spiegel*, No. 13, 26/3/1990. As to Kohl's real views see his Bundestag speech on the subject on 8 March 1990 (also Thatcher, *The Downing Street Years*, 322). I wonder whether the misunderstanding might not have been caused by the different meanings of 'Grenzen' applied by Kohl and Thatcher. Kohl was certainly not prepared to guarantee the inner-German border. There is no doubt that, for a while, the Prime Minister hoped that the CSCE settlement of European borders would also apply to the inner-German frontier.
[88] *Daily Telegraph*, 27/3/1989.

St Catherine's College. But he was pleasantly surprised by her friendly address, in which she praised his determination to stay in NATO and claimed that she had always been in favour of German unification.[89] No doubt the exchange of views on that occasion eased relations between the two governments considerably. The Prime Minister was greatly relieved when Kohl assured her that he would not trade unification against neutrality and, moreover, that a united Germany's economic centre of gravity would remain along the Rhine and in the south-west. She was also satisfied with the resolutions of both the *Bundestag* and the *Volkskammer* concerning the Oder-Neiße issue. When Kohl had informed her about his plan in early March she had congratulated him on his handling of this delicate matter ('höchst staatsmännische Schritte').[90] To Kohl's frustration Mitterrand proved to be less amenable since he backed further Polish demands.

MARGARET THATCHER AND THE GERMAN NATIONAL CHARACTER

Around the same time two influential historians tried to reassure the British public that there was nothing to fear from the 'ghost of Bismarck'. No 'Fourth Reich' was in the offing, as Conor Cruise O'Brien, former editor of the *Observer* had claimed in a notorious article in *The Times* at the end of October 1989.[91] Paul Kennedy, the eminent British historian now teaching at Yale and foremost expert on Anglo-German relations, emphasized that this time Germany was being united from below, not from above, by 'peaceful pressure, not force of arms'.[92] Being close to Washington's decision-makers, Kennedy knew that the new Germany would also remain embedded in the western security system. Hugh Trevor-Roper, one of an older generation of historians, was more guarded, but equally reassuring: 'I believe', Lord Dacre said in the Lords, 'there has been a fundamental change in the German mentality since 1945, owing to a fundamental change in German historical attitudes, historical teaching, and historical tradition.'[93] The problem was that the British mentality, reinforced rather than traumatized by the war, had not been transformed to the same extent.

---

[89] See H. J. Küsters and D. Hofmann (eds.), *Deutsche Einheit*, 137; also Kohl, *Ich wollte Deutschlands Einheit*, 340–2.   [90] Küsters and Hofmann (eds.), ibid., 920 (7/3/1990).
[91] Published in H. James and M. Stone (eds.), *When the Wall Came Down: Reactions to German Unification* (London, 1992), 221–3. James also published two of his newspaper articles in this edition. In an odd sense they are both reassuring in that they draw attention to the enormous problems arising from the merger of the two unequal economies.
[92] *Sunday Correspondence*, 18/3/1990.   [93] Published in the *Daily Telegraph*, 24/3/1989.

As one observer who was subjected to a history lesson by Mrs Thatcher commented: 'Long memories don't help.'[94] There was a striking discrepancy between the professional historian's perception of the past and a popular or tabloid picture of Clio. No doubt Margaret Thatcher, who took pride in being close to the instincts, the 'feelings', of ordinary people (once referred to in Germany as 'gesundes Volksempfinden'), belonged to the second category. 'Once a German always a German' was her favourite short-cut approach to German history.[95] In her memoirs she admits that she does not believe in collective guilt, but in national character[96]—again a very popular but somewhat misleading notion. What clearly worried her was the need to know whether the Germans could be trusted now that they were about to regain national unity and renewed power.[97]

This inquisitive disposition must have been the reason why she decided —or was open to the suggestion—to invite a group of expert historians to Chequers on 24 March, a week after the East German elections, to discuss the German question, or rather the problem with the Germans— in Vansittart's words 'the Germans in the plural'.[98] This cosy weekend seminar in the spring caused a sensation in mid-July when the minutes taken by Thatcher's foreign policy adviser, Charles Powell, were leaked to the *Independent on Sunday*.[99] The impact was compounded by a very offensive interview given by Nicholas Ridley, Thatcher's Secretary of State for Industry, to the *Spectator*, in which he gave vent to his anti-German sentiments in a saloon-bar manner.[100] He complained about the strength of the Deutschmark ('because of their habits') and maintained at the same time that monetary union was 'all a German racket disguised to take over the whole of Europe'. Kohl was following in Hitler's footsteps: 'He'll soon be coming here and trying to say that this is what we should do on the banking front and this is what our taxes should be. I mean, he'll soon be trying to take over everything.' The interviewer, Dominic Lawson, son

---

[94] G. R. Urban, *Diplomacy and Disillusion at the Court of Margaret Thatcher: An Insider's View* (London, 1996), 133.   [95] Ibid., 104–5.

[96] Thatcher, *The Downing Street Years*, 791.

[97] According to Urban, *Diplomacy and Disillusion*, 34, the Prime Minister 'went on and on telling' the participants at the Chequers summit: 'Yes, yes, but can you *trust* them?'

[98] See R. Vansittart's pamphlet *Black Record. Germans Past and Present*, which had been reprinted several times in 1941 and might have been read by Margaret Thatcher as a teenager.

[99] Reprinted in James and Stone (eds.), *When the Wall Came Down*, 233–9. German version: *Der Spiegel*, No. 29 (16/7/1990). The Prime Minister, when questioned in Parliament by Roy Hattersley, stood by Powell without further ado on the grounds that he was a civil servant, not a cabinet minister like Ridley who was forced to resign. See *H.C. Deb.*, vol. 176, 857 (17 July 1990). The exchange is also reproduced in Urban, *Diplomacy and Disillusion*, 158–9.

[100] 'Saying the Unsayable about the Germans', the *Spectator*, 14/7/1990. Urban, ibid., 153, comments: 'Ridley, of course, richly deserved sacking, but M.T.'s own views about Germany are, alas, in no way different from his.'

of a former Thatcher chancellor, mused that Mr Ridley's confidence in expressing his views on the German threat 'must owe a little something to the knowledge that they are not significantly different from those of the Prime Minister who originally opposed German unification'. The British press was unanimous in its rejection of Ridley's remarks. His choice of words reminded *The Times* of 'teenage hooliganism'.[101] Ridley had to resign in order to dispel the impression that the Prime Minister shared his views. The leaked minutes of the Chequers seminar made this assumption all the more credible. Three of the six participants distanced themselves from Powell's unfortunately phrased summary in an attempt to protect the Prime Minister as well as their own reputations. Significantly, all their public protestations and explanations appeared in the ultra-respectable *Frankfurter Allgemeine Zeitung*.[102]

One of the most offensive passages in the Chequers memorandum was a list of German character traits. Apart from a strong inclination to self-pity and a longing to be liked: '*angst*, aggressiveness, assertiveness, bullying, egotism, inferiority complex, sentimentality'. Powell had to perform a balancing act between pleasing his mistress and accommodating the Foreign Office which clearly hoped to calm the Prime Minister down for the sake of better Anglo-German relations. The most comprehensive account of the confrontation between Margaret Thatcher and her chosen experts on Germany, amongst them two distinguished American scholars, is by one of the least-known participants, George Urban, former director of Radio Free Europe and adviser to the Prime Minister on Eastern Europe. Nowhere else is the actual agenda published and it is almost more revealing than the protocol of the seminar itself.[103] The initial questionnaire was heavily loaded, with constant references to 'the Germans', their 'national ambitions', their 'mission in Central and Eastern Europe', their 'drive to master all the German-speaking peoples', etc. All these questions implied the dubious assumption that surfaced in the final minutes: 'We could not expect a united Germany to think and act in exactly the same way as the Federal Republic which we had known for the last 45 years.'[104] Urban tells us that all participants, despite their very different backgrounds, came to the same conclusion: 'The PM's "instincts" were extremely wide of the mark'.[105] In other words, they all tried desperately to talk Mrs Thatcher out of her basic anti-German feelings or, as Urban

---

[101] See summary of press reactions in H. Süssmuth and C. Peters, 'Die Vereinigung Deutschlands im Spiegel der englischen Tageszeitungen. Eine Momentaufnahme', in H. Süssmuth (ed.), *Deutschlandbilder* (Baden-Baden, 1996), 267–80, esp. 276–7.

[102] Timothy Garton Ash, 'Wie es eigentlich war' (18 July 1990); Norman Stone, 'Recht geredet' (19 July 1990); Fritz Stern, 'Die zweite Chance' (26 July 1989).

[103] Urban, *Diplomacy and Disillusion*, 147–9.

[104] Chequers Memorandum (see footnote 99).

[105] Urban, *Diplomacy and Disillusion*, 128, 103.

puts it, 'her Alf Garnett version of history'. The 'overall message' in Powell's memorandum was also meant to be positive, however condescending in tone: 'We should be nice to the Germans.'[106] From Urban's reminiscences it is clear that this was indeed the educational purpose pursued by the Foreign Office. While there is no mention of the Chequers seminar or the Ridley Affair in Thatcher's memoirs, in German publications these incidents are given too much prominence.[107] They can be interpreted as evidence of a deep-seated unease about German unification in high places. But this is hardly surprising. What matters much more are the consequences: Nicholas Ridley had embarrassed his colleagues and had to go. Over a period of time the Prime Minister had done the same and was, in due course, forced out of office.

THE 'TWO PLUS FOUR' AGREEMENT ON GERMAN UNIFICATION

For Europe and the rest of the world, especially the United States, the squabbles in the British press were of no relevance whatsoever compared with the news at about the same time that during Kohl's visit to the Caucasus in mid-July 1990 Gorbachev had eventually made the final and all-important concession: NATO membership for the whole of Germany and the withdrawal of Soviet troops within three to four years.[108] This paved the way for German unification on terms acceptable to the western powers and was the great triumph of a man whom Margaret Thatcher had dismissed as an overweight, plodding politician from the deepest sticks of Germany.[109] No doubt he was fully aware of what had been going on behind the scenes to persuade Gorbachev. It was now the West's responsibility to control Germany. The continued presence of US troops in Germany was more of a means to appease British and French anxieties than to address German security concerns. For good reasons, however, this hidden agenda was never spelled out. Margaret Thatcher congratulated Kohl on his success and did not wait for long before cashing in on the new peace dividend by announcing a substantial reduction in British troops stationed

---

[106] Chequers Memorandum (see footnote 99).

[107] Including my own article: 'Englische Spekulationen über die Deutschen', in G. Trautmann (ed.), *Die häßlichen Deutschen? Deutschland im Spiegel der westlichen und östlichen Nachbarn* (Darmstadt, 1990), 194–208. See also G. Heydemann, 'Partner oder Konkurrent? Das britische Deutschlandbild während des Wiedervereinigungsprozesses 1989–1991', in F. Bosbach (ed.), *Feindbilder* (Cologne, 1992), 201–34. A more balanced picture of the British press clearly emerges from Süssmuth and Peters (see above, n. 101).

[108] See Kohl, *Ich wollte Deutschlands Einheit*, 421–44; Teltschik, *329 Tage*, 313–45. See also H. Klein, *Es begann im Kaukasus. Der entscheidende Schritt in die Einheit Deutschlands* (Berlin, 1991).   [109] Urban, *Diplomacy and Disillusion*, 131.

in Germany.[110] Moreover, with the withdrawal of Soviet troops from East Germany the British garrison in West Berlin could be disbanded.

After the German–Russian understanding was reached in Gorbachev's dacha, the rest of the 'two plus four' negotiations seemed a mere formality. However, on the eve of 12 September, when the final treaty was to be signed, the British delegate John Weston threw a spanner into the works, probably on behalf of Downing Street. He insisted on the need for NATO manoeuvres in East Germany following the withdrawal of the Red Army.[111] Having made one concession after the other, the Russians objected to the large-scale deployment of foreign, i.e. non-German, troops in the eastern territory. Even though the American negotiator seemed to back Weston, Foreign Minister Genscher and his team were very angry and frustrated by what they called the 'British problem'.[112] When the Russians cancelled the signing ceremony scheduled for the next day Genscher woke up James Baker in the middle of the night to enlist his help in salvaging the situation. In the end a compromise was worked out which left it to the discretion of the German government to define the notion of 'deployment'. Again the British, in trying to prove their loyalty to the Americans, were exposed as trouble-makers. It was a fitting end to the whole unification process in which Britain had given the impression of trying to hold on to her waning influence by means of procrastination. Future research, based on official documents, will show whether this is a superficial impression created by Mrs Thatcher's handbag-waving protestations, or indeed the lasting verdict on Britain's contribution to the eventful years of 1989/90.

Whatever newspapers had ventured to predict in the course of twelve months, however much the government had tried to slow down the pace of reunification, by 3 October 1990 a sense of sober realism had set in. It was an occasion for taking stock: along with the five new *Länder*, the old Federal Republic had acquired a huge heap of financial, economic and social problems. The reconstituted Germany looked decidedly less menacing than just a year earlier. Three of the major British newspapers, the *Daily Telegraph*, the *Financial Times*, and the *Guardian* realized that the Federal Republic might well be preoccupied with internal reconstruction for some time to come.[113] In many ways, German unification proved to be a burden, certainly in the short term, rather than an asset. Moreover, in the long-run German independence would be further curtailed by European integration.

---

[110] H. J. Küsters and D. Hofmann (eds.), *Deutsche Einheit*, Doc. 357, 1377; and Doc. 368, 1410–11.

[111] Genscher, *Erinnerungen*, 869–76; Kiessler and Elbe, *Ein runder Tisch*, 209–13.

[112] Zelikow and Rice, *Germany Unified*, 361. It looks as though the US negotiator Robert Zoellick had backed the British position rather than initiating the move himself. In this sense it was a 'British problem'.

[113] See Süssmuth and Peters, 'Die Vereinigung Deutschlands', 277–9.

PART II

The Post-Cold War Relationship:
Politics and Security since 1990

5

Britain, Germany, and the Deepening of Europe: The Role of Domestic Norms and Institutions

JIM BULLER AND CHARLIE JEFFERY

The parallel Intergovernmental Conferences (IGCs) on Economic and Monetary Union (EMU) and Political Union which culminated in the Maastricht Summit in December 1991 produced the most significant extension of the scope of European integration since the Rome Treaties. This in part continued the impetus established by the Single European Act and the 1992 Single Market Programme it spawned, with further steps in economic integration. In particular EMU came to be seen as necessary to consolidate the Single Market and maintain Europe's competitiveness in an increasingly internationalized economic environment. In addition, the end of the cold war, and German unification in particular, added a new slant to the integration process. The end of the cold war 'unbound' a German 'Gulliver'[1] hitherto tied down by the sclerotic nature of cold war international relations. This image of an unrestrained Germany revived one of the founding philosophies of the European integration process: integrate in order to bind German power into multilateral structures.[2] The result was a French-sponsored and Commission-driven acceleration of the EMU agenda, based on the premise of taming German economic power, as vested in the Bundesbank, in the framework of a European Central Bank. Germany's leadership under Chancellor Helmut Kohl, keen to reiterate a now united Germany's pro-integrationist credentials, acquiesced in this agenda—but on the condition that parallel steps be made towards Political Union. The two IGCs on EMU and Political Union were thus launched in an unprecedented atmosphere of urgency and improvisation. As a result, their agendas became unusually

---

[1] The terminology is that of S. Bulmer and W. Paterson, 'West Germany's Role in Europe: Man-Mountain or Semi-Gulliver?', *Journal of Common Market Studies* 28 (1989); and W. Paterson, 'Gulliver Unbound: The Changing Context of Foreign Policy', in G. Smith *et al.* (eds.), *Developments in German Politics* (London, 1992).

[2] See D. Spence, 'The European Community and German Unification', in C. Jeffery and R. Sturm (eds.), *Federalism, Unification and European Integration* (London, 1993), 140–1.

fluid and open, and they ultimately produced a clear timetable and method for implementing EMU while also extending far beyond the original economic agenda into new initiatives in policy integration and institutional design.

British and German responses to this accelerated deepening of European integration in the 1990s have been markedly different. As already indicated in Chancellor Kohl's opening of the Political Union agenda, deepening is a process with which German policy-making elites have felt at ease and for which they have been capable of offering leadership. The situation in the UK has presented a stark contrast. Successive Conservative governments under Margaret Thatcher and John Major were beset by persistent divisions over the nature and direction of the integration process, and amply and repeatedly confirmed the perception of the UK as the 'awkward partner'[3] in the European integration process. Only with the election of the 'New' Labour government under Prime Minister Tony Blair has a strong prospect of an enduring positive engagement of the UK with the EU emerged.

This chapter presents an explanation for these divergent responses to the agenda of deepening integration which is rooted in domestic politics. It argues that the domestic political norms and institutions in which policy-making elites are schooled condition and shape their engagement in European co-operation.[4] It proposes that domestic institutions and norms serve to equip, even empower, German policy-makers in the EU's co-operative decision-making processes (section one), while the domestic political experience British policy-makers take with them into European decision-making processes are ill-suited to the rules of the game of EU governance (section two). A nuance is added in the British case in that, for much of the 1990s, the unease of British policy-makers in the European environment was projected outwards in a revival of prejudices about Germany and German power in Europe (section three). The final section explores the potential for change in the established patterns of European diplomacy which some commentators have identified with the advent of the Blair government in the UK, which may lead to a 'more German' form of interaction with the EU.

---

[3] S. George, *An Awkward Partner: Britain in the European Community* (Oxford, 1998).

[4] A number of the lines of argument developed draw from the discussion of the interaction of interests, institutions and identity in European diplomacy in S. Bulmer, C. Jeffery and W. Paterson, 'Deutschlands europäische Diplomatie: die Entwicklung des regionalen Milieus', in W. Weidenfeld (ed.), *Deutsche Europapolitik. Optionen wirksamer Interessenvertretung* (Bonn, 1998), 11–102, which itself drew on S. Bulmer, 'Britain and Germany in the European Union: British Realism and German Institutionalism?', paper presented to the *Conference of Europeanists*, Chicago, 14–16 March 1996; and S. Bulmer. 'Shaping the Rules? The Constitutive Politics of the European Union and German Power', in P. Katzenstein (ed.), *Tamed Power: Germany in Europe* (Ithaca, NY, 1997), 49–79.

GERMANY: EUROPEAN CO-OPERATION AS WARM BATH

German unification in 1990 initially led to considerable popular and academic debate[5] about whether the new Germany would move away from its 'ostentatious modesty', the 'culture of reticence' and the 'leadership-avoidance reflex' which had previously characterized its role in the European integration process. It was anticipated that the removal of the residual, post-war, externally imposed constraints on the projection of German power which German unification brought with it would allow Germany to act in a less modest and reticent way in the European arena. It was expected that Europe's economic giant would at last begin to punch its weight in European politics in a more calculated and overt pursuit of national interest.

Until the SPD–Green victory in the German general election in September 1998 such anticipations had not been borne out. Under Helmut Kohl but also, it appears, under Gerhard Schröder's new leadership united Germany has remained wedded to multilateral co-operation in the EU, and has failed to develop its European policies in line with the realist, national interest-driven conceptions of power some commentators had expected to come to the fore after unification.

This pre- to post-unity continuity in German European integration policy shifted at least the academic debate towards alternative approaches to understanding German policy more focused on internal than external conditions as explanatory factors.[6] As this strand of the debate has matured, it has focused increasingly explicitly on domestic norms and institutions.[7] Fundamental here is the commitment of German policy-making elites to multilateral co-operation. To quote Jeff Anderson and John Goodman:

Over the course of forty years, West Germany's reliance on a web of international institutions to achieve its foreign policy goals, born of an instrumental

---

[5] As reviewed in C. Jeffery, 'A Giant with Feet of Clay? United Germany in the European Union', *University of Birmingham Discussion Papers in German Studies*, IGS95/6 (1995), 1–3.

[6] A vivid depiction of this broad shift in approach is given in the interchange between Markovits and Reich and Goldberger. See A. Markovits and S. Reich, 'Should Europe Fear the Germans?', *German Politics and Society* 23 (1991), 1–20; B. Goldberger, 'Why Europe Should not Fear the Germans', *German Politics* 2 (1993), 288–310; A. Markovits and S. Reich, 'A Realistic Appraisal? A Rejoinder to Goldberger', *German Politics* 3 (1994), 129–32.

[7] See e.g. P. J. Katzenstein, *Tamed Power: Germany in Europe* (Ithaca, NY, 1997), and 'Germany and Mitteleuropa: An Introduction', in P. J. Katzenstein (ed.), *Mitteleuropa: Between Europe and Germany* (Oxford, 1997); Bulmer, Jeffery and Paterson, 'Deutschlands europäische Diplomatie. Die Entwicklung des regionalen Milieus'.

choice among painfully few alternatives, became so complete as to cause these institutions to become embedded in the very definition of state interests and strategies.[8]

Chief among these institutions had been those of European integration, which, from the German perspective, had successfully performed a threefold function: to secure and entrench West Germany's post-war international rehabilitation; to provide a positive framework of trade and competition for the export-led West German economy; and to embed an enduring Franco-German peace. These successes led to the embedding of the commitment to European integration as a deeply held value among German policy-makers 'concerning the rules of the game of post-war European politics'.[9] This value was internalized in a consensus extending across all the main political parties, all the relevant political institutions and, in a general 'permissive' sense, in public opinion on the goal of closer European integration.[10] It had, as Klaus Goetz wrote, become imprinted on the 'genetic code' of German politics.[11]

The commitment to the value of closer integration has not been undermined following German unification. The Maastricht negotiations provided ample confirmation. If unification had raised fears that a united Germany/Gulliver would break out from its bonds, the German view was that 'we should exploit [this] fear before it diminishes'[12] to spur on the intensifying debates on EMU and Political Union. The subsequent commitment to subsume the DM into the single European currency and to extend European co-operation into the new EU pillars of Common Foreign and Security Policy (CFSP) and Justice and Home Affairs could hardly have provided a stronger affirmation that the 'new' Germany would uphold the multilateralist values of its West German predecessor. With apologies to George Orwell, one could almost envisage German policy elites responding to the new post-cold war environment with the mantra: 'unilateralism bad, multilateralism good'.

It is not, however, merely that German policy elites subscribe to the positive value of European co-operation; they are also good at the process of co-operation. This skill can be understood in terms of the

---

[8] J. Anderson and J. Goodman, 'Mars or Minerva? A United Germany in a Post-cold war Europe', in R. Keohane, J. Nye, and S. Hoffmann (eds.), *After the cold war: International Institutions and State Strategies in Europe, 1989–1991* (Cambridge, Mass., 1993), 23–62.

[9] Bulmer, 'Shaping the Rules? The Constitutive Politics of the European Union and German Power', 67.

[10] S. Bulmer and W. Paterson, *The Federal Republic of Germany and the European Community* (London, 1987), 22 and 108–22.

[11] K. Goetz, 'Integration Policy in a Europeanised State: Germany and the Intergovernmental Conference', *Journal of European Public Policy* 3 (1996), 24.

[12] Quoted in D. Spence, 'Enlargement without Accession: The EC's Response to German Unification', *RIIA Discussion Papers* 35 (1991), 8.

congruence Simon Bulmer has pointed to between the German domestic and the European arenas in terms of institutional structures and the norms which shape institutional interaction.[13] Domestically, Germany is characterized by institutional pluralism, a legacy of the conscious decision to disperse the *loci* of political power in the constitution-building process of 1948–9. As Peter Katzenstein put it, Germany is a 'semi-sovereign' state, lacking a single authoritative location of political power.[14] 'Semi-sovereignty' is most evident in the deconcentration of power through the structures of the German federal system, but also in the relative autonomy of, and absence of effective co-ordination structures among, national ministries; in the role of the Constitutional Court in constitutional adjudication; and in the roles of 'para-public' institutions charged with performing functions on behalf of the state, foremost among which is the Bundesbank.

To make dispersed institutional structures work together effectively requires 'lubricants'. Two vital political norms provide much of the lubrication.[15] First, German government is highly rule-bound, embedded in a *Rechtsstaat* tradition invested with new vigour and authority following the arbitrary abuses of the rule of law in the Third Reich. This is reflected most obviously in an over-detailed constitution, which—especially if the supplementary legislation frequently required in the constitution to clarify constitutional norms is taken into account—meticulously structures institutional interaction. Characteristic too is a ramified courts structure, with the Constitutional Court at its apex, much-exploited in a culture of legal adjudication to clarify differences of interpretation of political structure and procedure.

Second, German government is highly consensual. Institutional pluralism requires co-operation and agreement across institutions if public policies are effectively to be delivered. And this broadly happens. An emphasis on technical policy expertise supports a 'search for a rationalist consensus',[16] while the relative stability of German policy communities—itself a product of the tightly delineated rules of German politics—allows policy actors to develop the regularized relationships with each other which facilitate the delivery of consensus. The consensus approach pervades not just institutional interactions but also, with few exceptions, German

---

[13] Bulmer, 'Shaping the Rules? The Constitutive Politics of the European Union and German Power', 61–8.

[14] P. Katzenstein, *Policy and Politics in West Germany. The Growth of a Semi-Sovereign State* (Philadelphia, 1987).

[15] See Bulmer, 'Shaping the Rules? The Constitutive Politics of the European Union and German Power', 67–8.

[16] K. Dyson, 'West Germany: The Search for a Rationalist Consensus', in J. Richardson (ed.), *Policy Styles in Western Europe* (London, 1982).

party politics, both within coalitions and across government–opposition divides.

The congruence with the EU is immediately evident. The EU displays the institutional plurality of fifteen member states, interacting in the various ministerial Councils (without much overall co-ordination between them) and with the various Commission Directorates-General, and doing so by reference to the rules set out by treaty, and with a *modus operandi* of consensus facilitated by a number of enduring relationships—that of Germany with France at the forefront. In other words, there is at the European level an institutional environment and a set of lubricating norms broadly similar to those which exist in German domestic politics, and 'which is congenial to German negotiators'.[17]

The congruence issue can be taken even further. Germany's multilateralist vocation, rooted in the value of European co-operation, has led it probably more than any other member state to seek and/or accept multilateral EU co-operation as a means of addressing political problems. This has led on the one hand to a gradual extension of the fields of policy from which the advantages of German–EU congruence can be drawn. It can also offer opportunities for what Bulmer, Jeffery, and Paterson have termed 'institutional export',[18] i.e. the supply of institutional models from the domestic arena which then set the parameters for policy-making at the European level. The Maastricht Treaty process provided a number of examples of this phenomenon of institutional export. First, in a direct sense, the content of the Treaty was concretely shaped by German policy actors. This applied first to the success of the German Länder in sensitizing the treaty foundations of the EU at least in part to their concerns, as self-proclaimed representatives of a 'third' regional level, to embed the regional level in European decision-making processes (via the Committee of the Regions, the opening up of the Council of Ministers in certain cases to regional ministers empowered to lead their countries delegations, and the embedding of the principle of subsidiarity in the treaty).[19] It also applied, more prominently, to EMU. On the one hand, Germany's commitment to the EMU project powerfully reflects its vocation of deepening multilateral co-operation even in an area of vital economic and symbolic concern; on the other hand, the Bundesbank's model of monetary policy management was proposed as the institutional design for European monetary co-operation—and was then adopted enthusiastically by at least some member states keen to 'import' German

---

[17] Bulmer, Jeffery, and Paterson, 'Deutschlands europäische Diplomatie. Die Entwicklung des regionalen Milieus', 14–15.   [18] Ibid. 32–40.
[19] C. Jeffery, 'The Länder Strike Back. Structures and Procedures of European Integration Policy-Making in the German Federal System', *University of Leicester Discussion Papers in Federal Studies*, FS94/4 (1994), 7–12.

monetary rigour.[20] Needless to say it is a design with which German policy elites will feel comfortable, and which seems set indirectly to advantage and empower them in the future EU monetary policy decision-making process.

The Maastricht process also produced examples of 'indirect' institutional export in the course of the domestic debates on the ratification of the treaty. In two ways, these debates led to the embedding of the goal of European integration in Germany's domestic constitutional structure in ways which set down markers for the nature and scope of future integration initiatives. First, the Länder were successful in securing a constitutional amendment as a *quid pro quo* for their ratification of Maastricht which required future integration steps to respect the federal structure within Germany. And the Constitutional Court, called upon to adjudicate on the validity of the Treaty in German constitutional law, ruled that this and future integration initiatives could only be valid in Germany if they complied with the fundamental principles of the German constitution.[21] These constitutional manoeuvrings around Maastricht have had the effect of imposing internally grounded constraints on Germany's external partners. Together with the more direct examples of institutional export noted above, they consolidate a pattern in which the internal peculiarities of the German system of government shape—and empower German policy actors in—EU decision-making. Institutional export completes a virtuous circle: institutional congruence empowers German policy elites while institutional export extends the scope of institutional congruence.

But this is a rather different expression of power than that which realist commentators expected to see projected by post-unity Germany. It is a form of 'soft'[22] institutional power, far removed from a realist politics of overt pursuit of national interest which serves to mobilize a bias in Germany's favour in the character of EU governance.[23]

THE UK: EUROPEAN CO-OPERATION AS COLD SHOWER

The UK provides a stark contrast to what Bulmer has called this 'strikingly good fit'[24] between German and EU governance. While Germany has been deeply embedded in the fabric of multilateral co-operation in the EU, the UK has been enduringly dubbed Europe's 'awkward partner'.

---

[20] Bulmer, Jeffery, and Paterson, 'Deutschlands europäische Diplomatie. Die Entwicklung des regionalen Milieus', 33–5.   [21] Ibid. 35–40.

[22] See J. Anderson, 'Hard Interests, Soft Power and Germany's Changing Role in Europe', in Katzenstein, *Tamed Power: Germany in Europe*.

[23] Bulmer, 'Shaping the Rules? The Constitutive Politics of the European Union and German Power', 50.   [24] Ibid. 76.

This of course is Stephen George's phrase, and refers to the political style adopted by successive UK governments in EU decision-making.[25] Above all, George is concerned with the continual refusal of British leaders to accept the EU's methods of doing business: linkages across policy issues, concession of position, building compromise, and so on—all the paraphernalia inherent in the EU's particular form of multilateral co-operation. Much of the explanation for this can be found in the strikingly bad fit between UK and EU governance. Most fundamentally, there is at the normative level no entrenched sense that multilateral co-operation is a good thing, a value in itself. This is of course in part a reflection of the UK's international history: overseas empire, perceived closeness to the USA, but above all a geographical location which has insulated the UK from being as deeply and persistently immersed as its continental neighbours in the territorial conflicts on mainland Europe which were the main inspiration after World War II for the commitment to multilateral co-operation through European integration. This UK *Sonderweg* allowed a sense of pride to entrench itself in British political elites which was focused on the UK's singular constitutional structure, and on a notion of (unbroken) national sovereignty which sits uneasily with notions of multilateralism. Given this historical experience, British elites have never consistently shared—or sought to build—a consensus on the possible benefits of multilateralism. There has always been a strong element, straddling the main party-political divide, which could easily chant an Orwellian mantra of 'unilateralism good, multilateralism bad'.

Domestic institutions and norms provide additional explanations for the failure to develop a more embracing integrationist consensus. Geographical location also plays a role here. The absence of domestic revolution and foreign occupation insulated the UK from all the pressures on the European mainland over the last two centuries for constitutionally formalized, limited government. The gradual, unbroken development of British institutions over this period is what decisively sets the UK apart from its European neighbours; the legacy is a unique, democratically updated system of seventeenth-century government. A number of the institutional structures and norms of this system of government are worth noting, first and foremost its centralization, as captured in the constitutional doctrine of parliamentary sovereignty. This doctrine tends to an unusual degree to concentrate decision-making power in the hands of any central government capable of maintaining a parliamentary majority. Checks and balances are few and, in the absence of a fully codified

---

[25] 'I intended the title of my book to convey nothing more than that Britain had proved a difficult partner for the other member states to deal with, and that British governments had often been clumsy in handling their relationships with other members.' S. George, 'A Reply to Buller', *Politics* 15 (1995), 43.

constitution, weak, and typically located in convention and case law rather than a higher quality of constitutional law.

This has important implications for the norms which guide the operation of UK institutions. Gaining control of the sovereign parliament is the big prize, in effect the only prize worth having, and the winner takes all. The result is an adversarial, party-centred politics focused on that prize and untutored in—because it has no need of—compromise and consensus-building. The incongruence with the EU is immediately evident. The UK's institutional configuration and norms of political interaction are miles removed from those of the EU: institutional centralization versus institutional pluralism; politics by convention versus legal formalism; adversity versus consensus.

These are two patterns of governance which—unlike the German case—do not mesh well. Germany is advantaged and empowered in EU decision-making because the rules of the EU game are similar—increasingly similar as German domestic institutions are 'exported'—to those in the German domestic arena. In this context Simon Bulmer has likened the experience of German policy elites entering negotiations in Brussels to that of settling into a 'warm bath'. If, however, UK policy elites enter EU decision-making fora with a mindset shaped by the rules of the UK game, the experience is 'closer to a cold shower'.[26] The winner takes all mentality, rooted in unique British conceptions of sovereignty, combined with the tradition of adversarial politics, have militated against the definition of clear strategies of European co-operation. 'Lacking the stabilising anchor of a consistent strategy', the tendency has been to improvise, often in confrontational manner, in interaction with other member states:[27] Wilson's renegotiation of the terms of UK membership in the 1970s; Thatcher's budgetary handbagging in the 1980s; Major's BSE-inspired non-cooperation in the 1990s. While this kind of single-minded pursuit of specifically national issues may at times succeed, it does little for the UK's longer-term position; it militates against the long-term relationship-building—as exemplified by the robustness of the Franco-German relationship in the EU—which tends to drive integration initiatives forward. In other words, the next time an issue of specific importance to the UK emerges, British policy-makers run the danger of finding themselves friendless.

Even when UK governments have had spells of constructive co-operation, they have not lasted, largely because too little effort—or understanding—is invested in cultivating the long-term co-operative

[26] Bulmer, 'Shaping the Rules? The Constitutive Politics of the European Union and German Power', 50.
[27] S. Padgett, 'The Failure of Britain's European Policy: Reactions to German Unification and European Union', unpublished paper (1994), 1.

relations which are capable of transcending a range of policy issues. A key example was the Single Market, which in some respects can be seen as an instance of successful UK institutional export in the form of market liberalization. It is illuminating here to quote Adam Fergusson, adviser to the then Foreign Secretary Sir Geoffrey Howe:

It was understood quite early on that if you want to get anything done, you really have to align yourself with other European governments. This is the drift of all continental politics, where coalitions and compromises are very important. Of course this was rejected by Margaret [Thatcher] when she first got into power, saying that compromise and consensus is for 'wimps'. But she was persuaded that it was only when you had two or three other member states working your way that you were likely to get somewhere.[28]

Looking beyond this startling discovery by the UK government that coalition-building, compromise, and consensus were the *modus operandi* in Europe, it is characteristic that the co-operative approach did not last. The UK's main ally in pushing through the Single Market was Germany. The UK only wanted the Single Market; Germany saw it as part of a wider project linked to other issues, in particular, in due course, EMU. The statement of intent on working towards EMU which was included, with German support, in the Preamble of the Single European Act was seen by Thatcher as a betrayal and led to the withdrawal of the UK back into 'awkwardness'. To quote Fergusson again:

The German episode was one of the first occasions that we tried to do it [i.e. build coalitions and compromises]. But after Milan [the summit in June 1985 at which the supposed 'betrayal' took place], it was difficult to get her to appreciate that this was worth doing at all.[29]

THE UK AND THE 'SCAPEGOATING' OF GERMANY IN A DEEPENING EUROPE

Another potent nuance in the nature of the UK's 'incongruent' engagement with the EU was added by Germany's unification in 1990. As the trade-off, noted above, between German unification and the deepening of European integration became clear, alarm bells sounded in Downing Street. This linkage represented for Prime Minister Thatcher an unpalatable combination of undesirables: deeper European integration, not least following the Single European Act episode, was not on the UK agenda; nor, for a Prime Minister still harbouring wartime resentments about Germany, was German unity seen as a positive development:

---

[28] Interview with Jim Buller, 27/9/1995. See also Ch. 2 by J. Smith and G. Edwards in this book.   [29] Ibid.

There are things that people of your generation and mine ought never to forget. We've been through the war and we know perfectly well what the Germans are like, and what dictators can do, and how national character doesn't basically change.[30]

Thatcher's response was to try to limit the damage: in conversations with Gorbachev on how the unification process might be prevented (something described by one former senior UK diplomat[31] as an act of 'high treason' to Germany); and in her attempts to anchor German unity in the framework of the looser CSCE process rather than through closer European integration. These efforts proved to be in vain, and Thatcher found herself increasingly isolated both in the EC, as it moved towards the IGCs which culminated at Maastricht, and in her own party which—above all because of the European integration issue—deposed her in 1990.

Although Thatcher's political career effectively ended at that point, her last years in office left two important and potent legacies for British European policy: the linkage between deeper European integration and Germany; and the public expression—and therefore partial legitimization—of historical anti-German prejudice. The early stages of John Major's Prime Ministership did not reveal evidence of this linkage. Major had announced the intention of working 'in the heart of Europe' and of introducing a more positive tone into the UK's European policy. Although little changed in the actual substance of policy, Major certainly brought with him a friendlier and less dogmatic approach. This was illustrated in the Maastricht negotiations as Major, like Thatcher, sought to prevent further integration initiatives but did so in a more pragmatic way, as manifested in the opt-out/in solutions for EMU and the Social Chapter. He also had a softer personal touch, as reflected in the close personal relationship he developed with Helmut Kohl and the easier diplomatic relationship which ensued between the UK and Germany.[32]

The British–German honeymoon was a short one, swept away by the Exchange Rate Mechanism (ERM) crisis in September 1992 in a way which led to the revival of the Thatcher legacy on Germany and European integration. The ejection of the pound from the ERM in 1992 and its subsequent, rapid devaluation were a personal humiliation for Major, who had repeatedly, and right up to the ERM crisis stated that 'devaluation would be a betrayal of our future'.[33] The causes of the ERM crisis

---

[30] Mrs Thatcher in conversation with George Urban, quoted in 'The Alf Garnett version of history', *Independent*, 7/10/1996.

[31] In a comment to Charlie Jeffery. See also Ch. 4; and above all J. Major, *The Autobiography* (London, 1999) and N. Lamont, *In Office* (London, 1999).

[32] For John Major's European policy, see e.g. A. Seldon, *Major: a political life* (London, 1997), 163–8, 226–7, 238 ff. by I. Kettenacher.

[33] Quoted in Padgett, 'The Failure of Britain's European Policy: Reactions to German Unification and European Union', 13. See also Ch. 11 by I. Begg and M. Wood.

were mixed.[34] Much can be attributed to the rigorous, post-unity monetary policy of the Bundesbank, which was externalized onto Germany's
EU partners, together with the clumsy public statements of some Bundes-
bankers, which certainly helped to undermine market confidence in
the pound. British policy had also not been especially adept. For years
the phase 'we will only join the ERM when the time is right' had been
recited, only for the UK to join at an especially unfavourable moment of
world-wide currency instability and an over-valued pound in October 1990.
The UK government had also refused, despite high interest rates and
domestic recession, to seek a realignment of the pound in the ERM. The
net result was the dramatic loss of confidence in the pound and the
ruthless speculative attacks which ejected it from the ERM.[35]

The solution chosen by the UK government in explaining the crisis was
one which played down any British policy contributions to the crisis and
blamed the Germans. The German Ambassador was summoned demonstratively to Downing Street and a publicity offensive launched which
was taken up avidly by the conservative press and right-wing Conservative Party backbenchers. Germany was as a result presented systematically
and more or less officially as the scapegoat for a complex European
policy problem.

The nature of the withdrawal from the ERM and from responsibility
for the devaluation of the pound decisively shaped the next years of the
Major government. The ERM trauma both quashed Major's previous Euro-
constructiveness and encouraged the euro-sceptic right wing of his party.
The euro-sceptics also grew in political weight in a period when Major's
in any case slim parliamentary majority was eroded further by a series
of by-election defeats. A group of 'rebels' who had repeatedly voted against
Major in a series of European policy divisions in parliament—including
the ratification of Maastricht—were temporarily expelled from the
parliamentary Conservative Party, and then formed the core electorate
supporting John Redwood in his unsuccessful challenge in 1995 to take
the leadership of the Conservative Party from Major.

The foundation of the generously-financed, anti-EU Referendum Party
by Sir James Goldsmith in 1996 stoked up the pressures on Major further,
narrowing his government's room for manoeuvre on European policy issues.
Karl Lamers, Foreign Policy Spokesman of the CDU, and a close colleague of Chancellor Kohl was correct in March 1996 when stating that

    [34] For fuller accounts of the ERM crisis, see M. Harmon and D. Heisenberg, 'Explaining
the European Currency Crisis of September 1992', *German Politics and Society* 29 (1993), 19–51;
A. Busch, 'The Crisis in the EMS', *Government and Opposition* 29 (1994), 80–96.
    [35] See H. Young, *This Blessed Plot: Britain and Europe from Churchill to Blair* (London, 1998),
436–43.

the Major government was 'incapable of action in European policy'.[36] It was, to be more precise, certainly incapable of constructive action, forced rather—even more than in the Thatcher era—to restrict itself to a reactive stance on others' initiatives, and then usually negatively given that the domestic (i.e. internal Conservative Party) hurdles to a more positive engagement were set too high. Examples included: Major's rejection of the Belgian Prime Minister Jean-Luc Dehaene's appointment as President of the European Commission; his government's position in the discussions in the Reflection Group set up to prepare the agenda for the 1996–7 IGC, where the UK was in a minority of one on around fifty separate issues;[37] and the subsequent White Paper on the IGC, which was also permeated by an odour of refusal.[38]

Major's European policy became, in other words, a 'two-front war', in which the domestic engagement with his own party was at least as difficult as interaction with the other member states of the EU. Germany played a useful role here as a metaphor and shorthand for the wider European issue in the domestic arena. In a thinly disguised comment on German attitudes on the European social policy agenda, Major complained that 'it is the ambition of nearly all the rest of our European partners to bring much of their domestic social legislation under the Social Chapter, in order to remove their competitive disadvantage against the United Kingdom'.[39] EMU, according to Sir Richard Body, a euro-sceptical backbencher, was a German 'obsession with a superstate in which Germany is master and the rest are puppets'.[40] Moreover, opposition in the EU in 1996 to lifting the BSE-inspired export ban on British beef was regarded as 'political and to the benefit of French, German and Dutch farmers'.[41]

The use of the German scapegoat as a metaphor for a European project over which the Conservative government was enmeshed in a two-front war unfortunately led to a revival of a Germany discourse rooted in World War Two. On BSE, the former Minister and now disgraced ex-MP, Neil Hamilton managed in a triumph of offensiveness to bring in the Holocaust: 'Chancellor Kohl had proposed a "final solution" to the BSE problem involving the "unnecessary slaughter" of large parts of the British herd'.[42] More remarkable still were the British reactions to the

---

[36] *Frankfurter Allgemeine Zeitung*, 16/3/1996.
[37] C. Jeffery, 'Britische Positionen zur Regierungskonferenz 1996—Ein Wandel in Sicht?', in *Maastricht II—Zum Erfolg verurteilt? Herausforderung und Perspektiven der europäischen Integration* (Erfurt, 1996), 32. See also Ch. 13 in this book.
[38] *A Partnership of Nations. The British Approach to the European Union Intergovernmental Conference 1996*, Cm. 3181 (London, 1996).
[39] Quoted in K. Hughes, *What Role for Britain in the EU? Prospects for the Late 1990s* (London, 1996), 11.   [40] Quoted in the *Independent*, 11/2/1996.
[41] Quoted in *the Independent*, 2/5/1996.   [42] Quoted in ibid.

presentation of Kohl's standard speech on European integration in Leuven, Belgium, in February 1996. His speech was essentially the same as many others he had given, in particular his juxtaposition of the successes of European integration and the question of peace and war in Europe. The only novelty was his emphasis on the necessity of EMU amid growing controversies about the convergence criteria set out at Maastricht. The reactions in the UK press and in the Conservative Party were extraordinary: 'Only in Britain, it seems, was the Chancellor's sinister message— the Panzer are ready to roll unless you accept EMU—correctly decoded and amplified to the level of a major international incident.'[43] The speech was also reported as being presented in a 'lurid' way[44] and—contrary to the perceptions of those who attended it—'in the most strident terms',[45] although Kohl is not known for achieving emotional heights in his presentational style. The presentation of the Leuven speech in the UK was, in other words, more or less an invention. More importantly, this could only have happened in a European policy atmosphere in which Germany was being used as a shorthand for euro-scepticism, and in which it had become acceptable to express and propagate anti-German prejudice. As the leader of the Liberal Democrats put it:

One of the worst aspects of the current political debate is that it has become acceptable in Conservative circles to talk about Germany and the Germans in the same tone which English politicians reserved for the Jews 80 years ago and for the Irish a century ago.[46]

This 'sullenly xenophobic'[47] instrumentalization of Germany as a cipher for British difficulties with the European integration process of the 1990s revealed another distinguishing feature of UK European policy-making: in the absence of a clear strategic anchor guiding European policy, policy is left 'at the mercy of the vicissitudes of domestic politics',[48] and vulnerable to the persistent intra-party differences—in both major parties —over the benefits and purpose of European integration. The response observable during the Major government might be termed a modernized form of nineteenth-century social imperialism: try to appease your internal tensions by embarking on external adventure and confrontation. Needless to say, resorting so nakedly to the instrumentalization of the EU, in its German disguise, reflects the weakness of the UK commitment to and the absence of a far-reaching consensus on the idea of multilateral co-operation.

---

[43] Quoted in the *Independent*, 11/2/1996.
[44] E.g. The *Independent*, 6/2/1998; *Guardian*, 12/2/1998.   [45] *Independent*, 3/2/1998.
[46] Quoted in the *Independent*, 7/3/1996.   [47] Ibid.
[48] Padgett, 'The Failure of Britain's European Policy: Reactions to German Unification and European Union', 1.

THE BLAIR GOVERNMENT: CONSTRUCTIVE ENGAGEMENT THROUGH THE 'EUROPEANIZATION' OF DOMESTIC POLITICS?

Major's intra-party splits proved his nemesis in the UK general election of 1 May 1997. The open and virulent differences within the Conservative Party over European integration were repeatedly revealed during the election campaign, weakening the Conservatives credibility—a weakness skilfully exploited by the highly disciplined 'New Labour' of Tony Blair.[49] Blair's signal phrase on Europe on entering government was that of 'constructive engagement' in the EU. Recalling Major's equivalent 'heart of Europe' message, the question begs itself whether constructive engagement will, as under Major, dissipate into the UK syndrome of obstructionist bickering. The initial steps of the government were clearly adjudged as genuinely constructive: the commitment to sign up to the Social Chapter, the pro-EMU industrialist Lord Simon's appointment as European Trade Minister, Bank of England operational autonomy, a positive role at the Amsterdam Summit, the Chancellor of the Exchequer, Gordon Brown's, public flirtation with EMU. However, the early dynamism seems to have evaporated, particularly in the context of a lacklustre British Presidency of the EU in the first half of 1998. However, Blair will certainly not face the internal party difficulties which plagued Major. And Gordon Brown's integrationist credentials will certainly help to keep constructive engagement at the very least on a slow boil.

It is possible, though, that the Blair government will, perhaps unwittingly, establish a longer-term basis for a UK acceptance of the *modus operandi* of multilateral co-operation in the EU. Neal Ascherson wrote in the direct aftermath of Labour's election victory of Blair's 'polite revolution': 'Not the economy or society this time, but the way we are governed, the very spirit of democracy, the notion of where power comes from and what gives anyone the right to rule others.'[50] The Blair government's programme of constitutional and institutional reform is unprecedentedly radical: devolution, justiciable human rights in domestic law, freedom of information, House of Lords reform, proportional representation. This is, as Ascherson enthused, an 'almost recklessly bold programme'.[51]

Even if Labour did not in the end implement each and every part of this programme, the effect would still be radical enough to undermine

---

[49] See W. Paterson and C. Jeffery, 'Großbritannien nach dem Machtwechsel. New Labour, Devolution und Europapolitik', *Konrad-Adenauer-Stiftung Arbeitspapiere* (1997).

[50] Neal Ascherson, 'Measure by Measure. Blair Plans the Polite Revolution', the *Independent on Sunday*, 4/5/1997, 19.   [51] Ibid.

the traditional constitutional doctrine of parliamentary sovereignty. If one creates through devolution new centres of democratic authority, if the people have legally enforceable human rights and freedom of information, if the House of Lords acquires some form of democratic mandate, and if one introduces proportional representation and the coalition government it implies, then Westminster is *de facto* if not *de jure* no longer sovereign. Its power is qualified, subjected to external limits; it is and will be forced to co-operate and seek compromise.

Ascherson likened this to a Europeanization of the British constitution, with the Blair programme 'deeply influenced by Europe, by the "rights culture" and consensus politics and decentralised government of the states which make up the European Union'.[52] This kind of constitutional Europeanization seems set also to influence the way in which the UK engages with its partners in the EU. A new constitutional settlement marked by dispersal of power will require new forms and norms of domestic political interaction. These will include a much fuller recourse to the law, for example in the adjudication of disputes over human rights or the distribution of competencies between UK authorities and the new devolved units of government. New forms of co-operation between institutions will also emerge, and the principle of co-operation will become all the more embedded the more complete the move towards proportional representation and the practice of coalition government proves to be.

As new institutional structures and new lubricating norms embed themselves, it is likely that they will find some external expression in the EU, tendentially replacing unilateralism and adverseness with a new 'export model' rooted in internal power-sharing and co-operation, and rather more likely than the current rhetoric of the Blair government to embed a constructively engaged UK enduringly in the heart of European decision-making. In other words, UK policy-makers may in the coming years come to terms with the structures and ethos of power-sharing in a deepening EU. They may stop being the awkward partners and shift from periodic bouts of obstructionism to enduring positive partnership. One day they may even happily jump together with the Germans into the long hot bath of EU multilateralism.

[52] Ibid.

6

The Eastern Enlargement of the European Union

JOHN PINDER

In May 1948 the Congress of Europe at The Hague affirmed the aim of 'union or federation' for all European democracies.[1] Winston Churchill, after observing that the eastern part of Europe was disappearing behind an Iron Curtain, had already said in September 1947 that 'we must build a kind of United States of Europe', adding that 'the first step in the re-creation of the European family must be a partnership between France and Germany . . . France and Germany must take the lead together'. But he did not envisage British participation in it: 'Britain and the British Commonwealth' were, like the United States of America, to be 'the friends and sponsors' of the new Europe.[2] With remarkable prescience, he prefigured a pattern that was to endure for four decades: French and German leadership in the uniting of Western Europe, with the Central and East Europeans locked into the Soviet system. Britain, with the importance of the Commonwealth fading and unsure of its place in the world, was however to be neither a generous sponsor nor, following its accession, a constructive member of the European Community.

This was the background against which from 1989 onwards the Central and East Europeans won the freedom to choose democracy and, with it, to realize the vision of the Hague Congress by seeking to join the European Union. It is easy enough to agree that their membership of a well-functioning Union will contribute to the security and prosperity of Europe as a whole. But it is not so easy to secure consensus on the great changes required to bring this about. On the eastern side, there is the transformation from the Soviet system to the market economy and pluralist democracy. For the Union, there is the upsetting of vested interests through reform of the agricultural policy and the structural funds; there

[1] W. Lipgens and W. Loth (eds.), *Documents on the History of European Integration*, vol. 4, *Transnational Organizations of Political Parties and Pressure Groups in the Struggle for European Union, 1945–1950* (Berlin and New York, 1991), 346.

[2] W. Lipgens and W. Loth (eds.), *Documents on the History of European Integration*, vol. 3, *The Struggle for European Union by Political Parties and Pressure Groups in Western European Countries 1945–1950* (Berlin and New York, 1988), 662–6.

is the need to reform the institutions to ensure that the enlarged Union really will function well; and there is the prospect of shifts in power relationships as the number of member states increases from fifteen to thirty or more, as the Union's population rises from 350 million to half a billion, and as its centre of gravity shifts to Central from Western Europe, to Germany from France. The prospect of these changes evoked differing reactions from Britain, Germany, and Germany's principal partner, France.

These reactions were aptly summarized from the vantage point of the Netherlands not long after the turning point of 1989. Britain was seen to favour a wider European Community, above all in order to put a brake on further integration. France wanted to check widening and sought deeper integration, with emphasis on monetary union and stronger intergovernmental institutions, particularly involving heads of government. Germany, unlike Britain and France, saw no intrinsic contradiction between widening and deepening. Germany was both eager for enlargement and accepted the prospect of the single currency if combined with greater powers for the European Parliament.[3]

Geography places Germany centrally, with neighbours all round it; and the last two centuries have brought wars all round, from Napoleon's invasions up to the two world wars. The cataclysm of World War Two induced an accelerated learning process, with commitment to parliamentary democracy, market economy, the European Community and Franco-German partnership as well as the Atlantic Alliance; and this brought Germany unprecedented prosperity and peace, including in 1990 peaceful German unification. But with the collapse of the Soviet empire came potential instability among the neighbours to the east, giving Germans a powerful motive for anchoring them in the safe haven of the European Union. As President Herzog put it: 'If we do not stabilise the East, the East will destabilise us.'[4] Germans' profound awareness of the benefits of integration makes them at the same time particularly sensitive to the risk that widening could, unless accompanied by deepening, have a disintegrative effect. Their commitment to parliamentary democracy, which has served them so well, leads them to emphasize the need for a strong European Parliament. The partnership with France, combined with the commitment to integration, induced the German government to accept the project for the single currency.

---

[3] F. Alting von Geusau, *De som der delen: Europa voor en na de omwenteling* (Amsterdam, 1991), 148–9.

[4] Roman Herzog, 'Die Globalisierung der deutschen Außenpolitik ist unvermeidlich', Rede des Bundespräsidenten beim Festakt zum 40. Jahrestag der Deutschen Gesellschaft für Auswärtige Politik, *Bulletin des Presse- und Informationsamtes der Bundesregierung*, No. 20, 15/3/1995, pp. 161–5; cited in B. Lippert, K. Hughes, H. Grabbe, and P. Beckert, *Conflict or Co-operation in the Enlarged European Union? British and German Interests* (London, 1999).

Geography and history have made the French acutely aware of the power of their neighbour across the Rhine. They tried, after their defeat by Germany in 1871, to deal with the German problem by means of alliances, and after World War One through repression. Having learnt following the end of World War Two that neither policy worked, the French launched the project of the European Community in order to bind Germany as an equal partner within supranational institutions. Enormously successful, this has become the great French project of the second half of the twentieth century and anything that might threaten it is fiercely resisted. The prospect of enlarging the Community to include ten or more Central and East European countries was seen as just such a threat, with the potential for making Germany the central power in a looser and weaker Community. So the initial French reaction to widening was negative. President Mitterrand said that it would take 'decades and decades'.[5] France pressed for deepening instead, with emphasis on the single currency project though with some resistance to Germany's desire to strengthen the European Parliament. But commitment to the Franco-German partnership induces the French as well as the Germans to deal with such tensions through a process of 'pragmatic compromise'.[6] They have learnt to accommodate such differences.

For the British, the sea as their shield against invasion together with the policy of balance of power had been enough to avert dominance by a united Continent. Contrary to German and French experience, World War Two did not induce a radical review of British views as to the appropriate relationship between European states. Intergovernmental and diplomatic dealings were still preferred to institutions or policy instruments with federal characteristics. The British have been neo-realists rather than institutionalists; and they have preferred widening to deepening. There has nevertheless been a learning curve of accommodation to growing interdependence within Europe. The curve has had its downs as well as its ups; and the upward parts have not been steep. But learning there has been. The contribution of the Community and Union to prosperity and security in Western Europe is largely recognized. Imperial illusions have faded. For a quarter of a century the Wilson, Callaghan, Thatcher, and Major governments showed indifference or hostility to most proposals for deepening. But before them Edward Heath was much more positive and Tony Blair's government, elected in May 1997, is considerably more positive too. Britain continues to differ from the French, Germans, and most other member states regarding the relationship between deepening and widening. But there is a measure of convergence

[5] Cited in *Der Spiegel* 42 (1991), 24.
[6] H. Mayer, 'Early at the Beach and Claiming Territory? The Evolution of German Ideas on a New European Order', *International Affairs* 73/4 (1997), 723.

too. Precisely what this involves can be demonstrated by examining how their differing stances interacted in the decade following 1989.

TO ACCESSION VIA EUROPE AGREEMENTS: BRITAIN AND GERMANY AGREE

There was general agreement that the Community should respond positively to the transformation in Central and Eastern Europe which started in 1989. There was also wide agreement as to the measures that should then be taken, including trade and co-operation agreements, the general scheme of preferences, the PHARE programme to aid the process of transformation, and establishment of the European Bank for Reconstruction and Development. But there was one outstanding exception: Prime Minister Thatcher bitterly resisted German unification and hence also the immediate entry of the former GDR into the Community via its incorporation into the Federal Republic. President Mitterrand's first reaction was similar. But he rapidly accepted 'pragmatic compromise' in the interests of the Franco-German partnership: French support for German unification was consolidated by Chancellor Kohl's commitment to the single currency project. Thatcher's stand was, on the contrary, to cast its shadow on Anglo-German relations.[7]

With this crucial exception, Britain and Germany saw eye to eye on the Community's initial responses to the changes in Central and Eastern Europe, then both pressed for the replacement of the trade and co-operation agreements by the Europe Agreements. Already by the time of the European Council meeting in Dublin in June 1990 there was a British proposal for association agreements with the Central and East Europeans. By August, the Commission proposed 'Europe Agreements' for 'countries giving practical evidence of commitment to economic and political reforms', i.e. to market economies and liberal democracies, and suggested that Czechoslovakia, Hungary, and Poland had already done so.[8] In December the Council authorized the Commission to begin negotiations with them. The backbone of each agreement was industrial free trade between the parties, to be completed by the Union over a period of five years and by the associate in ten years, complemented by free movement of capital and free trade in services. Provision for agricultural trade and free movement of people was restrictive. There was to be co-operation in a wide range of economic, financial, social, cultural, and political fields.

---

[7] On Britain and German unification, see Ch. 4.

[8] Commission of the European Communities, *Association Agreements with the Countries of Central and Eastern Europe*, Communication from the Commission to the Council and Parliament, COM/90/398 final (Brussels, 27/8/1990).

Association institutions were established under each agreement for ministers, senior officials and members of parliament of the EU and the associated state.

By 1993 Europe Agreements had been concluded with Bulgaria and Romania as well as Hungary, Poland, and the by now separate Czech Republic and Slovakia. While Britain had given full support throughout, Germany had been the driving force; and it was Germany, backed by Britain, that pressed from August 1991 onwards, against resistance from the Commission and from France, for similar agreements with the newly independent Estonia, Latvia, and Lithuania.[9] With Slovenia following, there were by 1996 Europe Agreements with ten Central and East European states.

In addition to the usual protectionist pressures among the member states, negotiation of the agreements encountered a more general problem: the prospect of accession for the associates. As soon as the negotiation of Europe Agreements with the first wave of Central Europeans began, they announced their intention to seek full membership.[10] France and some other member states feared that this would weaken the Community; and the Commission had already asserted that accession was not among the objectives of the agreements.[11] In addition to sharing the fear that widening could lead to weakening, the Commission doubtless recalled the trouble caused by the inclusion of the aim of ultimate accession in the first association agreement, concluded with Greece in 1961, which had been followed two years later by the embarrassing refusal to include the same aim in the agreement with Turkey, about whose ultimate accession member states were more reserved. But there were fewer reservations about the principle of accession by Central and East Europeans and there was greater insistence on the part of Germany and Britain in particular, so the more reluctant member states were brought round through a series of steps to accept the aim of enlargement.

The first step was taken in 1991 in the preambles to the first Europe Agreements, 'recognising the fact that' the ultimate objective of the associates 'is to accede to the Community, and that this association, in the view of the parties, will help [them] to achieve this objective'.[12] The European Council at Maastricht in December 1991, in the margins of the fraught negotiations on the European Union Treaty, found time to

---

[9] Mayer, 'Early at the Beach and Claiming Territory?', 731.

[10] *Agence Europe*, 20/12/1990.

[11] Commission of the European Communities, *Association Agreements with the Countries of Central and Eastern Europe*.

[12] See e.g. 'Europe Agreement establishing an Association between the European Communities and their Member States for the one part and the Republic of Poland for the other part', *Official Journal of the European Communities* L348, vol. 36, 31/12/1993.

ask the Commission to present its next meeting with a report on the implications of enlargement; and this emphasized that 'widening must not be at the expense of deepening'.[13] The meeting in Edinburgh under British Presidency in December 1992 was again preoccupied with deepening, dealing *inter alia* with the problems arising from the Maastricht Treaty. However, it managed to agree that decisions would be reached at the following meeting in Copenhagen 'in order to prepare the associated countries for accession to the Union'.[14]

It was, then, in Copenhagen in June 1993 that the European Council explicitly adopted the aim of enlargement—'the associated countries in Central and Eastern Europe that so desire shall become members of the European Union'—and its requirements were spelt out. The candidates for accession must satisfy the political and economic conditions of democracy and market economy. They must also demonstrate 'adherence to the aims of political, economic and monetary union', words that certainly concealed differences between Germany and Britain as to the meaning of political union in particular. Enlargement would also depend on 'the Union's capacity to absorb new members, while maintaining the momentum of European integration':[15] more weasel words, for 'maintaining the momentum of European integration' certainly meant different things to the Germans and the British. The seeds of Anglo-German conflict over deepening were never far below the surface. Having come to full view in the Intergovernmental Conferences leading to the Maastricht Treaty, they were to emerge again in the IGC of 1996–7 which that Treaty had stipulated to complete some of its unfinished business, and which the European Council at Corfu in June 1994 decided should also create, before the enlargement negotiations begin, the 'institutional conditions for ensuring the proper functioning of the Union' after its enlargement.[16]

Meanwhile, however, British and Germans were to enjoy a wide measure of agreement on the 'route plan for the associated countries as they prepare for accession', which was adopted by the European Council under German Presidency at its meeting in Essen in December 1994.[17] This set down in detail the measures that the associates would have to take in the

---

[13] 'Europe and the Challenge of Enlargement', report presented by the Commission to the Lisbon European Council held on 26 and 27 June 1992, *Bulletin of the European Communities*, Supplement 3 (1992), 10.

[14] 'Edinburgh European Council: Conclusions of the Presidency', *Bulletin of the European Communities* 12 (1992), 37.

[15] 'Copenhagen European Council: Conclusions of the Presidency', *Bulletin of the European Communities* 6 (1993), 13.

[16] 'Corfu European Council: Conclusions of the Presidency', *Bulletin of the European Union* 6 (1994), 14.

[17] 'Report from the Council to the Essen European Council on a strategy to prepare for the accession of the associated CCEE', Annex 4 to 'Essen European Council: Conclusions of the Presidency', *Bulletin of the European Union* 12 (1994), 20.

relevant fields: single market legislation and regulation; competition policy; agricultural, environmental, transport policies; financial co-operation; culture, education and training; justice and home affairs; common foreign and security policy. It also developed the concept of 'structured dialogue', in the form of meetings of representatives of the EU member states and of all the Central and East European candidates together, at ministerial, official and parliamentary levels. From a German perspective, these meetings were useful though needing more thorough preparation and follow-up; and it was expected that the new series of European Conferences, with an annual meeting of the Heads of State and Government of the member and applicant states together with the President of the European Commission, would enhance the status of such dialogue.[18] The British government underlined the importance of the first meeting of the European Conference, which took place during the British Presidency in the first half of 1998.[19]

Meanwhile, the Commission had been asked to present its opinions on the individual applications immediately after the conclusion of the IGC, and to report on all aspects of enlargement together with the related matter of revising the Union's financing system. The opinions and the report were presented to the European Council in Luxemburg in December 1997; and both the British and Germans, unlike some of the Scandinavian and southern member states, had no difficulty in accepting the Commission's view that the first wave of accession negotiations be opened with the Czech Republic, Estonia, Hungary, Poland, and Slovenia as well as Cyprus.[20] They were also to find much common ground in their views on the implications of enlargement for the EU's policies and finances.

EU POLICIES AND ENLARGEMENT: MUCH AGREEMENT BUT SOME DIFFERENCES

The political imperative of enlargement has come to be appreciated throughout the Union, with the important rider that some member states, including Germany, have regarded deepening of the Union as a necessary condition whereas Britain has stubbornly resisted it: of which more later. But on the economic aspects Britain and Germany have largely agreed.

---

[18] B. Lippert and P. Becker, 'Bilanz und Zukunft des Strukturierten Dialogs', *Integration* 20/2 (1997), 56–71.

[19] *The British Presidency: Giving Europe Back to the People*, speech by the Foreign Secretary, the Rt Hon. Robin Cook, to the Institute for European Affairs, Dublin, 3/11/1997.

[20] See G. Avery and F. Cameron, *The Enlargement of the European Union* (Sheffield, 1998), 129.

Both have, for the last half-century, favoured freedom of trade, which will be consolidated in relation to Central and Eastern Europe by the move from Europe Agreements to membership. Germany has, moreover, a special interest in economic relations with its eastern neighbours. The Iron Curtain cut German trade in that direction to perhaps one-quarter of its natural level. Before the depression of the 1930s exports to the East, including what are now the CIS states, comprised 17 per cent of total German exports, but in 1989 only 4 per cent. The Federal Republic's exports to Denmark were greater than those to Czechoslovakia, Hungary, and Poland combined.[21] The potential rate of growth of the Union's exports to Central and Eastern Europe has been estimated at over 10 per cent a year;[22] and Germany's have risen particularly fast, already reaching 8.5 per cent of total German exports by 1996. The gain is in manufactures that are human-capital-intensive; and a loss of jobs among the less skilled is seen as an unavoidable consequence of economic globalization.[23] German industry has reacted to the latter by means of outward processing as well as by investment in Central and Eastern Europe. German investment in the associated countries has risen fast; and the stability and security guaranteed by membership will provide a further incentive. These economic interests, together with Germany's profound political interest in security to the east, are a most powerful combination.

Britain's trade with Central and Eastern Europe is much smaller than Germany's. The British will gain less and are moreover expected to be among the main losers of unskilled jobs as a result of it.[24] Though the Europe Agreements will already have accounted for much of this effect, the painful process of adjustment will continue. But imports from outside Europe are the main cause of this, and with Britain's generally liberal policy on international trade, protectionist pressures will not weaken British support for enlargement.

It is in the context of this shared liberal approach to the economic aspects of enlargement that Britain and Germany have found much agreement on the implications for EU policies in fields such as the structural funds and, eventually, agriculture. The European Commission's White Paper, 'Agenda 2000',[25] showed how much enlargement would expand the EU's

[21] O. Storf, *Business Risks and Opportunities in Eastern Europe and the Soviet Union*, paper for conference of the Centre for European Policy Studies (Brussels, Nov. 1990).

[22] R. Faini and R. Portes (eds.), *European Union Trade with Eastern Europe* (London, 1995), 93–4.

[23] C. Weise, 'Der EU Beitritt ostmitteleuropäischer Staaten: Ökonomische Chancen und Reformbedarf für die EU', *Integration*, 20/3 (1997), 175.

[24] G. Denton, *Enlarging the Union: The Intergovernmental Conference of the European Union 1996*, Federal Trust Papers No. 5 (London, 1996), 28.

[25] European Commission, 'Agenda 2000: For a Stronger and Wider Union', *Bulletin of the European Union*, Supplement 5 (1997).

budget unless these policies were reformed; and both Britain and Germany have resisted any growth of the budget faster than that of the Union's GDP. Thus, they have largely agreed about the reform of the structural funds and, after a lengthy period of dissension, of the agricultural policy. The White Paper also analysed the effect of enlargement on the annual rebate that has, since 1984, served as compensation for the high net cost of the budget to Britain resulting from the structure of the agricultural policy; and this was a potential source of conflict with the Germans, on whom the budget imposes a yet higher net cost. But agreement on that too was reached at the meeting of the European Council in Berlin, under German Presidency, on 24–5 March 1999.

The Commission's estimate of the extra budgetary cost that enlargement to all ten of the Central and East European applicants would impose on the agricultural policy was ecu 9–12bn., on top of the existing cost of ecu 40bn. which is about half of the Union's total budget.[26] Given the resistance of Britain and Germany to higher Union expenditure, they could both be expected to accept the proposal of the Commission's White Paper to restrict the agricultural costs of enlargement by 'deepening and extending the 1992 reform through further shifts from price support to direct payments, and developing a coherent rural policy to accompany this process'.[27] But whereas the British, while supporting the Commission's approach, deemed its proposals for price cuts insufficiently tough, the German minister for agriculture claimed there was 'no need for such a reform'.[28] The view of the German finance ministry was certainly different. But that of the agriculture minister reflected a reality of the CDU/CSU governing party: its dependence on the farm vote, and in particular the reliance of the CSU, which traditionally supplied the agriculture minister, on the votes of Bavarian farmers. Chancellor Kohl's custom was to let such differences between ministers on questions of European policy run their course until a decision at the European level was urgently required. But meanwhile, in the field of agriculture, disagreement between Britain and Germany was inevitable; and the outcome would have been such as to leave Britain not only dissatisfied but also attributing to Germany a share of the blame.

In October 1998, however, Gerhard Schröder replaced Helmut Kohl as Chancellor. Neither the SPD nor their Green partners were beholden to the agricultural lobby; and this was to prove a 'fundamental change'

---

[26] Commission of the European Communities, *Study on alternative strategies for the development of relations in the field of agriculture between the EU and associated countries with a view to future accession of these countries (Agriculture strategy paper)*, 'Fischler report', CSE (95) 607, Brussels, Dec. 1995. [27] 'Agenda 2000', 29.
[28] H. Grabbe and K. Hughes, *Enlarging the EU Eastwards* (London, 1998), 99; *Financial Times*, 7/1/1998.

for the future of these negotiations.[29] In January 1999, at the outset of the German Presidency of the EU Council for the first half of the year, Foreign Minister Joschka Fischer said that a 'root and branch reform of the common agricultural policy and a reduction in agricultural spending' were required;[30] and in the subsequent negotiations the German Presidency did seek a radical reform on the lines of the Commission's proposals. The British, though again preferring tougher cuts, were supportive, as were most of the other governments. But at the meeting of the European Council in Berlin in March 1999 at which agreement on the budgetary implications of Agenda 2000 was finally reached, President Chirac insisted on dilution of the reform. Failure to reach a settlement at that meeting on the European Council could have damaged both the Franco-German partnership and relations with the Central and East Europeans, and hence also Schröder's domestic political position. So he settled for what was probably an inadequate reform; and this time at least, the result of the 'fundamental change' in German policy was not so much in the settlement itself as in Anglo-German consensus regarding its negotiation.

Anglo-German consensus regarding the 'structural operations' (comprising the Cohesion Fund as well as the 'structural funds') did not depend on changes of government. These funds account for a third of the Union's budgetary expenditure and, since their main purpose is to help the development of less-favoured regions, enlargement to include the low-income countries of Central and Eastern Europe will have major implications for this part of the budget. The Commission proposed, in 'Agenda 2000', that the Union's financial perspective for the seven years 2000–6 should include ecu 45bn. for the five applicants due to accede during the course of that period and pointed out that all fifteen of the present member states would have to pay, whether by contributing more or receiving less than they would otherwise have done.[31] This was a signal for conflict between the net recipients from the structural funds, led by Spain, and the net payers, led by Germany and Britain. As the two largest net contributors to the Union's budget, both were determined to keep their future contributions as low as possible. Partly in response to their evident resolve, the Commission had by the time of the Berlin meeting of the European Council reduced its proposed allocation for the structural funds from the average of ecu 39bn. a year for the seven years included in the 'Agenda 2000' White Paper to a figure of 34bn. a year (denominated by now in euros). The British wanted it reduced below 29bn. euros

---

[29] C. Jenkins, *Paying for an Enlarged European Union* (London, 1999), 25.
[30] 'Statement by Joschka Fischer, President-in-Office of the Council, on the programme of the German Presidency and the situation in Kosovo', *Verbatim Report of Proceedings*, European Parliament, 12/1/1999, 4.   [31] 'Agenda 2000', 63, 67, 74 Table 3.

and were joined in this by the French, who had also become net contributors to the budget as a whole.[32] But Schröder, having to contend at
the Berlin European Council with a very determined Spanish leadership
of the net beneficiaries from the funds, finally secured agreement on an
annual allocation of 30.5bn. euros a year, made more palatable for the
British by special favours for parts of the UK such as Northern Ireland
and the Scottish Highlands and Islands.

Unlike the structural funds, the budgetary rebate was a source of
potential conflict between Britain and Germany. The British rebate was
a long-standing bone of contention, originating in the arrangements
for financing the common agricultural policy made before Britain joined
the Community. Britain had, during its accession negotiations, secured
an assurance from the existing member states that 'equitable solutions'
would be found if 'unacceptable situations' were to arise; and by the end
of the 1970s the net contribution was due to rise towards some 1 per cent
of GDP. For five years from 1979, when she became Prime Minister,
Mrs Thatcher fought single-mindedly for an 'equitable solution', generating much bitterness by using her ability to block the development of the
Community as a weapon in her battle. Finally, in 1984, she secured the
rebate, equivalent to about two-thirds of Britain's net contribution and
paid each year in due proportions by each of the member states.

Without that arrangement, the net British contribution would have
averaged not far short of 1 per cent of GDP in the years 1992–7; and the
rebate reduced it to 0.30 per cent. This became increasingly irksome for
Germany, whose net contribution over the same period was 0.67 per cent
and which was still suffering the effects of its own unification both in the
consequent burden on the German budget and in the sharp reduction of
average incomes per head.[33]

The Commission had explained, in 'Agenda 2000', why enlargement,
by altering the balance of the budget, would raise the question of the rebate,
but had not regarded the matter as urgent. It had suggested a gradual
reduction of the rebate when British average incomes should rise above
the average for the Union as a whole, which would be likely to occur after
the first phase of enlargement. The Commission therefore proposed a
review immediately after that enlargement had taken place, which might
result in an 'adjustment of the financial key', requiring less from high net
contributors such as Germany, or a 'generalized system of corrections'.[34]
But pressure from Germany intensified, as well as from Austria, the

[32] *Financial Times*, 27–28/3/1999.
[33] The figures for net contributions are given in the European Commission's 'Agenda 2000:
Financing the European Union—Commission report on the operation of the own resources
system', Supplement 2/98, *Bulletin of the European Union*, Annex 8, Table 5.
[34] 'Agenda 2000', 67–9.

Netherlands, and Sweden, whose net contributions exceeded Britain's 0.30 per cent of GDP, and from other member states which had never been happy about the rebate. By October 1998, the Commission in its report on *Financing the European Union* had become 'decidedly less optimistic'.[35] The British government continued to insist that the rebate must not be touched and it looked as if conflict between Britain and Germany would be hard to resolve.

Schröder decided, however, to settle the question at the Berlin European Council with a necessary minimum of changes. The British agreed to 'technical adjustments' to neutralize any 'windfall gains from changes to the financial system', which were estimated at 220m. euros. The German contribution to the rebate, which had previously been reduced by one-third from its 'normal' level, was now cut by three-quarters, as were the Austrian, Dutch and Swedish contributors; and these arrangements were to stand until 2006.[36]

It was perhaps not surprising that Blair called Schröder's chairmanship 'brilliant'.[37] Schröder was able to claim that he had been able to 'stop and reverse the rising trend in Germany's net contributions' to the budget.[38] But he had also taken full account of British interests, largely no doubt in order to achieve a positive outcome from his first Presidency of the European Council, but also perhaps because there was greater underlying harmony between his government and Blair's than there had been between those of their predecessors.

DEEPENING WITH WIDENING: ON COLLISION COURSE

It was under German Presidency that the European Council decided in June 1988 to set up the Delors Committee to propose 'concrete stages leading towards' the objective of economic and monetary union.[39] EMU was not the most comfortable element of integration for Germany, but Kohl saw it as both a building block for a federal Europe and necessary in order to keep the Franco-German partnership pointing in that direction. The resulting Delors report proposed the establishment of EMU in three stages, the third of which would create the single currency and the European Central Bank.[40] For Germany, as we have seen, EMU should

---

[35] Jenkins, *Paying for an Enlarged European Union*, 12

[36] 'Berlin European Council: Conclusions of the Presidency', *Bulletin of the European Union* 3 (1999).   [37] *Financial Times*, 27–28/3/1999.

[38] 'Government Policy Statement' by Gerhard Schröder on the conclusion of the EU summit meeting in Berlin and on the NATO operation in Yugoslavia, Bonn, 26/3/1999.

[39] Committee for the Study of Economic and Monetary Union, 'Foreword', *Report on economic and monetary union in the European Community*, 'Delors report' (Luxembourg, 1989).

[40] See Ch. 13.

be accompanied by the power of co-decision for the European Parliament with the Council. Foreign and security policy would also have to be co-ordinated, leading by stages to a European defence pillar within Nato.[41] For France, the single currency was the keystone of the great project of anchoring Germany in the European Community, as well as the means of regaining a share in the monetary autonomy that had been lost to the Bundesbank.

All this was anathema to Thatcher, who envisaged a Community limited to a single market, with institutions and foreign policy co-operation run on intergovernmental lines. It is useful to examine her reactions to the relationship between deepening and widening the Community in some detail, as her stamp was to remain on British policy and hence on Anglo-German relations regarding enlargement until the general election of May 1997, and in some respects beyond. She reacted promptly to the launching of the EMU project with her speech at Bruges in September 1988, in which she attacked attempts to 'suppress nationhood', to fit old nations into an 'identikit European personality', with decisions to be 'taken by an appointed bureaucracy' in a 'European super-state exercising a new dominance from Brussels'.[42] It was to be expected that this would be seen in Germany as a far from polite attack on a concept of the Community of which Kohl, like most of the German political class, was a foremost proponent; and the feeling grew in Bonn that 'Britain could not be trusted on Europe'.[43] German unification added a very sharp edge to this divide. Kohl wanted it to be combined with deepening the Community in order to ensure stability. 'If we don't link German unification with European unity, if what we undertook in Maastricht fails and we don't achieve European Union in the last decade of this terrible century, we will revert to nationalist disputes in Europe next century.'[44]

Thatcher did not want German unification nor did she want Kohl's version of European unity, let alone the two together. In September 1989, soon after the movement towards German unification began, she told Mikhail Gorbachev she was 'apprehensive' and found that he did not want it 'either'. She sought allies to put a stop to it. By February 1990, Kohl had persuaded Gorbachev, with the help as she put it of a 'huge sum' of money, to accept both German unification and the united Germany's

[41] See Ch. 8. See also a statement by Foreign Minister Kinkel, the *Independent*, 4/11/1996.
[42] The Rt Hon. Margaret Thatcher, *Britain and Europe*, text of the speech delivered in Bruges by the Prime Minister on 20/9/1988 (London, 1988), 4.
[43] T. Kielinger, cited in A. Watson, 'Thatcher and Kohl: Old Rivalries Revisited', in M. Bond, J. Smith and W. Wallace (eds.), *Eminent Europeans: Personalities who shaped contemporary Europe* (London, 1996), 267.
[44] *International Herald Tribune*, 8/6/1992, cited in H. Miall, *Shaping the New Europe*, Chatham House Papers (London, 1993), 85.

membership of Nato.[45] In the same month she 'tried to explain' to President Bush that not only should Germany stay in Nato and the US in Europe but also that to 'help balance Germany' in Europe, 'looking well into the future, only the Soviet Union—or its successor—could provide such a balance.' Bush, she found, 'failed to understand' that she was discussing 'a long-term balance of power in Europe rather than proposing an alternative alliance to Nato'. But the misunderstanding surely had deeper roots. Bush had a few weeks earlier made it clear that he preferred the path of European integration rather than what she called her 'Bruges goal of European development'.[46] He saw European integration, rather than the balance of power, as the way to contain the power of the united Germany. There was only one other ally with whom Thatcher could hope to restore balance of power to its traditional central place: France.

Mitterrand's initial reaction to the prospect of German unification was similar to Thatcher's. But he soon demonstrated that he was unwilling to 'change the direction of his whole foreign policy' and chose instead to move ahead 'faster towards a federal Europe in order to tie down the German giant', rather than to 'abandon this approach and return to that associated with General de Gaulle—the defence of sovereignty and striking up of alliances to secure French interests'.[47]

Thatcher could not impede German unification. But she hoped to prevent the concomitant deepening of the Community. While recognizing that many Germans 'want to see Germany locked into a federal Europe', she was convinced that Germany 'would be more rather than less likely to dominate in such a framework'. She also thought that her more flexible Europe 'would be much more accommodating to the countries of the post-communist world' and that they would provide her with potential allies in her 'crusade for a wider, looser Europe'.[48] With the exception of the Czech premier, Vaclav Klaus, however, scant support for her view was forthcoming from political leaders of the Central and East Europeans. A more typical reaction came from a Czech specialist in European affairs: that in Nato and the European Community, Germany had 'given up large parts of its sovereignty, which, especially for its Eastern neighbours, represents a guarantee of utmost importance'.[49]

Kohl's reaction to Thatcher's behaviour was that she was 'pre-Churchillian' rather than 'post-Churchillian', evidently because her thinking had not progressed beyond the concept of the balance of power, regardless of its potential for damage and conflict.[50] He may also have

---

[45] M. Thatcher, *The Downing Street Years* (London, 1993), 792, 798.
[46] Ibid. 795, 799.   [47] Ibid. 795.   [48] Ibid. 759, 791.
[49] J. Stepanovsky, 'International Relations in Central and Eastern Europe', in Forschungsinstitut der Deutschen Gesellschaft für Auswärtige Politik, *Central and Eastern Europe in Transition* (Bonn, 1991), 35.   [50] Watson, 'Thatcher and Kohl', 271.

recalled Churchill's vision of Franco-German partnership leading beyond the balance of power to a 'kind of United States of Europe', which had heralded the transition from the old Europe to the new. At a more mundane level this episode, combined with the notorious seminar on Germany that Thatcher held at Chequers, served to decrease 'German trust in British politicians' yet further, to the extent that it was seen at the time as a 'crucial turning point' for Britain in Europe.[51] This conflict over the question of deepening as a complement to widening had reached a pitch at which it threatened not only Anglo-German relations but also the future of enlargement and of the European Union itself. While Thatcher's 'instinctive anti-Germanism'[52] exacerbated the conflict, it was also fuelled by romantic nationalism on the right wing of the Conservative Party and by the traditional view of diplomacy that had flourished among British diplomats during her years in power. So it was sustained throughout the subsequent period of Conservative government.

Thatcher herself was to continue fighting the battle until her resignation in November 1990. While the Irish Presidency called a special European Council in April 'to consider events in eastern Europe and the implications for the Community of German unification', she noted that 'for others this was just an opportunity to keep up the federalist momentum' and she wanted to 'open up the divisions between the French and the Germans.'[53] But unlike Churchill, she failed to appreciate the significance of the Franco-German partnership. The French and Germans, convinced that it was the basis for the peaceful and prosperous European Community, were not about to let their differences stand in the way of their proposals to deepen it. The French continued to insist on the single currency and the Germans continued to accept it, so the IGC on EMU was convened. Both Germans and French wanted a common foreign and security policy with some majority voting and both wanted to strengthen the Community institutions, even if the French preferred to do so through the Council and European Council while the Germans wanted to strengthen the European Parliament too. Thus, the European Council in June 1990 decided to hold an IGC on political union alongside the one on EMU. Thatcher was hostile to all these things as well as to the Franco-German partnership, which she was to call an 'axis' and a 'juggernaut'.[54]

The turbulence generated by Thatcher's reactions to German unification, as well as to the proposals for deepening the Community in response to this, were a major cause of her resignation in November 1990. She had failed to understand the nature of relations between the member

[51] H. Wallace, 'At Odds with Europe', *Political Studies* 45/4 (1997), 680.
[52] Watson, 'Thatcher and Kohl', 266.
[53] Thatcher, *The Downing Street Years*, 760, 761.   [54] Ibid. 759, 762.

states in the Community, the significance of the Franco-German partnership, the merits of German policy as seen by the Americans and the French
as well as other Community partners, or the views of Central and East
Europeans regarding Germany and the European Community. Her attitude
to Europe had provoked the resignations of no fewer than four of her
most senior ministers—Michael Heseltine, Geoffrey Howe, Nigel Lawson,
Leon Brittan—and had contributed to her loss of the support of the
Conservative Party in the House of Commons. While the excesses of her
behaviour proved unacceptable, the preference for intergovernmental
relations and hence for widening without deepening lived on. She had
fostered a strand of right-wing nationalism whose influence grew in the
Conservative Party and press; and the traditional view of diplomacy, which
had come to prevail in the Foreign Service, was not discouraged by Douglas
Hurd, who had become her Foreign Secretary in October 1989 and was
to retain the post until 1995.

Major did not match his desire to be 'at the heart of Europe' with
support for the proposals to deepen the Community which Kohl,
Mitterrand, and most of its other political leaders regarded as a necessary condition of enlargement. His main contribution to the Maastricht
Treaty was to weaken the single currency project, as well as Britain's
relationship with Germany, by securing the British opt-out from EMU
as well as from the Social Chapter. He did accept, which Thatcher would
scarcely have done, the Treaty's provisions to strengthen the European
Parliament, in particular through the co-decision procedure and the
right to approve the appointment of the Commission. This helped to ease
German worries about the democratic deficit. But Major resisted German
proposals for stronger arrangements for foreign policy co-operation,
failing to appreciate that Germany's intention to recognize Croatia
unilaterally, which was declared in the run-up to the Maastricht negotiations, was a result of the weakness of those arrangements, from which
the conclusion can be drawn that 'German power will become more
evident where European institutions prove to be too weak'.[55]

The relative importance that Major attached to enlargement on the
one hand and keeping the Union's institutions weak on the other was
demonstrated during the negotiation on the weighting that member states'
votes were to have in the Council after enlargement to include Austria,
Finland, and Sweden. In principle Britain strongly supported enlargement.
But Hurd feared that Britain's negotiating leverage would be weakened
if the weighting that the other member states wanted was to be adopted.
Major was on the point of vetoing the change because this was seen by

[55] Bulmer and Paterson, 'Germany in the European Union', 18. See also Mayer, 'Early at
the Beach', 724; and Miall, *Shaping the New Europe*, 94.

Conservative Eurosceptics as a test of his readiness to 'stand up for British interests'. This would have been tantamount to vetoing the enlargement. But eventually a face-saving formula was devised and he cast his veto instead on the candidacy of the Belgian Jean-Luc Dehaene for the Presidency of the Commission, preferring Jacques Santer from Luxemburg instead.[56] Major doubtless shared the view that the more intergovernmental the institutions the better British interests would be served. This conviction as well as the Eurosceptics' use of his small majority in parliament to hold him hostage made him unwilling to adopt policies that would have improved Britain's relationship with Germany and most of the other member states. He made it quite clear that, for him, widening should not be accompanied by deepening. Major claimed that 'Britain successfully used the Maastricht negotiations to reassert the authority of national governments'. He insisted that the European Parliament was not 'the future democratic focus of the Union' and that this 'should remain the case'. Nor did he find it necessary to express a minimum of respect for his partners' principal project, averring that if they recited 'the mantra of full economic and monetary union' it would have 'all the quaintness of a rain dance and about the same potency'—words that themselves read quaintly in 1999.[57]

A year later Wolfgang Schäuble, Chairman of the CDU/CSU Parliamentary Party in the Bundestag, and its Foreign Affairs Spokesman, Karl Lamers, published a paper proposing that a core group of Germany, France, and the Benelux countries proceed with deeper integration, as a way of circumventing the British block on deepening.[58] Not long afterwards, a former British ambassador to Bonn was to say that 'Britain and Germany are far apart, indeed on collision courses.'[59] This was borne out both in the British government's derogatory attitude to EMU and, with respect to institutions, in the comportment of its representative in the Reflection Group preparing for the IGC that began in 1996, who opposed almost all proposals seen by Germans as helping to deepen the Union. Whereas, for example, 'a large majority', certainly including the German representative, was for co-decision, 'one member', clearly the British one, 'in principle, opposed any extension'; and 'a large majority' was

[56] Wallace, 'At Odds with Europe', 683.

[57] The Rt Hon. John Major, 'Raise your Eyes, There is a Land Beyond', *The Economist*, 25/9/1993, 24, 27; and *Europe: A Future that Works*, William and Mary Lecture given at the University, Leiden, 7/9/1994.

[58] W. Schäuble and K. Lamers, *Überlegungen zur Europäischen Politik* (Bonn: CDU/CSU Fraktion des Deutschen Bundestages, 1/9/1994), reproduced in English as 'Reflections on European Policy', in K. Lamers, *A German Agenda for the European Union* (London, 1994), 11–24.

[59] Sir Oliver Wright, *Robert Birley Memorial Lecture*, cited in Watson, 'Thatcher and Kohl', 265.

likewise prepared to consider qualified majority voting in the Council as the general rule, but 'one member saw no case' for extending it.[60] Thus the idea of 'flexibility' became prominent in the preparations for the IGC, reflecting the desire of a core group of member states, and of Germany in particular, to deepen their integration before the eastern enlargement, without being impeded by the British veto.[61] With Germany, along with France and other core states, convinced that widening must be accompanied by deepening, to which Britain was opposed, the collision appeared to be rapidly approaching.

FROM 1997: CONVERGENCE AND A HAPPY ENDING?

By the time the European Council met in Amsterdam in June 1997 to conclude the IGC, John Major's government had been replaced by the New Labour government led by Tony Blair. After over seventeen years in opposition, the Labour Party had swung round from a policy of taking Britain out of the Community to one of constructive engagement. The policy document on Europe, adopted by the Party Conference in 1995, had approved for example the extension of qualified majority voting in the Council in the fields of industrial, regional, social, and environmental policy, together with co-decision wherever qualified majority voting applied: very similar to the current German policy on these matters.[62]

The Amsterdam Treaty did indeed extend co-decision so that it will apply to over half of Union legislation. On qualified majority voting, however, Kohl was at that time, owing to domestic political pressures, unwilling to go as far as Blair.[63] Moreover, Belgium, frustrated in its desire to secure this strengthening of the institutions, refused to accept the re-weighting of Council votes in favour of the larger countries that they deemed necessary before the accession of a number of smaller countries from Central and Eastern Europe. So a Protocol to the Treaty requires a new IGC to be held, to review the 'composition and functioning of the institutions', at least a year before the number of member states exceeds twenty, i.e. before the next enlargement.

The Amsterdam Treaty also provided for 'flexibility' under the name of 'closer co-operation', enabling a group of member states to use

---

[60] European Commission, *Reflection Group's Report*, SN 520/95 (Brussels, 5/12/1995), para. 86, 100.

[61] M. Piepenschneider, 'Die Positionen der Mitgliedstaaten und EU-Organe im Überblick. Standpunkte, Spielmaterial und Sprengsätze', in M. Jopp and O. Schmuck (eds.), *Die Reform der Europäischen Union. Analysen—Positionen—Dokumente zur Regierungskonferenz 1996/97* (Bonn, 1996), 79.

[62] Labour Party, *The future of the European Union*, Report to the Party Conference on Labour's position in preparation for the Intergovernmental Conference 1996 (London, 1995).

[63] A. Duff, *The Treaty of Amsterdam: Text and Commentary* (London, 1997), 155–6.

the Union institutions for new measures of integration that others are not willing to share. With the new British approach to Europe, 'flexibility' is not likely to lead to divergence between Britain and Germany as regards Community affairs except, so long as Britain stands apart from the single currency, with respect to the euro and economic policy co-ordination connected with it. But there was less convergence between Britain and Germany with respect to the Union's other two 'pillars' relating to Common Foreign and Security Policy and to Justice and Home Affairs. Here Blair insisted on retaining the British veto intact and on opting out from the Schengen Agreements.

Measures to deepen the Union by strengthening its powers and institutions are seen in Germany as an essential concomitant of widening to include the countries of Central and Eastern Europe. British and German attitudes towards deepening are therefore a determinant of the relationship between the two countries in the approach to enlargement. Nearly two years after Blair became Prime Minister and half a year after Schröder became Chancellor, the Berlin European Council of March 1999 demonstrated much agreement about the policy implications of enlargement. Evidence of convergence in attitudes towards deepening was less definite, though there were some promising indications.

Blair's refusal at Amsterdam to move towards adoption of the 'Schengen *acquis*', comprising a large body of measures of police and judicial co-operation as well as the abolition of frontier controls, was a disappointment for Germany. But while the insistence on retaining frontier controls on the movement of people between Britain and the Continental member states remained, the British government subsequently took a major step in announcing its wish to adopt all the rest of the Schengen *acquis*.[64] Germans, for their part, also have their concerns about the movement of people across frontiers. The *Bundesarbeitsministerium* (the Federal Ministry of Employment) has estimated that between one-third and two-thirds of a million people a year will want to seek work in Germany after the Central and East European states have joined the Union; and the largest number will come from Poland, which is to join in the first wave. Private estimates have been nearly twice as high.[65] In order to soften the impact, which is likely to be concentrated in particular sectors such as the building industry, Germany is likely to want a long transitional period during which controls remain on the movement of labour from Central to Eastern Europe; and German governments will not be well placed to complain about remaining British frontier controls.

[64] See statement by the Minister of State for Home Affairs at the European Parliament, *Agence Europe*, No. 7451, 23/4/1999.

[65] C. Weise, 'Der EU Beitritt ostmitteleuropäischer Staaten', 176; P. Becker, 'Der Nutzen der Osterweiterung für die Europäische Union', *Integration* 21/4 (1998), 233, 237 n. 13.

As regards the Common Foreign and Security Policy (CFSP), which is particularly important in the context of enlargement, divergence has also been diminishing. Already at Amsterdam, Britain and Germany were in agreement on most of the amendments for making the CFSP more effective and improving the capacity for analysis and planning.[66] But while Germany and France both wanted to move towards qualified majority voting and to merge the Western European Union (WEU) into the European Union, Blair held fast to the veto and insisted that WEU remain separate. While the British policy on majority voting has not changed since then, there has been considerable movement of policy on defence. Initiatives taken by Blair in this direction at an informal meeting of the European Council at Portschach in September and an Anglo-French meeting at St Malo in November 1998 were welcomed by Joschka Fischer in his speech as German Foreign Minister to the European Parliament at the beginning of the German Presidency of the EU Council in January 1999;[67] and in May the EU foreign and defence ministers agreed, with British consent, on the principle of the merger with WEU. Concern about relations with the United States regarding policy towards the Balkans and aspects of the bombing of Yugoslavia also strengthened the British desire to forge an effective European defence identity.[68]

An underlying motive for the change of British policy on defence was the fear that Britain would lose influence within the EU as a result of its opting out of the single currency and the hope that a strong participation in European defence arrangements would provide a means of redress. The Labour government indicated soon after coming to power that it favoured British participation in EMU, but insisted that the economic conditions must be right.[69] There is also the crucial political condition of success in the promised referendum on joining the single currency; and opinion polls have not been encouraging. Prolonged British abstention from the euro would be seen in Germany as weakening the Union in the context of enlargement and would consequently impair the prospect of close partnership between the two countries.

Before Labour came to power, the fear that Britain would block the strengthening of the Union which Germany regarded as essential for a successful enlargement was the main motive for German interest in new arrangements for 'flexibility', allowing a group of member states to

---

[66] M. Jopp, A. Maurer and O. Schmuck (eds.), *Die Europäische Union nach Amsterdam. Analysen und Stellungnahmen zum neuen EU-Vertrag* (Bonn, 1998), 293.

[67] Statement by Joschka Fischer, 12/1/1999, 7.

[68] See e.g. the positions taken by Foreign Secretary Robin Cook, *Financial Times*, 13/5/1999, 14/5/1999.

[69] Speech by Gordon Brown, Chancellor of the Exchequer, to the Royal Institute of International Affairs, London, 17/7/1997.

proceed with projects for deepening within the Union but without the participation of all of them. Given the present trend of British policy, flexibility is not likely to be used as a way of circumventing British obstruction in Community affairs, but the principle is already in operation in the outstanding case of EMU. If British failure to adopt the euro lasts beyond, say, 2003, flexibility is likely to grow in significance, thus sharpening the difference between the majority of member states, including Germany, and a minority including Britain. But provided that Britain does participate fully in EMU, that is not likely to occur; and with this commitment behind them, the British are more likely to appreciate the need for deepening through institutional reform.

There are still fundamental differences between British and German attitudes to reform of the Union's institutions. The conviction remains among the German political class that the Union should continue its progress towards federal institutions, with the citizens' representatives in the European Parliament sharing power on a basis of equality with the states' representatives in the Council, who should increasingly adopt majority voting. In Britain, while most accept the necessity of the Commission, Court, and Parliament, the preference is for predominance of the member states' governments and for the principle of unanimity to retain its importance in the Council.

In his address to the European Parliament in January 1999, Joschka Fischer affirmed that the need for institutional reform was becoming urgent, to enable the Union to 'avoid institutional collapse' in the context of enlargement and to 'maintain its ability to act with twenty one or more members'. The key to this would be the Union's 'willingness to accept majority decisions in as many areas as possible'; unanimity should remain over the longer term only for questions such as treaty amendment. It would also be necessary to strengthen the Union's democratic character by according co-decision rights to the Parliament in all areas where the Council can adopt laws by majority voting, which already applies to the bulk of the Union's legislation. It was interesting, in view of the part that the Parliament was soon to play in securing the Commission's resignation in March 1999, that he suggested a greater role for it in the election of the Commission than had been prescribed in the Treaty of Amsterdam. He also proposed that the Union draft a charter of fundamental rights and mentioned favourably the idea of 'a European Constitution'. Progress in such directions should be made in the forthcoming IGC which he expected to be held 'around the year 2001'.[70] While Chancellor Schröder is doubtless less committed to such views than his predecessor, this remains the German policy. It reflects the predominant

[70] Statement by Joschka Fischer, 12/1/1999, 5–6.

view of Germany's political class and there is no reason to suppose that it will be reversed.

Britain has, to the contrary, preferred a minimalist agenda for the IGC, focused on the number of Commissioners and the weighting of votes in the Council. British policy on these is likely to be similar to that of Germany. But although the Labour Party Conference in 1997 came close in some respects to the German proposals subsequently enunciated by Fischer, the Labour government has distanced itself from them. Blair has stressed instead the importance of the veto and of preventing the extension of majority voting into areas where it 'might cause damage'; and he has not been sympathetic to proposals for extending co-decision. Following the resignation of the Commission, indeed, in which the European Parliament played the decisive part, he emphasized the role of member states, their governments, and the Council in controlling the Commission at the expense of the role of the Parliament.[71]

While British Eurosceptics tend to regard the difference between Britain and Germany about federal developments in the Union's institutions as fundamental, pro-Europeans such as the Labour government tend to minimize their significance. In this respect the Eurosceptics may be closer to the mark. Fischer expressed the mainstream German view that a large extension of majority voting in the Council and a full right of co-decision for the Parliament will be essential if the eastern enlargement is to produce a successful and democratic Union; and there is profound conviction that its success is essential for both German and European security. Continued British opposition to these institutional reforms will be problematic for relations between the two countries even if the Labour government is less intransigent than its Conservative predecessor. The remaining disergence may be due at least in part to Blair's gradual approach to turning public opinion round. But it may also reflect a more fundamental difference as to the proper relationship between the member states and the European Union. In so far as that difference carries the greater weight, the convergence between British and German policies which impinge on enlargement will continue to lack an essential element. But it can at least reasonably be hoped that, just as the change of government in Germany has removed a source of friction over the common agricultural policy, so the change of government in Britain will eventually come to reduce the potential for conflict over institutional reform, so that convergence can advance far enough to ensure a happy ending to this sometimes strange, and always eventful, history.

---

[71] *House of Commons, Parliamentary Debates*, 18/6/1997, 313–14; and 16/3/1999, 891–2 and 897.

7

The American Dimension: Britain, Germany, and the Reinforcement of US Hegemony in Europe in the 1990s

VALUR INGIMUNDARSON

When Henry Luce, the publisher of *Time-Life*, proclaimed the dawning of the American Century in 1941, he did not only foresee the defeat of Germany and Japan in World War II but also the political and economic predominance of the United States in the post-war period. True, his characterization lost much of its glow and force in the 1970s and 1980s, when the United States witnessed the erosion of its political credibility due to the Vietnam War and its competitive advantage in many economic areas at the expense of Japan and Germany. But with the millennium approaching, it is impossible to deny that the United States has consolidated its global leadership position. Dire prognoses of US decline—some sort of 'imperial overstretch'[1]—and a retreat into isolation have been silenced by a rejuvenated economy and vigorous and, at times, aggressive diplomacy.

This development was by no means apparent in 1990–1. Apart from the Gulf War, the United States was a reluctant world power, and the economic recession at home spurred calls for introspection and a domestic agenda. The Bush Administration certainly played a key role in German reunification, but it did not want to become engaged in the Yugoslav crisis or to end the strategic uncertainty following the collapse of communism in Eastern Europe. The Americans were, in other words, slow to spell out their precise role in a European post-cold war setting. Towards the end of the 1990s the picture was much clearer: the United States had not only reaffirmed its status as an economic superpower but has also reinforced its political and military hegemony in Europe.

It will be argued here that the interplay between the United States, on the one hand, and Britain and Germany, on the other, played a decisive role in shaping developments regarding European integration in the 1990s. In the absence of cold war certainties, the process itself was highly

---

[1] This is the thesis of P. Kennedy's book *The Rise and Fall of Great Powers: Economic Change and Military Conflict from 1500 to 2000* (New York, 1987).

volatile. But what ultimately mattered was that the British and Germans agreed on the need to maintain a strong US presence in Europe despite the lack of a Soviet threat. The purpose of this chapter is to show how this was achieved by examining four developments: the European integration process; the debate over a distinct European defence identity; the Yugoslav crisis; and NATO's eastern expansion.

A comparison of the foreign policies of Britain and Germany since German reunification in 1990 reveals three strands: first, one detects a strong sense of continuity, with the collapse of the Soviet Bloc having no major impact on the direction of either state. Second, the British and the Germans still hold conflicting visions regarding European integration, even if the Labour government has taken a far more constructive view of it than its Conservative predecessor. Among the EU states, Germany has consistently been the most enthusiastic supporter of closer political and economic union. Britain, on the other hand, has expressed scepticism of political integration and stressed the economic rationale for European co-operation. Third, both governments view the relationship with the United States as the vital component of their respective foreign policies.

Conversely, Britain and Germany have remained the most loyal partners of the United States in Europe in the post-cold war period, even if they have had genuine differences over some issues, such as the war in Bosnia. The Americans see both states as advocates of more economic liberalization and deregulation within the European Union. Apart from being the largest European trade and investment partner of the United States, Britain has always enjoyed the benefits from its 'special relationship'. The US–German relationship lacks this cultural intimacy for historical and cultural–linguistic reasons. But, since World War II, Germany has occupied a primary role in US foreign policy, with the bulk of American military forces in Europe stationed on German soil. Germany cannot support the United States as strongly as Britain on many foreign policy issues because of its political commitment to France. These twin foreign policy pillars are considered equally important. But, mindful that among their allies the Unites States was by far the most supportive of German unification, the Germans have been fully committed to the transatlantic relationship in the post-cold war era.

Indeed, despite their membership in the European Union, Britain and Germany have closer relations with the United States than with each other. For one thing, there has always been a strong anti-German bias in British politics due to Germany's wartime role. Influential British historians such as A. J. P. Taylor continued well into the post-war period to promote the theory that the division of Germany was 'the kindest policy toward the Germans themselves'. A reunited Germany would either 'resume the march towards European domination' or its power would be 'compulsorily reduced by foreign interference, if the wartime allies had the sense to come together again in time'.[2] This view was widely shared within the British establishment, even if cold war prerogatives prevented it from being disseminated freely. A. J. P. Taylor changed his mind and abandoned his efforts to portray German history as an unbroken line from Luther to Hitler. Still, in 1989 it became clear that notions of a specifically German national character were by no means dead within Britain; on the contrary, they were circulating at the top of the British government. Prime Minister Margaret Thatcher could not hide her dissatisfaction, when German Chancellor Helmut Kohl presented his ten-point plan for German reunification following the fall of the Berlin Wall. Her relationship with Helmut Kohl had, of course, neither been close nor cordial, and by raising the spectre of a German nationalist revival and future hegemonic aspirations in Europe, she enlisted the support of French President François Mitterrand—albeit for a short time—in her efforts to resist West Germany's absorption of a defunct East Germany. Playing on nationalist sentiments and, no less important, historical memory, the anti-German British press did not fail to do its share. In early 1990, an astounding number of Britons, in fact 53 per cent, feared the recurrence of fascism in Germany. Indeed, support for German reunification was far lower in Britain than in the United States or France, even though the percentage of those in favour was substantially higher than of those opposing it.[3]

Although the French backed away from their initial opposition to German reunification, they were, like the British, fearful of a German-dominated Europe. The Americans acted, in fact, as if they had already drawn that conclusion six months before the collapse of East Germany, when George Bush offered West Germany the famous 'partnership in leadership' status. But after the revolutionary events of 1989, Kohl sought to calm British and French worries. The Maastricht Treaty of 1991—with its provisions for a common foreign policy, the abolition of internal borders, a common currency, and universal social provisions—was, as for example Hans-Peter Schwarz has argued, a *quid pro quo* arrangement by which Germany could attain the assent of Britain and France to German reunification.[4]

The French wanted to prevent the creation of a duopoly in Europe based on US political and military hegemony and German economic

[2] A. J. P. Taylor, *The Course of German History*, rev. edn. (New York, 1962), 9–10.

[3] R. Davy, 'Großbritannien und die Deutsche Frage', *Europa-Archiv* 45/4 (1990), 140. See also the article by Lothar Kettenacker in this book.

[4] H.-P. Schwarz, 'Germany's National and European Interests', *Daedalus* 123/2 (1994), 84 (also reprinted in A. Baring (ed.), *Germany's New Position in Europe: Problems and Perspectives* (Oxford, 1994), 107–30.); see also J. Brechtefeld, 'Europe's Double Transformation Crisis', *International Relations* 13/4 (1997), 36. On the Maastricht Treaty, see also below, Ch. 13.

predominance.[5] In 1990 there were, indeed, fears of a German *Sonderweg*, the rekindling of a Bismarckian *Realpolitik* or 'Rapallo' with Germany assuming the role of the arbiter between East and West and playing them off against each other at will. As if to belabour the point, the French are fond of quoting the dictum of Thomas Mann: 'We want a European Germany but not a German Europe.'[6] These worries proved to be grossly exaggerated. German unification under Kohl in 1990 had very little in common with that under Bismarck in 1871. There were no border disputes, no wars, and Germany's most important allies accepted it, albeit without any enthusiasm. When Soviet President Michael Gorbachev acquiesced to President Bush's and Helmut Kohl's pressure for Germany's accession to NATO, the remaining obstacles were removed. To be sure, the British and the French were almost as unhappy as the Soviets at the prospect of German reunification. But although they assumed a central role as occupying powers, they exercised no initiative during the debate over German reunification. They were, as Tony Judt put it, 'cast aside when their usefulness had expired'.[7] The two-plus-four negotiations were conducted in an atmosphere of cordiality, and the Germans worked very well with the British—who had come around to the US position—and the Americans to ensure a mutually acceptable framework for Germany's entry into NATO.[8]

THE AMBIVALENCE OF US SUPPORT FOR EUROPEAN INTEGRATION

While the Maastricht Treaty was a device to Europeanize a reunited Germany, it is mistaken to view it solely in terms of a price paid by the Kohl Government. It reflected a historical vision pursued by German leaders since Konrad Adenauer aimed at achieving political rehabilitation abroad and economic prosperity at home. A unified Germany has shown no appetite for assuming a hegemonic role in Europe.[9] Its contribution to the Gulf War was solely in the form of money, and its military

[5] W. Woyke, 'Außenpolitische Kontinuität—aber auch Veränderungen. Fünf Jahre deutsche Außenpolitik', in R. Altenhof and E. Jesse (eds.), *Das wiedervereinigte Deutschland. Zwischenbilanz und Perspektiven* (Munich, 1995), 373–5.

[6] D. Vernet, 'Europäisches Deutschland oder deutsches Europa?' *Internationale Politik* 52/2 (Feb. 1997), 15. See also K. Larres, 'Germany and the West: The "Rapallo Factor" in German Foreign Policy from the 1950s to the 1990s', in K. Larres and P. Panayi (eds.), *The Federal Republic of Germany since 1949: Politics, Society and Economy before and after Unification* (London, 1996), 278–326.　　[7] T. Judt, 'New Germany, Old NATO', *New York Review of Books*, 29/5/1997.

[8] For the American involvement in German reunification, see P. Zelikow and C. Rice, *Germany Unified and Europe Transformed: A Study in Statecraft* (Cambridge, Mass., and London, 1995).

[9] M. C. Brands, 'Überforderung durch Machtzunahme. Deutschland als integrierende oder zentrifugale Kraft', *Internationale Politik* 52/2 (1997), 34.

presence in Bosnia has been modest. To be sure, Germany's full participation in NATO's air strikes in the Kosovo crisis in 1999 represented a major break with the past. That this was done under a Red–Green coalition government is, of course, all the more remarkable. But the purpose was not to stake out a European leadership position. Germany wanted to prove itself a loyal member of NATO as part of a humanitarian mission to prevent the horrors of Bosnia from happening in Kosovo. This is not to deny that German reunification represented a real redistribution of powers within the European system. Germany regained some of its pre-World War II size and reclaimed its predominant economic position in Central and Eastern Europe.[10] But with the sole exception of the recognition of Croatia and Slovenia, its foreign policy has not been marked by any unilateralist tendencies.

For the British, like the French, one of the main benefits of the Maastricht Treaty was Germany's commitment to multilateralism. But as a blueprint for Europe, it represented the direct opposite of what the British had envisioned.[11] Margaret Thatcher and other European leaders clearly underestimated the degree to which the adoption of the Single Market Programme in 1985 would act as a catalyst for political integration.[12] That the Maastricht Treaty echoed a Franco-German agenda, not a British one, was clear from the beginning. It was precisely for this reason that Prime Minister John Major insisted on opt-out clauses. But when the Maastricht Treaty was concluded, Germany's vision of a supranational Europe seemed to be prevailing. Britain frequently saw itself isolated within Europe as a result of the Franco-German axis. This trend reached its climax in September 1992 when Britain was forced to devalue the pound and to withdraw from the European Exchange Rate Mechanism (ERM).[13]

The United States had traditionally supported the European integration process. Indeed, during the late 1940s and 1950s, it did so with considerably more fervour than the Europeans themselves.[14] From the mid-1960s on, however, US governments became more selective in its policies toward Europe. Charles De Gaulle's challenge to what has been dubbed an Atlantic framework as expressed in US political and economic hegemony was partly responsible for this shift. The decline of US economic

---

[10] See M. N. Hampton, 'Institutions and Learning: Explaining Incremental German Foreign Policy Innovation', *European Security* 5/4 (Winter 1996), 552–3; see also R. Niblett, 'Disunion: Competing Visions of Integration', *The Washington Quarterly* 20/1 (1996), 93–5.

[11] See G. Brock, 'Geht von Deutschland eine Bedrohung aus?', *Internationale Politik* 52/2 (1997), 24–5.

[12] R. Niblett, 'Disunion: Competing Visions of Integration', 96–9; see also M. Calingaert, *European Integration Revisited: Progress, Prospects, and US Interests* (Boulder, Colo., 1996), 19–20.   [13] See also Ch. 11.

[14] Geir Lundestad, *'Empire' by Integration: The United States and European Integration, 1945–1997* (Oxford and New York, 1998), 42.

supremacy and France's questioning of American predominance in NATO forced the Americans to rethink their unreserved backing of European integration schemes. And in the 1970s, the Americans largely ignored the slow progress toward political and economic union.[15] During the 1980s, the United States was sceptical of several pan-European initiatives and was intent on countering any dilution of its hegemonic military role in NATO. As Geir Lundestad has argued, the Reagan Administration feared the economic and political consequences of Europe's push toward the Single Market. Indeed, it was less supportive of the European integration process than any previous or later administrations.[16] The Bush Administration adopted a more positive stance, but in 1990–1, it had little to offer the Europeans. The perception of economic decline due to chronic budget deficits, wage stagnation, and social problems had severely discredited the Anglo-Saxon model. Other countries looked to the 'social market economies' of Germany and Japan for guidance. True, the United States managed to reassert itself as the only military superpower in the Gulf War, but its weakness as an economic superpower had been exposed, when it pressured Germany and Japan to pay for a substantial part of the costs involved. And while the Bush Administration saw the obvious merit in anchoring a reunited Germany in a European framework and successfully negotiated compromises with the European Community on trade disputes, it did not have a say in shaping the European integration agenda.

Germany, in contrast, was showing increasing self-confidence in the wake of unification. In 1991, it played a large role in concluding the Maastricht Treaty, paving the way for closer European integration. It forced the EC to recognize Croatia and Slovenia despite serious misgivings abroad. And together with Mitterrand, Chancellor Kohl proposed an independent defence capability under future EU jurisdiction. Germany seemed to be intent on setting a fairly ambitious foreign policy agenda within a European framework together with France—and, significantly, without Britain. There was one problem, however: it was not clear where the United States with its status as a quasi-European power would fit into this picture.

Since the 1950s, the main thrust of Germany's foreign policy had been directed toward balancing pro-French and pro-American perspectives. The close relationship with the French has in the last few decades enjoyed much popular support. Similarly, a clear majority of Germans have consistently ranked the close relations with the US favourably, even

---

[15] Ibid. 154; also K. Larres, 'Torn between Idealism and Egotism: The United States and European Integration, 1945–1990', *Irish Journal of American Studies* 8 (1999).

[16] Lundestad, *'Empire' by Integration*, 168; Larres, 'Torn between Idealism and Egotism'.

during periods of intensive anti-American sentiment.[17] In 1991–2, the question arose whether Germany was moving too close to France at the expense of the United States—whether the delicate balance between the twin pillars of its foreign policy was being upset. The Americans were surely less than enthusiastic about some aspects of the Franco-German agenda. The Reagan and Bush Administrations were, for example, initially sceptical of the Single Market and questioned the prospects of its success. From the point of view of US–European relations, it counted on a system of bilateral treaties. The Americans only gave this initiative conditional support, although it was clearly consistent with their goal of promoting closer European integration.

In the end, however, the United States[18] put aside lingering suspicions about a Fortress Europe, when it became convinced that the Single Market would not be 'free on the inside, protectionist on the outside'.[19] It is true that trade friction between the United States and Europe over agriculture and other issues is far from being resolved, and a serious transatlantic rift over unilateralist US trade policies, especially the Helms –Burton laws, was only narrowly averted. But the 1995 New Transatlantic Agenda arrangement on US–EU co-operation in many areas will probably lessen the intensity of future disputes. The British and German commitment to trade liberalization—one of America's economic priorities —was of major significance in the development of the structure of the Single Market. And since the European Union remains its largest trade and investment partner, this outcome was, of course, extremely beneficial to the United States. In a farewell address in 1996 as US representative to the EU, Stuart E. Eizenstat could claim with obvious satisfaction that the 'EU is far more open to US and foreign business today than a decade ago'.[20]

Another issue was also resolved to the liking of the United States with the firm support of the British: namely, the German–French idea of a distinctively European Security and Defence identity (ESDI). In October 1991, Kohl and Mitterrand suggested the creation of a Franco-German corps—an embryonic Western European army. The purpose was to form an 'organic' relationship between the Western European Union (WEU) and the soon-to-be formed EU. The Bush Administration was not at all pleased with what became later known as the Eurocorps, fearing that it

---

[17] E. Noelle-Neumann, 'Öffentliche Meinung und Außenpolitik. Die fehlende Debatte in Deutschland', *Internationale Politik* 50/8 (Aug. 1995), 5.

[18] G. van Well, 'Die europäische Einigung und die USA', *Europa-Archiv* 46/18 (1991), 531–2; see also A. Falke, 'Veränderte amerikanische Einstellung zur EG. Der Binnenmarkt und die Gatt-Verhandlungen', *Europa-Archiv* 46/6 (1991), 192.

[19] S. E. Eizenstat, 'Farewell Remarks to the EU Committee of the American Chamber of Commerce', 8/2/1996, US Department of State, Internet Information [http://www.state_gov.useu].

[20] Ibid.

would undermine NATO and, by extension, Washington's predominant role in it. The proposal was, of course, perfectly consistent with the Maastricht Treaty, with its emphasis on closer European co-ordination. But other European nations, especially the British and the Dutch, did not want to have anything to do with it on the grounds that it competed with NATO. The WEU had been dormant for almost thirty years and its role within NATO had never been adequately defined.[21] To be sure, it had been reactivated by the Rome Declaration of October 1984, but it was only seen as being supportive of existing NATO obligations. Ever since the French vetoed the creation of the European Defence Community (EDC) in 1954, the UK has been sceptical of the viability of a European-based security and defence identity outside NATO. Germany was out of the picture, not only for historical reasons but also because of its total dependency on the United States militarily. France, on the other hand, seemed to place more emphasis on preserving its own independent nuclear capability than with sharing it with others. From the British perspective, NATO and American military might were the best solution to the problem of European defence.[22]

Still, it could be argued that the end of the cold war justified a reassessment of this policy. After all, the Franco-German push for a separate European defence organisation coincided with a reduction in the strength of US troops in Europe. But the British were only willing to let the WEU play a subordinate role to NATO and successfully headed off weak European attempts to elevate its status. They were able to do this because of their long-standing role as a leading player in NATO and due to their close relationship with the United States in the military field; a relationship that, after all, includes nuclear weapons collaboration and the sharing of intelligence information. The British Major Government was criticized by the German Government for taking a narrow view of the WEU's future and for an excessive fear of alienating the United States.[23] But the Americans had made it clear that they were sceptical of the formation of a separate European defence identity because it could weaken NATO. In that sense, the British position was closer to American thinking than the German. The British, however, were not only motivated by a desire to strengthen the transatlantic relationship; their position was also fully compatible with their minimalist vision of Europe. As it turned out, it prevailed: the Eurocorps numbering over 50,000 soldiers was integrated

[21] See Brechtefeld, 'Europe's Double Transformation Crisis', 36.

[22] See G. Wyn Rees, *The Western European Union at the Crossroads: Between Trans-Atlantic Solidarity and European Integration* (Boulder, Colo., 1998); A. Deighton, *Western European Union 1954–1997: Defence, Security, Integration* (Oxford, 1997); and below, Ch. 8.

[23] See G. Wyn Rees, 'Britain and the Western European Union', *European Security* 5/4 (Winter 1996), 530–2; also P. H. Gordon, 'Does the WEU Have A Role?', *The Washington Quarterly* 20/1 (Winter 1996), 125–40.

into NATO. The Anglo-French air command and the Mediterranean rapid reaction force are also evidence of the fairly small steps taken toward closer European co-operation on defence.[24] However, the Americans succeeded with their desire that the EU would not be given a fully independent role in European defence matters. In late 1998, during the Vienna EU summit and particularly in the course of bilateral Anglo-French discussions there were some indications regarding a strengthening of the EU's defence re-sponsibilities. The decision of the Blair government to reopen the Euro-pean defence debate in 1998 partly served the purpose of bringing home the point that the inability of the Europeans to do anything in Kosovo without calling on the Americans undermined Europe's credibility in foreign affairs. The Franco-British agreement at St Malo on 3 December 1998 underscored this commitment. Although this was just a small step towards the construction of a true European defence identity, the Kosovo crisis accelerated this trend.[25] The Europeans found themselves totally dependent on the American war effort. This should not have come as a surprise given the fact that the gulf between US and European defence spending has been widening since the end of the cold war. Yet, the pressure to strengthen the European pillar has increased after the disturbing experience in Kosovo.[26] It is intended to abolish the WEU in its present form and to use it as a structural basis for a new European Security Identity within the EU.

BOSNIA: EUROPEAN STUMBLING AND AN AMERICAN SHOW

The third issue which the Americans largely resolved on their own terms within the European context was the war in Bosnia. The Dayton Accords of 1995 reasserted US hegemonic role in Europe and dashed any Maastricht hopes of an independent foreign policy. It also provided a test case for the conflicting approaches of Britain and its Franco-German allies toward a separate European defence identity.[27] When the Yugoslavian crisis unfolded in 1991, to the surprise of many it was Germany that took the lead by calling for the participation of the EU, the Conference on Security and Co-operation in Europe (CSCE), and the WEU to find a peaceful settlement. Bonn was also instrumental in pressuring the EU

---

[24] Niblett, 'Disunion: Competing Visions of Integration', 94–5.

[25] See e.g. *Financial Times*, 29–30/5/1999.

[26] On the prelude to the Kosovo crisis, see e.g. T. Judah, 'Kosovo's Road to War', *Survival* 41/2 (1999), 5–18; Mark Danner, 'Endgame in Kosovo', *The New York Review of Books*, 6/5/1999. See also T. Judah, *The Serbs: History, Myths, and the Destruction of Yugoslavia* (New Haven, 1997). See also below, Ch. 8.

[27] See Rees, 'Britain and the Western European Union', 530–2.

into recognizing the independence of Croatia and Slovenia during the summer of 1991.[28]

The United States, which had opposed the break-up of Yugoslavia, was harshly critical of this action. But, although the Germans and the EU could certainly be faulted for failing to extract anything in return for the recognition of Croatia and Slovenia,[29] the United States was hardly in a position to lecture other countries about the Balkan conflict. It had chosen to abdicate leadership in the early stages of the war, despite Yugoslavia having played an important role in America's cold war strategy in Europe. The much-quoted comment by Secretary of State, James Baker, that 'We got no dog in this fight' captured the essence of the passive role of the Bush Administration during the first 18 months of the war.[30] The unexpectedly easy military triumph in the Gulf War did little to change that perception. There was simply no interest in risking the political rewards of the Gulf victory by projecting American power into the Balkans. It was also an indication that the United States would act differently in a post-cold war setting and adopt a selective strategy with respect to conflict areas.

This is not to say that the Europeans acted more wisely. In 1990, the Americans, at least, tried to convince the Europeans about the need to consider the Yugoslav crisis at NATO and CSCE meetings, but met with no success. The Germans and the British warned the Americans not to overreach, and, on a less diplomatic note, the French accused them of 'overdramatizing' the situation. What followed was, of course, an unmitigated disaster: the break-up of Yugoslavia in 1991 and savage wars in the Balkans.[31] But it was only after four and a half years of fighting, leaving about two hundred thousand dead and breeding three million refugees, that the United States became directly involved in the Yugoslav conflict.

It has been argued that the Americans could have halted the war in Croatia in the autumn of 1991, 'the autumn of sieges', with relatively minor costs and prevented the outbreak of the Bosnian war in 1992. Although only a few months earlier Bush had declared that the 'Vietnam syndrome' was 'buried once and for all', the Americans believed that a credible threat of force could send the United States down a slippery slope of full engagement without domestic support.[32] Thus in 1991, the Americans passed the responsibility for Yugoslavia to the Europeans. In the euphoric

---

[28] See S. Lefebvre and B. Lombardi, 'Germany and Peace Enforcement: Participating in IFOR', *European Security* 5/4 (Winter 1996), 564–5.

[29] See S. L. Woodward, *Balkan Tragedy: Chaos and Dissolution after the cold war* (Washington, DC, 1995), 395–6.

[30] Quoted in M. Danner: 'The US and the Yugoslav Catastrophe', *The New York Review of Books*, 20/11/1997.

[31] See e.g. D. Rohde, *Endgame: The Betrayal and Fall of Srebrenica, Europe's Worst Massacre since World War II* (New York, 1997); N. Cigar, *Genocide in Bosnia: The Policy of Ethnic Cleansing* (Austin, 1995).

[32] See Danner, 'The US and the Yugoslav Catastrophe'.

days after Maastricht, the Europeans accepted this role with an odd sense
of enthusiasm. Brimming with self-confidence, Foreign Minister Jacques Poos
of Luxemburg declared—in words surely destined to outlive himself as
Mark Danner has pointed out—that this would be 'the Hour of Europe'.
But by handing the problem to the European Community, which had no
collective defence arm, instead of NATO, the Americans had, as Danner
put it, 'ensured that no forceful action could be threatened'.[33]

For this reason, US criticism of the Germans for pressing for the
recognition of Slovenia and Croatia lacked credibility. The German
action was premature, although it only confirmed political realities in the
former Yugoslavia. But if the Balkan conflict had been a priority for
the Americans, they could have exerted pressure on the Germans to
abandon or, at least, postpone the recognition of Slovenia and Croatia.
They had done so many times before and they had usually prevailed.
However, the Bush Administration never considered the Yugoslav conflict a matter of US vital interest. The Clinton Administration initially
continued this policy despite its rhetoric to the contrary. The Bosnian
war was not deemed to justify the risk of soldiers' lives but to warrant
diplomatic attention.[34] Yet when a somewhat more realistic proposal
emerged, the Vance–Owen plan, which foresaw the division of Bosnia into
ten ethnically controlled cantons for the Serbs, Croats, and Muslims, the
Americans, in effect, rejected it.

The differences between the United States and the European Union,
including the British and the Germans, over the response to the conflict
in 1993–4 only deepened the paralysis. During the continued squabbling
over the Vance–Owen plan, the imposition of a no-fly zone, and the
tightening of sanctions, the Americans produced one proposal to solve
the Bosnian conflict: the 'lift and strike' option. But the demand for
lifting the Bosnian arms embargo and for allowing for NATO air strikes
if the Serbs did not stop their aggression fell on deaf ears. To the Europeans, Clinton's rhetoric had accomplished nothing except to convince
the Bosnian leaders that the Americans would intervene on their behalf.
That the British and French were faced with real problems was unques-
tionable: in the case of Serbian intervention, they were concerned about
the safety of their own troops taking part in the United Nations peacekeeping mission (UNPROFOR) in Bosnia. Germany fully supported
the position of France and Britain to strengthen the UN presence in
Bosnia in 1995 and publicly opposed the American push for arming the
Bosnians.[35] It was unrealistic for the Americans to expect the Europeans
to go along with 'a lift and strike' policy while ruling out the option of
contributing troops of their own. But the British and French refusal to

---

[33] Ibid.   [34] Woodward, *Balkan Tragedy*, 397.
[35] See Lefebvre and Lombardi, 'Germany and Peace Enforcement: Participating in IFOR',
564–5.

see the conflict in Bosnia as a result of Serbian aggression certainly did not make things easier. In his account of his mediating role in the Balkan conflict, David Owen is very critical of the Clinton Administration for its support of the Bosnians in 1993–4.[36] But his tendency to blame the war on all factions in Bosnia and his reluctance to single out the Serbs as the most active aggressor undermines his case. The Germans, at least, stood with the Americans on the issue of Serbian war guilt, even if they opposed the arming of the Bosnian Muslims. What was ultimately needed to break the US–European stalemate in 1995 was the fall of UN-declared safe havens, such as Srebrenica, and the Marketplace Massacre in Sarajevo. These savage acts paved the way for direct US involvement and later to the Dayton Accords brokered by the chief American mediator, Richard Holbrooke.[37]

The criticism of the German decision to sanction the break-up of Yugoslavia by pushing for Croatian and Slovenian independence sapped the diplomatic strength of the Kohl Government. But its proposal to create the Contact Group in 1994, comprising the United States, France, Britain, Germany, and Russia, mitigated serious policy differences on Bosnia. Nor should one belittle the historic decision in 1995 to participate in NATO military support for the redeployment of UNPROFOR to more defensible locations in Bosnia. This was followed by the approval of the *Bundestag* to assign roughly 1,500 German troops to protect and support the UN Rapid Reaction Force (RRF), marking the first time that Germany has assigned combat units to a UN mission. Soon German fighter-bombers flew their first combat mission since World War II, taking reconnaissance photos over Bosnia. And in the wake of the Dayton Accords, Kohl decided to contribute a 4,000-strong military contingent to the NATO-led Implementation Force (IFOR) and later 3,000 troops, including for the first time armoured infantry units, as part of the Stabilization Force (SFOR). These measures were not commensurate with Germany's status as the third largest economic power in the world, but given the historical memories conjured up in the Balkans about German atrocities during World War II and about Nazi collaboration, it was a very difficult decision. The Kohl Government managed to reach a political consensus about sending German troops abroad, a task that no previous German government had achieved.

After taking the side of the French during the critical period before Dayton, the Germans were quite satisfied with letting the United States take the lead in the former Yugoslavia. US sponsorship of the peace

---

[36] See D. Owen, *Balkan Odyssey: An Uncompromising Personal Account of the International Peace Efforts Following the Breakup of the Former Yugoslavia* (New York, 1995), 106.

[37] See M. Danner, 'America and the Bosnian Genocide', *The New York Review of Books*, 4/12/1997. For Holbrooke's interpretation of the events leading to the Dayton accords see his *To End a War* (New York, 1998).

process has also alleviated much German concern about the unwillingness and inability of the Clinton Administration to play a global leadership role. Having abandoned their efforts to create a separate European identity, the Germans fully supported the NATO mission in Bosnia. Indeed, the Kohl Government came to see the Bosnian crisis as a way for NATO to reassert is relevance.[38] But it was also, of course, an admission of its own failure. The Germans, like the other Europeans, had originally seen the Yugoslav crisis as a European issue despite widespread reluctance to become militarily involved. The Balkan wars effectively buried half-baked ideas of making the WEU a major defence player. Prior to the spread of the war to Bosnia, the British had successfully prevented the adoption of a French proposal for WEU intervention. But it was only after much timidity that the British Major Government supported the NATO decision to use force against the Bosnian Serbs, in the summer of 1995, when they were violating the UN-declared Safe Areas.[39] By this time, the United States was spearheading the efforts to reach a Balkan settlement, and the British like the Germans fully supported Americans leadership on this issue. Thus the net result was the same: both Germany and Britain assumed their respective roles as junior partners in the American scheme of things. At the same time, the Bosnian experience had reinforced a powerful perception of a European dependency on the United States.[40] The Kosovo crisis had the same effect in a military sense. The Americans were in total command from the beginning, contributing the bulk of the war planes for the air attacks against the Yugoslav Federation. But given the many mistakes NATO committed in the conflict, the Americans have paid a political price. In contrast to the Bosnian experience, which seemed to vindicate US military strategy, the air campaign against the Yugoslav Federation was deeply flawed. What prolonged the war was the assymetrical and confusing nature of the military operations and the reluctance to consider the option of introducing ground troops; there was great concern to keep Western military casualties at an absolute minimum.

THE UNITED STATES AND THE PROCESS OF NATO EXPANSION

The question of NATO expansion was another example of how the United States determined the terms of the outcome at the expense of the

---

[38] See Lefebvre and Lombardi, 'Germany and Peace Enforcement: Participating in IFOR', 582.

[39] For the Major government's policy in the former Yugoslavia, see e.g. A. Seldon, *Major: a political life* (London, 1997), 303 ff., esp. 558–60, 592–4; and J. Major, *The Autobiography* (London, 1999). [40] See Rees, 'Britain and the Western European Union', 533–4.

Europeans. As with other major issues confronting the United States after the cold war, the Americans were slow to act. The Bush Administration effectively put off any decision on the question of inviting former Warsaw Pact members to join NATO. The Clinton Administration was also hesitant in the beginning. The Germans tend to credit Volker Rühe, the Minister of Defence, with influencing the evolution of American policy. In a widely noted speech in 1993, he publicly called for NATO expansion, with special priority given to Poland. But while Rühe managed to keep the issue alive, the Clinton Administration's policy was probably more driven by domestic political pressures than by a commitment to what Peter Rudolf has termed a mixture of 'neo-Wilsonian ambitions with residual realpolitik about European stability'.[41] At first, the Clinton Administration adopted an incremental approach, not least because of a lack of consensus in Washington. For realists in the geopolitical tradition, the strategic vacuum in East Central Europe had to be filled by NATO. Otherwise Germany or Russia might be forced to step in, with the consequences of a dangerous German–Russian rivalry. Critics of enlargement, however, believed that it would have a very negative impact on American–Russian co-operation, especially denuclearization, and divide the western alliance in the absence of a Soviet strategic threat. Echoing a unilateralist strand within the United States, some even supported American disengagement on the grounds that the time had come for the Europeans to take care of their own defence.

Straddling the issue, the Clinton Administration pursued a middle course with its Partnership for Peace proposal. Although NATO adopted it in January 1994,[42] it received decidedly mixed reviews. In line with the Kohl Government's push for European integration, the Germans had hoped to link early NATO expansion to that of the EU. This proposition was meant to be reassuring for Germany's neighbours, meaning that Germany with or without Russia had no intention of filling the geopolitical vacuum created in Central and Eastern Europe by the collapse of the Soviet Union. In the United States, the Partnership for Peace was also sharply criticized for its ambiguity both within the strategic community and by influential Republican Congressmen. To cap it all, the Clinton Administration was feeling much pressure from Polish-Americans to allow for Polish accession to NATO.

It was largely due to these domestic developments that the Clinton Administration decided to take the plunge: in January 1994, Clinton declared during a visit to Prague that NATO's enlargement to the east was inevitable. It would help to consolidate new democracies and

---

[41] P. Rudolf, 'The Future of the United States as a European Power: The Case of NATO Enlargement', *European Security* 5/2 (Summer 1996), 175–8.   [42] Ibid.

prevent new great power rivalries in Europe. As it turned out, other NATO members were less enthusiastic than the Americans and the Germans. The French warned of 'premature expansion' and the British expressed caution. One reason may have been a desire on the part of the French and British not to cede too much influence to the Germans in East Central Europe. They did not want, however, to stand in the way of NATO expansion, accepting the momentum of the process. When the Germans sensed that there was resistance to enlargement, especially from Russia, they began to retreat. In the fall of 1994, they reacted to American pressure for enlargement by pointing to the need for a parallel EU expansion. The argument itself was valid: the best way to consolidate the democratic gains in East Central Europe was undoubtedly to integrate them economically into the European Union. However, the EU had no desire to do so: from the Maastricht project for monetary union to the more recent Schengen Accords, facilitating movements within the EU, the member countries have been erecting barriers and imposing conditions for the East Central Europeans.[43]

When the Germans finally agreed to decouple the two integration processes, they insisted that no candidates for early NATO membership should be singled out. Kohl did not want to involve the Baltic states in the process out of fear that it would alienate Russian President Boris Yeltsin. The Americans went along with that, since they believed that only three East Central European nations were really qualified for early membership: Poland, the Czech Republic, and Hungary. Madeleine Albright, who, after serving as US representative to the UN, assumed the position of Secretary of State in 1997, had played an important role in pushing the NATO enlargement issue for political as well as personal reasons (her Czech ancestry). After putting NATO expansion on the top of the political agenda in 1996, the Clinton Administration, finally, managed to get Yeltsin's acquiescence at the Portugal summit in the spring of 1997. By then, the United States was facing an awkward situation: it suddenly found itself advocating a slower process than the others by pressing for the admission of only three candidates. In Portugal, nine out of sixteen countries declared their support for including Slovenia and Rumania. Indeed, only Iceland—which does not even have its own army—initially supported the American idea of limiting the first new members to three. Germany and Britain kept their options open; however both appeared to be prepared to accept a compromise. The rest of the story is well known: during the Madrid Summit, the Americans pressured NATO to accept only the Poles, Czechs, and the Hungarians (who eventually joined in March 1999). The debate exposed serious differences over the role of the United

---

[43] See also Ch. 6 by John Pinder.

States as the world's sole remaining superpower and criticism of what was seen as growing American heavy-handedness. As was to be expected the British stood with the Americans in the dispute, but in addition to Iceland, only Norway and Denmark favoured the US position. Germany decided to support France, but characteristically it blinked first when faced with American pressure. As Dutch Foreign Minister Hans van Mierlo put it: 'The countries favouring five new members had to quickly face up to the reality that that was not possible, especially after Germany gave up the fight.'[44] In this case as in the others discussed here, the Germans and British proved to be reliable US allies, who facilitated the outcome favoured by the United States. Is it too early to speculate on NATO's eastern enlargement in the wake of the Kosovo crisis. At NATO's 50th anniversary summit at the end of April 1999, the alliance reaffirmed its commitment to the enlargement process. And the Americans, Germans, and British are certainly among the most pro-expansionist members of NATO. But it is far more likely that the alliance will adopt a wait-and-see attitude in light of the Kosovo experience. (See also Ch. 8 by Emil J. Hirchner)

CONCLUSION

The reinforcement of America's hegemony in Europe during the 1990s was not only due to a willingness to play a global leadership role in the post-cold war period after much initial hesitation and soul-searching following the collapse of communism. American ascendancy was also closely linked to the perceived failure of the European integration process in the security sphere. During this period, America's two most reliable allies in Europe, Britain and Germany, offered two competing visions of Europe. In 1990–1, Germany was setting the agenda in co-operation with the French. It had achieved political reunification without major foreign policy complications, and its economy was the envy of the world. Germany's victory in the World Cup in 1990 symbolized its new-found self-confidence. In contrast Britain was facing mounting economic difficulties and its Euro-scepticism was widely condemned by its EU partners.

Two factors changed all that. First, the problems associated with German unification—especially the large costs involved and high unemployment in the former East Germany—diverted Germany's attention from its ambitious European agenda. Second, the recession in Europe seriously dampened popular support and enthusiasm for further European integration.

---

[44] Statement by Hans Mierlo, Madrid, 8/7/1997: CNN, Internet Information [http://cnn.com/world].

While few subscribed to Britain's minimalist blueprint for Europe, there was a clear tendency to question the Franco-German maximalist version. As it turned out, Britain's withdrawal from the ERM proved to be a blessing in disguise. Whereas Germany's structural economic problems grew worse from 1993 to 1998, by 1996/97 the British had been the first European nation to come out of the recession with a relatively vibrant and competitive economy. The unemployment rate was also substantially below the average of 11 per cent across European Union.

European voters were looking to their national governments for recovery, but constrained by the stringent monetary policies pursued for the sake of monetary union, they could do little to spur economic growth. Another reason for public disenchantment with deeper European integration was and still is the lack of a clear definition of its end-point. During the cold war, West European integration was a sub-plot of the bipolar strategic stalemate.[45] The potential hegemonic power, Germany, was divided, although it was allowed to play a central if not overbearing role in Western European integration. Helmut Kohl had staked out his position on deeper European integration in no uncertain terms: it was a question of peace or war in Europe. John Major was quick to contradict this vision by maintaining that Europe had, in fact, abandoned the concept of its original founders and that the nation-state remained the legitimate focus of popular loyalty. In some respects, Tony Blair's European agenda differs from that of his predecessor. Britain has largely abandoned its obstructive behaviour in the European Union. While the Labour Party's emphasis is still on the economic benefits of European co-operation, it is now prepared to strengthen the European defence pillar within the EU without undermining US military hegemony in Europe.[46]

Buoyed by added economic strength, Britain's position vis-à-vis Europe is much stronger than it was in 1990. The Anglo-Saxon economic model has been resurrected.[47] Germany and, especially, Japan have ceased to function as the economic role models of the world. But the questions of further European political union, including European defence, have not been settled. It remains, for example, to be seen whether EMU will serve as a catalyst for further integration. As was the case with Maastricht, the outcome is bound to have an impact on the US role in Europe. True, the failure to develop a separate European defence identity, to end the war in Bosnia, to exercise leadership in the Kosovo crisis, and to have a say on NATO expansion is a testimony to Europe's weakness at the moment. That Germany's efforts to attain a permanent seat on the UN Security

[45] See Niblett, 'Disunion: Competing Visions of Integration', 93–5.
[46] Speech by Gordon Brown to the British–American Chamber of Commerce, New York, 5/12/1996: British Information Service, New York, Internet Information [http://www.britain-info.org].
[47] See also Ch. 9 by Jeremy Leaman.

Council have gone nowhere despite US support is an indication of the modest role still played in international affairs by the largest European economic power. But there is considerable unease about Washington's dominant role in Europe. Together with the successful launching of EMU in January 1999, any further growth of American influence could well galvanize the European integration movement. As usual, the French are unhappy about what they consider excessive US influence in Europe. The American refusal to give up NATO's Southern Command in return for France's return to NATO's military structure only reinforced French suspicions. During the NATO Maastricht meeting in October 1997 the French declared that they would not return to the fold under the existing circumstances. The French surely committed a diplomatic blunder by failing to ask for the reward before declaring their intention. But the Americans should have realized that the French would have to get something in return for reversing De Gaulle's historic decision to pull France out of the military structure of NATO in 1966. The Europeans, including the Germans, the British, and the French were also united in rejecting American cost estimates of NATO expansion.[48] But despite futile efforts to develop a separate European defence identity, the French have been more willing to expand their co-operation with NATO during this decade. And as the St Malo initiative and the Kosovo experience suggest, the Europeans intend to increase their capability of acting independently of Americans in potentially minor regional conflicts in Europe.

The British, and the Germans have shown no inclinations for experiments in defence matters. The close chemistry between Kohl and Clinton was a source of stability, even if the US–German relationship was not as strong on lower diplomatic levels. There is nothing to suggest that there will be a fundamental change in German foreign policy as a result of the defeat of Kohl in the 1998 parliamentary elections and the formation of a Social Democratic–Green coalition government. Both Chancellor Gerhard Schröder and his Foreign Minister Joschka Fischer have pursued continuity in Germany's foreign policy. Germany's full participation in the military intervention in Kosovo was a clear example of that. The Germans will support a strong US military presence in Europe as long as no European defence structure exists. As a German newspaper observed after the Maastricht meeting: 'It is true that the [construction] of Europe can be achieved only with France, but security only together with the United States.'[49] Despite recent British–French steps towards more military co-operation and the formation of a joint force capable of acting independently of the United States, the British Labour Government does not

---

[48] *The Financial Times*, 15/10/1997. For US cost estimates, see e.g. *The Washington Post*, 3/10/1997.   [49] *Tagesspiegel*, 10/10/1997.

want a new European security mechanism to serve as a vehicle to strengthen the EU at the expense of NATO. Despite the frosty relationship between Major and Clinton due to the efforts of the Conservative Party to intervene on behalf of the Republican Party in the 1992 presidential elections, it did not affect the close relations between the Americans and British on issues of mutual interests. Indeed, the Anglo-American 'special relationship' has been rejuvenated by the personal relationship between Clinton and Blair since the latter's election victory in May 1997. But the Germans and British know that their security policies hinge above all on one premise: on the continued willingness of the United States to act as a 'benign hegemon' in Europe. As we have seen, European divisions and distrust in the post-cold war period have only perpetuated US predominance. And yet, it raises the question of whether the EU can really expect, in the long run, to have one currency but more than fifteen armies.[50]

[50] See *Il Mundo*, 2/10/1997.

8

NATO or WEU? Security Policy since 1990

EMIL J. KIRCHNER

Changes in threat perceptions since 1990, and growing concerns about military and non-military aspects of security provoke questions over the extent to which NATO can or should remain the dominant security provider of the western world. It also raises the question about the extent to which the Western European Union (WEU), either alone or in conjunction with the European Union, can or should be responsible for security. Debate about these questions not only takes place in the US, Britain, France, and Germany, where divided opinions prevail within and between countries; it is also discussed in the Russian Federation where the questions of enlargement of NATO and WEU remain particularly controversial.[1] After all, the eastern enlargement of NATO in March 1999 to include Poland, Hungary, and the Czech Republic was viewed with great dismay in Moscow. Moreover, NATO's bombing of Serbia and Serbian positions in Kosovo which began shortly afterwards on 24 March and lasted until 10 June led to the most severe crisis in Russian–NATO relations since the end of the cold war.

Although controversies about the war in Kosovo within the West superseded the discussion about the role of the EU and the WEU within the western security system, this issue has not gone away. Important in this context is that the intense debate in the early 1990s about 'either' NATO 'or' WEU has given way to NATO 'as well as' WEU. Helpful as this might be for those favouring continued American commitment to Europe or shying away from the enormous costs associated with a military upgrading of WEU,[2] it still leaves unresolved the old problems between the two about leadership, division of labour, rules of joint or separate engagement, and burden sharing. Differences among the key

---

[1] For further details of this debate see J. Sperling and E. Kirchner (eds.), *Recasting the European Order: Security Architecture and Economic Cooperation* (Manchester, 1997). For the WEU's recent history, see G. Wyn Rees, *The Western European Union at the Crossroads: Between Trans-Atlantic Solidarity and European Integration* (Boulder, Colo., 1998). See also Ch. 6 by J. Pinder in this book.

[2] See R. Seidelmann, 'Costs, Risks, and Benefits of a Global Military Capability for the European Union', *Defence and Peace Economics* 8 (1997), 123–43.

actors in both organizations occur (and are likely to continue) at three levels. The first is over threat perception. Conflicts, like the Gulf, Bosnia, the Great Lakes, and indeed Kosovo involve different interests among member states and therefore different responses.[3] At a second level these differences reflect tensions over leadership, trust, and cost.[4] Leadership is tied to the perennial question over the role of the US in Europe and whether or not the US is a European power. This resonates with the issue of trust among the main European actors: Britain, France, and Germany. Since 1990 it also involves consideration of Russia as either a stable or reliable partner in the establishment of a European order. Matters of leadership and trust affect cost consideration, e.g. for what purposes can American military assets be shared by its European allies or how should cost-sharing be arranged. The latter issue relates to the third level of differences and invokes the notion of economic competition between the US and the Europeans. The introduction of the euro on 1 January 1999, the enlargement of NATO in March 1999 and the looming enlargement of the EU are bound to further heighten rather than reduce these tensions.

The following will explore areas where either a meaningful division of labour is emerging between NATO and WEU or effective co-operation can be envisaged between the two. This will be done by examining how the two organizations, either individually or jointly, deal with: (*a*) ethnic conflicts in Central and Eastern Europe; (*b*) promote democracy and market stability in these countries; and (*c*) approach enlargement. However, before we do this a brief review will be provided of how the two organizations have developed since 1990.

THE EVOLVING RELATIONSHIP BETWEEN NATO AND WEU

In response to the by now well-rehearsed changes which have taken place in Central and Eastern Europe since 1989 culminating in the unification of Germany and the break-up of the Soviet Union, a lot of posturing initially occurred between the major actors within NATO and WEU. Whereas in 1990/1 countries like France and Germany, had either expected or hoped that WEU, as an integral part of the EU's common foreign

---

[3] See P. Schmidt, 'Germany, France and NATO', *Strategic Studies Institute; Strategic Outreach Roundtable Paper and Conference Report* (US Army War College, Oct. 1994); A. Lee Williams and G. Lee Williams, 'NATO's Future in the Balance: Time for a Rethink?', *University Advisory Committee of the Atlantic Council of the United Kingdom* (London, 1995).
[4] S. Sloan, 'Transatlantic Relations: Stormy Weather on the Way to Enlargement', *NATO Review* 45/5 (1997), 12–17.

and security policy (CFSP) would replace NATO as the primary security organisation, this view diminished in the mid-1990s and was not regarded
as a credible alternative in the late 1990s. Reasons for this could be found
in: (*a*) inability on the part of the Europeans, either through WEU or the
CFSP of the EU, to resolve the Bosnian conflict; (*b*) disagreements over
the strengthening of WEU, capable of taking on NATO-like military missions; and (*c*) differences between Britain and France in their assessment
of the future of either Russia or Germany, and the continued role of the
US in Europe. On the other hand, the perception that NATO could carry
on as before 1989, and deal with issues of ethnic conflict and democracy
as well as market stability, and maintain appropriate defence expenditures
has also receded. It appears that the most viable proposition is a more
coherent or effective sharing of security responsibilities between NATO
and WEU/EU.

Yet, it is one thing to agree to such a sharing in principle, it is quite
another matter do so in practice, as the following examples illustrate.
Both organizations have expanded their task, but not necessarily in
union; both have engaged in joint peacemaking and peacekeeping missions in Bosnia, but without providing a blueprint for similar operations
in the future (e.g. in the aftermath of the war in Kosovo); and both have
decided to share military assets through the formula of Combined Joint
Task Forces (CJTF), but without establishing appropriate ground rules.
Let us briefly look at these points.

NATO's main task of the 1990s—its eastward expansion—led to the
new Strategic Concept of 1991 which described the new risks facing NATO
as 'multi-faceted and multi-directional'. The centrepiece of this strategy
was the Allied Rapid Reaction Corps (ARRC), which was meant to become
NATO's crisis management contingency planning structure. When fully
operational, the headquarters were expected to be able to command up
to four divisions with 80,000 troops drawn from up to thirteen nations.
A further NATO task expansion was added with the 1994 US/NATO
decision to make CJTF available, primarily for operations by European
members of NATO.

With regard to WEU developments, the Maastricht Treaty of 1991
proposed a more concrete role for WEU as a defence agency working
alongside the EU, proposing the eventual establishment of a European
Security and Defence Identity (ESDI). But the Treaty on European Union
also stressed that any arrangement should be compatible with NATO.
Under this 'hinge principle' the WEU was to become the defence component of the EU, while at the same time it was regarded as the instrument for strengthening the European pillar of NATO. In response to the
Maastricht recommendations, the WEU decided at the St Petersberg
summit of June 1992 to strengthen its virtually non-existent operational

capabilities by outlining a procedure for the assignment of forces from member states and the creation of a planning cell. The latter would deal with command, control and communications arrangements for operational missions and preparing contingency plans for operations. Under these arrangements the WEU would be activated only for specific purposes rather than constituted as a standing operational force. When carrying out peacemaking or peacekeeping operations, the WEU would be working with the UN and OSCE, the Organization for Security and Co-operation in Europe. St Petersberg also spelled out areas for WEU humanitarian and rescue tasks.

Organizationally, this new security agenda was made operational by the introduction of Forces Answerable to WEU (FAWEU), in which WEU could call upon military groupings, including Eurocorps, the NATO-dedicated Anglo-Dutch amphibious force, and national groupings. The main Eurocorps was expected to comprise a military strength of 50,000 from France, Germany, Belgium, and Spain. However, this Eurocorps seemed less well suited for rapid deployment and mobile operations outside Europe and lacked equipment logistics, intelligence gathering, and airlift capability. The Torejon satellite interpretation Centre, established by WEU in 1993 to promote satellite intelligence gathering and analysis, was suffering from a shortage of funds and tasks.

What remained unclear, even after the Amsterdam Treaty of 1997, was how the relationship between WEU and EU would develop, e.g. whether WEU would become an integral part of the EU. On the other hand, as shown below, the link with NATO was also unclear, because of uncertainties over CJTF. Prior to the outbreak of the war in Kosovo in March 1999, Britain as well as Denmark, Ireland and Sweden opposed attempts to include WEU in the EU, or to give the EU any military responsibility. Whereas France and Germany together with the Benelux countries and Italy sought to endow the EU with a common defence policy, Britain was only prepared to provide WEU with a gradual role in the formulation of a defence policy, but not a role regarding matters relating to a common defence policy. This was consistent with British desires to prevent WEU from acquiring an independent command structure or an integrated military command.[5] Moreover, it illustrated the gulf which existed among the key EU partners on this subject and raised questions whether majority voting can ever be introduced for CFSP decisions.

Both NATO and WEU tried initially in separate ways to respond to the Bosnian conflict in providing forces for the monitoring of maritime

---

[5] A. Forster, 'The Ratchet of European Defence: Britain and the Reactivation of Western European Union, 1984–1991, in A. Deighton, *Western European Union 1954–1997: Defence, Security, Integration* (Oxford, 1997), 40.

and air embargoes of weapons (which, incidentally, also constituted NATO's first out-of-area operation) and peacekeeping initiatives. They soon realized however that duplication or lack of co-ordination was impeding their missions and decided to combine efforts through operation Sharp Guard. Even this operation suffered from drawbacks, such as insufficient support from ground forces, lack of American contribution to these ground forces, and the eventual pull-out by the Americans from the entire operation in 1994 over disagreements with its European allies regarding the weapons embargo against Bosnia. The Bosnian conflict demonstrated the difficulties for both NATO and WEU to find sufficient organizational consensus for the rules of engagement, and to work with a complex organization such as the UN, which was the main legitimizer of peacemaking or peacekeeping operations. The lesson was learnt during the 1999 Kosovo conflict: both the UN and the WEU were largely ignored and clearly subordinated to NATO.

Thus, the NATO agreement of January 1994 for the establishment of CJTF had not been able to give the European dimension greater importance. The agreement recognized the need for the development of a European Defence and Security Identity and the sharing by the US of military assets (infrastructure, logistics and communications for operations) with its European allies, presumably under the joint control of NATO and WEU. This assured the Americans as their preferred formula was for the CJTFs being 'separable but not separate' from NATO. The US continued viewing the WEU as either duplicating NATO missions or as possibly dragging Americans against their will into conflicts along Europe's periphery. It could also be seen as WEU picking up either what the US did not want to get involved in, or what NATO, in a general sense, did not want to undertake. But it left both unfulfilled expectations on the part of the French and uncertainties, despite an energetic attempt at NATO's ministerial meeting in Berlin in 1996, over the implementation of the CJTF. France saw the CJTF as a mechanism that allowed Europeans to act militarily outside American control. It therefore campaigned for a separate command structure for CJTF. This was in line with French arguments that NATO's integrated military structure gave too much authority to the Supreme Allied Commander in Europoe (SACEUR) and too little to political authorities in member states in Europe.[6] France also sought to reduce NATO to a classical alliance with political commitments but without any substance to bolster those commitments. The US would be a last resort, to be called upon when European stability was disrupted to such an extent that the Europeans could no longer deal with the situation themselves.[7]

---

[6] J. Wyllie, *European Security in the New Political Environment* (Harlow, 1997), 103.
[7] N. Gnesotto, 'Lessons of Yugoslavia', *Chaillot Papers* 14 (March 1994), 27.

Britain, on the other hand, viewed the CJTF as a device for sustaining the relevance of NATO's integrated military structure to new tasks in a complex world, while avoiding the creation of wasteful rival structures.

The validity of the French position was not necessarily undermined by their attempts, especially between 1994 and 1996, to move closer to NATO,[8] or by Franco-German willingness to place Eurocorps under NATO command in certain situations. Rather what this signalled, together with Spain's intention to join the integrated structure of NATO in the very near future,[9] was partly the desire to move away from the assumption that the WEU would replace NATO, and partly the intention to bargain with the US to get as much flexibility over WEU operations as possible.

While this flexible or attempted autonomy is bound to be subject to internal considerations, both within WEU and the EU, involving British as well as Scandinavian concerns, it will also be affected by the transatlantic economic relationship. The latter was until 1989 overshadowed by the transatlantic security relationship, which was embedded in a bipolar context. In the future issues of economic rivalry will increasingly interact with issues of burden-sharing over military objectives and engagements. This is likely to sharpen the issue of how much control the Americans intend to retain over CJTF or how costs for these operations are to be shared between the Americans and the Europeans.

Two sets of issues can be envisaged in which those strains are likely to escalate. The first concerns ethnic conflicts in Central and Eastern Europe, like those in Bosnia or in Kosova. The second involves attempts to create or foster a stable political environment in Central and Eastern Europe, in which non-military issues of security will play an important role, and consideration will have to be given to the dual enlargement of the EU and NATO. These points will be elaborated below.

MEETING ETHNIC CONFLICTS

The end of the cold war led to the development of new circumstances in threats and threat perception. Besides being faced with the task of helping to promote the process of democratisation and market reform, the most immediate task NATO and WEU had to confront were ethnic conflicts in Central and Eastern Europe. However, whereas during the cold war there had been a clear hierarchy of power among the security institutions, no such hierarchy prevailed when faced with ethnic conflicts, particularly in Bosnia.[10] Three immediate consequences surfaced. First,

---

[8] Wyllie, *European Security in the New Political Environment*, 21.
[9] Javier Solana, 'Preparing for the Madrid Summit', *NATO Review* 45/2 (1997), 3–6.
[10] C. Bertram, 'Why NATO must enlarge', *NATO Review* 45/2 (1997), 14–16.

it became unclear as to who was in charge: the UN, NATO, WEU, OSCE, EU? This was epitomized in June 1991, when Jacques Poos, chairman of the EU Foreign Ministers, declared 'if there is any problem Europe can solve, it is Yugoslavia'.[11]

Second, duplication of WEU and NATO peacemaking missions became apparent. Starting in 1992, both NATO and WEU individually supported the UN in its peacemaking efforts, primarily to enforce UN arms embargo and economic sanctions. However, in 1993, the two realized that combined efforts were to be preferred and joined forces in the operation Sharp Guard, in order to patrol the Adriatic to enforce the embargo on Serbia; to monitor Bosnian air space, provide humanitarian assistance; and control heavy weapons in Bosnia.

Third, the cohesion of NATO became affected, when in 1994 the US decided unilaterally to pull out of the enforcement of the NATO arms embargo on former Yugoslavia over disagreement with the British, French, and Russians. Prior to that, decision-making in NATO had been cumbersome due to the unanimity requirement in the NATO Council and because of the need for UN legitimisation, which gave the Russians powers of a veto.

This resulted in several years of complex interweaving of diverse international perspectives, concerns, and commitments, and hopeless international bungling—with near-catastrophic consequences.[12] Overall as Wyllie argues, there was confusion about the relationship between operational capabilities, the political will to use them and the political wisdom of deploying them.[13] In the end, the American-inspired Dayton agreement of 1995 stopped further large-scale killings in Bosnia and closed the chapter on attempts by the Bosnian Serbs to establish a Greater Serbia in the shape of a set of 'independent' or formally linked territories. But Dayton also approved of two crucial aspects, which presumably the Americans had objected to in the ill-fated Vance–Owen plan of 1993, namely ethnic cleansing (an 'ethnically cleansed' Serb entity was established in a part of Bosnia) and the acquisition through force of contiguous territory for the Serbs in Bosnia. This unfavourable outcome happened, according to Gow, in the face of the collective weakness of the western powers.[14]

The Bosnian conflict did not produce a diplomatic solution, since the protagonists fought it out on the battlefield, particularly in 1994/5. It resulted in the spectacular defeat of the Bosnian Serbs by the combined Croat and Muslim forces. Neither can it be said that NATO played a major role in the ending of this conflict, though it helped that a workable NATO

---

[11] Quoted in Wyllie, *European Security in the New Political Environment*, 29.
[12] See J. Gow, *Triumph of the Lack of Will: International Diplomacy and the Yugoslav War* (London, 1997).   [13] Wyllie, *European Security in the New Political Environment*, 22.
[14] Gow, *Triumph of the Lack of Will*.

framework for implementing the Dayton agreement was available, and that the US participated with ground forces. Moreover, since Dayton, the NATO led operations in the form of IFOR and SFOR can be deemed a success. This is particularly the case with SFOR whose brief from the UN in 1996 was to deter renewed hostilities and contribute to the secure environment necessary to consolidate the peace. It assembled a force of 31,000, managed to persuade thirty-six countries to participate, and was to last for eighteen months (until the end of June 1998). Political oversight was held by the North Atlantic Council in consultation with non-NATO contributing countries. Of significance was the participation of a Russian airborne brigade, with a personnel of 1,500. IFOR/SFOR helped to advance the adoption of new NATO procedures, involving all sixteen allies in the direction and conduct of military operations. Clearly this strengthened NATO's political and military cohesion and paved the way towards a future NATO command structure in which all allies, or a significant proportion, can respond to new missions.[15]

Yet, in spite of these achievements the future of NATO peacekeeping missions seemed uncertain in the late 1990s. One reason was that 'out of area' missions tended to have a divisive rather than cohesive effect.[16] Initially, the war in Kosovo appeared to confirm this. However, as soon became clear, throughout the conflict a fairly united NATO front could be upheld—despite severe misgivings against the bombing of Serbia on the part of Greece, Italy, and the new Red–Green government in Germany. Successful conflict prevention and conflict termination however requires unity of political purpose and of diplomatic or military action,[17] but such a common response seems only possible in very exceptional circumstances. Thus whilst IFOR and SFOR provided a test for the organizations' operational development, it has not become a blueprint for further NATO peacekeeping operations.

The second factor which might affect future NATO peacekeeping missions are doubts over US willingness to deploy ground forces in future NATO operations. Already, there seemed to be some doubt over whether the US would extend its ground forces beyond SFOR's June 1998 deadline, or whether they would ask the Europeans to take sole responsibility, possibly in the shape of a CJTF operation. In the end, a scaled-down US commitment occurred. European governments appeared to be reluctant to continue without NATO operations or American commitment; fearing that if anything went wrong they would get the blame for it.[18] Such European unwillingness to take sole charge, could undermine their pleas

---

[15] G. Schulte, 'Bringing Peace to Bosnia: A Basis for the Future?', *NATO Review* 45/2 (1997), 25.   [16] Bertram, 'Why NATO Must Enlarge', 14–16.
[17] Schulte, 'Bringing Peace to Bosnia: A Basis for the Future?', 22–6.
[18] Sloan, 'Transatlantic Relations: Stormy Weather on the Way to Enlargement', 14.

for greater autonomy of CJTF operations. Moreover, as far as the war in Kosovo was concerned, despite the British Labour government's relatively early willingness to deploy ground troops, for weeks NATO, most EU countries, and above all the USA refused to contemplate the deployment of troops before NATO's prolonged and extensive bombing campaign had more or less wiped out any serious Serb resistance in Kosovo. Yet, once the Serbian resistance in Kosovo was overcome and an agreement with the Yugoslavian military leadership to leave Kosovo had been concluded, the willingness to commit NATO peacekeeping troops was never in doubt; the WEU, however, played hardly any role whatsoever during the Kosovo conflict.

Two consequences emerge from the undertaking of peacekeeping missions by NATO and the WEU. First, duplication in planning and administration seems unavoidable. There will be two planning staffs, for two military organizations which share some of the units for the same or similar missions. Secondly, there could be tension between the formal tasking and the relative capacities of both organizations: whereas NATO has a restricted mission but greater military capability, the WEU has fewer restrictions but more limited military capabilities. Importantly, the EU through CFSP has the capacity to request the WEU to undertake security actions on behalf of the EU, as happened in the case of the policing and administering of Mostar. In addition, the St Petersberg declaration lays down provisions for humanitarian activities.

With NATO and WEU facing problems, what about the EU? Whilst the EU has responded with a host of economic and diplomatic measures to upheavals and developments in Central and Eastern Europe states, it has not been able either on its own or in conjunction with the WEU, to respond with effective military measures to conflicts such as that in Bosnia or Kosovo. Lack of consensus, inadequate preparation by and relations with the WEU, and ambiguous lines of demarcation between the UN, NATO, and the OSCE have largely prevented such undertakings.[19] The EU has moved away from a predominantly economic model of foreign policy in the conflicts in Bosnia and Kosovo, but it has not moved fully to a position that can be described as a political model. As Wyllie points out, the abortive Poos attempt with regard to former Yugoslavia can be seen as an abdication of Europe's opportunity and responsibility in its own sphere of influence. This does not bode well for a cohesive EU security over issues of a less vital character.[20]

However, the EU attempted to learn from its failure in Bosnia and to some extent succeeded in playing a more coherent and effective part

---

[19] See Sperling and Kirchner (eds.), *Recasting the European Order*, ch. 3.
[20] Wyllie, *European Security in the New Political Environment*, 28.

during the Kosovo war—above all, by co-ordinating relief efforts for the hundred of thousands of refugees in Albania, Macedonia, and Montenegro. Yet, the lion's share of the war in Kosovo was undoubtedly born by the USA and NATO. Thus, the war encouraged efforts to develop a distinct European defence structure. Above all, there were serious considerations to extend the Anglo-French St Malo agreement on a European defence platform of December 1998. Both Paris and London, the only two European nations with substantial military potential, envisaged developing a European defence capability which was capable of acting in co-ordination with NATO without necessarily involving the United States. After all, European priorities may well be increasingly different from American aims. This was confirmed during the NATO meeting in Washington in April 1999: it was spelled out that European NATO members might well act on their own in the future. Although St Malo had always meant to be the beginning of a broader structure which would include other EU countries (including Germany), the Kosovo war dramatically speeded up these plans. It also appeared to indicate that the French were turning away from the idea that the WEU ought to be the core of a common European defence identity.[21]

Indeed, during the 73rd Franco-German summit in Toulouse in late May 1999 both countries made it clear that they were determined 'to contribute all their weight so that the EU equips itself with the necessary autonomous means to decide and deal with crises'. This may well lead to the build-up of a rapid European reaction force, possibly around the Franco-German brigade established in 1993 which also includes Belgium, Luxemburg, and Spain.[22] The European Council summit meeting in early June 1999 in Cologne largely confirmed these developments. Not only was Javier Solana, NATO's outgoing Secretary General, selected as the man responsible for pushing ahead with the development of a Common European Foreign and Defence Policy, it was also decided by all EU members including Britain to incorporate the WEU into the EU. Above all, this includes the so-called 'Petersberg tasks', the responsibilities for peacekeeping and humanitarian intervention.

There is however more to security and stability than peacemaking or peacekeeping missions. Nowadays much depends on conflict prevention or the establishment of democratic regimes and market reforms. It is here where NATO can help,[23] but where a substantially greater contribution

---

[21] A Council of European defence ministers and more intensive co-operation in weapons planning and procurement was also envisaged. See *Financial Times*, 29–30/5/1999.

[22] See *Financial Times*, 31/5/1999, 2.

[23] Note e.g. NATO's response to the outbreak of hostilities in Kosova in March 1998: 'The North Atlantic Council condemns unreservedly the violent repression of non-violent expression of political views as well as terrorist acts to achieve political goals. [It] calls on all sides to take immediate steps to reduce tensions, and for the two sides to enter without preconditions

might be expected from the EU and WEU. The following will demonstrate why.

PROMOTING DEMOCRACIES AND STABILIZING MARKETS

Among the distinct foreign policy objectives of the West after 1989 have been the establishment of democratic regimes in Central and East European countries (based on the rule of law, a pluralist system and respect for human rights), and the introduction of market-based economies in the region. The logic is that peace and stability depend on democracy and prosperity. In a wider sense democracies are considered in the Kantian mode as 'peace-loving' and as fostering security.[24] This is accompanied by a feeling that 'hard' defence alone may well be inadequate to deal with the rapidly changing notions of what constitutes a threat to peace involving, for example, immigration/migration, narcotics, organized crime, terrorism, and environmental problems.

The question is how best to achieve this. Both NATO and the EU use norm-setting methods to foster democratic aims as expressed in conditions for either membership or Euro Agreements.[25] However, the EU has greater possibilities for complementing these methods with trade, finance, technical assistance, and macroeconomic measures.[26] It can also employ more effectively political and legal methods; aspects in which NATO seems ill-equipped to function.[27]

Partly to prevent the events in Bosnia and Kosovo from recurring elsewhere in Eastern Europe, and partly to promote stability in the region, the EU has concluded partnership and co-operation agreements with

into a serious dialogue in order to develop a mutually acceptable political solution for Kosova within the Federal Republic of Yugoslavia.' *NATO Press Release*, 5/3/1998.

[24] For an overview of the 'democratic peace' proposition, see B. Russett, *Grasping the Democratic Peace* (Princeton, 1993); J. L. Ray, *Democracy and International Conflict* (Columbia, SC, 1995); and S. Chan, 'In Search of Democratic Peace: Problems and Promises', *Mershon International Studies Review* 41 (1997), 59–91.

[25] On various occasions since 1990, such as in the Association Agreements, later named Euro Agreements, and the 1993 Copenhagen declaration, the EU has reminded Central and East European states of the obligation to introduce democratic forms. This point was once again emphasized in the Agenda 2000 report of the European Commission which calls on membership aspirants to: (*a*) establish institutional stability as a guarantee for democracy and the legal order; (*b*) protect human rights as well as minorities; (*c*) strengthen the administration, including central and local institutions; and (*d*) improve the functioning of government and NGO's involved in the transition, including local and public services. See European Commission, 'Agenda 2000: for a Stronger and Wider Europe', *Bulletin of the European Union*, Supplement 5/97.

[26] See Sperling and Kirchner (eds.), *Recasting the European Order*.

[27] See M. Kahl, 'European Integration, European Security, and the Transformation in Central Europe', *Journal of European Integration* 20/2–3 (1997), 184.

Kazakhstan, Kyrgyzstan, Ukraine, and Russia and is preparing association agreements with for example Albania and Macedonia. The aims of
these agreements are to provide a solid global framework for the development of deeper bilateral relations and to assist these countries in effect-
ing democratic reforms and bringing their laws into line with the legal
norms of the Council of Europe. They cover political dialogue in addition to trade in goods and services, capital, intellectual and industrial
property protection, and economic co-operation. They also stress democratic values, respect for human rights and a market economy as essential elements of the partnership. Finally, they emphasize the importance
of regional competition to safeguard the future prosperity and stability
of these countries. Most of these EU efforts have been channelled through
the TACIS programme of technical assistance to the countries of the
former Soviet Union, established in 1991.

In the same vein, the EU established in 1993 a European Stability
Pact in an effort to reinforce stability to the east of the EU. It can be
considered as an exercise in preventive diplomacy. Its aims include a
guarantee of the rights of minorities and the inviolability of frontiers in
Europe. It therefore implies that Central and East European countries
should resolve their conflicts before joining the EU. It builds on the activities within the PHARE and TACIS economic assistance programmes,
and the Europe Agreements, which have been concluded with several of
the Central and Eastern European states. The Pact would help to tie
together the existing European security and human rights organizations,
the OSCE, the Council of Europe, NATO and the WEU. But besides
holding a high level international conference and a series of 'round
tables', this Pact has not amounted to much.

To complement these efforts and to prepare for the second round
of entrants to the EU from Central and Eastern Europe, especially with
regard to issues of drug trafficking, money laundering, and terrorism, in
1998 the EU introduced a programme, endowed with 100 m. euro to fight
organized crime and corruption in these countries.

ENLARGEMENT

Enlargement can be considered as another tool in trends to promote democratization and market reform. However, with various forms on offer for
widening the European political and security space, there is a question
whether the forming of multiple, interdependent security frameworks
are interlocking or interblocking. This relates to issues of boundaries
(membership inclusion) and to co-operation among the security institutions. To a large extent this will depend on the degree to which American
interests coincide with some of its European partners.

It is the aim of NATO, WEU, and the EU to create in Europe a common space of security and stability. Subsequently, all three organizations try to offer security protection to Central and East European states and in turn invite these states to participate in a range of security tasks, including peacekeeping, disaster relief, and combating terrorism and drug trafficking. All three have emphasized that no country would, *a priori*, be permanently excluded, and that each could accede in accordance with predetermined criteria. However, the three make different security packages available, ranging from traditional collective security guarantees to security provisions via the economic and diplomatic route. This will make not only the element of choice difficult but also consideration of subsequent developments. The issue of choice will involve two key aspects for the US, the EU, and Central and Eastern Europe. First, will or can NATO expand beyond the three new members who joined in March 1999 (Poland, Hungary, Czech Republic)? Second, what are the consequences of NATO expansion for the establishment of the EU' s CFSP?

(a) EU expansion

With uncertainties over whether NATO will expand beyond the accession of Poland, Hungary, and the Czech Republic, there is significant debate about whether EU membership without NATO membership can provide the security guarantees desired by Central and East European countries. Different answers are being provided for the short term and the long term. Whereas Francke sees a replacement of NATO's classical collective defence article through CFSP only as a long term prospect,[28] Freedman and Menon argue that CFSP can already be considered a 'security community' in the sense that there is a degree of mutual solidarity based on shared values and awareness that an attack on one would directly affect all, even where there is not always the firmness of an alliance obligation to come to the aid of a partner under threat.[29] Hence, while not a substitute for NATO, EU expansion could increase the security of those states outside NATO for the near future, especially with regard to Russia, since any Russian intervention in an EU-member state would have serious consequences for its relations with Europe as a whole. Moreover, given its mainly economic characteristics, the EU could be considered less provocative to Russia and less divisive to Central and East Europe. In contrast, when Poland, Hungary, and the Czech Republic were admitted to NATO, this might have achieved the opposite effect to what was intended:

---

[28] K. Francke, 'Balancing transatlantic relations', *NATO Review* 45/5 (1997), 19.

[29] L. Freedman and A. Menon, 'Conclusion: Defence, States and Integration', in J. Howorth and A. Menon (eds.), *The European Union and National Defence Policy* (London and New York, 1997), 166.

'offering security guarantees to countries which do not need them may heighten the insecurity of those who (lying in the orbit of the former Soviet Union) do need them but cannot get them.'[30] Thus, a security community based on 'creeping enlargement' can have advantages over alliances providing traditional security guarantees.

However, WEU or EU enlargement, whether in their own right, or as an advance guard for NATO membership, is not without difficulties. Two issues seem particularly pertinent: Turkey, and the challenges to the EU of rapid enlargement in terms of new border problems, costs, and decision-making. US pressure for an accelerated process of Turkey's EU accession have been met with stiff resistance by leading EU members, particularly Germany. Though domestic reasons are the most important criteria, there are also external concerns. The domestic reservations centre on Turkey's human rights record with respect to the Kurdish minority, its state of economic development and the subsequent aid or subsidies necessary for integration, and fears over the potential high number of migrants. External issues involve the dispute with Greece over Cyprus. Greece has threatened to block other Central and East European applic-ants from EU entry, unless Cyprus is admitted. Turkey insists on separate negotiations for the northern part of Cyprus, and, failing that, threatens to annex that territory into Turkey. Whether the proposal for joint participation of both linguistic communities, in the form of a 'Cyprus Delegation', will solve the issues remains to be seen. Turkey might trade-off concessions on Cyprus for a 'clearer' timescale on its own EU admission. Yet, should Turkey be admitted eventually, there also would be, besides the domestic issues mentioned above, concerns over poten-tially unmanageable frontiers with Iran, Iraq, Syria, Georgia, and Armenia. On the other hand, non-admittance bears the danger of severely exacer-bating Turkey's internal problems.

The first and second wave of EU enlargements will raise important secur-ity issues such as environmental issues (for example, the Chernobyl nuclear power plant in the Ukraine) as well as questions of migration, drug trafficking, money laundering, and terrorism. The Schengen process will come under pressure. Some efforts are being made to prepare the second wave of applicants, e.g. the 'pre-ins programme'. All this will force the EU to take a much clearer stand on what role it should play in Central and Eastern Europe, for example whether it should keep its interests strictly in the economic sphere or add some kind of security dimension. In turn this will pose considerations about decision-making, effectiveness, and costs. However, in view of declining defence expenditures, substantial differences among EU partners about an upgrading of the EU's defence and security

---

[30] Ibid.

dimension, as well as the desire on the part of Central and Eastern Europe to obtain traditional security guarantees, attention turns once again to NATO.

(b) NATO expansion

The question of further NATO expansion beyond admitting Poland, Hungary, and the Czech Republic depends substantially on US attitudes and to some extent on Russian consent or co-operation. Views seem to differ in the US with regard to NATO's relationship with Russia. The Clinton administration is determined to expand NATO as widely as possible, irrespective of Russian reservations and has even hinted that eventually Russia could be admitted.[31] In contrast, voices of concern emerged within the US elite, most explicitly expressed in an open letter by a group of former US Senators and an ex-National Security Adviser in February 1998:

Antagonism is sure to grow if the alliance extends ever closer to Russian territory. . . . we will have misplaced our priorities during a critical window of opportunity to gain Russian co-operation in controlling nuclear arsenals and preventing proliferation . . . The Senate would be wise to link NATO and EU. If that link is made, it is essential to stipulate that admission to the EU is no sufficient qualification for entry into NATO, which should weigh any future applicant against the contributions and burdens its members would entail . . . What is called for is a definite, if not permanent, pause in this process.[32]

In some ways these reservations seemed surprising given that Russian co-operation had been secured through both the SFOR arrangements and the 1997 Founding Act between NATO and Russia. Under the former, Russia participates with one Brigade in IFOR/SFOR peacekeeping missions in Bosnia. Under the latter, a number of institutional arrangements have been made such as the establishment of a Permanent Joint Council, an Euro-Atlantic Community, and a NATO Assembly–Federal Assembly of Russia. It also entailed concessions for Russia by declaring that no nuclear weapons would be deployed on the territory of new member states. The Act signified that security is indivisible, which was also recognised in the special agreement NATO signed with the Ukraine. In view of this

---

[31] e.g., Strobe Talbot, American Deputy Secretary of State, strongly supported the view that 'no emerging democracy should be excluded because of size, geopolitical situation or historical experience. That goes for very small states such as the Baltic, and it goes for the very largest, that is, for Russia'. It is a message that Bill Clinton has given to Russian President Boris Yeltsin in their private meetings, according to Mr Talbott. Quoted in Jim Hoagland, 'NATO Is in Transition, So Why not Talk about It?', *International Herald Tribune*, 19/3/1998.

[32] See H. Baker, S. Nunn, B. Scowcroft, and A. Frye, 'Enlarge the European Union before NATO', Letter printed first in *The New York Times*, reprinted in *International Herald Tribune*, 6/2/1998.

co-operation, American concerns over Russia might be a deflection from their real reservation, namely to avoid commitments to both boundless new troubles and excessive costs. However, the war in Kosovo and its aftermath put NATO's relationship with Russia under severe strain and it is an open question whether the relative closeness achieved in the early to mid-1990s can be resurrected.

The factor of cost loomed large in the conditions which Hungary, Poland, and the Czech Republic were asked to fulfil by 1999, namely to modify their civil–military relations radically, to change force structure completely, to replace weapons systems, and to retain its personnel.[33] This raised concerns over whether they would be able to bear the associated financial cost or if they would need financial help; and in the latter case, who would pay for it?

There is however fear that decisions by NATO, or for that matter the EU, to admit some further countries and continue excluding others, might give the wrong signals to Russia. In other words, such decisions could lead Russia to consider those in the waiting room as relegated to a Russian zone of influence[34] and might encourage Moscow to exert political and military pressure against neighbouring states, the former members of the Soviet Union which Moscow regards as its 'near abroad'.[35] Already, there have been complaints by the Baltic countries that norms stipulated for NATO membership with regard to the resolution of border disputes and observance of human rights principles were negatively influenced by Russian refusal to resolve their boundary disputes and Russians claims of victimization of Russian minorities in Estonia and Latvia.[36]

Yet, any delay in NATO's further eastern enlargement could also affect WEU expansion, as there is a convention that only NATO members can be full WEU members. On the other hand, the Maastricht Treaty agreed that all EU members could have some form of membership with WEU. WEU's Association Partnership appears a poor substitute for full membership.[37] Neither does it seem as suggested by Bertram that an intensification of the Partnership for Peace (PfP) or associate member status of NATO would do the trick.[38] But, while full NATO

[33] See D. R. Herspring, 'After NATO Expansion: The East European Militaries', *Problems of Post-Communism* 45/1 (1998), 10–20.

[34] See Bertram, 'Why NATO Must Enlarge', 16.

[35] See M. M. Balmaceda, 'Ukraine, Russia, and European Security: Thinking Beyond NATO Expansion', *Problems of Post-Communism* 45/1 (1998) 21–29.

[36] See R. J. Krickus, 'The Case for Including the Baltics in NATO', *Problems of Post-Communism* 45/1 (1998), 3–8.

[37] The St Petersberg summit established a Forum for Consultation with nine Central and East European states to structure dialogue and consolidate the security architecture of post-cold war Europe and the CFSP.   [38] See Bertram, 'Why NATO Must Enlarge', 14–16.

membership is desirable for Central and Eastern European countries, it also has implications for all those organizations involved with European security.

(c) Consequences of NATO enlargement

NATO enlargement effects the other security organizations: it demotes the status of EU/WEU or OSCE; reinstates military aspects over economic or diplomatic ones; and continues dependence on US defence and security. As Seidelmann points out NATO enlargement represents 'the continuation of political and military dependency on the US; a military perception and military solution of Europe's basic security problems; and a lost opportunity to streamline a competitive, duplicating and counterproductive European security architecture'.[39]

Through NATO enlargement, so it seems, the EU will miss an historic opportunity to complement its well-developed economic profile with a political and security dimension. The EU might thus for a considerable time remain a halfway house with enticing prospects for solving regional problems and establishing a European order, but in the meantime severely weakened by perceptions in Central and Eastern Europe of military inadequacy, by internal differences over a military upgrading of WEU, and by continued American military leadership and control. To overcome this dilemma, a parallel approach is needed in which a European pillar in NATO is maintained while CFSP or WEU are strengthened. The challenge is thus how to minimize US dependence and exploit the limits of the American role in Europe; after all it is clear that the Americans do not want to become involved in every European conflict. This became increasingly obvious in the aftermath of the Bosnian crisis, and, on account of the lukewarm attitude of the Clinton administration, the Congress, and American public opinion to ever deeper involvement in the Balkans, it also became particularly apparent during the Kosovo war.

IMPLICATIONS FOR ANGLO-GERMAN SECURITY POLICY[40]

Different security interests and strategies seem to prevail between the UK, which favours a strong Atlanticist orientation, and Germany, which sees

[39] R. Seidelmann, 'NATO's Enlargement as a Policy of Lost Opportunities', *Journal of European Integration* 20/2–3 (1997), 244–5.

[40] The following section draws on the article by J. Sperling and E. Kirchner, 'The security architectures and institutional futures of post-1989 Europe', *Journal of European Public Policy*, 4/2 (June, 1997), 155–70.

the Atlantic Alliance as one of several viable security structures. It is important to note, however, that Germany, particularly during the stewardship
of the Kohl government, has moved away from its earlier foreign policy
logic, which anticipated the eventual subordination of NATO to the OSCE.
NATO has once again become the institutional address for German
security co-operation.[41] The dividing line between the Anglo-Saxon and
the German architecture is located in the anticipated institutional forms
of the second pillar of the Atlantic Alliance. The Germans favour a
solution that parallels progress towards the pooling of sovereignty in the
EU which could have the unintended consequence of diplomatic drift and
the eventual estrangement of the two pillars of the alliance, but meets
France's minimum demand of some progress towards an independent
European security identity.

The difference between the British and German positions centres on
the future of WEU. The British position is that the WEU should remain
independent of the EU and intergovernmental. The British fear that any
institutional subordination of the WEU to the EU would have a corros-
ive effect upon the alliance, encourage the disassociation of the United
States and Europe, and degrade British security and influence. The British
argue that the disparate treaty obligations of the EU and WEU, particularly Article 5 (which stipulates a collective security guarantee) of the
WEU Treaty, counsel against transforming the WEU into a pillar of
the EU—the institutional option, preferred by France and Germany.
Recently, some movement towards a recognition of the British, French,
and German views could be observed. Each country now reserves the
right of ultimate control over the disposition and use of national armed
forces. However, the British oppose the Franco-German proposal to make
majority voting in the CSFP more palatable with a system of 'constructive abstention' where no state would be obliged to take part in a joint
action against its will, but could not prevent others from doing so.
Residual autonomy in defence has not given way to the efficiencies and
benefits of pooled sovereignty. Given its preferred mix of military and
economic aspects of security and flexibility in the institutional design
of a European security order, the German architecture appears to best fit
the needs and current security requirements of the United States, the
Russian Federation, and the other European powers, particularly France.
However, in view of the veto requirements for both the merging of the
WEU with the EU and the military upgrading of WEU, it is probably
the British view which will determine European security policy, at least
in the immediate future.

[41] See H. P. Schwarz, 'Germany's National and European Interests', in A. Baring (ed.),
Germany's New Position in Europe: Problems and Perspectives (Oxford, 1994), 107–30.

CONCLUSION

For a long time the WEU was in the shadow of NATO and played a sub-ordinate role. The end of the cold war has presented both organizations with new challenges (ethnic conflicts in out-of-area regions, economic and democratic reform programmes in Central and Eastern Europe, refugees and migration flows, environmental hazards, Islamic fundamentalism, etc.) which in turn affect the relationship between the two organizations. This relationship is further influenced by increasing economic competition between the US and the EU, on the one hand, and growing pan-European co-operation, on the other. With the EU striving towards greater economic and political integration, and both NATO and the EU enlarging, the pivotal position of WEU will be put to a hard test. Will the WEU be drawn more deeply into the orbit of the EU and used as a tool of EU policy strategies, or pulled by the centrifugal forces of a strengthened NATO and provide, with the assistance of CJTF, the geographic legs for 'out-of-area' security operations?

While the long-term prospects for the EU appear good, NATO holds the trump cards in the short to medium term. The decision to enlarge NATO, and engagements in the Gulf, in Bosnia (though more in a peacekeeping than crisis management role in the case of Bosnia), and corresponding failures of the EU's CFSP in Bosnia, and of course NATO's activities during the war in Kosovo have clearly elevated NATO in security terms above the EU. As Freedman and Menon point out no substantial military operation is possible without the support of the US and certainly not in the face of its opposition.[42] Reflections of this shift in perception can be found in both US and European attitudes towards NATO. There is a growing US view that far from being a cold war relic, NATO should be the cornerstone of an evolving security order in Europe, e.g. remain vital for ensuing arms control, for maintaining the kind of industrial base that provides a solid defence and for providing the institutional home for coalitions to meet crises beyond Europe.[43] On the European side there is a visible reduction of calls for a redefinition of NATO's role. To match American superiority in infrastructure and military capabilities (satellite intelligence, air power and integrated battlefield information systems) would require enormous costs and efforts, as well as cohesion, on the part of the Europeans. There is no evidence that either will happen: falling rather than rising defence expenditures are the practice in Western Europe. For the time being, particular interests rather than common interests dictate how conflicts are viewed or are to be resolved, e.g. the UN weapons

---

[42] Freedman and Menon, 'Conclusion: Defence, States and Integration'.
[43] See letter by Baker *et al.* 'Enlarge the European Union before NATO'.

inspection crisis in Iraq in 1998.[44] Therefore, the EU discrepancy between economic strength and political/military weakness is bound to continue, with the likely consequence of continued dependence on and dominance by the US. This was confirmed by the war in Kosovo in 1999. Although the performance of the European countries was less factionalized (at least on the surface) than in the Gulf War and the Bosnian wars in the early and mid-1990s, it became obvious, however, that it was Washington which was in charge of the overall NATO operation in Serbia. It was also the USA which contributed most of the alliance's overwhelming airpower.

Whilst the continuation of this state of affairs is likely to constitute the essence of US–EU relations in the coming years, it is clear that it does not sufficiently meet the requirements for a new European security order. The latter requires further strengthening of WEU–NATO relations, and a more effective blending of economic and security interests among the three major security players, the US, EU/WEU and Russia. However, it does appear as if the EU is determined to obtain a greater security and foreign policy role albeit in close co-operation with NATO.

[44] The UK was accused, especially by the Dutch, of abusing its role as chairman of the EU Presidency, e.g. by openly siding with the US and by deliberately keeping EU colleagues in the dark over policy on Iraq; this it was claimed was hampering EU efforts to forge a CFSP. See I. Traynor and S. Bates, 'Iraq Crisis: Dutch Attack Blair for Siding with US', *Guardian*, 19/2/1998.

PART III

The Post-Cold War Relationship:
The Economic and Social Dimension
since 1990

9

Industrial and Commercial Cultures in Britain and Germany: Rivalry or Reconcilability?

JEREMY LEAMAN

A recent survey of opinion polls on German attitudes towards Britain paints an interesting, if predictable picture. Britain features strongly as an 'important partner' (behind the USA and France) but is almost entirely absent from the list of significant economic threats.[1] Inasmuch as such polls can be seen to represent 'a' common view, they reflect still the typical ambivalence of German attitudes in the post-war period, confident in the success of their economic culture and institutions but mindful of Germany's structural subordination in foreign and security policy and its need to demonstrate a commitment to multilateralism: the economic giant content (mostly) to remain a political dwarf.

This convenient pattern of relations, mirrored in British attitudes towards Germany and sustained by the cold war, has clearly been disturbed by the astonishing events of the late 1980s and early 1990s—unification and the end of bipolarity—and by the intensification of longer-term structural developments in economic affairs and national demography. Indeed, the hitherto unthinkable has happened: the acknowledged dominant economy of Europe has consistently underperformed, compared to its counterparts in the EU and the wider OECD—and not just as a result of unification. Lower than average rates of GDP growth have been insufficient to halt a persistent rise in unemployment (1981: 5.5 per cent; 1989: 7.9 per cent; 1997: 11.2 per cent)[2] to a level which is currently much higher than in Britain. Domestic demand for both consumer and investment goods is stagnating; what is left of the German growth engine is being fuelled almost exclusively by exports, helped by a weaker DM. Talk of the 'English disease'—of lower productivity, low investment, low growth and lousy industrial relations—has given way to an obsessive concern with Germany's perceived problem as a 'location'

---

[1] W. Dobler, 'Britain's Image in Germany: A Survey of Poll Results on German Attitudes towards Britain and other EU Member Countries', *German Politics* 6/3 (1997), 152 ff.
[2] The overall rate is 11.2 per cent; unemployment in the West stands at 9.5 per cent, and at 18.2 per cent in the East.

for economic activity (*Standortdebatte*). This is matched by a badly concealed smugness on the part of British politicians about Anglo-Saxon virtues. The result has been a sudden explosion of political and academic interest in the threats to the German 'model' and the rival merits of British 'flexibility'.[3] A recent, comprehensive survey of the 'pitfalls and potentials' of Anglo-German business collaboration also revealed more positive perceptions of British commercial prowess, while still drawing out the persistent weaknesses of British industrial culture.[4]

While the vulnerability of Germany's economic 'model' has become increasingly apparent, unification and the opening-up of Central Europe have, if anything, strengthened Germany's profile as a middle power in terms of both geo-politics and geo-economics: the Federal Republic has moved from the eastern flank of a trading and security block to the centre of a reunited and liberalized continent. Its position, size, wealth, and traditional profile in Eastern Europe have given it a new and powerful leverage in European politics; its export dependency has sharpened the traditional focus on its 'vital interests' in the East.[5] At the same time, the so-called 'reform states' have copied key elements of Germany's political economy to underpin their transformation process, notably universal banks and independent central banking. The politico-economic potential for Germany of trade and investment in Central and Eastern Europe has been at the centre of much of the political and economic manoeuvring since 1990: the Maastricht programme, the collapse of Yugoslavia and the eastern expansion of the EU all bear the imprint of Germany's new-found influence and interest articulation.

The economic relations between Britain and Germany since unification have, therefore, to be viewed both in the historical context of a cold war partnership with all its relative certainties and also under the quite new circumstances of economic failure and political uncertainty. This chapter will thus sketch these relations, first in terms of the similarities and contrasts of two economic cultures, secondly, in terms of the common pursuit of the new neo-liberal orthodoxy from the early 1980s onwards, and thirdly, in terms of the current 'crisis of the German model'.

[3] For an overview of the debate see: H. Uterwedde, 'Le Modèle allemand. Fin ou recommencement?', *Documents. Revue des Questions Allemandes* 3 (1996), 8–14; S. Casper and S. Vitols, 'The German Model in the 1990s: Problems and Prospects', *Industry and Innovation* 4/1 (1997), 1–13; J. Grahl and P. Teague, 'Is the European Social Model Fragmenting?', *New Political Economy* 2/3 (1997), 405–26; C. Lane, 'Trade Assocations and Inter-firm Relations in Britain and Germany', in R. J. Bennett (ed.), *Trade Associations in Britain and Germany: Responding to Internationalisation and the EU* (London, 1997), 23–32; W. Streeck, 'German Capitalism: Does it Exist? Can it Survive?', *New Political Economy* 2/2 (1997), 237–56.

[4] D. Ebster-Grosz and D. Pugh, *Anglo-German Business Collaboration: Pitfalls and Potentials* (London, 1996).

[5] For survey respondents, 'eastern Europe and Russia topped the list of Germany's "vital interests" in the 1990s followed by France and the United States'. See Dobler, 'Britain's Image in Germany', 157.

PERFORMANCE OF RIVAL MODELS

Germany and Britain manifest marked similarities as well as significant contrasts. Up to 1990 they had a roughly similar land mass and an almost identical size of population and population density. As Table 9.1 shows, many similarities persist. Both countries now have highly mechanized systems of agriculture, have long and impressive traditions as trading nations and are thus strongly dependent on exports. The two main contrasts relate to the exceptionally high proportion of the working population in Germany still employed in manufacturing (37 per cent) compared to British levels (27.8 per cent), which are closer to the OECD average, and, secondly, to Britain's persistent trade deficit which contrasts unfavourably with Germany's persistent surplus.

TABLE 9.1. *Key Economic Data for Germany and Britain (1997)*

Category	Germany	Britain
Area	357,000 km^2	240,000 km^2
Agricultural Land	17.162 million ha	17.175 million ha
Population	81.422 million	58.395 million
Inhabitants/km^2	228	239
Working Population	49%	50%
of which percentage working in:		
Agriculture, forestry, fishing	3.3%	2.1%
Manufacturing	37%	27.8%
Services	59.7%	70.1%
Foreign Trade		
Imports	381,636 mill $	226,172 mill $
per capita	4,687 $	3,893 $
Exports	427,136 mill $	204,009 $
per capita	5,246 $	3,512 $
Balance of Trade	45.5 billion $	−22.163 bill $
Price Index (1991=100)	102	110.4
GDP Index at market prices (1990=100)	123	121
State Consumption (% of GDP)	19.5%	21.6%
Private Consumption (% of GDP)	57.3%	63.9%
Investment Ratio (% of GDP)	19.9%	15.6%

Source: Statistisches Jahrbuch der Bundesrepublik Deutschland; OECD Country Surveys

Germany's trading performance since the Second World War has been consistently impressive and is clearly not unrelated to the fact that manufacturing production and employment retains an exceptionally high presence within the national economy; it has been easier hitherto to trade goods in contrast to services. Germany's structural surpluses have meant that, by and large, it has not had to employ high interest rates either to defend the exchange rate or to increase foreign demand for domestic securities. Such a policy has certainly been a long-term disadvantage for the British economy with its structural deficits.

In 1997 Britain was Germany's third largest trading partner with 8.2 per cent of German trade behind France (11.4 per cent) and the USA (8.6 per cent); this compares to just 4.1 per cent in 1958. Characteristically, Britain has run a consistent trade deficit with Germany since the 1950s, in common with all other EU countries except the Netherlands.

The growing trade interdependence between Britain and other EU countries on the one hand and Germany on the other is thus unequal in respect of net flows, but also in terms of the quality of goods traded. The composition of trade flows between Britain and Germany underscores the historical disparity of economic performance of the two countries, as Table 9.2 reveals. Within the overall trade deficit, there is a rough balance in the exchange of foodstuffs, raw materials, semi-finished goods and pre-products but a colossal disparity in the exchange of end products. This pattern is replicated in Germany's general trading relationships, underlining the success of trading strategies at both micro- and macro-levels based on the principle of maximizing added value between inputs (imports) and outputs (exports). Within the context of a world market where the supply of non-finished goods is more competitive than that of (high grade) finished goods, it is not surprising that Germany has generally benefited from rising terms of trade.

The trading disparities between Britain and Germany can be accounted for, in the first instance, in terms of the historical determinants of their respective economic cultures. British trading success derived in large measure from the structural advantages of early industrialization, maritime power, and the benefits of formal imperialism; its relative decline can be traced back to the evaporation of these advantages, to the complacency of its institutions and the failure to adapt to the changed circumstances. The dominance of Britain's financial institutions over productive sectors, which marked its political economy in the twentieth century, derived from the openness, spontaneity and liberality of British capitalism in the eighteenth and nineteenth centuries, but produced the oft-bemoaned short-termism of Britain's corporate sector, the low investment ratio, and the high level of private consumption as proportions of GDP.

TABLE 9.2. *German–British Trade according to Product Type (1995)*

Product Type	British Exports to FRG (DM m.)	German Exports to UK (DM m.)
Foodstuffs/Agricultural products	1,232.23	2,336.6
Raw Materials	3,563.75	268.66
of which Crude Oil	*3,302.81*	—
Semi-finished Products	2,333.16	2,431.87
Pre-products	5,335.09	8,801.84
of which chemicals	*1,298.29*	*1,596.70*
of which plastics	*1,049.78*	*2,259.67*
End Products	25,968.70	42,693.56
of which motor vehicles	*7,175.09*	*14,025.35*
of which electrical goods	*5,666.61*	*8,122.76*
of which pharmaceuticals	*1,282.74*	*1,135.5*
of which photochemicals	*3,666.69*	*299.13*
Manufacturing Total	37,200.71	54,195.64
Total All Goods	40,404.67	58,195.64

Source: Federal Office of Statistics

Germany's trading success, on the other hand, derived from the specific constraints of late industrialization, the consequent absence of a formal empire and the harnessing of craft and scientific skills within a set of protective hierarchies. A mercantilist state nurtured enterprises with a modern, effective economic and educational infrastructure, trade diplomacy and protective tariffs, while industrial and financial capital made up for the initial weakness of capital markets by developing a unique set of relationships based on the universal bank. Industrial stock was held and traded by the big banks and less by private individuals; banks and industrial enterprises exchanged directors to sit on their respective supervisory boards; small shareholders channelled their representation through the banks' proxy voting system. The marriage of industry and banking via reciprocal equity holdings, illegal in other major industrialized countries, contributed in large measure to the longer-term perspective of German capitalism, to a lower level of risk, particularly for larger corporations and therefore a greater preparedness to develop innovative, far-sighted investment strategies.

Germany's *organized capitalism* was further strengthened by the widespread use of cartels to prevent the negative effects of competition.[6]

[6] The 1925 Programme of the Reich Federation of German Industry stressed the advantages of a 'healthy and responsible cartel activity', which contrasted with operation of free competition which 'would destroy means of production and bring about unemployment', cited in K. Pritzkoleit, *Das kommandierte Wunder* (Vienna, 1959), 613.

The strength and political effectiveness of modern Germany's trade associations are rooted in the cartel tradition, even if their role has been modified by the Federal Republic's more rigorous policing of cartels. Up until 1945, the state, trade associations, and cartels in Germany operated on the basis of both a defensive nationalism and co-operative corporatism. The hierarchies altered, allowing first a brief inclusion of labour interests in decision-making in the Weimar Republic and then a subordination of both labour and small business to the will of the cartel leaders in the 'Third Reich'. However, the perceived benefits of co-operation survived the historical disasters of the first half of the twentieth century and re-emerged after the Second World War within a new democratic framework.

The post-war 'German model' is a strange hybrid creature, retaining a number of the original protective and risk-avoiding features of the past but obliged to shed certain discredited elements of statism and to accept the constraints of US free trade and anti-trust ideology. Commentators are frequently too eager to dignify this hybrid with the label of 'ordo-liberalism', proceeding from the assumption that one can subsume any element of 'Ordnungspolitik'—the institutional and statutory frameworks of labour law, trade associations, training, monetary policy, planning, environmental law, contract law and quality standards—under the label of 'ordo-liberalism'. In fact, ordo-liberalism was always a rather quaint minority branch of German economic thinking, based on Walter Eucken's 'Freiburg School' and rooted ideologically in anti-monopolism;[7] yes, it eschewed Keynesian interventionism and stressed the key role of monetary policy, but its utopian emphasis on the efficacy of market prices, derived from the dynamic competition of small enterprises and guaranteed by state competition policy, bears little resemblance to the heavily juridified systems of consensual risk-avoidance and quality assurance which have characterized the German way of doing things in the post-war period.

A recent comparative study of contract law and inter-firm co-operation in Germany and Britain[8] contrasts the 'voluntarist' system in the UK, which is light on regulation and exposes small suppliers to high risks, to Germany's tighter contract law. The latter (in the shape of Article 242 of the Civil Code) includes a specific reference to good faith and commits contractual parties to tighter quality standards and payment procedures. Most significantly, it is the individual trade associations in Germany that are normally responsible for the setting of standard contract terms; they 'also have the power to seek injunctions against firms which attempt to impose unlawful contract terms upon others'.[9] German trade associations have higher levels of membership than their British counterparts, offer

[7] See J. Leaman, *The Political Economy of West Germany 1945–1985* (London, 1988), ch. 2.

[8] Summarized by S. Deakin, in 'Contract Law and Inter-firm Co-operation: The Role of Good Faith', *Signal* (Autumn 1997), 3 ff.   [9] Ibid. 3.

a wider range of services and function, according to Deakin, as quasi-gatekeepers for entry to the trade, thus helping 'to entrench a high level of performance as the norm for most firms'.[10] Germany's tightly-knit network of business associations operates additionally on three levels: as industrial associations, associations of employers, and as chambers of industry and commerce; the latter have mandatory membership and function as para-public institutions, co-ordinating apprenticeship and in-service training with state bodies. Trade associations are acknowledged by the state as both representative and effective lobbyists and consequently as valuable partners in framing national policy on economic, trade, training, research, labour, and social affairs.[11] British associations are less coherently linked, less well resourced and hence less effective as vehicles for interest articulation than their German counterparts. As a consequence, larger British companies have tended to develop their own lobbying arrangements at national and international level, while Germany's big companies still channel the majority of their lobbying through their respective associations.[12]

There is thus a degree of inter-firm co-operation in Germany which is acknowledged to be more effective commercially and politically than Britain's 'flexible' system. It represents a fundamental distinction between the two economic cultures: 'What in Britain would be taken already as a mark of cartel-like relationships, is highly valued in Germany as a structural mechanism for binding individual interests into a common order of the collectively represented objectives of a particular branch.'[13]

Another interesting contrastive feature of the two economic cultures is the function of law in social relations. First, Germany's written constitution predefines general rules of private and commercial activity and the channels for legislation, litigation, and jurisdiction, where the British legal system operates predominantly according to cumulative case law. Second, Germany's legal system has distinct, specialized branches covering criminal law, commercial law, labour law, administrative law, and constitutional law. Together with the standard- and norm-setting powers of business associations as para-public institutions, legal statutes help to embed codes of behaviour which operate in large measure without recourse to litigation. There is strong cultural pressure to comply with statutory rules, to seek co-operative or consensual or arbitrated agreements before recourse to law in Germany, which contrasts frequently with

---

[10] Ibid. 4.
[11] R. J. Bennett, 'Trade Associations: Britain and Germany Compared', in Bennett (ed.), *Trade Associations in Britain and Germany*, 12–22.
[12] Lane, 'Trade Assocations and Inter-firm Relations in Britain and Germany', 23–32.
[13] R. Bachmann, 'Wettbewerbsfähigkeit auf dem Prüfstand: Das britische und das deutsche Wirtschaftsmodell im Vergleich', *Signal* (Autumn 1997), 6.

the British business and industrial relations environment where legal action is a 'matter of first, rather than last, resort'.[14] Even when legal action is taken, as in labour law for example, the procedural priority of the adjudicating panel (Labour Judge, employer's representative, trade union representative) is to seek a consensual solution between parties rather than to impose a judgement. For employers in Germany, therefore, participation in co-operative and consensus-seeking institutions has been seen as a valuable contribution to the furtherance of commercial interests, where the expense of maintaining them is outweighed by the benefits of pooled information, lobbying, a skilled, productive and loyal workforce.

REFORMING CAPITALISM: BRITAIN, GERMANY AND THE NEW ORTHODOXIES

The stagflationary crises of the mid- and late 1970s produced a fundamental reappraisal of state economic policy-making and the virtual abandonment of Keynesianism by the OECD and by academic economists. It was displaced in the first instance by monetarism, joined then rapidly by the stable mates of neo-liberalism and supply-sidism. The postwar British state had long been committed to a rather haphazard variant of interventionist welfarism à la Keynes, while Germany discovered Keynesianism (too) late in 1967. Moreover, with the inflationary surge of 1969–72 Bonn was forced to jettison its policy principles (and its chief architect, Karl Schiller) by the independent Bundesbank, even before the first oil crisis. West Germany, in one sense, returned to the virtuous orthodoxy of 'Ordnungspolitik' under Helmut Schmidt, acquiring the new badge of 'Modell Deutschland' on the way, while Britain's transition to monetarism was altogether more brutal, as evidenced by the 1976 IMF episode.[15] The broader adoption of neo-liberal recipes by Helmut Kohl in 1982 was nevertheless trumpeted as loudly if not louder than by Margaret Thatcher in 1979 under the banner of the 'great change' (*Wende*). This is odd in the sense that Britain had a far greater distance to move in terms of privatization—since most of Germany's utilities apart from the railways and telecommunications were already in private hands—whereas both countries had excessively complex tax systems and Germany's regulatory culture was deemed by the OECD to be particularly dense and inimical to market-pricing.[16]

---

[14] Deakin, 'Contract Law and Inter-firm Co-operation', 4.
[15] See J. Leaman, 'Central Banking and the Crisis of Social Democracy—A Comparative Analysis of British and German Views', *German Politics* 4/3 (1995), 31 ff.
[16] See OECD, *Progress in Structural Reform* (Paris, 1990), 21 ff.

The fundamental thrust of the neo-liberal revolution was towards a redistribution of net national product (national income) away from labour and the state towards capital. Privatizing state assets, revising taxation law, and deregulating retail opening hours, telecommunications, financial institutions, and social provision were either secondary to or instrumental in the weakening of the power of organized labour or the state to claim larger slices of the social cake. It is important to bear this in mind when reviewing the implementation and relative success of neo-liberal reforms in Britain and Germany in the 1980s.

Helmut Kohl's accession to power in October 1982 coincided with the second year of deep recession in Germany following the second Oil Crisis. It was facilitated by serious conflict between the independent Bundesbank and Helmut Schmidt's Social Democrats (senior partners in the coalition with the FDP) and by the FDP's shift in allegiance in the Federal Parliament's first successful 'constructive vote of no confidence'. Together with the centre-right majority in the Bundesrat (Upper House), this produced a new constellation of political forces based on a neo-liberal consensus. The rhetoric of the *Wende* was very much in line with that of the Thatcher and Reagan administrations and stressed the need to boost entrepreneurial competitiveness through cost-relief measures and regulatory reform.[17] The intellectual logic of the new radicalism was based on the virtuous circle of cost-relief creating higher rates of profit, leading to higher levels of investment, higher levels of productivity, higher employment, and stronger macro-economic growth; this logic owed much to the assumption in Say's Law that an optimally structured supply would generate its own demand. An equally bold assumption informed the notion, popularized by Reagan, that reducing rates of corporate taxation would increase the state's tax yield from such taxes (the so-called 'Laffer-Curve'), thus also helping to solve the structural problem of increasing state borrowing and overall debt as a percentage of GDP.

This neo-liberal agenda was supported vigorously by business and employers' associations in both Britain and Germany. The scale of reform in Britain was (inevitably) destined to be more radical. As noted above, the proportion of productive assets in the hands of the state was considerably greater than in Germany; social welfare in Britain was based predominantly on state transfers rather than on statutory social insurance and was thus more accessible to radical modification. Furthermore, Britain's centralized system of government, unconstrained by a written constitution, contrasts strongly with Germany's extreme federalism, in which policy formulation and implementation is hampered by a severe

---

[17] See J. Leaman, 'The Rhetoric and Logic of the *Wende*', *German Politics* 2/1 (1993), 124–35.

separation of powers (regional government and independent central bank) and by a system of constitutional checks on all policy actors in the shape of the Federal Constitutional Court. The progress of privatization, deregulation and taxation reform in Britain thus came to be envied by neo-liberal reformers in Germany; furthermore it was taken as a kind of benchmark for 'structural reform' by organizations like the OECD:[18] 'On the one hand Great Britain as the prototype of a flexible national economy, on the other hand the Federal Republic as an example of the patient plagued by "sclerosis".'[19]

The flexibility v. sclerosis polarity has become a fixed feature of orthodox thinking in Germany since the early 1980s, underpinning the arguments which have been constantly repeated in the rolling debate about Germany as a location for investment. The polarity is nevertheless a parody of economic realities which does little to illuminate Germany's and Britain's real structural problems. First, as observed above, Germany's economic performance as a manufacturing and trading nation is still superior to that of Britain and other representatives of the so-called Anglo-Saxon model, evidenced in consistent structural trading surpluses in contrast to the chronic trading deficits of the UK and the US. Some sclerosis, it could be said, if it does not hinder the country out-trading other countries or generating more industrial patents per capita than anywhere else!

Second, the rhetoric of sclerosis, of lagging behind the reform zealots of Britain and the US, conceals the real advances made in Germany in the area of redistributive politics, a core objective of neo-liberal policy. It is true that the institutional framework of industrial relations in Germany has changed little, in comparison with the far-reaching reforms of labour law in Britain. Collective bargaining, co-determination, employment protection, social security and strike laws are still firmly in place in Germany, despite some modifications; trade union membership also remains high. In Britain, on the other hand, a series of Employment Acts in the 1980s curtailed trade union power, reduced employment protection and benefit entitlements; closed shops and wages councils have been largely abolished, collective bargaining now covers less than 50 per cent of the employed population, giving way to decentralized systems of wage determination; trade union membership has slumped. Nevertheless, in Germany the gross profits ratio (the share of income from capital in national income) has risen just as much as in other countries,

---

[18] See OECD, *Progress in Structural Reform*; OECD, *Economic Survey—United Kingdom* (Paris, 1994).

[19] A. Heise, 'Neoliberale Empfehlungen zur Beschäftigungspolitik in Theorie und Praxis: Großbritannien und Deutschland im Vergleich', *WSI-Mitteilungen* 11/1997, 759 ff.

including Britain.[20] This has been achieved within or rather through the surviving institutional framework. State taxation policy has furthermore reduced the tax-take from capital from 35 per cent in 1960 (27 per cent in 1980) to 11 per cent of total taxation in 1995, while increasing the yield from wages and salaries from 12 per cent to around 35 per cent.[21] The change to net distribution ratios is thus even more spectacular, reinforcing the success of neo-liberal policies in favour of capital.

What neither policy regime in Britain or Germany has been able to deliver are the other major elements of the virtuous circle, notably increases in the investment ratio (i.e. the reinvestment of additional profits) and reductions in structural unemployment.[22] Arne Heise uses the comparison of Britain and Germany to test the validity of a wide set of neo-liberal hypotheses and demonstrates convincingly that they are fatally flawed. In particular, the assumed benefit for low-skilled workers to be derived from wider wage differentials are not borne out by data relating to Britain after 1979.[23] There is, however, a strong correlation between the declining investment ratio in both countries and the rising rate of unemployment.[24] Nevertheless, and particularly in the wake of Germany's unification crisis, the virtues of the British 'model' of low regulation, weak trade unions, decentralized bargaining procedures, and a cheaper social state are being loudly trumpeted by some sections of the employers' community. The Federation of German Industry (BDI) under Hans-Olaf Henkel has used the British example of low corporate taxes and high direct investment as central arguments against the maintenance of Germany's consensus model, 'yesterday's model'.[25] Henkel pleads for the application of the principle of 'subsidiarity' to wage agreements and applauds both the open flouting of branch-based agreements by East German enterprises and the weakness of trade unions in the East. He eschews 'round tables'—the long-standing symbol of corporatist institutions—expressing a preference for 'sharp-edged decisions'. He thus sets himself starkly outside the co-operative model of 'social partnership', breaking ranks both with the consensual approach of the Employers Federation (BDA) under Dieter Hundt and with its principle of industry-wide collective bargaining. Henkel's own firm, IBM, was withdrawn demonstratively from the BDA. In 1995 and 1996 there was significant conflict between Henkel and the then president of the BDA, Klaus Murmann; the latter saw grave

---

[20] The structurally adjusted wages ratio declined by 7 per cent in Germany between 1982 and 1994; see C. Schäfer, 'Mit falschen Verteilungs-'Götzen' zu echten Standortproblemen', *WSI-Mitteilungen*, 10/1996, 597 ff.

[21] D. Eißel, 'Reichtum unter der Steuerschraube?' in E. U. Huster (ed.) *Reichtum* (Frankfurt/M., 1997), 148.

[22] Heise, 'Neoliberale Empfehlungen zur Beschäftigungspolitik in Theorie und Praxis 758–70.   [23] Ibid. 763 ff.

[24] Ibid. 766.   [25] Thus Henkel in an interview with *Der Spiegel* No. 1 (1998), 74.

dangers in the abandonment of national agreements, in terms of increased negotiating costs and the risk of enterprise-based conflict.[26]

To the outsider, there is something suspiciously theatrical about the public spats between Henkel's BDI and the adherents of consensualism, be they in government, opposition, the BDA, or the trade unions. Even if Henkel's more outlandish statements and demands are not openly supported by conservative voices outside the BDI, he is clearly in tune with the neo-liberal orthodoxy of academic economists.[27] Furthermore he maintains an intensity of discourse which keeps the debate about social models on the front burner and—as in the good police interrogation tradition—makes the less strident neo-liberal reforms appear more reasonable and conciliatory. The erosion of the German 'model' will continue but appear to be less drastic than the dark plans of the demagogue Henkel. The recently floated proposal to merge the BDI and the BDA under the presidency of the 'more conciliatory' Dieter Hundt would fit well into this theatrical scenario.[28] Heise's critique of the 'sclerosis-flexibility' polarity and of neo-liberalism as macro-policy and ideology is well complemented by comparative studies of the micro-level, e.g. by Ebster-Grosz and Pugh or Casper and Vitols. Neither study draws the simplistic conclusion of a stark alternative—either the British model or further decline via German sclerosis. Instead, both seek to identify strengths and weaknesses that can be addressed by 'incremental adaptation' or by collaboration. The extensive study by Ebster-Grosz and Pugh of the relationship between British and German subsidiaries of German and British parent companies provides an illuminating picture of the dysfunctional features of the clash of two economic cultures but above all of the creative advantages of collaboration, of commercial synergies. They stress in particular the specific advantages of the British 'liberal' environment and the German 'structured' environment for specific branches of the economy or indeed specific operations within the same company: innovative products with short lead-in times thrive best in the quick-response British environment with its easier access to tailor-made short-term financing. Research-intensive products—in chemicals or pharmaceuticals—thrive best in Germany's structured environment, with its lower levels of distributed profits and longer-term financial security. Within the individual enterprise, German planning skills can complement British innovative skills, British marketing can dovetail with German after-sales service. Within this comparative framework, Ebster-Grosz and Pugh are at pains to avoid caricatures: while there are stark differences in economic culture

[26] See *Die Welt*, 12/6/1996: 'Murmann stolpert über Streit mit BDI'.
[27] See e.g. the comments by Herbert Hax, one of the group of five independent economic advisors in the Council of Economic Experts, *Die Welt*, 6/1/1998.
[28] See *Der Spiegel*, No. 2 (1998).

(in relation to skills training and financial institutions) many of the distinctions are relative.[29] Casper and Vitols identify significant residual strengths of the German model, concluding that Germany's 'competitiveness problem . . . has been exaggerated', that neo-liberal claims of 'structural barriers' are 'inaccurate or only partially true' and that perceived weaknesses in high-technology innovation are compensated by advantages in medium technology sectors.[30]

The public debate about rival models has tended to stress the export of German capital and its acquisitions in other investment locations, flagging up—in the case of UK acquisitions—the celebrated examples of BMW's takeover of Rover, VW of Rolls Royce, Dresdner Bank of Kleinwort Benson or Deutsche Bank of Morgan Grenfell. Again the public perception is misleading. Corporate restructuring has indeed increased the activity of German corporations in mergers and acquisitions and there is a net outflow of investment capital from Germany. However, in relation to direct investment flows between Britain and Germany, the available data show that 'British companies have consistently been acquiring more companies in Germany than vice versa'.[31] This applies to the period 1989 to 1996 and the trend indicates, if anything, an intensification of British interest in German companies. At a general level, the data reveal that corporate strategy does not reflect any wholesale preference for the 'liberal' environment of the UK. More specifically British companies would not seem to be deterred by the ostensible disadvantages of *Standort Deutschland* qua 'over-regulation' and high costs. Müller-Stewens and Schäfer stress rather the attractiveness of German labour skills and the technological competence of the German small and medium-sized enterprise sector as well as the geo-economic advantages of Germany's central position in a reunified European market.[32]

CONCLUSION

The debate about the rival claims of the Anglo-Saxon cum British and the European cum German 'models' must be seen within the context of a more fundamental distributional conflict taking place on a global

---

[29] See Ebster-Grosz and Pugh, *Anglo-German Business Collaboration*, esp. 201–29.

[30] S. Casper and S. Vitols, 'The German Model in the 1990s: Problems and Prospects', *Industry and Innovation* 4/1 (1997), 10, 8 ff.; see also D. Soskice, 'German Technology Policy, Innovation and National Institutional Frameworks', *Industry and Innovation* 4/1 (1997), 75–96.

[31] See G. Müller-Stewens and M. Schäfer, 'The German Market for Corporate Control: Structural Development, Cross-Border Activities and Key Players', in G. Owen and A. Richter (eds.), *Corporate Restructuring in Britain and Germany* (London, 1997), 37. [32] Ibid.

scale. The agenda and often brutish-simplistic style of the debate reflects the power shift away from organized labour and the nation state and towards the international (transnational) corporation. The bargaining weakness of both trade union and political actors is underscored by the rootedness of global mass unemployment and the fiscal crises driven by associated welfare costs. Capital can and does choose its investment locations, unions and states have fewer choices and are forced in consequence to engage in a process of wage and tax disarmament, a process which is fatally competitive. Furthermore the prospect of a twenty-first century in which global consumption needs can be serviced by 20 per cent of the potential workforce, leaving 80 per cent dependent on private and public alms,[33] underscores the extreme political vulnerability of the European consensual model and suggests that the clamorous espousal of British 'flexibility' by German industrialists will win the day, unless the process is firmly resisted.

In the absence of co-ordinated supra-national re-regulation of global capital, i.e. in the continuing 'location cannibalism' (Altvater) of competitive economic disarmament by unions and states[34] and notwithstanding the current resilience of the German consensual system, the British model would, in the short term, certainly seem to offer a greater institutional adaptability to the processes of 'modernization' and lean production. Above all, the speed of implementation at the level of capital and labour markets and of political agencies is arguably much higher in Britain than the ponderous procedures encountered in Germany. The paralysis of German taxation reform (promised now for three decades) contrasts with the rapid restructuring of British corporate taxation under Mrs Thatcher. Even if effective levels of business taxation are no higher in Germany than elsewhere in Europe, the persistence of high marginal rates provides ammunition for extravagant critiques à la Henkel.

In the medium term, however, the British 'model' is no more than a catalyst for accelerating the negative sum-game of competitive disarmament. Most of the supporters of the German model cited in this chapter concede that it is in need of reform but reject the wholesale adoption of the British alternative as naive and perilous, tantamount to throwing the baby out with the bathwater:[35] 'The big fault of many European economies—the labour market record—can be put right in ways which are consistent with the social liberal traditions of Europe, and without adopting the more laissez-faire and individualistic approach

[33] H. P. Martin and H. Schumann, *Die Globalisierungsfalle. Der Angriff auf Demokratie und Wohlstand* (Reinbek bei Hamburg, 1996), 12 ff.

[34] E. Altvater, 'A Contest without Victors: Politics in the Context of the Geo-Economy', *Journal of Area Studies* 7 (1995), 65.

[35] See C. Huhne, 'Don't throw the baby out . . .', *New Statesman*, 2/1/1998, 24 ff.

of the US.'[36] The salvaging of core elements of the German/European model is feasible but these optimistic conclusions are predicated on, or they at least imply a process of supra-national resistance. However, few of the spirited defences of consensualism explain the ways in which this model can address the core problems that will persist into the 21st century, affecting Britain, Germany and most other industrialized nations:

- the crisis of accumulation will continue: capacity surpluses and stagnating demand will continue to deter investment in additional capacity and thus in additional jobs;
- growth will be nowhere near sufficient to prevent further increases in structural unemployment;
- economic concentration will continue both to increase unemployment and distributional disparities both nationally and internationally;
- environmental problems will persist.

On the whole, there are good grounds for asserting that a politico-economic system which—like Germany's—is inclusive of a broad range of interests and opinion is better equipped both institutionally and culturally to face these enormous challenges.

[36] Ibid. 25; see also Casper and Vitols, 'The German Model in the 1990s', 10 ff.; J. Grahl and P. Teague, 'Is the European Social Model Fragmenting?', *New Political Economy* 2/3 (1997), 422 ff., and 'The Crisis of Economic Citizenship in the EU. Lean Production and the German Model', in M. Roche and R. van Berkel (eds.), *European Citizenship and Social Exclusion* (Aldershot, 1997); C. Lane, 'Is Germany Following the British Path? A Comparative Analysis of Stability and Change', *Industrial Relations Journal* 25/3 (1994), 195 ff.; Uterwedde, 'Le modèle allemand. Fin ou recommencement?', 8–14.

10

European Union Social Policy: German and British Perspectives on Industrial Citizenship

ELIZABETH MEEHAN

European Union (EU) social policy is not, as it is in states, directly redistributive. EU policy instruments provide a regulatory framework for the operation of state social policies in certain fields. This framework has come about for reasons specific to integration and does not cover the normal spectrum of intervention. These reasons include the needs to: reduce impediments, including nationality-based discrimination, to the free movement of labour; make integration more attractive to ordinary people; and reconcile the goal of economic and social cohesion with dislocations arising from the creation of a single European market.

In contrast to some of its member states, the EU has no enforceable social policy provisions specifically aimed at equality for indigenous ethnic minority communities. Provisions relating to migrants from countries outside the EU are dealt with, not as matters of social policy, but—hitherto—under the Justice and Home Affairs pillar of the Maastricht Treaty. Both of these are set to change under the Amsterdam Treaty which provides a constitutional basis for the enactment of EU legislation to outlaw ethnic and racial discrimination and which will bring the treatment of migrants from 'third countries' under the aegis of Community instead of intergovernmental institutions.

The main successes in securing agreement over EU social policy have been the co-ordination of social security arrangements for migrant workers and, irrespective of migration, in the fields of sex equality and occupational health and safety. The main controversy over social policy has been in the field of industrial citizenship. Since industrial citizenship is significant to competing conceptions of European integration and since Germany and the United Kingdom (UK) are central to this conflict, this chapter will concentrate on that aspect of social policy.

Recent literature reveals three understandings of developments in industrial and social citizenship in the EU. One suggestion is that there

The author would like to thank Mary Browne for her generous assistance with sources.

is a hybrid of liberal and social-democratic approaches to welfare rights and a conservative, corporatist approach to industrial rights.[1] Second, there are negative readings of hybridity. For example, the weakness of the Community Charter of Fundamental Social Rights of Workers has been attributed to a clash between the 'liberal' and 'social' state, exemplified respectively by the UK and Germany.[2] It is also argued that, while the EU's approach to social protection is still more similar to that of northern countries than the UK, there are pressures on other member states to introduce more coercive systems, though not necessarily in the British pattern.[3] Third, there is said to be a contest in which, according to one conclusion, Germany's approach prevails or, according to another, the UK's. For example, Haseler predicts 'serious pressures upon Britain to adapt to continental European (primarily German) economic culture—to continental ways of industry and industrial relations'.[4] Conversely, Streeck argues that the Europeanization of the German model of industrial citizenship is a lost battle and that European provisions threaten not Britain but Germany.[5] And Duff suggests that, notwithstanding the repositioning of social policy in the heart of Treaty provisions, the relevant Amsterdam chapters reflect a shift to liberal opinion—initially associated mainly with Britain but now, to some extent, exported to Germany.[6]

This chapter will conclude that a hybrid model has not been displaced by a contest in which either the British or the German approach has been 'Europeanized' wholly at the expense of the other and, indeed, that the perception of a contest between national traditions may be misguided. The chapter opens with an outline of why industrial and social rights have come to be seen as a necessary component of equal citizenship. It then discusses the place of industrial and social rights in the so-called 'Rhenish' and 'Anglo-Saxon' models of capitalism. After that, developments in EU industrial citizenship and social policy are analysed. It is then argued that

---

[1] P. Close, *Citizenship, Europe and Change* (Basingstoke, 1995), 201–6.

[2] B. Hepple, 'The Implementation of the Community Charter of Fundamental Social Rights', *The Modern Law Review* 53/5 (1990), 643–54, 653. See also B. Hepple, 'Social Rights in the European Economic Community: A British Perspective', *Comparative Labor Law Journal* 11/4 (1990), 425–40.

[3] J. Cook, 'Restructuring Social Rights in the EU. Does a Flexible Employment and Benefits Regime Entrench Exclusion and Inequality?', in M. Roche and R. van Berkel (eds.), *European Citizenship and Social Exclusion* (Aldershot, 1997), 151–68, at 161.

[4] S. Haseler, *The English Tribe: Identity, Nation and Europe* (Basingstoke, 1996), 169–72.

[5] W. Streeck, 'Citizenship Under Regime Competition: The Case of the European Works Councils', *European Integration on-line Papers* (EIoP) 1/005 (1997) [http://eiop.or.at/eiop/texte /1997-005a.htm. 1–24]. Grahl and Teague also discern the diminution of the German model, though, perhaps less starkly than Streeck. See J. Grahl and P. Teague, 'The Crisis of Economic Citizenship in the EU: Lean Production and the German Model', in M. Roche and R. van Berkel (eds.), *European Citizenship and Social Exclusion*, 67–82, esp. 68.

[6] A. Duff, *The Treaty of Amsterdam: Text and Commentary* (London, 1997), 63–5, 72–3; see also below, Ch. 13.

the depth of differences—over integration *per se* and industrial citizenship —between the two countries means that German approaches have not disappeared. It is unlikely, however, that the UK will have to adopt a 'Europeanized' version of German industrial rights. Instead, as suggested in conclusion, both countries, in partnership with other member states, may have to develop something specific to the EU.

INDUSTRIAL AND SOCIAL CITIZENSHIP

The idea that there is an industrial element to the notion of citizenship derives from various critiques of early models of political participation in which even radicals insisted that the accumulation of property indicated fitness for taking part in public life.[7] In the early twentieth century, it began to be argued that the connection between unequal property relations and political inequality was not a matter of ownership but control. Workers' lives, and thus their autonomy, were controlled, not by distant shareholders, but salaried employees. Constraints upon their personal development had not been transformed by the transfer of ownership from private to public hands, either under communism or by the nationalization of industries in social-democratic regimes.

The ideas of advocates both of workers' control and participatory democracy came together in several ways. They identified similar conventional justifications for elite dominance; that is, the natural possession of craft or wisdom by some people but not all. The challenge to this was similar in both sets of ideas; that management skills and political arts could both be understood if opportunities for doing so were provided—by 'opening the books' and publishing 'social audits'. Participatory democrats revived John Stuart Mill's idea that workplace democracy could provide an outlet for the expression of people's inherently political natures—difficult to achieve in representative democracies compared to the smaller polities of Greek city states. Participation in familiar spheres could be instrumental in the development of aspirations and skills for wider political transformations. And, if lack of control rather than ownership was, indeed, the source of political inequality, then sharing control was a crucial means of equalizing citizenship.

Critiques of the property basis of older conceptions of citizenship also led to justifications for social security entitlements and services. If the need to scrabble for subsistence impeded the development of the intellectual qualities required for the exercise of disinterested judgement, excluding

---

[7] E. Meehan, *Citizenship and the European Community* (London, 1993), esp. ch. 5.

people was not the only answer. Instead, their material deprivation could be addressed. One version of the idea that social rights are essential to equal citizenship assumes that they enable individuals to pursue their own lawful pursuits. Another holds that a fair distribution of social justice is the basis of a solidaristic or common moral order.

Many accounts of citizenship distinguish between forms of universalization that are genuine extensions of power and those which are introduced to pre-empt radical social transformations. Bismarckian reforms in Germany could be construed as the latter.[8] Whether or not modern German and British rights fall into the former or latter categories is beyond the scope of this chapter. But it should be noted that industrial and social rights have a different place in the 'Rhenish' and 'Anglo-Saxon' models of economic organization.

MODELS OF ECONOMIC ORGANIZATION AND THE PLACE OF INDUSTRIAL CITIZENSHIP AND SOCIAL RIGHTS

The 'Rhenish' model, found in Switzerland, Germany, the Benelux countries, and Japan, rests on the idea that prosperity demands consensus, the pursuit of collective success, and concern for the long-term. The 'Anglo-Saxon' model, associated with the United States of America and the UK, is characterized as being driven by the need to provide opportunities for individual success and short-term profit.[9] The two models are sometimes contrasted as 'organized capitalism' versus 'disorganized capitalism';[10] in this volume, Leaman (Ch. 9) refers to flexibility versus a structured or consensus model.

---

[8] If the tide has turned from Germany being a model to be emulated to one to be circumvented, the current direction of influence over modern social rights is in marked contrast to the direction of influence when they were first regarded as necessary. In the 19th cent., Germany was something of a model for the UK in its demonstration that social rights could be extended in the absence of universal political rights (see F. Twine, *Citizenship and Social Rights: The Interdependence of Self and Society*, London, 1994, 103). In coming to believe that an 'uncoordinated and fragmentary approach to social problems' would not do, British reformers looked to Germany's more systematic innovations in education and Bismarck's compulsory insurance schemes (see G. Finlayson, *Citizen, State, and Social Welfare in Britain 1830–1990*, Oxford, 1994, 163–4). As Churchill put it, Germany was better placed than the UK for it was organized 'not only for war but also for peace' (ibid.) and his outlook gained 'increasing acceptance' in the UK during the first decade of the 20th cent., by then in combination with the promise of governments elected to introduce social rights for the purpose of reducing economic and social inequality (Twine, loc. cit.).

[9] Marquand, drawing on Michel Albert in D. Marquand, *The New Reckoning: Capitalism, States and Citizens* (Oxford, 1997), 181–5; Haseler, *The English Tribe*, 169–72.

[10] Marquand, *The New Reckoning*, ch. 9.

Within these broad approaches to economic organization are a number of industrial relations models. Though they may sometimes coexist, in different sectors within one country, it could be argued that, under the 'Rhenish' approach, industrial relations follow what Cassells calls the partnership/new industrial relations model in which

union management dialogue moves beyond collective bargaining alone to embrace business and product plans and strategies, and the design or re-design of production systems, linked to ongoing flexibility in work processes, new payment systems and more investment in training and development.[11]

The effects on industrial relations of responses by economic and political leaders to international competition [and, in the case of Germany to unification] have been less marked in Germany than in the UK. Indeed, the German system remains relatively intact as a result of willingness of trade unions to use institutions of partnership to accommodate more flexibility.[12] As a result of greater enthusiasm among UK employers and policy-makers for flexibilization as a response to global pressures, there are elements of all of Cassells's other models of industrial relations.[13] These are the reduction of statutory or other regulation of managerial action and labour markets, some elements of the non-union human resource model and remnants of the adversarial model.

Connections between the development of systems of industrial relations and notions of citizenship differ in the two countries. T. H. Marshall argued that the British trade union movement created a secondary system of citizenship: an industrial citizenship sitting alongside and buttressing political citizenship. It concerned itself primarily with collective bargaining and the defence of social rights.[14] It referred to more than a socio-economic extension of individualistic citizenship to facilitate the pursuit of personal ends because it involved the collective exercise of freedom of contract. But it was different from innovations in most other liberal-democracies where, according to Streeck, industrial citizenship was and is seen as the means of institutionalizing participation.[15]

Thus, the representation of antagonistic interests through a single channel has been more important in British industrial relations than industrial democracy as practised in the dual German system.[16] Despite

---

[11] P. Cassells, 'Welfare, Security and Economic Performance', in D. Foden and P. Morris (eds.), *The Search for Equity* (London, 1998), 114–21, at 121.

[12] J. Visser and J. van Ruysseveldt, 'Robust Corporatism, Still? Industrial Relations in Germany', in J. van Ruysseveldt and J. Visser (eds.), *Industrial Relations in Europe: Traditions and Transitions* (London, 1996), 124–74, at 162.

[13] Cassells, 'Welfare, Security and Economic Performance', 121.

[14] This aspect of T. H. Marshall's influential work is discussed by Streeck in 'Citizenship under Regime Competition', 5.   [15] Ibid. 5–6.

[16] J. Visser and J. van Ruysseveldt, 'From Pluralism to Where? Industrial Relations in Great Britain', in J. van Ruysseveldt and J. Visser (eds.), *Industrial Relations in Europe*, 42–81, at 44.

workers' control movements in Britain after 1918 and again in the 1960s and 1970s, the management of firms by workers has never become wider than a handful of experiments in job enrichment schemes and employee 'buy-outs'. The findings of one public enquiry on participation at the strategic level were rejected by trades unions.[17] The perceived strength of trade unions in defending interests came to be seen by rightward-moving labour governments and new-right conservatives as an important cause of British decline. Thus, policy focused on reducing collective bargaining rights and statutory regulation rather than encouraging something like the German system of co-determination. Ironically, however, the now weakened British unions have begun to be interested in Germany and the Europeanization of the German model.

In the German case, participation occurs at two levels: one 'interferes with the rights of property' (co-determination and company law), the other modifies the managerial prerogative in day-to-day company activities (regulation of the employment relationship and labour market law).[18] The common and antagonistic interests of the two sides of industry are institutionalized separately. While questions of pay and hours are dealt with through collective bargaining, German workers are represented on works councils and company boards where they participate in day-to-day and strategic decision-making respectively. Despite criticism during the 1970s that this dual system 'stifl[ed] industrial militancy and suppress[ed] class conflict',[19] it has survived as the model Haseler expects will have to be accepted by the UK.[20]

While Britain once saw Germany as exemplary in the solution of social problems,[21] the 'Anglo-Saxon' model is imbued with the new-right critique of social rights. Though associated with the USA, the critique is also a recognizable descendant of the old English preference for negative liberties over positive rights. In this approach, the duty of the state to maintain individual well-being or success is limited to the removal of arbitrary coercion or statutory impediments. Since the constraints of poverty cannot be attributed to the actions of any particular person but arise from the impersonal operations of the market, there can be no rights-based justification to intervene. Moreover, compensation by the state for material inequality entails depriving others of part of their income through taxation—a form of coercion, which also, in the long-run, weakens the prosperity of all by inhibiting 'trickle-down' effects.

[17] Ibid.   [18] Streeck, 'Citizenship Under Regime Competition', 5–6.
[19] O. Jacobi, B. Keller and W. Müller-Jentsch, 'Germany: Codetermining the Future?', in A. Ferner and R. Hyman (eds.), *Industrial Relations in the New Europe* (Oxford, 1992), 220–69, at 221.   [20] Haseler, *The English Tribe*, 169–72.
[21] See n. 8 above.

This is not to say that the 'Anglo-Saxon' model has eliminated state provision in the UK. Governments inherit the obligations of their predecessors and have to attend to public opinion. Moreover, new-right theory can accommodate intervention if it is based, not on rights, but on grounds of minimal justice or instrumentality and if it is realized through other means. Such means include the 'marketization' of services and the treatment of citizens as consumers. The point is that social provision in this approach is a matter of contingency rather than inherent in a conception of citizenship. Though social provision in Germany is instrumental to its consensual economic culture, social security and services are safer in their being regarded as essential to long-term collective well-being— instead of thought of as inhibiting profits and individual success.

In the history of social policy and citizenship in the EU, aspirations for industrial citizenship and a non-contingent approach to social rights can be seen, including the idea that the EU is not only a sphere for pursuing individual ends but also a collective moral order. But, as noted, the question now arises as to whether these are being 'squeezed out' in a contest between the 'Rhenish' and 'Anglo-Saxon' models.

INDUSTRIAL CITIZENSHIP AND SOCIAL RIGHTS IN THE EU

The European industrial citizenship project has three historical phases.[22] First, there were aspirations to harmonization in the 1970s, through both company and labour law—in effect, the Europeanization of the German model.[23] Then, in the 1980s, efforts were made to by-pass the property dimension, industrial rights being brought under ambit of labour law.[24] Subsidiarity was anticipated in that national differences were acknowledged as legitimate. Third, in the 1990s, co-ordination was sought to ensure that such differences did not undermine the integrated market, the means of this being the supranational regulation of national systems of labour law and the encouragement of voluntary agreements.

The most ambitious of EU moves, in the first two phases, towards industrial citizenship are still, if vulnerably, on the agenda. It is these that Haseler has in mind when he speaks of pressures upon the UK to transform its arrangements along these lines of German co-determination.[25]

---

[22] W. Streeck, 'Industrial Citizenship under Regime Competition: the Case of the European Works Councils', *Journal of European Public Policy* 4/4 (1997), 643–64, at 646.
[23] Streeck, 'Citizenship Under Regime Competition', 8.   [24] Ibid.
[25] Haseler, *The English Tribe*, 169–72.

(a) Industrial Citizenship—the First Phase

During the 1970s, European aspirations to industrial citizenship were under-pinned by a version of state-building and an assumption that harmonization was possible only if undertaken at the highest level. In the light of social upheavals in the late 1960s, it was assumed that the project would have to match German standards.[26] Defending the highest national standards on a transnational basis was motivated, not only by pan-Europeanism, but also by the need to ensure that companies could not evade con-sultation by claiming that this took place at headquarters in a country other than Germany.[27] Two methods were attempted: reform of company law to bring about workers' rights of participation and of labour law to modify managerial prerogatives over the employment relationship. In response to the German government, the first phase of EU industrial citizenship envisaged a two-tier board, combining company and work-place participation. But the idea of a 'wholesale adoption of the German model' waned as German business organisations began to reassess the costs of integration at the highest standards *vis-à-vis* the costs of living with diversity.[28]

(b) Industrial Citizenship—the Second Phase and the Origins of Phase Three

The second phase marks the 'failure to expand co-determination from Germany to the other members'.[29] In this period can be seen the discovery of what later was to be called 'subsidiarity'. Attempting to bypass hos-tility in the 1970s among other member states to the German model, the 'Vredeling Directive' of 1980 (1980/C297/3) sought to generalize mat-ters of consultation and information which had already been agreed to in limited situations of redundancy and the transfer of undertakings (the 'Acquired Rights' Directive). Commission Vice-President Vredeling's proposals would have compelled transnational and complex national companies to inform their staff of the structure of the enterprise, its situation and the development of employment and investment. Instead of finding consensus, the proposals provoked new hostility from business and in the Council of Ministers where the British were expected to exercise the veto.[30] The draft Directive was suspended in 1986. As its

[26] Streeck, 'Citizenship Under Regime Competition', 6, and 'Industrial Citizenship under Regime Competition', 645.　　　　　　　　　　　　　　　　　　　　　　　[27] Ibid.

[28] Ibid. 648.

[29] W. Streeck and P. C. Schmitter, 'From National Corporatism to Transnational Pluralism: Organized Interests in the Single European Market', *Politics and Society* 19/2 (1991), 133–164, at 139.

[30] G. Falkner, 'European Works Councils and the Maastricht Social Agreement: Towards a New Policy Style?', *Journal of European Public Policy* 3/2 (1996), 192–208.

failure became increasingly likely, company law was reconsidered, though not limited to the German system. In 1983, four models of participation were proposed; a choice between a two-tier board, single board, works council, or any other agreed structure.[31] But, in the absence of progress, discussion was also suspended in 1986.

The issue did not disappear, however, since governmental fears continued in Germany that German firms might escape national law by using potentially less strict European law and, in 1989, a revised version of a European Company Statute (ECS) was drafted. This emerged from the provisions of the Action Programme which accompanied the Declaration on Fundamental Social Rights for Workers (together, usually known as the Social Charter). The programme's proposals covered rights to information, consultation and participation, particularly in companies incorporated at the European level.[32] These were opposed by other countries, including the UK, which feared being forced to accept the German model. In 1991 another version of the ECS was drafted in which the 1983 option of a works council was dropped and substituted by 'Social Dialogue'.[33] In the hope of circumventing a British veto, the proposals were divided into company statutes and worker participation so that they could be based on separate Treaty provisions, thereby permitting qualified majority voting instead of requiring unanimity. The Commission hoped that a link could be maintained by the two sets of proposals being decided upon simultaneously.[34] As Streeck points out, the 'less noticed' corollary of this device was that it also ruled out a German veto in the event of European company law on incorporation without worker participation.[35] Despite the device to enable qualified majority voting, no legislation was achieved.

However, these efforts coincided with other developments, which anticipate the voluntarism with which Streeck characterizes the third phase. The growing momentum towards an 'ever closer union' was accompanied by a wider interest in the roles of citizens and social partners. The 1985 Adonnino Report highlighted the need for citizens to be included in decision-making.[36] Some 'Social Dialogue' took place, though inconclusively, in the Val Duchesse talks.[37] The peak organizations of employers (UNICE and CEEP) and unions (ETUC) did reach opinions on macro-economic policy, growth and employment in 1987 but discussion then petered out. The Single European Act formalized 'Social Dialogue'

---

[31] Streeck, 'Citizenship Under Regime Competition', 9.
[32] G. Ross, 'The European Community and Social Policy: Regional Blocs and a Humane Social Order', *Studies in Political Economy* 40/2 (1993), 41–73, 54–5.
[33] Streeck, 'Citizenship Under Regime Competition', 9–11.   [34] Ibid. 9.   [35] Ibid.
[36] 'A Peoples' Europe', *Bulletin of the European Communities*, Supplement 7/85 (Luxemburg, 1985).   [37] Ross, 'The European Community and Social Policy', 53–4.

and authorized it as a basis of European-wide agreements, if the two sides thought it appropriate.[38] In the climate of the new company law proposals in 1989, 'Social Dialogue' was relaunched in the same year,[39] this time to see if agreement could be reached over the Charter's proposals for participation. Three possible models were discussed: representation on boards of either the German or Dutch type; representation through works councils; or, as in British practice, through collective bargaining. Agreement was reached on the incorporation of companies but not participation, where employers wanted to set out broad principles but where the ETUC was seeking concrete proposals.[40]

From the Commission's point of view, both EMU and social cohesion (or its absence) implied further Treaty revisions.[41] In noting disparities in systems of industrial relations, its staff highlighted the need to respect 'positive diversity', while also 'moving forward'.[42] This led to a new approach to 'Social Dialogue'. Rejected at first, it was finally agreed that the Commission would 'signal its intentions' and 'solicit negotiated proposals from the social partners'.[43] If suitable suggestions were produced, they would be converted into a 'framework agreement' (instead of leading to legislation). If accepted in the Council of Ministers, framework agreements would have force of law. The Commission would make legislative proposals only if the social partners could not reach agreement. In the event, two such agreements have been translated into Directives: on maximum working hours and on the rights of part-time workers. In the case of the former, the British government has angered the TUC by enshrining it on the basis that individuals might volunteer to work longer hours.[44]

(c) Industrial Citizenship—the Full Articulation of Phase Three

In the wake of the Maastricht Treaty, but coming originally from the Social Charter, a European Works Council Directive was agreed in 1994. Under it, national law should require national firms with branches in other countries to negotiate with their whole European workforce. If agreement cannot be reached, companies must set up a European Works Council.

According to Streeck, its fanfare was overblown in comparison to its modest ambitions.[45] Provisions for participation are about information rather than real consultation. There are no rights (associated with property, company statutes, and co-determination) to contribute to strategic decision-making. Even merely as an innovation in regulating the

---

[38] Ibid. 53.   [39] Ibid. 54.   [40] Ibid. 54–5.
[41] Ibid. 59.   [42] Ibid. 56–7.   [43] Ibid. 67–9.
[44] The *Independent*, 9/4/1998.
[45] Streeck, 'Citizenship Under Regime Competition', 10–12.

employment relationship, it does not introduce a transnational regime of equal rights. As Streeck points out: it excludes workers in firms with no multinational operations. It also creates a system in which there are pan-European rights for workers in branches of firms operating in more than one country which sit alongside pre-existing systems of weaker or stronger (depending on the country) national rights. Justified by reference to subsidiarity, the setting of standards and the details of how national and European systems may coexist are left to voluntary negotiation or national governments.

Streeck argues that fragmentation, while apparently protecting stronger systems of rights, may come to erode German standards rather than raise those in weaker systems such as the British.[46] Among other things, he believes that representatives of the 'home country workforce', because of familiarity and numerical dominance, are likely, at first, to be more influential than those of 'foreign-based workforces' in European extensions of national works councils. In Germany, since the Directive is based on labour law not company law, representation 'on a large company board will remain confined to its German workforce', even if most of the company's workforce is employed outside Germany. European Works Councils in Germany will coexist with traditional, national central works councils which will have better contacts with management and the relevant trade union.

On the other hand, foreign-based workforces which have European rights in countries with weak domestic rights are likely to resist unequal access to information and influence between themselves and home country workforces with strong rights such as those in Germany. In seeking to upgrade their situations, weaker foreign-based workforce representatives may collude with management to weaken the stronger system. Indeed, Streeck suggests that this is already happening in the German case, where he observes the initiation of alliances between non-German workers and management in companies with German headquarters to upgrade works councils *vis-à-vis* co-determination arrangements—thereby marginalizing the latter.[47] According to Streeck, this fragmentation of interests is causing the isolation of German unions in the ETUC—though perhaps less than he suggests, given the new British union interest, mentioned earlier, in the German system.[48] The fragmentation is also weakening the unity of German unions and government in seeing the need for the EU to promote industrial rights through company law and co-determination.

Thus, the German government seems to have moved slightly closer to that of the UK. The latter, even under the Labour Party, is refusing to

---

[46] Ibid. 13–14.   [47] Ibid. 14.
[48] Visser and van Ruysseveldt, 'From Pluralism to Where?', 44.

accept the further extension of workers' rights of consultation that is being called for by Continental unions, because it fears the possibility of mass redundancies during the introduction of the single currency.[49]

(d) Social Rights

As noted earlier, social rights are part of the British conception of industrial citizenship and, together with worker participation, they are central to the so-called 'Rhenish' model. After an inauspicious start—except in the regulation of different national social security systems to avoid disadvantage to migrant workers, in sex equality, and in various 'soft law' provisions[50]—social rights acquired an increasing importance. This was reflected in the SEA, the Social Charter, and, albeit ambiguously, in the Maastricht Treaty.[51] In and since the SEA, the EU acquired new competencies in, for example, occupational health and safety. But, as in the past, social protection must be compatible with the 'economic constitution of community'. This contrasts with the outlook of T. H. Marshall for whom, as Majone points out, social policy represents the use of 'political power to supersede or supplement the operations of the economic system'.[52] Nevertheless, some EU policies are 'well above the lowest common denominators' and cover some 'areas neglected in national systems'.[53]

Such ambivalence is illustrated by Goma's observation of the Maastricht Treaty's positive and negative potential for the decommodification of labour.[54] The Treaty 'opened the way for a high level of welfare integration' but 'social policy is unevenly Europeanised, equality and its redistributional dimension under permanent stress, half-hearted and work oriented'. European social policy differs from national provisions because it is 'linked not to solidarity building but economic restructuring'. Such a view is partly shared by Marquand and Scharpf who argue that the SEM is an attempt to allow market forces to bring about investment and growth.[55] This was the deliberate intention of democratically accountable national governments, which are no longer able to maintain welfare programmes that previously were taken for granted. While it would be self-defeating, therefore, to reinstate such provisions through harmonization at a higher level of governance, most governments and the Commission

---

[49] *The Week*, 21/3/1998, 4.

[50] Meehan, *Citizenship and the European Community*, chs. 4–6.

[51] G. Majone, 'The European Community between Social Policy and Social Regulation', *Journal of Common Market Studies* 31/2 (1993), 153–71, at 153–4.   [52] Ibid. 156.

[53] Ibid. 166–8.

[54] R. Goma, 'The Social Dimension of the European Union: a New Type of Welfare System?', *Journal of European Public Policy* 3/2(1996), 209–30, at 222 and 227–8.

[55] Marquand, *The New Reckoning*, 157; F. Scharpf, 'Economic Integration, Democracy and the Welfare State', *Journal of European Public Policy* 4/1 (1997), 18–36, at 27.

see the need for a social dimension to avoid 'social dumping'. This is a fear that is strongest in Germany[56] and a solution that is least acceptable in the UK. Though the Labour government elected in 1997 ended the UK opt-out of the Social Chapter of the Maastricht Treaty, it has no great taste for 'a raft' of new social legislation.[57] Despite the German fear, Duff's account of the Amsterdam Treaty suggests that the Continental consensus amongst Social-Democrats, Christian-Democrats, and Commission personnel—that there cannot be economic prosperity without a satisfactory social dimension—is not immune to British scepticism of such an approach.[58]

OUTLOOKS IN GERMANY AND THE UK TO INTEGRATION AND ITS SIGNIFICANCE FOR INDUSTRIAL DEMOCRACY

Differences between German and British outlooks to the place of industrial democracy in the EU run parallel to their different contributions to and experiences of integration. The development of modern Germany and of European integration are mutually reinforcing—the opposite of British experience.

In the German case, the links run in two directions: on the one hand, Sperling suggests that 'German economic culture has become the economic culture of Europe';[59] on the other hand, the German polity has been Europeanized. This contrasts with a reluctant growth of understanding in the UK that its future necessarily lay in membership of the then European Communities. Despite the eventual cross-party consensus that this was so, there is a continuing sense—especially in the Conservative Party— that power and cherished institutions and practices are diminished rather than enhanced by integration.

Goetz concedes that it is possible to interpret certain actions by the Länder, the Bundesrat, Bundestag, and the Constitutional Court as intended to arrest the Federal government's Europeanification of Germany and the Germanification of Europe.[60] But he also suggests that these moves do not represent a serious challenge to a widespread consensus in favour of both these effects. He points out that the 1949 Basic Law made post-war Germany 'open to integration' from the start, stating

---

[56] Ross, 'The European Community and Social Policy', 60–1.
[57] Institute of European Affairs, *IGC Update*, No. 8 (Dublin, 1997).
[58] Duff, *The Treaty of Amsterdam*.
[59] Quoted in K. H. Goetz, 'Integration Policy in a Europeanised State: Germany and the Intergovernmental Conference', *Journal of European Public Policy* 3/1 (1996), 23–44, at 31.
[60] Ibid. 25–33.

as it does that Germany was to be 'an equal partner in a united Europe' and permitted by Article 24:1 to 'transfer sovereign powers to intergovernmental institutions'.[61] The new Article 23, replacing the now obsolete objective of German reunification, articulates Germany's undertaking to participate in the development of union in Europe—a union committed to 'democratic, rule-of-law, social and federal principles'.[62] Goetz suggests that this Article is sometimes taken to indicate the possibility of rupture between Germany and other member states, should the latter lead the EU away from German understandings of these concepts. But he is not persuaded either that the European agenda endangers German values and practices or that the constitutional stipulation limits Germany's 'in-built integrationist orientation'.

From the beginning, German unions were more in favour of European integration that than those of UK[63]—at least until the British Labour Party changed its EU policy and Jacques Delors addressed the Trades Union Congress (TUC) in 1986. German unions were part of the national consensus about the importance of the EU to the national interest. They also hoped for common European standards, not only to avoid 'social dumping', but also because the EU could be deployed domestically to help workers' representatives to meet new demands. Such demands include those of women who increasingly entered the labour market but for whom law and practice continued to be very traditional.[64] There were regular national conferences between government and labour on the SEM.[65]

Since 1992, while British unions have acquired an orientation towards European activism,[66] German attitudes have become more ambivalent; or, at least, are viewed more ambivalently in the literature. According to Weiss, German unions are not averse to EU regulation because they believe that, since their standards surpass those of the EU, except in the case of gender, the EU does not affect them adversely. He believes that German unions would challenge any attempt to modify worker participation, while, at the same time, recognizing that the German system cannot be forced on others.[67] On the other hand, Streeck believes that German unions had little influence on the 1992 project and, therefore, on the risk to workers' participation brought about by the transnational mergers occasioned by the SEM.[68] Despite declining influence on government and the potential

---

[61] Ibid. 37.   [62] Ibid. 38.

[63] W. Streeck, 'More Uncertainties: German Unions Facing 1992', *Industrial Relations* 30/3 (1991), 317–48, at 321.   [64] Ibid. 333–4.

[65] M. Weiss, 'Labour Law and Industrial Relations in Europe 1992: A German Perspective', *Comparative Labor Law Journal* 11/4 (1990), 411–24, at 415.

[66] B. Wemdon, 'British Trade Union Responses to European Integration', *Journal of European Public Policy* 1/2 (1994), 243–61; Visser and van Ruysseveldt, 'From Pluralism to Where?', 44.

[67] Weiss, 'Labour Law and Industrial Relations in Europe 1992', 416–21.

[68] Streeck, 'More Uncertainties: German Unions Facing 1992', 337.

for a diminished EU industrial citizenship to erode German standards, unions retain a vague hope that stronger integration at a higher level could be a defence. But the fragmentation of industrial citizenship practices and the isolation of Germany in the ETUC mean that German unions have no EU strategy except co-operation with national unions elsewhere.[69]

From the governmental standpoint, Leaman suggests (above, Ch. 9) that Germany accepted French hopes for EMU in exchange for France's agreeing to the export of Germany's industrial or economic model. German Christian-Democrats supported the Social Charter and related policies because of the belief that social partnership and consensus are the prerequisites, not only of their economy, but also—like the Delors-led Commission—of successful deregulation in Europe.[70] But the Franco-German axis, mediated by the state at any given time of the relationship between either of them and the UK, is not always the driving force.[71] And, indeed, British governments had some support for their stance of seeking deregulation without the amelioration of social policy. The Social Charter was seen by new-right conservatives as 'corporatist or even Marxist'.[72] Usually, UNICE (the Union of Industrial and Employers' Confederations of Europe) was on the same side as the UK—over works councils, the Social Charter and social policy in general. Some member states may have been covertly grateful for aspects of the British agenda.[73] As already indicated, the deregulatory agenda has been accepted sufficiently in Germany so as to weaken the consensus between government and unions.

Nevertheless, although British and German outlooks have turned towards each other, differences remain which will affect the EU agenda on workers' rights and the means of maintaining social consensus. Haseler suggests that, while the British understand high social costs to imply uncompetitiveness, the Continental view is that, since Europe will never be able to match low social costs in Asia, there is little point in making this a primary goal.[74] This rests on two deeper differences identified by Marquand.[75] The first of these is that the 'Anglo-Saxon' approach construes interference with the market by the state or voluntary associations as merely slowing down necessary adjustment processes in which losers are necessarily swept aside. Conversely, in the Continental approach, success needs not only crude positive and negative incentives, but also

---

[69] J. Hoffmann, 'Trade Union reform in Germany: Some Analytical and Critical Remarks Concerning the Current Debate', *Transfer* 1 (1995), 98–113, at 111.

[70] Marquand, *The New Reckoning*, 157, 181–5.

[71] S. George, 'The Approach of the British Government to the 1996 Intergovernmental Conference of the European Union', *Journal of European Public Policy* 3/1 (1996), 45–62, at 50–1.   [72] Marquand, *The New Reckoning*, 157.

[73] J. Grahl and P. Teague, *1992 The Big Market: the Future of the European Community* (London, 1990), 298–9, 300–1.   [74] Haseler, *The English Tribe*, 171.

[75] Marquand, *The New Reckoning*, 158, 185.

persuasion and negotiation—leading, therefore, to a trade-off between 'strict allocative efficiency' and 'social peace and political consensus'.[76] The second deeper difference noted by Marquand lies in differing conceptions of the individual. In drawing upon the English conception to account for differences over EU social policy between Germany and the UK, he argues that the British prioritize individuals in themselves whereas, in the German conception, individuals are shaped by their community. The latter characterization is also reflected in Haseler's quotation of Thomas Mann's view that the 'uniqueness of German individualism was its compatibility with . . . the social principle—the fusion of rights with collectivities, an aspect of post-war German success in companies and industrial organisation'.[77]

CONCLUSION

It is necessary now to re-address the assessments with which this chapter opened. Is EU policy on industrial and social rights: a congenial hybrid; a lowest common denominator consensus that satisfies no one; or dominated either by German or British conceptions? The answer may be all or none or that, in any case, to seek a definitive judgement may be beside the point.

The jury is out on the question of the Europeanization of either the German or British model. Haseler argues that Mann's 'social principle' and the American-inspired Basic Law mean that Germany is Europe's stable democratic core.[78] Conversely, Streeck's argument that a regime of weak supranational rights is undermining strong national rights implies that the British outlook is gaining ground.[79] Duff's commentary on the Amsterdam Treaty indicates that this may represent not the defeat of the German model but acknowledgement by German political and economic elites of some force in the British position; in other words, a hybrid or minimal consensus.[80]

Whether the political scope for common policies is congenial or unsatisfactory to the participants will rest on an uneasy interplay of coexistent systems. The survival of both traditions is reflected in divergent responses to the Social Charter[81] and to flexibilization pressures.

---

[76] It may be worth noting in connection with these contrasting outlooks that Visser and van Ruysseveldt find that the 'rigidities' of German partnership have, in fact, facilitated diversification, whereas deregulation in the UK has been paid for at the high price of the country becoming an economy with low costs but also low wages and low productivity. Visser and van Ruysseveldt, 'From Pluralism to Where?' and 'Robust Corporatism Still?', 80–1, 160–2.

[77] Haseler, *The English Tribe*, 148.   [78] Ibid. 148–9.

[79] Streeck, 'Citizenship Under Regime Competition', 4–6.

[80] Duff, *The Treaty of Amsterdam*.   [81] Marquand, *The New Reckoning*, 158.

According to some accounts, Germans unions have more control than UK counterparts in their negotiation of team-working so that schemes are not cosmetic forms of job enrichment. Indeed—though this is also disputed—'modernisation pacts' are said to equate to 'co-determination on the shop-floor'.[82] Leaman (above, Ch. 9) shows that pressures for more flexibility and lower social costs are accompanied in Germany by a concern 'not to throw out the baby with the bathwater'. On the other hand, the hopes of British unions of the EU and representation in it by a new British government are being disappointed by an approach, which, while it may differ in style from before, offers little of substance. Perhaps the Commission will be hospitable to the maintenance on a European basis of aspects of the German approach for as long as its Social Affairs Commissioner remains Padraig Flynn from the Republic of Ireland—a man accustomed in his own country to consensus institutions; that is, a degree of corporatism in the upper house, industrial relations resolved through compact, and partnership in economic policy-making.[83] Indeed, the partnership basis of the success of the 'Celtic tiger' is becoming of interest outside Ireland.[84]

Interest in the Irish case suggests that a preoccupation with the respective fates of the 'Rhenish' and 'Anglo-Saxon' models may now be redundant. As Peter Cassells, the General Secretary of the Irish Congress of Trade Unions, suggests, new approaches are needed which take account of transformations in technologies, values, and politics.[85] He argues that 'Social Dialogue' has so far failed to produce a means of modernization through 'striking a balance between flexibility and security and between individualism and partnership'. A proper partnership would need to be sustained by five principles which: (i) recognize the interdependence of countries and of groups within countries; (ii) reflect appreciation of the value of co-operation; (iii) embody greater respect for workers and entrepreneurs; (iv) are capable of producing higher levels of trust between workers and management; and (v) display commitment to fair sharing, which takes account of a changing pattern of winners and losers.

If Cassells is right about 'Social Dialogue', it will be necessary also to reconstruct the basic concept of industrial citizenship and the presupposi-

---

[82] Hoffmann, 'Trade Union Reform in Germany', 102. A more sober assessment can be found in Grahl and Teague, 'The Crisis of Economic Citizenship', 76.

[83] R. O'Donnell, 'Modernisation and Social Partnership', in R. Wilson (ed.), *New Thinking for New Times* (Belfast, 1995), 24–33. Whether the replacement of Padraig Flynn by Anna Diamantopoulou from Greece in late 1999, when the new EU commission led by Romano Prodi took office, will result in any substantial policy changes remains to be seen.

[84] Contribution by Peter Cassells, General Secretary of the Irish Congress of Trade Unions during a debate at a seminar entitled 'Ireland and Europe: Reflections on 25 Years Membership', session on Economics (Dublin: Institute of European Affairs, 19/11/1998).

[85] Cassells, 'Welfare, Security and Economic Performance', 1, 122–3.

tions of EU social policy. Both continue to assume a pattern of long service in, by and large, the same industry and possibly in the same firm—assumptions that are increasingly out of kilter with peoples' experiences. Changes in experience are being acknowledged. Hence, participants in German co-determination are extending their concerns from strategic organizational matters into basic income schemes to overcome the linking of social security benefits with traditional notions of 'normal working'. And there is increasing interest in Swedish-style share-ownership schemes for workers.[86] Such innovations also require attention to principles and values, as Leisink and Pixley warn, but might indicate future possibilities in the EU.[87]

According to Majone, all redistributive policies affecting capital, labour, and welfare require democratic legitimization which remains more achievable at the national level.[88] To Scharpf this neglects the paradox for welfare states that the economic integration which is necessary to national prosperity also reduces the effectiveness of national democratic self-determination. He sees this as the core problem confronting democratic governance in Europe.[89] One way forward, possibly indicated by German interest in basic income and share-owning schemes, might be to develop further European innovations in the 'portability' of rights. 'Portability' is already recognized in social security and voting provisions for migrants between countries. It could be construed as being a feature of the 'acquired rights' carried by workers when they 'migrate' in their own countries from one employer to another in the event of a transfer of undertakings. A 'bottom-up' elaboration of a system entitling all individuals to consultation and income maintenance may be more fruitful than continuing to try to circumvent the clash between two national meta-understandings of industrial and social rights. This would, indeed, be a retreat at the EU level from the property dimension of industrial citizenship but not necessarily undemocratic if founded on inclusive norms and principles of partnership.

---

[86] Hoffman, 'Trade Union Reform in Germany', 108.

[87] P. Leisink, 'Work and Citizenship in Europe', in M. Roche and R. van Berkel (eds.) *European Citizenship and Social Exclusion*, 51–66; J. Pixley, 'Employment and Social Identity. Theoretical Issues', in ibid. 119–34.

[88] Majone, 'The European Community between Social Policy and Social Regulation', 159–63, 167–8.

[89] Scharpf, 'Economic Integration, Democracy and the Welfare State', 22–3.

11

The Creation of the Single Market and Britain's Withdrawal from the EMS

IAIN BEGG AND MICHAEL WOOD

Britain's uneasy relations with its EU partners, especially Germany and France, have noticeably improved since the election of the Labour government in May 1997. The subsequent decision by Britain to forego entry into the European Monetary Union (EMU) in the first wave has, apparently, been accepted without acrimony by the other member states, and British support for European employment initiatives, and its adoption of the social chapter have been welcomed. All of this suggests that what has often been a fractious relationship is in one of its more constructive phases.

There have, however, also been dire periods when antagonism to Europe has been pervasive. British ambivalence about the EU is captured in the possibly apocryphal comments attributed to Russell Bretherton, the Board of Trade representative at the 1955 Messina conference which paved the way for the Treaty of Rome. His words on leaving the meeting early are said to have been:

I leave Messina happy, because even if you keep on meeting you will not agree, if you agree nothing will result, and if anything results it will be a disaster.[1]

Two recent episodes in European integration exemplify the ups and downs in Britain's links with its EC/EU partners. The first is the single market, now widely seen as a successful initiative that helped to overturn the 'eurosclerosis' of the early 1980s. The intellectual inspiration for this chimed with the market-orientated approach of the Thatcher government and one of the key figures in promoting it was the British Commissioner, Lord Cockfield. Although 20/20 hindsight has engendered some disquiet about the loss of sovereignty consequent upon the Single European Act, the single market continues to be seen in a positive light.

Iain Begg would like to express his gratitude to the ESRC for financial support for researching this chapter.

[1] Sir William Nicoll claims to have traced the statement not to Bretherton but to the French delegate Deniaud (reported in the *European Business Journal* 7/3 (1995), 63).

The contrast with the second episode—the European Monetary System (EMS), especially Britain's withdrawal from it in 1992—could not be more stark. From its inception in 1979, Britain held out against full EMS membership on the grounds that economic conditions for membership were not met. The eventual entry in 1990 was plainly at an inappropriate exchange rate, and the policy shifts occasioned by withdrawal in 1992 manifestly ate away the credibility of the Tory government for sound economic management.[2] The fall-out from this episode continues to affect British politics acutely, and has undoubtedly made the decision on full economic and monetary union (EMU) more difficult.

This chapter reviews the process of creating the single market and the events surrounding Britain's withdrawal from the EMS in 1992. It then discusses likely developments in the regulatory and monetary domains in the lights of these and relates them to British and German perspectives on European integration.

MEMBER STATES AND THE EUROPEAN 'PROJECT'

The impetus for advances in European integration has tended to come from different member states at different times. Even though the outcome has usually been a compromise which does not recognizably conform to the 'style' or preferences of any single member state, the balance of influence is often evident. Thus, cohesion has been championed by the southern member states, EU environmental policy appears to owe more to Dutch and German influence than to others,[3] while French priorities are visible in EU technology policy.

It can be argued that EU monetary arrangements, up to a point, reflect German aims and values, while the single market is very much Britain's 'thing' in the EU. It is instructive, in this regard, that completion of the single market is one of the few major initiatives in European construction that has not seen Britain dragging its heels. From doubts about the ECSC and the formation of the EEC through to the delay in agreeing the social chapter, and, now the opt-out from EMU, Britain has been the laggard. That the single market should be the exception to this testifies to its significance.

British ambivalence about the EMS is a matter of record and many of the reasons for it are well known. The doctrine that 'the time is not ripe' was frequently adduced to justify staying-out and could be defended

---

[2] The supreme irony here is that subsequent events suggest that economic policy from 1992 onwards was exemplary. The memoirs by John Major, *The Autobiography* (London, 1999), and Norman Lamont, *In Office* (London, 1999), appeared too late to be considered here.

[3] A. Weale, 'Environmental Rules and Rule-Making in the European Union', *Journal of European Public Policy* 3 (1996), 594–611.

on the grounds that in the early years of the system UK monetary policy conditions differed sharply from other member states. Inflation rates in the 1970s had been well above those in Germany, the monetarist approach of the first phase of the Thatcher government was clearly at odds with other countries, and the pound had become, at least partly, a petro-currency. These and other factors led to large fluctuations in the nominal exchange rate which also had a significant impact on the real exchange rate.

But British doubts about the EMS could also be seen as a manifestation of an approach to European integration which has always stressed the calculation of economic costs and benefits, rather than political aims. With EMS, the advantages of stability were not seen as sufficient to offset the risks that British policy would be unacceptably constrained. In particular, the aim of closer political union that partly motivated Giscard and Schmidt to introduce the EMS played little part in the UK stance, and eventually became a reason in its own right for resisting it. The announcement in October 1997 by the Chancellor of the Exchequer of the 'five economic tests' that have to be passed for Britain to take part in stage 3 of EMU, yet again echoes the cost–benefit approach.

THE CREATION OF THE SINGLE MARKET

The move towards the single market can, therefore, be portrayed as the anomaly in Britain's relationship with its EU partners. In many ways it is not that surprising. UK advocacy of the single market was entirely consistent with the Thatcher government's drive to give greater power to 'the market' in the economic governance of the country. Domestically, this manifested itself in a number of ways: extensive privatization of state-owned industries and assets; the introduction of market mechanisms in major public services; and a concerted effort to deregulate the labour market. The single market was (and remains) popular with British politicians precisely because it was seen as a means of promoting similar changes in other EU countries and of forestalling any attempts by 'Brussels' to impose regulations that would be inimical to greater competition. The attraction of this package to the UK was that it implied a free-trade area and a level-playing field with which the UK would be comfortable, while also restricting the scope for the Commission to impose rules. Moreover, it held out the promise of significant gains in allocative efficiency in the EU economy, although it has not yielded the economic transformation so glowingly trailed in the Cecchini report.[4]

---

[4] P. Cecchini, *The European Challenge* (Aldershot, 1988).

The deregulatory thrust was also consistent with the underlying ambition of unwinding socialism, whereas the social chapter was routinely condemned by Tory politicians as socialism by the back door. Bulmer argues that the political dimension of the single market programme was always crucial. Although often portrayed by Britain as, to borrow Bulmer's term, 'a free-standing initiative' the reality is that it was part of a complex intergovernmental bargain involving the settlement of the budget question in 1984 at Fontainebleau, the beefing-up of the Structural Funds, and action on environmental and technology policies.[5] The concept of 'competition between rules', in which good regulatory systems would drive out bad ones is yet another illustration of the competitive market philosophy behind the single market.[6]

The prospective gains from the single market were, arguably, always exaggerated. After the Panglossian hyperbole of the 'Costs of non-Europe' studies, it is instructive that the European Commission's 1996 review of the single market has produced much more sober estimates of its benefits, suggesting that it has added only slightly to GDP and employment.[7] This has not, however, deterred politicians and commentators from singing its praises. No Commission document is complete without a call-to-arms to reinforce the single market. It is the facet of European integration that is, seemingly, immune from criticism. Furlong and Cox observe that 'what was surprising, and what requires explanation, was the unprecedented success of this project'.[8]

How, then, has it achieved this state of grace? Its great strength was that it took an existing principle—free movement within the customs union—and sought to assure its more effective realization. The '1992' programme was, from the outset, limited in its ambitions to what was then adjudged to be politically feasible. Such features of integrated national markets as common rules on corporate governance and accounting, or an integrated corporate taxation regime were deemed to be unattainable. Even harmonization of VAT and excise duties—part of the original Cockfield package—has not occurred because of member state objections, although there has been movement in this direction.

According to its architect, Lord Cockfield, the enactment of the single market programme was facilitated by four innovative features of the process. First, the decision by the Milan European Council to publish the White Paper—in itself a novelty that reflected a British approach to

---

[5] S. Bulmer, 'Setting and influencing the rules', in D. G. Mayes (ed.), *The Evolution of the Single European Market* (Cheltenham, 1997), 30–48.
  [6] S. Woolcock, 'Competition between rules', in Mayes (ed.), *The Evolution of the Single Market*, 66–86.   [7] M. Monti, *The Single Market and Tomorrow's Europe* (London, 1997).
  [8] P. Furlong and A. Cox (eds.), *The European Union at the Crossroads: Problems in Implementing the Single Market Project* (Boston, Lincs., 1995).

policy-making—setting out the 300 measures required for completion of the internal market provided a very clear framework and road map. Second, setting the target date of 1992, not only gave a manageable deadline for the whole process, but also helped to galvanize the various interests to act. Cockfield's third factor was the notion that there was a philosophical coherence to the whole programme that could engender support. This was complemented by a fourth consideration, namely that the removal of barriers was intrinsically desirable and manifestly consistent with the basic aims of the Treaty of Rome. Who, after all, could be seen to oppose the removal of barriers to the free movement of goods services, capital and labour? In addition, Europe could be seen to be swimming with, and not against, a global movement towards freer markets and trade.[9]

Many of the major components of the single market programme tilted EU practice towards the British approach. Greater transparency in public procurement, liberalization of financial markets with less pre-scriptive forms of regulation and the drive to reduce administrative barriers of various kinds are all examples of single market measures that coincided with British domestic policies. Yet it would be wrong to regard the entire programme as consistent with British views. Harmonization (later watered-down to 'approximation') of VAT and of excise duties, and scrapping of border controls are single market measures that Britain has strongly resisted. Indeed, the Amsterdam Treaty appears to end once and for all any thought that the UK and Ireland will sign-up to the abolition of border controls (the Schengen *acquis*, now incorporated into the Treaty). In defiance of the liberalizing rhetoric, many of the measures— for example in the area of environmental policy—imposed more stringent regulatory controls.

All markets function according to rules, whether tacit or formal. Without rules, economic agents simply would not know how to interact with one another. What the single market programme has done is to recast the rules in the EU market, rather than to sweep them away. Although simplification and harmonization clearly formed part of the single market agenda, Wilks sees the process that the EU went through as more than an updating of regulations that had either lost their relevance or were incompatible with the spirit of the common market. Instead, he argues that what has happened is a reinvention of the structures of EU capital-ism.[10] It is interesting in this regard to contrast the narrow focus of the English term regulation with the much more expansive sense of the French *régulation* school or the German term *Ordnungspolitik* which defies straightforward translation into English.

---

[9] A. Cockfield, *The European Union: Creating the Single Market* (Chichester, 1994).
[10] S. Wilks, 'Regulatory Compliance and Capitalist Diversity in Europe', *Journal of European Public Policy* 3 (1996), 536–59.

WITHDRAWAL FROM EMS

Currency realignments have always been traumatic for the UK, not least because of a political setting in which devaluation has been seen as a defeat for the government in power. Whether in the 1931 decision to go off the gold standard or the 1967 devaluation, the authority of the government of the day was undermined by what, in dispassionate terms, were rational policy decisions. In 1992, when Britain withdrew from the exchange rate mechanism of the EMS,[11] the economy had just been through a prolonged recession that had seen GDP fall by some 3.5 per cent from its peak in the second quarter of 1990. Although the Conservative Party led by John Major had only recently (and somewhat unexpectedly) won a general election, the government was increasingly divided over Europe and uneasy about the economic strategy it was following.

Membership of the European Exchange Rate Mechanism (ERM), which had finally been accepted two years before, was a central plank of the government's policy. But it was far from universally accepted, despite the generally favourable reception that the 1990 decision to join had received. Indeed, the Chancellor in 1992, Norman Lamont, has since made it clear that it was very much against his better judgement that he had persevered with ERM membership.

Monetary policy in the UK from 1979 to 1992 went through a number of phases, an outcome of which was a volatile exchange rate. Figure 11.1, which plots the annual average exchange rates against the dollar and the DM from 1979 to 1996, shows that the exchange rate soared in the early 1980s, collapsed to reach a low point against the dollar in 1985/6, rose again in the late 1980s, then fell by some 15 per cent after the 1992 withdrawal from the EMS, only to return to its EMS parity in 1997. By any standard, this is exceptional volatility for an economy apparently closely integrated with its EU partners. Although the 'petro-currency' status conferred on the currency by North Sea oil was a contributory factor, the main reason for this volatility was the conduct of monetary policy.

After the watershed 1979 election in the UK, the government imposed an overtly monetarist policy aimed at breaking inflation expectations. High interest rates, reinforced by the rise in oil prices drove the currency to levels at which UK exporters became hopelessly uncompetitive, triggering a steep recession. Subsequently, the relaxation of monetary policy supported an economic recovery that lasted until 1990. This period of expansion saw a dilution of strict monetarism followed by a period during which the Chancellor, Nigel Lawson, shadowed the DM to the

---

[11] To put it politely; some might use the word 'ejected'.

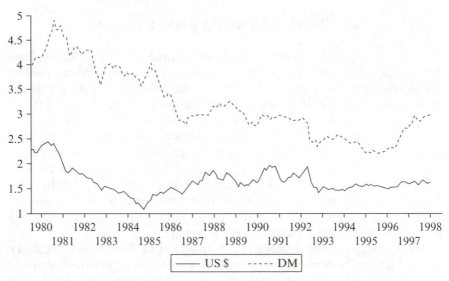

FIG. 11.1. The volatile exchange rate (units of currency per pound, monthly)

evident discomfiture of his Prime Minister, a policy that culminated in his acrimonious resignation from the government.

As inflation accelerated in the late 1980s, interest rates were pushed progressively higher, with the result that the economy was again tipped into recession. The decision to join the exchange rate mechanism was eventually taken in 1990 by John Major as Chancellor. In 1989, his predecessor Lawson had joined forces with the Foreign Secretary, Sir Geoffrey Howe, to demand that Mrs Thatcher agree to join the exchange rate mechanism. This gave rise to the so-called Madrid conditions—essentially another variant on 'when the time is ripe'. By autumn 1990, however, Mrs Thatcher's political position was increasingly precarious and she finally conceded and the UK joined the ERM at a parity of DM 2.90 to the pound. Ironically, in view of what followed, the immediate effect was to allow a cut in interest rates and the decision was widely welcomed, although concern was expressed that the rate was perhaps too high.

With hindsight, the timing could scarcely have been worse. The UK economy had dipped into recession in the second quarter of 1990 and would suffer a steep and extended decline in output. There are differing explanations for the recession, but it is widely accepted that a significant contributory factor was the deregulation of financial markets that had occurred during the previous decade. Personal sector indebtedness had soared on the back of easy access to credit leading to rapid asset price

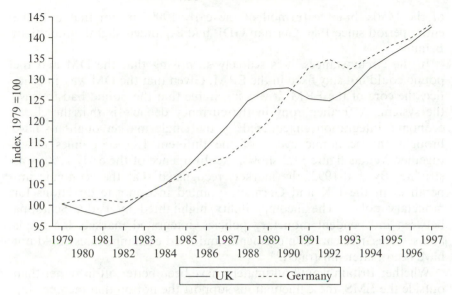

FIG. 11.2. German and British GDP trends (at constant prices)

inflation. Political delays in tightening monetary policy meant that when policy was eventually reversed, its effects were more severe. The first stirrings of recovery would not be seen until the middle of 1992.

Germany, meanwhile, was experiencing a continuing boom, fuelled by the surge in aggregate demand associated with the massive fiscal transfers to the *Neue Länder*. Fiscal and monetary policy in Germany became increasingly antagonistic, with successive interest rate hikes by the Bundesbank eventually bringing the boom to a shuddering halt in 1993. Because of the time it took to bring fiscal and monetary policy back into balance, German recovery was slow and hesitant.

The early 1990s consequently saw the UK and German economies become de-synchronized. It can be argued that this arose because of 'asymmetric' shocks in both: the fall-out from financial liberalization in the UK, and the effects of unification in Germany. As Figure 11.2 shows, the two economies had followed a broadly similar cyclical trend for much of the period since the EMS was created. But from 1989 onwards these trends diverged sharply. The chart shows that the long British expansion of the 1980s ended at precisely the point at which German growth was at its most rapid. Then, as the British economy started to recover in 1992, it was the turn of the German economy to run into the buffers. Yet, for most of the rest of the period the GDP trends of the two countries are broadly similar. German growth was lower than Britain's for most of the 1980s, but the turmoil of the early 1990s meant that over the entire period since 1980 German GDP had expanded slightly more than Britain's.

In the circumstances, it is scarcely surprising that the DM and the pound could not stay fixed in the ERM. Given that the DM was, in practice, the core of the ERM, it was inevitable that the pound had to leave the system. A further irony in the currency debacle is that the closer economic integration engendered by the single market ought to have brought the economic cycles of the different EU economies closer together. Yet, as figure 11.2 shows, the divergence of the early 1990s was striking. By mid-1992, the markets recognized that the economic imperatives in the UK and Germany pointed in opposite directions for monetary policy. The incompatibility highlighted by Padoa-Schioppa between independent monetary policies, integrated markets for goods and services, free capital movements, and fixed exchange rates could not have been better illustrated.[12]

Whether Britain would, ultimately, have been better off in rather than outside the EMS, these fluctuations support the notion that membership would have imposed severe strains on the economy. Britain's reluctance to join was generally presented as an objection based on economic costs and benefits, but towards the end of the 1980s, the debate became increasingly political. In particular, it engendered great bitterness between the rival factions within the Tory party. In September 1992, when the pressures for change made British withdrawal from the ERM inevitable, much was made of the lack of support for Britain from the German authorities. Stories rapidly surfaced about the lack of chemistry between Chancellor Lamont and the President of the Bundesbank, Helmut Schlesinger. But the notion that this explains the withdrawal of the pound from EMS is belied by the contrast between the UK experience and subsequent German support for France when the franc came under speculative attack in 1993. All the evidence suggests that it was exchange rate fundamentals rather than personalities which counted.

The ERM withdrawal has, inevitably, conditioned UK attitudes towards monetary union. It has fostered the belief that the UK economy is sufficiently distinct from those of the other EU member states to make participation in the Euro foolhardy. The apparent confluence of the UK and US economic cycles has even revived the notion that the UK is better off aligning itself across the Atlantic than the English Channel. However, there is little substance to much of this and the debate is conducted with more heat than light.

---

[12] T. Padoa-Schioppa, *The Road to Monetary Union in Europe: The Emperor, the Kings, and the Genies* (Oxford, 1994).

AN ASSESSMENT OF THE SINGLE MARKET AND EMS

The single market and the EMS can be thought of as, respectively, the British and German European 'projects' of the 1980s How well did they work? In most respects, the single market continues to be regarded as a success. Thus, Lord Cockfield the European Commissioner whose 1985 White Paper launched the single market sought to debunk critics of the single market in the following terms in a recent pamphlet: 'What matters is that the main structure of the single market is in place—somewhat later than it might have been, but there all the same.'[13] Despite the turmoil of 1992/3, the European Monetary System has, in the final analysis, played its assigned role in moving the EU towards monetary union.

To the extent that there are criticisms of the single market, they focus on unfinished business or the recalcitrance of member states in either the implementation or the enforcement of rules. Nor has the rather more muted assessment of the benefits in the 1996 review diminished enthusiasm. The underlying perception remains that the benefits can only increase if the single market is more fully realized so that vigilance is needed to prevent backsliding.

This generally favourable assessment does, however, need to be qualified. The consistency of the single market is not always ideal. The new approach to legislation that derived from the switch to mutual recognition has been described as 'indirect rule' and has opened up the possibility of differences in the transposition and enforcement of rules.[14] There are also, perhaps inevitably, unintended outcomes of EU rules. Thus, in public procurement, Hartley *et al.* point to the cumbersome nature of the tendering procedures demanded by EU rules and contend that this reduces rather than increases the efficiency of public sector purchasing by imposing greater costs on procurer and supplier alike.[15] Sanderson criticizes the 1997 Green Paper on public procurement as a missed opportunity to correct the excesses of the single market approach.[16]

The overwhelming success of the SEM is the speed at which it has become so much a part of orthodox thinking. Voices raised against it now appear as special interest group pleading. What is clear is that success is likely to be easier during more favourable macro-economic conditions,

[13] Philip Morris Institute, *Is the Single Market Working?* (Brussels, 1996).
[14] T. Daintith (ed.), *Implementing EC Law in the United Kingdom: Structures for Indirect Rule* (Chichester, 1995).
[15] K. Hartley, M. Uttley, and A. Cox, 'European Community Public Procurement Policy: Contract Awards and the Problems of Implementation', in P. Furlong and A. Cox (eds.), *The European Union at the Crossroads*, 161–86.
[16] J. Sanderson, 'The EU Green Paper on Public Procurement: A Better Way Forward or a Missed Opportunity', *European Business Journal* 10/2 (1998), 64–70.

particularly if growth is sustained. In this sense, the early 1990s' reces-sions have been difficult periods for many member states. Recession, retrenchment, and subtle protectionism can all too easily go hand in hand.

Trade volumes between members have increased by 20–30 per cent in manufacturing goods, and not at the expense of non-EU producers, whose imports from 1980–93 have increased from 12 to 14 per cent. In addition, the SEM has made the EU attractive as a location. It absorbed 44 per cent of global foreign investment flows in the early 1990s compared to 28 per cent in the middle of the 1980s. It has probably had a positive effect on investment and the Commission estimates that Community income is around 1 per cent higher than it would otherwise have been. Industry and commerce generally report that the abolition of many border controls and formalities is progressing well, although VAT is still seen as a bigger problem than it should be. Mutual recognition of technical standards, a potential nightmare, is working well enough.

Progress is much more advanced in mature product markets than in services. This is to be expected, but needs to be addressed as so much employment (about 70 per cent) is in services. For some service sectors the framework is now in place, such as air transport, telecommunications, banking, insurance, and some broadcasting, although implementation re-mains problematic. Distortions of investment decisions and cross-border transactions in some service markets are still widespread. This is partly explained by structural and behavioural impediments, but regulatory or administrative obstacles still apply.

A separate criticism of the single market programme is that it followed a competitive, 'neo-liberal' agenda too rigidly and failed to provide for the construction of a social dimension to European integration. The playing-field may have been levelled in respect of regulatory matters, but not in the rewards to workers, hence the widespread fears of social dumping. Germany has, on the whole, supported a social dimension to the single market, but it has been strongly resisted by the UK under he Tories. Since the general election of May 1997 the rhetoric of the new Labour government has been softer, but the UK continues to emphasize flexibility as a key aim.

Turning to the EMS, the overall verdict must be that it has served its purpose. It has largely succeeded in securing exchange rate stability in the EU and played its appointed part in bringing about monetary union. This contrasts with the experience of the 1970s when the Werner plan for monetary union went awry.[17] The monetary disciplines associated with EMS have also been influential in reducing inflation rates across the EU.

---

[17] A. Steinherr (ed.), *Thirty Years of European Monetary Integration: From the Werner Plan to EMU* (London, 1994).

But the EMS can be criticized for having held down growth rates in countries such as France (see some of the work in Barrell[18]) and for the failure by governments to recognize and deal effectively with the strains resulting from diverging inflation rates in the late 1980s and early 1990s, and from German unification.

THE WAY FORWARD FOR THE SINGLE MARKET

Despite the flurry of legislation since 1985, much unfinished business remains, partly because of the scope of the single market project, but also because the areas which remain are more contentious and touch on member state sensitivities. Britain continues to be well placed to take the lead here not only because of its long-standing advocacy of the single market, but also because of its experience of significant structural reforms over the last two decades. Several current orientations in single market policy can be linked to British preoccupations.

One of the main targets identified by the Commission for further action to reinforce the single market is the public services received by its citizens. In the Commission's Communication, 'Services of General Interest in Europe' it notes that, 'Many [Europeans] even view general interest services as social rights that make an important contribution to economic and social cohesion. This is why general interest services are at the heart of the European model of society, as acknowledged by the Commission in its recent report on the reform of the European Treaties.'[19] In particular, the Commission has stressed the need for member states to emphasize universality and affordable service provision; the openness of competitive and efficient provision within the single market; the improvement of consumer choice, quality, and lower prices; and the evaluation and monitoring of operation, performance, and competitiveness, to establish best practice.

As in the creation of the single market these are all areas in which the United Kingdom is uniquely placed to lead the way after the extensive supply-side reforms of the last two decades. By dramatically changing the way it provides services, it has challenged much of the accepted orthodoxy of public sector provision itself. The European model of public services provision since the war has been one of public ownership and delivery, with the state acting simultaneously as regulator and supplier, market participant and defender of consumer interests. Changing this

[18] R. Barrell (ed.), *Economic Convergence and Monetary Union in Europe* (London, 1992).
[19] Commission of the European Communities, 'Commission Communication to the Council and to the European Parliament, Services of General Interest in Europe', COM(96)443 final version of 11/9/1996.

will never be easy as the slow progress has demonstrated in industries such as air transport, where issues of security, national sovereignty (and pride), and industrial policy are raised.

The emerging structure for the regulation of utilities, championed by 'Brussels', emphasizes the market rather than a public service orientation and aims to reduce the role of the state, but with some concessions to social objectives. Majone also suggests that the Commission, is moving towards an 'Anglo-Saxon' model of a 'regulatory state'.[20] This trend has been reinforced as the Commission sees regulatory issues, including utility reform, as a field in which it can have a real impact. Although the point should not be exaggerated, many of the emerging features again reflect British preferences and approaches, implying that the EU will move towards the British model for public service provision. As with the single market, however, the outcome is likely to see the model evolve, not least to avoid some of the pitfalls of the UK approach.[21]

In the UK approach, public ownership was seen as a major obstacle to real improvements in service provision, but there is less support for this elsewhere. Indeed, the status and ownership of public services has always been a national, not a community issue and Article 222 of the Treaty assures neutrality on matters of ownership. Article 3 however, states that competition, and a lack of internal market distortions are principal goals. Proposals to add 'a contribution to the promotion of services of general interest' to Article 3(u) of the Treaty show that the Commission is very keen that general interest services are something which the Community should take into account when drawing up its policies and planning its activities. Separation of regulatory authority from political power is a further example of following the UK approach.

The Commission's 1996 SLIM (Simpler Legislation for the Internal Market) initiative was confluent with the UK government's aim of reducing the burden of 'red tape', again highlighting the attractions of the deregulatory agenda for the UK. It is no coincidence that it was the Edinburgh European Council that agreed this. It is instructive, in this regard, that the single market continues to occupy a prominent position on the agenda of the Labour government elected in 1997. One of the prime objectives identified by the British in holding the Presidency of the EU in the first half of 1998, for instance, was to give fresh impetus to efforts to complete the single market. Indeed, some of the rhetoric about flexibility that characterized the government's first few months in office can also be seen as having its roots in the 'competitive market' philosophy of the single market.

[20] G. Majone (ed.), *Regulating Europe* (London, 1996).
[21] M. Wood, 'Being a Good European: Britain Leads the EU in Utility Regulation', *New Economy* 5 (1998), 53–7.

BRITISH AND GERMAN INFLUENCE IN EUROPE

The creation of the single market and the evolution of the EMS are phases in European integration that are informative about the relationship between, and the respective preoccupations of, Britain and Germany in European construction. In the light of subsequent developments, it can seem surprising that the UK agreed to the Single European Act and thus to extensive use of qualified majority voting. German acquiescence to single market measures that appeared distant from domestic practice in areas such as insurance is also, at first sight, surprising.

The approaches of both Britain and Germany to the SEM and EMS/EMU, give insights not only into how each country views these specific developments, but also how each would like to see the union itself evolve. For Germany, persuading the UK of the economic case for monetary union would always be difficult. The case outlined in such reports as the Commission's 1990 study, 'One Market, One Money' which attempted to quantify the benefits of EMU was never going to be enough to win over a highly sceptical and cautious Britain.[22] The economic arguments for the elimination of exchange transactions costs, of lower interest rates, of higher growth, and of the need to hold fewer currency reserves were all benefits that one might have assumed would be in harmony with British Government objectives, and in particular with the ruling Conservative Party's wishes. However, it was much more concerned with the loss of the exchange rate as an instrument of policy, the sacrifice of independent monetary policy, and the loss of any possible monetary financing of budgetary deficits. A single currency would also circumscribe its ability to deal with certain economic problems, and might force the UK to undergo painful economic measures to achieve adjustments to economic shocks. The pain and the experience of Britain's withdrawal from the ERM are likely to cast a very deep shadow over economic policy-making for a decade.

Although historically, devaluation has almost always been associated with the perception of a political failure by government, the ability to realign sterling has always been seen as a legitimate and occasionally desirable policy option, necessary to restore competitiveness and trade balance. The fact that British governments have been rather inept at using this option effectively, often hanging on to an overvalued pound for far too long, is easily forgotten. What is considered important by the British, is the view that to give up the ability to vary the currency would be to forego a key economic policy instrument, that once lost, could never be re-established. The reality is a little different. Successive devaluations have

---

[22] Commission of the European Communities, *One Market One Money* (Luxemburg, 1990).

only tended to bring short-term, not long-term gains in competitiveness. The latter have come about with structural and industrial reforms. Moreover the currency volatility shown in Figure 11.1 has added to the problems of British industry, not alleviated them.

The irony is that throughout 1999, the British government seemed unwilling, or unable, to reduce the value of sterling to placate exporters, yet seems determined to retain its right to do so if it chooses. The reality of EMU is that it is not a policy that will be initially won on economic grounds, but reflects a German view that it is a political priority, and that the direction and character of the process has reflected German values to have a real influence on European political integration. No country has been so affected by the transformations in Central and Eastern Europe as Germany. It has been at the forefront of absorbing, and responding to the uncertainties and challenges that have occurred in recent years. It was determined that these changes would be accommodated within a strengthened and politically deeper Union and to ensure that its neighbours should prosper. Prosperity will secure democracy and reduce any likely threat of extreme political turmoil. The trade and investment potential is also favourable.

In this context the connection between tying the most stable of East European countries into the Union and deepening become clear. EMU is therefore one important stage on this road. However, this approach is not without risk. Investment may move from Germany to member states with lower direct and indirect labour costs. If unemployment in poorer countries were to rise, pressure might grow for substantial financial transfers from Germany to other states. Pressure on the stretched German budget is also likely to continue. Fears about the loss of a strong DM have had to be assuaged by ensuring that EMU is fashioned in Germany's image. The convergence criteria; the nature, likely role, and location of the European Central Bank; and the sheer driving force for the project, have all had a German hallmark pressed upon them.

In contrast, the Single European Market was a project with which the UK could easily identify. No European economy had been through reforms as far-reaching as the UK. With the reform of labour relations, the adoption of flexible labour markets, privatization, utility reform, the support for market mechanisms, and a genuine willingness to embrace competition and reject protectionism and state-funded industry, Britain felt that here was a message that it wanted to spread. The SEM was also a project where Britain could exercise some real influence in a positive manner, in line with Union philosophy, but without ruffling domestic political opinion. By appearing to set a free and fair market environment such a policy would also reduce the possibility of bureaucratic regulations detaching Europe from an ever more open global economy.

British influence was so strong because it was based on an apparent track record of success. The image of a successful British Airways contrasting with the state subsidized Air France was evident. British restructuring of its coal industry contrasted with the German 'Kohlepfennig'.[23] In addition, Britain's zeal to combine new technology with independent, transparent regulation, showed just what could be achieved if the political will was present. Old arguments of 'natural industrial monopolies' were unsustainable when British consumers were enjoying the choice offered by a multitude of competing telecom companies, and gas and electricity supply were becoming fully competitive.

The perception in some British quarters that a single open market would be a market essentially free of regulation was never on the cards. The SEM has recast the rules, and added some more.[24] But here again the style has often been British, with the example of the office of the independent utility regulator holding great sway and influence.

And the future? Although the UK has rejected entry into EMU in the first wave, the balance of probability must now be that it will join. The painful history of the EMS seems on its way to being forgotten as the UK has espoused such 'German' notions as stability and operational independence for the central bank in conducting monetary policy, though not quite with the freedom conferred on the Bundesbank. Germany, in turn, seems increasingly enthusiastic about liberalizing public services and shifting towards Anglo-Saxon methods of regulation, but with the expectation that it will be embedded in a modified German social model. In fact, since the departure of Lafontaine from the Schröder government in March 1999, there are increasing indications of convergence between the philosophies underpinning the policies of the UK and Germany. Blair's 'third way' and Schröder's 'neue Mitte' appear to combine the zeal for market solutions with orthodoxy in macroeconomic stabilization policy, while redefining the role of the welfare state. The lesson to draw is, perhaps, that European integration has allowed both countries to observe, appraise, and adapt core features of the other's economic governance and to benefit from the exchange.

---

[23] An additional amount added to every unit of gas and electricity that is used to keep German coal mines operational.

[24] I. Begg, 'Introduction: Regulation in the European Union', *Journal of European Public Policy* 3 (1996), 525–35.

12

Financial Reporting and Accounting Harmonization in Germany and the UK: A Comparative Analysis

PATRICIA MCCOURT AND GEORGE W. RADCLIFFE

Divergence in financial reporting practice between Germany and the UK would not be regarded by many as a contentious issue or an important source of friction between the two countries either in public debate or in negotiation within the institutions of the European Union. In fact, however, the financial statements of enterprises have also been a significant and fundamental determinant of two variables which have been the subject of widespread and sometimes acrimonious debate in recent years, namely levels of investment and corporate taxation.

Efficient capital investment at national or international level is dependent upon reliable financial information. The primary source of this information is the financial statements produced by major economic entities. Assessment of these entities' comparative economic performance, as a prelude to investment, involves an analysis of their financial statements. Therefore, if national accounting practices differ significantly, international investment decisions may be distorted and accounting diversity may represent as significant an obstacle to the free movement of capital as many of the direct restrictions whose abolition was required by the 1957 EEC Treaty.[1]

The effective incidence and burden of a tax are usually debatable but it is indisputable that both the tax rate and the tax base are significant determinants of these. Since accounting profit is the basis for computing tax on business incomes in most jurisdictions including Germany and the UK, any divergence in national accounting practices will result in differences in the bases of business taxation. Therefore harmonization of corporate tax rates in the European Union may lead to increased inequity in the incidence of taxes if national accounting practices are not harmonized. As the Ruding Committee recognized, 'any proposals regarding harmon-

---

[1] EEC Treaty, Article 67(1), now consolidated (in part) as Article 56(1).

isation of tax rates would be ineffective without simultaneous harmoniza-tion of the tax base'.[2]

Efforts to effect some degree of harmonization of accounting practice within the European Union have centred on the Fourth[3] and Seventh[4] Company Law Directives which apply respectively to the accounts of indi-vidual companies and groups of companies. These have been implemented in the national laws of member states with varying degrees of enthusiasm, and in three cases, only after legal action was taken by the European Commission.[5] Implementation of the Directives has not resulted in a uniform set of prescriptive accounting rules applying throughout the European Union to which reporting entities in each member state must adhere. Instead the Fourth Directive, in particular, has provided only a harmonized legal framework of broad rules relating to presentation and disclosure in financial statements within which each member state may develop more detailed national accounting regulation.[6] It is this national flexibility which permits two fundamentally different financial reporting systems, such as those of the UK and Germany, to exist side by side.

REGULATORY FRAMEWORK OF ACCOUNTING IN THE UK

The contribution of legal rules to the development of accounting prin-ciples in the UK has been insignificant. Until the implementation in the Companies Acts of 1981[7] and 1989[8] of the detailed rules of the Fourth and Seventh Directives on the form and content of financial statements, statute prescribed only minimal accounting disclosures and accounting rules were encapsulated in a single statutory requirement that accounts should be 'full and fair'[9] or 'true and correct'[10] or, most recently, 'true and fair'.[11] This circumstance is of course entirely consistent with the

---

[2] The Ruding Committee was appointed by the European Commission to examine company taxation. Its conclusions were reported in *Conclusions and Recommendations of the Committee of Independent Experts on Company Taxation* (Luxemburg, 1992). [3] 78/66/EEC.
[4] 83/349/EEC.
[5] P. Thorell and G. Whittington, 'The Harmonization of Accounting within the EU: Problems, Perspectives and Strategies', *The European Accounting Review*, 3/2 (1994), 215–39.
[6] Harmonization may be defined as 'a process of increasing the compatibility of account-ing practices by setting bounds to their degree of variation', whereas standardization implies 'the imposition of a more rigid and narrow set of rules', D. Alexander and C. Nobes, *A European Introduction to Financial Accounting* (Hemel Hempstead, 1994), 87.
[7] Now consolidated as Companies Act (1985), Section 226 and Schedule 4.
[8] Now consolidated as Companies Act (1985), Section 227 and Schedule 4A.
[9] Joint Stock Companies Registration and Regulation Act (1844), Section 35.
[10] Companies (Consolidation) Act (1908), Section 113(2).
[11] Companies Act (1989), Section 226(2).

common law concept of the role of decided cases in interpreting and amplifying statutory rules. However case law provides scant interpretative clarification of the phrases referred to and the courts have preferred to adjudicate accounting issues on the facts, relying on expert evidence of professional accounting practice. As a result no binding rules of accounting law have been established by precedent. For example, it is most unlikely that early judicial *dicta* commending the creation of secret reserves would be approved today.[12] Similarly more recent judicial support for the historical cost principle despite its failure to reflect economic reality reflects an acceptance of current practice rather than the enunciation of some underlying principle.[13]

Before 1981 the main sources of detailed accounting rules were therefore guidelines on the preparation and presentation of financial statements issued by professional bodies, primarily Recommendations on Accounting Principles issued by the Council of the Institute of Chartered Accountants in England and Wales and, after 1971, Statements of Standard Accounting Practice (SSAPs) issued by the Accounting Standards Committee (ASC). These professional standards were not enforceable in law but their significance as evidence of accepted accounting practice was recognized by the courts.[14] The detailed statutory provisions of the Companies Act (1981) represented a clear departure from this pragmatic and ad hoc approach to the development of accounting rules. For the first time mandatory balance sheet and profit and loss account formats were prescribed and broad accounting principles were laid down by statute.

One immediate consequence was the possibility for the first time of a conflict between statutory accounting provisions and the rules of an accounting standard. The reference to 'realized profits' in the new legislation[15] presented an early problem because of a possible conflict with the accruals principle laid down in SSAP 2.[16] The issue was resolved by the insertion of a statutory requirement that realised profits should be determined 'in accordance with principles generally accepted, at the time

---

[12] 'The purpose of the balance sheet is primarily to show that the financial position of the company is as good as there stated, not to show that it is not or may not be better.' Per Mr Justice Buckley, in *Newton v. Birmingham Small Arms Co. Ltd.* (1906), 2, Chancery, p. 387.

[13] 'This figure in the balance sheet in accordance with what is very common practice does not appear as a valuation of the property as at the date of the balance sheet, but is cost less depreciation. Therefore, it does not seem to me that there is anything misleading about it.' Per Lord Justice Somervell, in *Re Press Caps, Ltd.*, Court of Appeal (1949) 1, All England Reports, p. 1015.

[14] 'while they (accounting standards) are not conclusive and they are not rigid rules, they are very strong evidence as to what is the proper standard which should be adopted', per Mr Justice Woolf, in *Lloyd Cheyham and Co. Ltd. v. Littlejohn and Co. Ltd.*, Queen's Bench Division (1987), Butterworth Company Law Cases, p. 313.

[15] Now consolidated as Companies Act (1985), Schedule 4, para. 12.

[16] Statement of Standard Accounting Practice No. 2, *Disclosure of Accounting Policies*, para. 14, Accounting Standards Committee, 1971.

when the accounts are prepared'.[17] This provision reveals both the considerable authority accorded to professional accounting practice by the UK legislator[18] and a recognition that accounting principles are not static. When the terms of a new accounting standard have conflicted with the statutory rules, the professional standard setters have justified the inconsistency by invoking the overriding statutory 'true and fair' requirement.[19] An example is the statement in SSAP 19 on the subject of investment properties that 'the application of this standard will usually be a departure, for the overriding purpose of giving a true and fair view, from the otherwise specific requirement of the law to provide depreciation on any fixed asset which has a limited useful economic life.'[20] This use of the override provision has not been challenged in the courts but might not be upheld in European Union law[21] given the clear view of the European Commission that the legislation may not be used by member states 'to introduce an accounting rule of a general nature which is contrary to provisions of the Directive'.[22]

Despite the enactment of the 1981 Companies Act, professional accounting standards clearly remained the primary source of accounting rules. Nevertheless, two important deficiencies in the arrangements for setting standards became apparent. First, since standards were not enforceable in law, the ASC was effectively compelled to seek compliance by relying on those who were at liberty to ignore them.[23] As a consequence, it often adopted a consensus view when framing standards and frequently made concessions to placate pressure groups.[24] Secondly, because of the lengthy consultative process required before the issue of new standards, the ASC often failed to provide timely authoritative guidance on the new accounting issues which were emerging in an increasingly complex

[17] Now consolidated as Companies Act (1985), Section 262(1).

[18] R. Instone, 'Realised Profits: Unrealised Consequences', *The Journal of Business Law*, March (1985), 106–14.

[19] Under Companies Act (1985), Section 226(5), departure from the statutory provisions is permitted if in special circumstances compliance with them is inconsistent with the requirement to give a true and fair view.

[20] Statement of Standard Accounting Practice No. 19, *Accounting for investment properties*, para. 17, Accounting Standards Committee, 1981.

[21] It has been suggested that the application of the true and fair override to a specific category of companies is justified by the reference in Article 2(5) of the Fourth Directive to the right of Member States to 'define the exceptional cases in question and lay down the relevant special rules'. See D. Alexander, 'Truer and Fairer: Uninvited Comments on Invited Comments', *The European Accounting Review* 5/3 (1996), 483–93.

[22] European Commission, *Interpretative Communication concerning Certain Articles of the Fourth and Seventh Council Directives on Accounting*, 20/1/1998 (98/C16/04), para. 6.

[23] M. Bromwich and A. Hopwood, 'Some Issues on Accounting Standard Setting: An Introductory Essay', in M. Bromwich and A. Hopwood (eds.), *Accounting Standard Setting: An International Perspective* (London, 1983), p. xii.

[24] G. Whittington, 'Accounting Standard Setting in the UK after 20 Years: A Critique of the Dearing and Solomons Reports', *Accounting and Business Research* 19/75 (1989), 195–205.

business environment. As a result the practice of creative accounting[25] was permitted to develop whereby some companies manipulated their annual profit figures, often by providing information which was correct in legal form but misleading in substance. This issue was brought to the public's attention when major corporations such as Polly Peck International went into liquidation shortly after disclosing significant profits in their financial statements.[26]

These perceived shortcomings led the accountancy profession to appoint the Dearing Committee in November 1987 'to review and make recommendations on the standard-setting process'.[27] The Dearing Committee's proposals for a standard-setting body with greater authority than the ASC and a committee which would provide immediate guidance on pressing accounting issues were accepted with alacrity by the profession. An Accounting Standards Board (ASB) made up of professionally qualified accountants was established and charged with the task of issuing Financial Reporting Standards (FRSs) with functions and authority similar to those of SSAPs.[28] The Urgent Issues Task Force (UITF), a committee of the ASB, was established in 1990 to provide swift guidance in areas 'where an accounting standard or a Companies Act provision exists, but where unsatisfactory or conflicting interpretations have developed or seem likely to develop'.[29] The UITF circumvents the often lengthy process of developing accounting standards by arriving at a consensus based on existing law and standards[30] which it sets out in statements of best practice known as Abstracts. An independent Financial Reporting Review Panel (FRRP), made up of accountants, bankers, and lawyers and chaired by a Queen's Counsel, was also established. Its aim was to investigate material departures from accounting standards and company

---

[25] Creative accounting involves manipulating financial statements by taking advantage of ambiguities and inconsistencies in accounting regulation to enhance corporate performance. Stock market pressure on companies to produce consistently good results has been cited as a primary cause of the growth of creative accounting during the 1980s, I. Griffiths, *Creative Accounting: How to Make Your Profits What You Want Them to Be* (London, 1986), 2.

[26] R. Dodge, *Foundations of Business Accounting* (London, 1993), 507–8, gives the following explanation. 'In September 1990 Polly Peck International published its interim results for the six months ended 30 June 1990 revealing a profit before tax of £110.5m. The total market value of the shares at that point was £1.05 bn. One month later the company was in the hands of the administrators, who announced that an immediate liquidation would result in the shareholders receiving nothing; there was a deficiency of £384m.' While 'the Polly Peck case was not instrumental in bringing about changes to standard setting . . . [in the UK] it is a good example of why these changes were needed'.

[27] Sir R. Dearing, *The Making of Accounting Standards, Report of the Review Committee* (London, 1989), p. ix.

[28] In addition the ASB was given the remit of reviewing the existing 25 SSAPs and revising or replacing them where appropriate.

[29] ASB, *Introduction to the First Consensus Pronouncements by the Urgent Issues Task Force* (1991).

[30] M. J. Mumford, 'United Kingdom', in D. Alexander and S. Archer (eds.), *European Accounting Guide*, 2nd edn. (Orlando, Fla., 1995), 920.

legislation (which are not justified under the overriding 'true and fair' requirement) in the financial statements of large private limited companies and public companies.[31]

The authority of professional accounting standards as a source of accounting rules was further reinforced when they were expressly recognized by statute for the first time in the Companies Act (1989). Large private limited companies and public companies were required to state 'whether the accounts have been prepared in accordance with applicable accounting standards' and to give 'particulars of any material departure from those standards and the reasons for it'.[32] This solution had been recommended by the Dearing Committee as preferable to the direct incorporation of standards into the law which would engender 'a legalistic approach and a reduction in the ability of the financial community to respond quickly to new developments'.[33]

The Act also provided for authorization of applications[34] by the FRRP to the courts for declarations that annual accounts do not comply with the statutory requirements and for orders requiring directors to prepare revised accounts.[35] In fact this power has never been used since in all the cases investigated to date directors have revised accounts voluntarily where necessary.[36] Persuasion by the FRRP reinforced by the threat of legal action therefore appears to have been effective thus far.[37] The FRRP's role is reactive rather than proactive in that it reviews only the

[31] The main difference between a public and a private limited company is that the former may offer its shares for subscription to the public at large while the latter may not. The share capitals of public limited companies are therefore usually larger than those of their private equivalents. Private limited companies are further classed as small, medium-sized or large by reference to the value of their turnover, balance sheet totals, and average number of employees.

[32] Companies Act (1985), Schedule 4 para. 36A (as amended by the Companies Act (1989)).

[33] Dearing, *The Making of Accounting Standards*, para. 10.2.

[34] The Companies (Defective Accounts) (Authorised Person) Order (1991), Statutory Instrument 1991/13, authorizes the Financial Reporting Review Panel Ltd. to act as agent of the Secretary of State for Trade and Industry in making application to a court in respect of defective accounts.

[35] Companies Act (1985), Section 245B(1) (as amended by the Companies Act (1989)).

[36] The procedure for voluntary revision of accounts is summarized in Companies Act (1985) Section 245 and the Companies (Revision of Defective Accounts and Report) Regulations (1990), Statutory Instrument 1990/2570.

[37] The Financial Reporting Review Panel perhaps came closest to applying to the court in respect of defective accounts in a case concerning the 1991 financial statements of Trafalgar House plc. The company's directors were asked to appear before the FRRP to explain, among other things, a transfer to fixed assets of trading properties held as current assets. This transfer meant that a deficit on revaluation of £68m in the value of the properties which the directors had anticipated did not have to be written off in the profit and loss account, thereby reducing reported profit. Though the transfer was within the law and the issue was not addressed directly in any accounting standards, it was deemed to be against the spirit of the law. Though initially unwilling, the directors of Trafalgar House plc eventually agreed to revise the financial statements. Companies may be discouraged from challenging a recommendation of the FRRP in court by the prospect of adverse publicity and substantial legal costs. Furthermore, before the case comes

financial statements of companies which have been referred to it. Its function is to police by providing evidence rather than to adjudicate on whether financial statements should be revised, which remains the prerogative of the courts alone.

Professional accounting standards are also a significant source of rules for the computation of taxable profit. Though the taxing statutes have always included detailed provisions on this subject, their scope has been confined in general to specific matters such as the deductibility of certain expenses[38] and reliefs for capital expenditure which replace the accounting depreciation charge.[39] Since a statutory definition of the 'full amount of the profits or gains of the year' which is the stated measure of trading subject to tax[40] was not provided until 1998, the courts have relied heavily on 'ordinary principles of commercial accounting'[41] in interpreting the phrase. A recent judgement of the Court of Appeal has confirmed that no binding rules of tax law for the computation of taxable profit have been established by case law precedent.[42] Instead the courts rely on expert evidence of prevailing accountancy practice so that accounting standards in effect prescribe rules for computing taxable profit. This dependence has been criticized on the grounds that standards permit too much choice and are designed to measure the performance rather than the tax liability of a business.[43]

Nevertheless, the inclusion for the first time in the Finance Act 1998 of an express requirement that taxable trading profit should be computed 'on an accounting basis which gives a true and fair view'[44] represents clear statutory endorsement of the courts' established practice of determining

---

to court, professional guidance may be published on the point at issue which may weaken the case of the company concerned. Such was the case when the Urgent Issues Task Force published Abstract 5, *Transfers from Current Assets to Fixed Assets*, in July 1992 which addressed the issue in contention in the Trafalgar House case. The above figure is taken from M. Davies, R. Paterson and A. Wilson, *UK GAAP: Generally Accepted Accounting Practice in the United Kingdom* (London, 1997), 690.

[38] For example Income and Corporation Taxes Act (1988) Section 74 gives details of deductions not allowable in computing taxable trading profit.

[39] The Capital Allowances Act (1990) provides for tax capital allowances in respect of expenditure on industrial buildings, plant and machinery and other capital assets.

[40] Income and Corporation Taxes Act (1988) Section 60(1).

[41] Per Lord Justice Clyde in *Whimster and Co. v. Commissioners of Inland Revenue*, Court of Session (1925) 12, Tax Cases, p. 823.

[42] 'Indeed, given the plain language of the legislation, I find it hard to understand how any judge-made rule could override the application of a generally accepted rule of commercial accountancy which (a) applied to the situation in question, (b) was not one of two or more rules applicable to the situation in question and (c) was not shown to be inconsistent with the true facts or otherwise inapt to determine the true profits or losses of the business.' Per Sir Thomas Bingham, Master of the Rolls, in *Gallagher v. Jones*, Court of Appeal (1993), Simons Tax Cases, p. 555.

[43] J. Freedman, 'Defining Taxable Profit in a Changing Accounting Environment', and G. Whittington, 'Tax Policy and Accounting Standards', *British Tax Review* 5 (1995), 434–44 and 452–60.   [44] Finance Act (1998), Section 42(1).

taxable profit by reference to accounting principles. Other recent tax statutes, like their company law equivalents, also reveal a clear intention by the legislator to enhance the authority of accounting practice. New provisions relating to the deduction and assessment of loan interest[45] follow accounting practice closely and the purpose of new legislation concerning rental payments on finance leases is expressly described as being to 'charge amounts of income determined by reference to those which fall for accounting purposes to be treated in accordance with normal accountancy practice as the income return on investment'.[46]

REGULATORY FRAMEWORK OF ACCOUNTING IN GERMANY

The primary source of accounting rules in Germany is the legal code. In accordance with civil law tradition, statutory rules are comprehensive and in theory the main function of the courts is to interpret rather than to develop the law. Nevertheless, the accounting statutes are not precise in every detail and the courts' role in refining the law (*Rechtsfortbildung*) permits some flexibility in response to changes in the business environment. In adjudicating accounting issues the courts take note of the expert commentary of lawyers and business academics as well as professional guidelines such as the Expert Opinions and Recommendations of the Institute of Auditors (*Institut der Wirtschaftsprüfer*, IdW). The authority of expert opinion in informing the process of statutory interpretation by the courts may be further enhanced by the establishment in 1998 of the German Accounting Standards Committee (*Deutsches Rechnungslegungs Standard Committee e.V.*, DRSC) which is required to establish an independent German Accounting Standards Board (*Deutscher Standardisierungsrat*, DSR). Membership of the DRSC is open to any company and to individuals with relevant qualifications or experience,[47] though eligibility for election to its executive organs is restricted to accountants, tax advisers, lawyers, and members of similar professions.[48] Nevertheless, the development and drafting of accounting rules is likely to remain primarily the responsibility of the Federal Ministry of Justice with the new bodies acting in an advisory capacity. The standard setting remit of the new Board will be confined to consolidated financial reporting by groups of companies and the contract authorizing the Board's establishment states specifically that standards which it draws up may not contradict legal provisions.[49]

---

[45] Finance Act (1996) Sections 80–105 and Schedules 8–15.
[46] Finance Act (1997) Schedule 12 para.1(2).   [47] Charter of the DRSC, §4(1).
[48] Charter of the DRSC, §6(2).
[49] Standardization Contract between Federal Ministry of Justice and the DRSC, Section 4(3).

Under the German Commercial Code (*Handelsgesetzbuch*) all enterprises are required to prepare financial statements which comply with 'principles of regular book-keeping' (*Grundsätze ordnungsmäßiger Buchführung*, GoB).[50] In interpreting this phrase the courts originally took cognizance of the accounting practices of reputable businessmen but many principles are now expressly prescribed in the Code.[51] However if there is no specifically applicable legal rule or if there is a conflict between two accounting principles, the courts interpret the GoB by reference to the purpose of the financial statements. This functional approach permits consideration of the interests of different users such as creditors and shareholders.[52]

The Accounting Directives Law (*Bilanzrichtliniengesetz*) (1985) which implemented the provisions of the EU's Fourth and Seventh Company Law Directives laid down a comprehensive code of accounting rules applicable to all corporations.[53] A specific consequence whose effect has been much debated was the incorporation into German law of the 'true and fair view' principle derived from UK company law.[54] The prevailing opinion is that the requirement may be fulfilled by additional disclosure in the notes to the accounts rather than by adjustment of the accounting figures[55] since the override provision of the Fourth Directive[56] was not expressly adopted by the German legislator. The Joint Stock Corporation Act (*Aktiengesetz*) prescribes additional accounting rules for stock corporations (*Aktiengesellschaften*, AG)[57] and limited partnerships with shares (*Kommanditgesellschaften auf Aktien*) (KgaA).[58] The Act Concerning Limited Liability Companies includes similar rules for limited liability companies (*Gesellschaften mit beschränkter Haftung*, GmbH).[59] Under the 1998 Law on Corporate Control and Transparency, disclosure requirements have recently been extended to include, for example, information

[50] *Handelsgesetzbuch*, 243(1).

[51] General principles of regular book-keeping such as completeness, correctness and consistency are laid down in *Handelsgesetzbuch*, 238, 239, 243, 246, 252, and 265. Accounting principles such as historical cost, going concern and accruals are described in *Handelsgesetzbuch* 252 and 253.

[52] D. Ordelheide and D. Pfaff, *European Financial Reporting: Germany* (London, 1994), 108.

[53] The rules are contained in *Handelsgesetzbuch* 264–335.

[54] *Handelsgesetzbuch* 264(2).

[55] A. Haller, 'The Relationship of Financial and Tax Accounting in Germany: A Major Reason for Accounting Disharmony in Europe', *International Journal of Accounting* 27 (1992), 310–23.

[56] Article 2(5) requires that in exceptional cases a provision of the Directive which is incompatible with the true and fair requirement 'must be departed from in order to give a true and fair view'.

[57] *Aktiengesetz* 17–19, 30, 32–5, 49, 57–71, 91–2, 142–5, 182–240, 256–61, 270.

[58] *Aktiengesetz* 286, 288.

[59] The Act is called *Gesetz betreffend die Gesellschaften mit beschränkter Haftung*; see 5, 19, 29–34, 41–3, 55–8.

on stock option plans[60] and management's assessment of future risks facing the corporation.[61]

A fundamental tenet of German accounting law is the 'authoritativeness principle' (*Maßgeblichkeitsprinzip*) which requires substantial identity between financial and tax accounting. The requirement in the tax statutes[62] that the computation of income for tax purposes must follow the commercial law GoB has two effects.[63] First, the 'abstract authoritativeness' principle implies that commercial accounting law which is consistent with the GoB and does not conflict with a rule of tax law must be applied in computing taxable profit. Second, under the 'formal authoritativeness' principle financial statements prepared for commercial purposes are binding for tax purposes. Therefore, where commercial law permits a choice among options for recognition or valuation of assets and liabilities, the option chosen in the financial balance sheet (*Handelsbilanz*) must also be used in computing taxable profit unless tax law requires otherwise. Tax law also prescribes[64] a 'reverse authoritativeness principle' (*umgekehrtes Maßgeblichkeitsprinzip*) which permits certain tax reliefs, for example special depreciation allowances, only if corresponding adjustments are made in the financial statements.[65]

The authoritativeness principle and in particular its reverse have been criticized as incompatible with a strict interpretation of the 'true and fair' requirement and an impediment to harmonization of rules for accounting and the computation of taxable income in the European Union.[66] Conversely, the principles are defended as simple, administratively efficient and economical, and equitable in that profits available for distribution to shareholders are calculated on the same basis as those used to calculate the share of the state as a sleeping partner in the business.[67] A significant effect of adherence to the principles is the importance of tax jurisprudence in determining GoB. The local fiscal courts (*Finanzgerichte*) and the higher Federal Fiscal Court (*Bundesfinanzhof*, BFH) are required to interpret all of the GoB whether expressly laid down in the Commercial Code or not. Because tax litigation is much more common than commercial accounting litigation, decisions of the BFH are a more important

---

[60] *Handelsgesetzbuch* 285(9a) and (10). The Law is called *Gesetz zur Kontrolle und Transparenz im Unternehmensbereich*.   [61] *Handelsgesetzbuch* 289(1) and 315(1).

[62] *Einkommenssteuergesetz* 5(1).

[63] D. Pfaff and T. Schröer, 'The Relationship between Financial and Tax Accounting in Germany—the Authoritativeness and Reverse Authoritativeness Principle', *The European Accounting Review* 5, Supplement (1996), 963–79.   [64] *Einkommenssteuergesetz* 5(1) S.2.

[65] Commercial law specifically permits the use of these tax induced values in financial statements (*Handelsgesetzbuch* 254, 279(2), 280(2)).

[66] Haller, 'The Relationship of Financial and Tax Accounting in Germany', 322.

[67] Pfaff and Schröer, 'The Relationship between Financial and Tax Accounting in Germany', 969–70.

source of accounting rules than those of the Federal Supreme Court (*Bundesgerichtshof*, BGH).

The courts may seek rulings from the European Court of Justice (ECJ) when European Union accounting law is in issue. For example, on a reference from the Second Chamber of the BGH, the ECJ recently held[68] that the practice of congruent dividend reporting was compatible with the requirement of the Fourth Directive that valuation should be prudent with only profits made at the balance sheet date included.[69] The course of the litigation reveals some uncertainty in European accounting jurisprudence in that the Court rejected the clear opinion of the Advocate General that congruent dividend reporting was precluded by the terms of the Fourth Directive.[70] It then subsequently amended its own judgement to correct 'obvious errors' by changing the conditions under which the practice may be permitted.[71]

The main function of consolidated accounts of groups of companies in Germany is the provision of information:[72] in accordance with the 'entity principle' (*Einheitsgrundsatz*) they should present a true and fair view of the group as a whole.[73] They have no direct effect on the calculation of profits available for distribution or taxable profit and, since the authoritativeness principles do not apply to them, conservative tax-based valuations used in the accounts of individual subsidiaries are seldom applied. As they will apply only to consolidated accounts, standards drawn up by the new German Accounting Standards Board, unlike their UK equivalents, will not affect the computation of taxable profit.

A growing practice among German multinational companies has been the preparation of two sets of consolidated financial statements, one of which is based on international accounting standards. The Law to Facilitate the Raising of Capital enacted in March 1998 now expressly permits German listed companies which are parents of a group to use internationally accepted accounting principles as the sole basis for preparing consolidated accounts.[74] This liberal legislation may prove

---

[68] Judgement of the European Court of Justice (Fifth Chamber), delivered 27 June 1996: Case C-234/94 Waltraud Tomberger v. Gebrüder von der Wettern GmbH.

[69] Fourth Directive, Art.31(1)(c)(aa).

[70] In his Opinion delivered on 25 January 1996 Advocate General Tesauro rejected the arguments of the German and UK governments that the exclusion of profits of a wholly owned subsidiary would be 'excessively restrictive and formalistic'. This rejection of congruent dividend reporting caused considerable concern in Germany.

[71] Among the conditions for congruent dividend reporting prescribed in the original decision were adoption of the subsidiary's accounts in general meeting before completion of the audit of the parent company's accounts and attribution of the dividend to the parent in the subsidiary's financial statements. These requirements were much criticized and are absent from the revised conditions listed in the corrective ruling of 10 July 1997.

[72] Ordelheide and Pfaff, *European Financial Reporting: Germany*, 167.

[73] *Handelsgesetzbuch* 297(3) S.1.

[74] *Handelsgesetzbuch* 292a. This Law is called *Kapitalaufnahmeerleichterungsgesetz*.

contentious in the event of a future conflict between the requirements of an international accounting standard and the terms of the Seventh Directive. As the Single Market Commissioner Mario Monti observed in 1996: 'It would therefore be impossible for a Member State to refer in national law directly to International Accounting Standards. This would create legal uncertainty and place the Member State concerned at the mercy of a process which neither it nor we can control. This would not be in conformity with European law.'[75]

THE ROLE OF FINANCIAL STATEMENTS IN GERMANY AND THE UK

The role of financial statements as an information source within an economy has a significant impact on the national system of accounting.[76] This influence is particularly evident when contrasting accounting systems in Germany and the UK. Businesses in the UK and in Germany prepare financial statements with different objectives in mind. In the UK corporate ownership is widely dispersed among uninformed owners[77] for whom the financial statements are the only source of information while in Germany a large proportion of shares in listed companies is held by institutional investors, including banks and insurance companies in particular. This greater concentration of corporate ownership in Germany is a consequence of differences in the way industrialization took place in the two countries.[78] Since German institutional investors are usually represented on the boards of directors they have direct access to the company's internal information.[79] The content of annual financial statements is therefore of less significance to them than to private investors. In contrast, in countries like the UK where capital markets are more important, accounting systems evolve which focus on full and fair disclosure in financial statements.[80] German companies also have a larger proportion of debt in their capital structure than their UK counterparts. Since the large banking institutions who are the main providers of debt finance

[75] Extract from a speech by Mario Monti to the European Federation of Financial Institutes, 21/6/1996, in Paris.

[76] H. Biener, 'What Is the Future of Mutual Recognition of Financial Statements and Is Comparability Really Necessary?', *The European Accounting Review* 3/2 (1994), 335–42.

[77] 20 per cent of adults own shares in the UK compared with 7 per cent in Germany. See F. Hyde, *The German Way: Aspects of Behaviour, Attitudes, and Customs in the German-Speaking World* (Lincolnswood, Ill., 1996).

[78] Sir G. Owen, 'Lessons for Britain from German Corporate Governance', *Accountancy*, April (1995), 75.

[79] Thorell and Whittington, 'The Harmonization of Accounting within the EU', 231.

[80] D. Cairns, 'What is the Future of Mutual Recognition of Financial Statements and is Comparability Really Necessary?' *The European Accounting Review* 3/2 (1994), 344.

are represented on corporate boards and often exercise considerable influence on companies' financial policies,[81] information published in financial statements is of limited significance to them.

The importance of protecting the providers of debt capital (*Gläubigerschutz*) ensures that conservatism is the overriding principle applied in determining distributable profit in German accounting. Application of the prudence principle (*Vorsichtsprinzip*), which requires that all losses but no profits should be anticipated, reassures lenders that German companies can adequately fund interest payments and loan redemptions. This conservative approach is further encouraged by the authoritativeness principles since lower accounting profits lead to reductions in corporation tax liabilities. By contrast, the importance of equity financing in the UK encourages listed companies to report earnings in the most favourable light. Since dividends, which are paid to shareholders usually twice a year, are based on distributable profits, the higher the profit figure, *ceteris paribus*, the higher the dividend income to the investor. Furthermore, equity shareholders benefit from capital appreciation of their investment when the share price of the company increases in response to favourable earnings announcements. In short, the better the reported earnings, the greater the likelihood of attracting investor capital.

Clear divergences between the conservative, tax-based, *Gläubigerschutz* approach to income determination in Germany and the investor-orientated, profit-maximizing approach in the UK, are often revealed in the application of radically different accounting treatments to identical transactions in the two countries. For example, the option to revalue tangible and financial fixed assets permitted by the EU's Fourth Company Law Directive[82] was not incorporated into German law which requires that asset values should not exceed original cost (historic cost).[83] The German legislator's conservative policy undoubtedly reflects a fundamental aversion, founded on the hyper-inflationary experiences between 1919 and 1923,[84] to any recognition of inflation in the legal code. Other significant aims were to avoid jeopardizing creditors' protection and prevent any increase in the corporate tax burden resulting from increased accounting earnings adopted for tax purposes in accordance with the authoritativeness principles. In contrast, the revaluation of fixed assets, in particular freehold and leasehold land and buildings, is explicitly recommended in the relevant UK accounting standard on the ground that this provides 'useful and relevant information to users of accounts'.[85]

---

[81] Ordelheide and Pfaff, *European Financial Reporting: Germany*, 44.
[82] Article 33(1).   [83] *Handelsgesetzbuch* 253(1).
[84] G. Seckler, 'Germany', in Alexander and Archer (eds.), *European Accounting Guide*, 223.
[85] Statement of Standard Accounting Practice No. 12, *Accounting for Depreciation*, para. 5, Accounting Standards Committee, 1977.

The marked difference between the accounting treatment of intangible fixed assets in Germany and the UK is a further illustration of the contrasting principles of conservatism and profit maximisation. These are non-financial assets which do not have physical substance but are still of value to a business, for example licences, franchises, and quotas. UK accounting rules permit, in certain circumstances, the inclusion in the balance sheet of intangible fixed assets which a company has produced itself.[86] The inclusion of these costs in the balance sheet ensures that earnings are not reduced and increases asset values reported in the company's financial statements. However, in Germany the cost of producing intangible fixed assets cannot be included as an asset (*Vermögensgegenstand*) and must be written off to the profit and loss account,[87] thereby reducing earnings.

Because of the conservatism of German accounting principles and the binding link between accounting and taxable profit established by the authoritative principles, it is often assumed that the balance sheets of most enterprises contain 'hidden reserves' (*stille Rücklagen*) representing undisclosed assets. This assessment was evidently accepted by the then German Minister of Finance, Oskar Lafontaine, who in November 1998 condemned the accumulation by enterprises of 'excessive tax free hidden reserves' as 'simply unacceptable and economic nonsense'.[88] A less negative attitude to such reserves is revealed in the comment of Herbert Biener, the secretary general of the new German Accounting Standards Committee, that 'understatement for its own sake is widely considered to be desirable, since the greater the understatement of assets the greater the margin of safety the assets provide as security for loans or other debts'.[89]

Empirical evidence of the existence of hidden reserves is difficult to substantiate. Average ratios of market capitalization to accounting value (or price/book ratios) of German and UK listed companies are similar, both having risen from 2:1 to 3:1 over the period from 1988 to 1997.[90] However this close identity does not confirm that the assets of German companies are not undervalued in financial statements compared with those of their UK counterparts since current and expected accounting figures are themselves significant determinants of market prices. A study by the *Deutsche Bundesbank* reveals that the enactment of the Accounting Directives Law in 1985 had no significant effect on asset valuations in

---

[86] Financial Reporting Standard 10, *Goodwill and Intangible Assets*, para. 14, Accounting Standards Board, 1997.   [87] *Handelsgesetzbuch* 248(2).

[88] Speech in the *Bundestag* debate on the draft Tax Relief Law, 13/11/1998.

[89] Biener, 'What is the Future of Mutual Recognition of Financial Statements', 338.

[90] L. S. Speidell, *International Accounting Standards versus U.S. GAAP: Should Analysts care?*, paper presented at the 1997 Annual Conference of the Association for Investment Management and Research, New Orleans, May 1997.

TABLE 12.1. *Depreciation charge as a percentage of net tangible fixed assets*

	1984	1985	1986	1987	1988	1989	1990	1991	1992	1993	1994	1995
Germany	16.2	16.4	16.3	20.2	20.9	21.2	21.6	21.8	22.1	22.4	22.5	21.6
UK	5.5	6.1	6.0	5.9	5.3	4.7	5.0	5.2	5.3	5.3	5.7	6.0

Source: OECD. Financial Statistics of Non-Financial Enterprises (Paris, 1996)

the balance sheets of German enterprises.[91] However, this may not be conclusive evidence of the absence of hidden reserves but merely an indication that the law did not result in any substantive change in German accounting practice. The minimal impact of the international debt crises of recent years on the balance sheets of German banks is cited as further evidence of substantial undisclosed reserves in the financial sector.[92]

Depreciation charges as a percentage of net tangible fixed assets provide perhaps the most visible measure of the relative conservatism of accounting valuation policies. The statistics in Table 12.1 show that depreciation rates applied by German companies have been approximately three times greater than those used by UK companies in recent years. This pattern is consistent with the adoption of conservative tax based 'wear and tear' (*Absetzung für Abnutzung*) rates in the financial statements of German companies and, in particular, the inclusion of special tax depreciation allowances (*steuerliche Sonderabschreibungen*) in accordance with the reverse authoritativeness principle.[93]

The effects of the prohibition in German law of capitalization of the costs of internally produced intangible fixed assets are reflected in the results of a study by the *Deutsche Bundesbank*.[94] These show that intangible assets made up approximately 7 per cent of the balance sheet totals of US companies in 1994 and 1995 but only 1 per cent of the totals of their German counterparts.

---

[91] Deutsche Bundesbank, 'The Effects of the Act Concerning the EC Annual Accounts Directive on the Figures of the Corporate Balance Sheet Statistics', *Deutsche Bundesbank Monthly Report*, October 1990, 18. The study shows that aggregate balance sheet totals of the 184 enterprises examined actually declined by 11 per cent from DM 551 bn. to DM 490 bn. after introduction of the Accounting Directives Law. However, this decline does not reflect a decrease in asset values but is explained by a change in presentation. Aggregate depreciation of DM 69 bn. which had been treated previously as a separate liability was now offset directly against the cost of the relevant assets.

[92] Ordelheide and Pfaff, *European Financial Reporting: Germany*, 157.

[93] *Handelsgesetzbuch*, para. 279(2), expressly permits the inclusion of such depreciation charges in financial statements despite their incompatibility with GoB.

[94] Deutsche Bundesbank, 'International Comparison of Corporate Profitability', *Deutsche Bundesbank Monthly Report*, Oct. 1997, 39.

THE IMPACT OF GLOBALIZATION

Increasing globalization of capital markets and business activities has led to many changes in the institutional and regulatory environment within which UK and German enterprises operate. The progressive abolition of restrictions on international capital movements, payments, and rights of establishment has allowed European multinational companies to look beyond traditional national sources of finance, whether banks or private investors. If domestic markets are unable to satisfy their capital requirements, they turn to international markets and in particular the sophisticated and efficient US stock exchanges as alternative providers.[95] Several German companies have followed the well-publicized example of Daimler-Benz AG in 1993 in seeking listing on the New York exchange.

To obtain a US listing companies must register with the Securities and Exchange Commission (SEC) which requires financial statements prepared in accordance with the generally accepted accounting practice (GAAP) in the United States. In the early 1990s several major German companies, supported by the German government, sought to persuade the SEC to accept accounts prepared on the basis of German accounting rules. Their case was based on the principles of equivalence and reciprocity since German stock exchanges accepted financial statements prepared in accordance with US GAAP. These arguments were rejected by the SEC whose principal objection was that the application of the *Gläubigerschutz* principle in German financial statements masks companies' true profits and therefore disadvantages shareholders. In fact the SEC is now the only supervisory body in the world which does not accept financial statements prepared in accordance with European law.[96]

Both UK and German companies listed on US stock exchanges must therefore prepare accounts based on US GAAP. Compliance is regarded by some as a surrender to US pressure: thus it was argued that acceptance of the requirement by Daimler-Benz AG in 1993 undermined the bargaining position of the German representatives who were seeking to negotiate a mutual recognition agreement.[97] Others consider the required revision of accounts both inconvenient and costly. Hugh Callum, Chief Financial Officer of SmithKline Beecham plc which is incorporated in the UK but listed in the US, points out: 'Running an Anglo-American multinational registered in the UK, and listed and reporting in the UK, the US, and Japan, I live in a veritable Tower of Babel of conflicting

---

[95] A. Wilson, 'Harmonization: Is It Now or Never for Europe?,' *Accountancy*, Nov. 1994, 98.

[96] Biener, 'What Is the Future of Mutual Recognition of Financial Statements', 341.

[97] A. Haller, 'International Accounting Harmonisation: American Hegemony or Mutual Recognition with Benchmarks? Comments and Additional Notes from a German Perspective', *The European Accounting Review* 4/2 (1995), 238.

accounting practices.'[98] However the prevailing positive view is perhaps reflected in the following statement by Heinrich von Pierer, President and Chief Executive Officer of Siemens AG in 1998: 'The planned conversion of our accounting system from the German HGB system to the US GAAP standard is a prerequisite for listing on a US stock exchange. Conversion to US GAAP naturally will make our financial statements comparable world-wide. As a true global player, we are meeting international standards. In addition, the new system will have a major effect on the transparency and shareholder-focus of our external publicity work.'[99]

It is difficult to draw clear conclusions from a comparison of financial results reported under US GAAP and under German or UK accounting practice. Far from corroborating the assumption of greater conservatism in German accounting, the reported results of Daimler-Benz AG in fact suggest the reverse. When the company revised its financial statements to comply with US GAAP, a profit for 1993 of DM 615 million arrived at using German accounting rules became a loss of DM 1,839 million while in 1995 and 1996 results under the two systems were almost identical.[100] Similarly there were no significant differences in the results of Veba AG in 1996 and 1997 calculated using US GAAP and German accounting rules.[101] A possible reason for the absence of divergence is provided in the 1997 Report of Veba AG which explains that 'the consolidated financial statements comply with US GAAP as far as permissible under German GAAP'. Therefore in the consolidated accounts drawn up under German principles (which have no effect on tax liability or distribution policy) many of the conservative tax-based options may be excluded. Furthermore, reported results of UK companies do not confirm the assumption that differences between UK and US GAAP are insignificant. A revision of the 1997 financial statements of SmithKline Beecham plc to comply with the SEC's requirements resulted in a decrease in profits from £1,079,000 under UK GAAP to £828,000 under US GAAP.[102]

Mutual recognition of particulars required on admission to listing on stock exchanges in the European Union was established in 1987:[103] companies are required to provide either individual or consolidated accounts which comply with the annual accounts Directives and give a true and fair view.[104] Therefore, despite the evident differences between UK and German accounting practice, financial statements drawn up in accordance with either will be accepted by stock exchanges in both

[98] Cairns, 'What Is the Future of Mutual Recognition of Financial Statements', 345.
[99] H. von Pierer, Speech at annual Press Conference of Siemens AG, Munich, 3/12/1998.
[100] Daimler-Benz AG, Annual Report 1996.   [101] Veba AG, Annual Report 1997.
[102] SmithKline Beecham plc, Annual Report 1997.
[103] Directive 87/345/EEC, Art. 1, amending Directive 80/390/EEC, Art.24.
[104] Directive 80/390/EEC, Annex 1, Ch.5.1.5.

jurisdictions. Nevertheless, German companies may choose to prepare consolidated accounts on the basis of international principles in order to reveal increased equity reserves: Schering AG adopted this policy when it was first quoted on the London stock exchange in 1986.[105]

Though the spread of US GAAP may be primarily a product of the search by large multinational companies for competitive advantage in capital markets, legislative changes such as the German Law to Facilitate the Raising of Capital will undoubtedly stimulate the process. Since internationally quoted German groups need no longer prepare separate consolidated financial statements for domestic and foreign investors, the influence of international accounting principles will be enhanced within the German business community. The foundation of the German Accounting Standards Committee, with the express 'aim of introducing and financing standardisation in accordance with the Anglo-American and international model'[106] for consolidated financial reports, will further accelerate this process. The fact that no similar concession is contemplated in the UK reflects the different perceived objectives of financial statements in the two countries. Though consolidated accounts are irrelevant for tax purposes in both jurisdictions, it is only in Germany that this is regarded as a ground for the application of different accounting rules. Since the provision of useful and accurate information to existing and potential investors is seen as the primary objective of financial statements in the UK, the use of different accounting principles in preparing the accounts of individual companies and groups would appear illogical and unjustifiable.

CONCLUSION

The freedom to prepare consolidated accounts using international accounting practice is widely regarded as a solution to the problem of restrictions on capital flows and distortion of investment decisions resulting from accounting diversity. The new approach to accounting harmonization adopted by the European Commission in 1995 was undoubtedly based on this rationale. The Commission accepted that the obligation of European companies seeking listing on certain international markets to prepare two sets of accounts was 'costly and the provision of different figures in different markets is confusing to investors and the public at large'.[107] Its solution was to facilitate the preparation of consolidated accounts on the basis of International Accounting Standards (IASs)

---

[105] Ordelheide and Pfaff, *European Financial Reporting: Germany*, 82.

[106] Preamble to the Charter of the DRSC.

[107] European Commission, *Communication: Accounting Harmonisation: A New Strategy vis-à-vis International Harmonisation* (COM(95) 508), para. 3.3.

drawn up by the International Accounting Standards Committee on which the Commission has observer status. The Contact Committee on the Accounting Directives considered that, subject to minor exceptions, these Standards were compatible with the Directives.[108] This conclusion clearly facilitated the development of the German Law to Facilitate the Raising of Capital. Nevertheless, the Commission has emphasized that if only one set of consolidated accounts is prepared, it must comply with the requirements of the EU's Seventh Company Law Directive: conformity with international standards alone will not satisfy that condition.[109] In particular, the right granted to member states by the Seventh Directive[110] to require or permit the use of different valuation methods in individual and consolidated accounts does not extend to bases which would conflict with those allowed under the Fourth Directive.

Though a convenient practical expedient, the use of different accounting principles in individual and consolidated accounts is difficult to justify on theoretical grounds since it seems illogical to assert that a true and fair view is provided when the same transaction by a subsidiary is treated differently in its own and in its parent's accounts. The argument that the 'entity principle' is sufficient justification for divergence seems untenable. A more practical objection concerns the exclusion of many small enterprises which do not prepare consolidated accounts. In Germany the new right to prepare financial statements based on international principles will apply to only a very small number of listed companies.

Moreover, the separation of individual and consolidated accounts does not effect a reconciliation between the divergent philosophies on which the accounting systems of Germany and the UK are based. The debate on the respective merits of each remains unresolved. Some believe that the UK model is preferable in that it leads to greater transparency in financial statements which assists users in making informed decisions.[111] Others take a decidedly negative view of investor-orientated financial statements insofar as their preparation fosters a culture of short-term gambling in which the highest and quickest return is sought to the detriment of companies' long-term development.[112]

---

[108] European Commission: Contact Committee on the Accounting Directives, *An Examination of the Conformity between the International Accounting Standards and the European Accounting Directives* (Luxemburg, 1996).

[109] European Commission, *Interpretative Communication concerning Certain Articles of the Fourth and Seventh Council Directives*, para. 61.   [110] Article 29(2)(a).

[111] W. P. Schuetze, 'What is the future of mutual recognition of financial statements and is comparability really necessary?', *The European Accounting Review* 3/2 (1994), 332. The reference is to the US but is equally applicable to the UK since both share similar capital-market based corporate structures and a similar system of accounting. However, it is worth pointing out that the UK's investor-orientated system did not always produce transparent financial statements as the example of Polly Peck International demonstrates.

[112] Biener, 'What Is the Future of Mutual Recognition of Financial Statements', 338.

Until a compromise is reached, harmonization of corporate tax rates in the European Union would lead to increased inequity if the true burden were lower in Germany than in the UK because taxable profits are computed using more conservative accounting practices. The resulting decreases in tax liabilities may be permanent or temporary, as when a charge is postponed by undervaluation of an asset but eventually crystallizes on its disposal. It is difficult to provide conclusive evidence of the effects of divergent accounting practices on corporate tax liabilities in Germany and the UK. During the period 1979 to 1994 corporate tax revenue amounted to 2 per cent of GDP on average in Germany but fluctuated between 2.5 per cent and 5 per cent of GDP in the UK,[113] though corporation tax rates were significantly higher in Germany. Clearly the contraction of the tax base in Germany resulting from conservative accounting practices may explain part of this difference but other factors such as the definition of corporate tax, the extent of its integration with personal taxation, the size of the incorporated and unincorporated business sectors and cyclical profitability in the corporate sector are also relevant. A closer alignment between the bases of corporation tax in Germany and the UK may result from implementation of the new German government's tax reform proposals announced in November 1998. A key feature of these is the extension of the tax base by the elimination or restriction of permitted reductions in asset valuations: thus a 'tax system with lower rates and fewer exceptions' will be established.[114]

In 1988 the European Commission prepared a far-reaching proposal for a directive on the harmonization of rules for the determination of taxable profits of enterprises which acknowledged the inadequacy of the Fourth Company Law Directive as a source of accounting rules because of the wide range of options permitted.[115] Indeed in a study of the Fourth Directive undertaken in 1986 for the Commission's Directorate General for Economic and Financial Affairs there is an admission that 'standardisation with respect to valuation was not attempted—or was even deliberately avoided'.[116] Though a limited European accounting jurisprudence is developing mainly as a result of references from German courts,[117] the rules established remain inadequate bases for the computation of tax

---

[113] L. Chennels and R. Griffiths, *Taxing Profits in a Changing World* (London, 1997).

[114] O. Lafontaine, Speech in the *Bundestag* debate, 13/11/1998.

[115] P. McCourt and G. Radcliffe, 'Les Relations Fiscalité-Comptabilité in France: A Model for Europe?', *British Tax Review* 5 (1995), 482.

[116] European Commission, *The Fourth Company Accounts Directive of 1978 and the Accounting Systems of the Federal Republic of Germany, France, Italy, the UK, the US and Japan* (Luxemburg, 1986).

[117] For example, the Cologne Tax Court has recently sought a preliminary ruling on the interpretation of Article 31 of the Fourth Directive in the case of Brühler Kreditbank eG v. Finanzamt Brühl (Case C-56/95).

liabilities. While wholesale tax harmonization in the European Union is now regarded as incompatible with the principle of subsidiarity, the elimination of 'harmful' tax competition is an agreed objective.[118] Until harmonized European accounting rules are established, any proposal for the elimination of unfair tax competition which is based on differences in nominal corporate tax rates must be open to question.

[118] Proposals to tackle harmful tax competition were unanimously agreed by European Union finance ministers on 1 Dec. 1997. An effective level of taxation which is significantly lower than the general level of taxation in the country concerned is one criterion for recognition of potentially harmful tax measures identified in the European Commission communication to the Council, *Towards Tax Co-ordination in the European Union: A Package to Deal with Harmful Tax Competition* (COM(97)495), Annex, para. E.

13

Negotiating the Intergovernmental Conferences: Maastricht, Amsterdam, and Beyond

ROBERT HARMSEN AND NICKOLAS REINHARDT

The 1990s have seen the adoption of two treaties marking, to varying degrees, the continued development of the European integration project. The Maastricht Treaty or Treaty on European Union was agreed in December 1991 and entered into force, after a turbulent ratification process, in November 1993. The Amsterdam Treaty was agreed in June 1997. Following a protracted but uneventful ratification process, this later treaty entered into force in May 1999. Both Treaties were the product of Intergovernmental Conferences or 'IGCs'.

An Intergovernmental Conference, as the name suggests, is a formal negotiation concerned with Treaty revision between the governments of the member states of the European Union. According to the terms set down in the Treaties themselves, these negotiations concern only the governments of the member states. The Commission, the European Parliament, and other interested parties may, of course, make representations and seek to influence the agenda. Indeed, they have occasionally done so to considerable effect. Nevertheless, it is the governments of the member states alone who must, unanimously, agree any change to the Treaties. The dynamics of the process are thus decisively 'intergovernmental' in the sense used in the integration theory literature.[1] The outcome of an IGC remains largely (though not entirely) explicable with reference to the convergence or divergence of the policy preferences of the member states.

The Maastricht Treaty was the product of two parallel IGCs, dealing with Economic and Monetary Union (EMU) and Political Union. Although both IGCs were concluded at the Maastricht summit in 1991,

[1] A. Moravcsik, 'Negotiating the Single European Act: National Interests and Conventional Statecraft in the European Community', *International Organization* 45/1 (1991), 19–56. See also A. Forster, 'Britain and the Negotiation of the Maastricht Treaty: A Critique of Liberal Intergovernmentalism', *Journal of Common Market Studies* 36/3 (1998), 347–68; and A. Moravcsik and K. Nicolaïdis, 'Explaining the Treaty of Amsterdam: Interests, Influence, Institutions', *Journal of Common Market Studies* 37/1 (1999), 59–85.

most commentators have stressed the relative autonomy of the two processes. Discussions on EMU predated those on Political Union and were
shaped, to a much larger extent, by the existence of a strong consensus
of values among key decision-makers.[2] The results of the negotiations
similarly reflected this distinction. While a detailed blueprint for EMU
was agreed at Maastricht, many of the major questions on Political Union
remained substantially unresolved.

The negotiations leading to the Amsterdam Treaty assumed a somewhat different form. Unlike Maastricht, the Amsterdam process consisted
of only a single IGC, concerned entirely with aspects of Political Union.
Although EMU formed a significant part of the background to the discussions, it was not formally on the IGC agenda. Amsterdam, in contrast to Maastricht, was also largely 'pre-programmed'. The Maastricht
Treaty had provided for the holding of an IGC in 1996 to discuss a number of unresolved issues. The Amsterdam Treaty negotiations thus often
appeared process-driven. The member states felt themselves obliged to
negotiate, and to reach a successful outcome, even though the holding of
such negotiations no longer necessarily corresponded to clear political
objectives.

The present chapter examines the positions and strategies adopted by
Germany and the United Kingdom during the course of the Maastricht
and Amsterdam Treaty negotiations. As such, the focus of this chapter
is not directly on Anglo-German bilateral relations. Rather, it seeks to
situate the two countries within the framework of a complex, increasingly
institutionalized multilateral bargaining process. The IGCs necessitate that
states engage in an ongoing process of coalition-building, attempting to
cobble together package deals acceptable to all participants. Neither
Germany nor the United Kingdom may escape from the constraints of
this process. It is clear, nevertheless, that they appear differentially placed
in terms of their ability to shape the nature and the outcome of these
negotiations. Successive German governments, working in tandem (if not
always in harmony) with their French counterparts, have played a central
role in defining the terms and pace of the integration process. Successive
UK governments, conversely, have appeared condemned (or, at least, have
condemned themselves) to the status of perpetual outsiders—confined for
the most part to reacting to initiatives which have taken shape elsewhere.

Separate sections below deal with each of the two Treaties. Reflecting
the relative autonomy of the two processes, separate subsections within

---

[2] The EMU policy community formed by national governments and central banks appears
to possess many of the attributes of an 'epistemic community' in which policy choices are
circumscribed by widely shared normative and causal belief structures. On the general concept,
see P. M. Haas, 'Introduction: Epistemic Communities and International Policy Co-ordination',
International Organization 46/1 (1992), 1–36.

each section examine EMU and Political Union. The conclusion then draws together these various strings, putting forward a general assessment of the two countries' relative influence across the two Treaties and three IGCs.

THE MAASTRICHT TREATY NEGOTIATIONS

(a) Economic and Monetary Union

Monetary union was officially declared an objective of the EC in 1969, but early moves to implement this goal had failed. The issue re-emerged in the mid-1980s as part of the Common Market programme. By then, the stabilizing effects of the European Monetary System (created in 1979) had generated a more favourable climate for institutional reforms.[3]

Although Chancellor Helmut Kohl was initially hesitant to enter into any international co-operation which might undermine the independence of the Deutsche Bundesbank,[4] he reviewed his position during the late 1980s in response to French and Italian criticism of Germany's dominance in the monetary field.[5] By taking a lead in the negotiations, Kohl could not only demonstrate his pro-integrationist credentials, but was also able to shape the talks in the process. In the spring of 1988, the German government set out a number of non-negotiable essentials for EMU which sought to reconcile the need for integration with Germany's concerns for monetary stability. The proposal envisaged tight public deficit controls and the creation of an independent European Central Bank charged with securing stable prices. Membership of EMU was to be made dependent on economic convergence. Moreover, Germany wanted to secure progress on the political dimension of European integration.[6]

Prime Minister Margaret Thatcher rejected EMU on the grounds that the project would infringe on Westminster's constitutional rights to carry out an independent economic policy. Her involvement in the negotiations therefore has to be explained by the dynamic and interlocking nature of the European bargaining process. If she had vetoed the exercise at this early stage, the other countries probably would have commenced their discussions outside the Community framework, depriving Britain of any

---

[3] See K. Dyson, *Elusive Union. The Process of Economic and Monetary Union in Europe* (London, 1994) and W. Sandholtz, 'Choosing Union: Monetary Politics and Maastricht', *International Organization* 47/1 (1993), 1–39.

[4] H. Kohl, 'Regierungserklärung zum Europäischen Rat in Luxemburg vom 5.12.1985', *Bulletin der Bundesregierung* (7/12/1985), 1213–17.

[5] 'M. Balladur veut accélerer la construction de l'Europe monétaire', *Le Monde*, 8/1/1988, and G. Amato, 'Un Motore per lo SME', *Il Sole 24 Ore*, 25/2/1988.

[6] For an overview of the German position, see W. Schönfelder and E. Thiel, *Ein Markt—Eine Währung. Die Verhandlungen zur Europäischen Wirtschafts- und Währungsunion* (Baden-Baden, 1994).

influence in the debate. The United Kingdom entered the negotiations on the basis that the EC should stall reforms until the Common Market had generated a market-based demand for monetary union.[7] Thatcher left little doubt that she did not believe this would be the case during her lifetime.[8]

The EMU negotiation process may be dated from June 1988 with the appointment of the Delors Committee by the European Council. The Committee, chaired by EC Commission President Jacques Delors and consisting largely of central bank governors, was charged with investigating the means by which monetary union could best be achieved. In April 1989 the Committee published its recommendations. At their June meeting in Madrid, eleven governments endorsed the group's findings as a blueprint for EMU. The British stood alone in their outright opposition to the proposals. The Delors Report (as it was known) was heavily influenced by Karl-Otto Pöhl, the Bundesbank's President. It stressed the need for an independent central bank, a clear commitment to price stability and the importance of strict public deficit controls. The report propagated a three-stage transition towards EMU, but failed to mention any specific dates, implying instead a lengthy period of economic adjustment. During the initial stage, all member states were to join the EMS and liberalize their capital markets. As part of Stage 2, some monetary policy functions should be transferred to a newly created European Central Bank (ECB). National authorities would nonetheless retain ultimate responsibility in monetary affairs. In the third and final stage, exchange rates were to be irrevocably fixed and the ECB given the exclusive authority over the then issued single currency. Binding rules were to limit public deficits.[9] By adopting the Report's proposals, all but one member state had essentially agreed on the fundamental principles of Economic and Monetary Union by June 1989.[10] The first stage of the Delors Report would begin in July 1990. Once the preparatory work on Stage 2 and 3 had sufficiently progressed, an intergovernmental conference (IGC) would be convened to decide on the necessary treaty revisions.

While endorsing Stage 1 of the Delors Report as a Common Market measure, the British government did not see the necessity for any institutional reforms, as proposed by Stages 2 and 3 of the recommendations.

---

[7] N. Lawson, 'What Sort of European Financial Area?', talk at the Royal Institute of International Affairs, London, 25/1/1989.

[8] 'Sceptical Champion of EC Monetary Integration', *Financial Times*, 1–2/7/1989.

[9] European Communities, *Report of the Committee for the Study of Economic and Monetary Union* (Luxemburg, 1989). See also N. Thygesen, 'The Delors Report and European Economic and Monetary Union', *International Affairs*, 65/4 (1989), 637–52.

[10] *European Presidency Conclusions* (Madrid, June 1989). See also the conclusions of the Economics and Finance Ministers at Ashford Castle, Ireland. 'Informal ECOFIN Council. Conclusions', *Agence Europe*, 2–3/4/1990, 5–8.

Instead, it sought to generate cross-national support for an alternative market-inspired route to monetary integration. Initially, Britain wanted to let national currencies compete freely against one another.[11] When this idea received a cool reception by the other governments, Britain launched its 'Hard-ECU-Plan' in June 1990.[12] This envisaged the creation of a thirteenth European currency to circulate parallel to the existing national denominations. The 'hard ECU' would be issued by a European Monetary Fund in exchange for national currencies. A government guarantee was to protect the new currency against devaluations, potentially making it an attractive investment and transaction medium. Although the plan went far to address the other member states' wishes for a common monetary institution and a common currency, it was submitted too late to influence the negotiations. By the summer of 1990 the political transformation process in Central and Eastern Europe and the prospect of German unification had strengthened the determination among the other governments to pursue a supranational route to monetary integration. This left Britain marginalized and let the Franco-German bargain shape the actual content of the Maastricht Treaty.

Following Britain's membership of the EMS in October 1990 and Thatcher's resignation the following month, there was a brief expectation that her successor John Major would take a more proactive stance at the negotiations. As it turned out, he was heavily constrained by his party's divisions over Europe.[13] In May 1991, the British government gradually retracted from its 'Hard-ECU-Plan' and concentrated instead on securing for itself a treaty 'opt-out' giving it the choice whether to join the final stage of EMU. This right was formally enshrined in a Protocol to the Maastricht Treaty in December 1991. Beyond that, the British delegation sided with Germany or France depending on the specific issue under discussion at the IGC.

Germany, the Netherlands, and Britain favoured tough and clearly definable economic criteria, which member states should meet before being eligible to join EMU. France, Italy, Spain, and the European Commission preferred looser standards, arguing that, as in the case of the EMS, monetary union would automatically lead to more convergence. Consequently, the first group of countries rejected premature institutional reforms and a specific timetable for monetary union, while the second propagated swift transitional arrangements. As German unification became

---

[11] See H.M. Treasury, *An Evolutionary Approach to Economic and Monetary Union* (London, Nov. 1989).

[12] 'Major's Plan for Monetary Union', *Financial Times*, 21/6/1990, and Bank of England, *The Hard ECU in Stage 2: Operational Requirements* (London, December 1990).

[13] For an account of the EMU discussions within the British government, see P. Stephens, *Politics and the Pound: The Tories, the Economy and Europe* (London, 1997).

increasingly inevitable, Helmut Kohl was prepared to give way to French pressures on the tempo of integration. At their summit in Strasbourg in December 1989, the governments decided that the IGC would be convened in the second half of 1990 and concluded by the end of 1991. A year later, January 1994 was set as the starting date for the second Stage of EMU. The Maastricht summit finally established 1 January 1999 as the latest possible date for Stage 3. In return for their approval of these dates, Germany, the Netherlands, and Britain secured general assent to tough conditions of economic convergence. Based on a Bundesbank submission,[14] each member state was required to fulfil four 'convergence criteria': a low inflation rate, low long-term interest rates, the avoidance of excessive public deficits, and a stable membership of the EMS for two years. The German side, including Britain, also secured French support on the transitional institutional arrangements. The creation of the European Central Bank would be postponed until Stage 3, allowing national authorities to retain full control over their own monetary affairs during the transition period. Instead a European Monetary Institute (EMI) was to be created and charged with technical preparations for the ECB.

Given that not all countries (including possibly Italy) could be expected to qualify for participation without severe austerity measures, the treaty potentially restricted monetary union to a core group of countries.[15] The looming conflict between firm timetables and economic convergence was to later overshadow the EMU implementation process, especially after it became clear in 1995 that Germany itself would find it difficult to qualify for monetary union.[16]

Whenever the negotiations turned to the final institutional design of EMU, the United Kingdom, France, and the European Commission favoured some degree of flexibility and political discretion, while Germany, the Netherlands and central bank representatives[17] preferred formalized rules of co-operation. Centrally, French projects for the creation of an 'economic government' (an economic policy-making body of political composition) conflicted with strong German insistence on establishing an absolute autonomy of action for the ECB. The United Kingdom, adopting an intermediate position, stressed only the need for a degree of

---

[14] 'Bundesbank Adds a Voice to Bonn's Go Slow Chorus on EMU', *Financial Times*, 21/9/1990.

[15] This point had already been acknowledged by the Deutsche Bundesbank in June 1990. 'Pöhl Suggests Dual-Speed Union', *Financial Times*, 12/6/1990.

[16] 'Deutsches Staatsdefizit überschreitet Eintrittskriterium für die Währungsunion', *Süddeutsche Zeitung*, 12/1/1996.

[17] See the Delors Report and the document submitted in April 1990 by the Monetary Committee of the EC, a technical committee consisting of representatives of the central banks and the Finance Ministries. 'Economic and Monetary Union', *Agence Europe Documents*, No. 1609 (3/4/1990).

national parliamentary control. Helmut Kohl's government also went further than most member states in its demands for tough automatic sanctions against countries running excessive public deficits. The United Kingdom adamantly rejected such plans on the basis that these not only challenged Britain's parliamentary sovereignty but also undermined the self-regulating strength of capital markets. In the end, the Maastricht Treaty did include the option of sanctions, but the procedure to invoke them remained lengthy, cumbersome and reliant on broad political assent.

Germany's influence in the EMU negotiations has often been described as 'hegemonic'.[18] This assessment seems especially valid in the context of the Delors Report and the initial phases of the bargaining process. Given the D-Mark's past track record of price stability and its pivot position in the EMS, this country had most to loose from EMU and could effectively lay down its preconditions for membership. The broad consensus on monetary policy-making in the EC since the 1980s made the German bargaining position generally acceptable to most member states. In the context of German unification, Chancellor Helmut Kohl none the less had to accept a number of Franco-German compromises, most notably over the timetable and the public deficit rules.[19] The question of fiscal discipline was especially sensitive as it linked the negotiations on Economic and Monetary Union to the broader issues of institutional reform and an expansion of Community competencies; topics being addressed in the parallel IGC on Political Union.

(b) Political Union

The initial movement towards the establishment of Economic and Monetary Union was not paralleled by comparable moves in the direction of Political Union. The formal preparatory work on EMU, dating from the appointment of the Delors Committee in June 1988, had no political counterpart. The convocation of an IGC on Economic and Monetary Union was not originally twinned with one on political union. While the Strasbourg European Council of December 1989 formally decided that an intergovernmental conference dealing with EMU would begin at the end of 1990, no comparable commitment was made as regards political union until some six months later at the June 1990 Dublin summit.

[18] K. Dyson and K. Featherstone, 'EMU and Economic Governance in Germany', *German Politics* 5/3 (1996), 337–9.

[19] For a critique of the 'hegemonic' explanation and an assessment of Germany's unattained bargaining preferences over EMU, see G. Garrett, 'The Politics of Maastricht', in B. Eichengreen and J. Frieden (eds.), *The Political Economy of European Monetary Unification* (Boulder, Colo., 1993), 49–53.

The initial absence of parallelism can, in good part, be put down to continued French reticence on the question of political union. While the German government had already clearly intimated at Strasbourg that it would seek to extract substantial advances on political union as the price for merging the D-mark into a common currency, the French government continued to conform to its traditional policy of seeking 'a strong Europe with weak institutions'. Although wishing to see a stronger European presence on the world stage, French preferences (like those of the United Kingdom) ran to the development of essentially intergovernmental forms of co-operation.

The early months of 1990, however, saw a major tactical shift by President François Mitterrand.[20] Faced with the inevitability of German unification and the absence of viable alternatives to deal with it, Mitterrand came to accept the need for the further deepening of the formal institutional structures of the European Community. From this tactical conversion, to which Delors acted as something of a midwife,[21] the joint Franco-German initiative that effectively launched the 1990–1 IGC on political union was born.

Although preceded by a Belgian memorandum of 19 March 1990 setting an agenda for the institutional reform of the European Community,[22] it was the Kohl–Mitterrand letter published on 19 April of that year which gave the process its major impetus.[23] The initial joint letter was quite limited, not extending much beyond a broad declaration of intent. Citing the dramatic changes then reshaping the political map of Europe and the rapid progress of economic integration, the German Chancellor and the French President called for the convocation of an IGC on political union to parallel that already agreed on EMU. At this stage, however, little detail was given as to the desired agenda for the conference.

A more detailed Franco-German blueprint for institutional reform was made public on 6 December 1990, in the form of a second Kohl –Mitterrand letter.[24] This letter, issued just prior to the formal launch of the parallel IGCs on EMU and political union, put forward proposals concerning both the institutional reform of the European Community and the development of a Common Foreign and Security Policy (CFSP).

---

[20] Mitterrand's change of tack is critically analysed in F. O. Giesbert, *François Mitterrand: Une Vie* (Paris, 1996), 584–8. Mitterrand himself glosses over the extent of the change in his posthumously published memoir *De l'Allemagne, De la France* (Paris, 1996), 83–6.

[21] See C. Grant, *Delors: Inside the House that Jacques Built* (London, 1994), 139–42.

[22] Reprinted in F. Laursen and S. Vanhoonacker (eds.), *The Intergovernmental Conference on Political Union: Institutional Reforms, New Policies and International Identity of the European Community* (Maastricht, 1992), 269–75.   [23] Reprinted in ibid. 276.

[24] Reprinted in ibid. 313–14.

On questions of institutional reform, the letter represented something of an awkward compromise between France's traditional intergovernmental preferences and Germany's resolute support for the establishment of more 'federal' structures. On the one hand, reflecting German priorities, the letter evoked the need for a major enlargement of the Community's sphere of competence, as well as the need for a substantial reinforcement of the role and powers of the European Parliament. At the same time, however, it was proposed to affirm and expand the role of the (intergovernmental) Council of Ministers. Indeed, the affirmation of the Council's role appeared sufficiently strong to draw an almost immediate rebuke from the 'pro-federal' Dutch government.[25] Tellingly, the German government was also party to an initiative in April 1991, with the Italian Government, which presented a much more forthright case for the expansion of the European Parliament's powers.[26]

While some differences also persisted between Paris and Bonn on foreign policy and defence issues, there was nonetheless a more genuine convergence on these questions than on the institutional reform agenda. The Franco-German tandem were thus able to put forward much more tangible proposals in this area. The Kohl–Mitterrand letter of 6 December 1990 already made clear the two countries' support for the development of a common foreign and security policy which would encompass all areas of external involvement, rather than merely those connected with the internal market. While accepting that unanimity would still tend to be the normal voting rule in the development of such a policy, it was none the less countenanced from the outset that some majority voting might be envisaged as regards the 'implementing arrangements' for agreed policies. It was also proposed that a 'clear organic relationship' be established between the West European Union (WEU) and the European Community, potentially leading to the ultimate merger of the WEU into the structures of Political Union.[27]

The Kohl–Mitterrand initiative on Political Union posed an obvious challenge to Mrs Thatcher's vision of Europe.[28] The initial response from London was, however, relatively muted.[29] Reflecting a realistic assessment that the UK could not stop the IGC process from being engaged, the

---

[25] Reprinted in ibid. 315–17.

[26] Reprinted in R. Corbett, *The Treaty of Maastricht* (Harlow, Essex, 1993), 242–3.

[27] The joint Franco-German proposals on foreign policy and defence were further elaborated in two later submissions, made public in February and October of 1991. The documents are reprinted in Laursen and Vanhoonacker (eds.), *The Intergovernmental Conference*, 333–5 and 415–18.

[28] See the tellingly titled 'Paris–Bonn Challenge to Thatcher on EC Unity', *The Times*, 20/4/1990.

[29] See S. George, *An Awkward Partner: Britain in the European Community*, 2nd edn. (Oxford, 1994), 216–18. See also 'Hurd Keeps Prime Minister Out of a Fight', *Financial Times*, 11/12/1989.

Government initially adopted a relatively constructive tone. Reservations were expressed and questions raised in a manner which sought to exercise an influence on a process regarded as undesirable, but apparently inevitable.

This attitude of 'sweet reasonableness' (to use Mrs Thatcher's own term)[30] was, none the less, to suffer an abrupt reversal at the time of the October 1990 Rome European Council meeting. Feeling somewhat ambushed by the Italian Council Presidency's insistence on reaching early agreement over the agenda for the IGCs, the UK Prime Minister gave vent to one of her sharpest 'anti-European' outbursts to date. Having situated her summit colleagues' plans for EMU firmly within 'cloud cuckoo land', the PM went on in the post-summit Commons debate famously to give her response to the further development of Political Union—'No, No, No'.[31]

It is against this backdrop that the European policy subsequently followed by John Major must be understood. Although much was made in the months after his accession to the premiership of Major's desire to put Britain 'at the heart of Europe',[32] little substantive change in UK policy could be detected. Rather, Major can be seen as renewing the tone of constructive, critical dialogue that had marked British policy prior to the Rome *débâcle*.

Under Major, as under Thatcher, UK policy in the run-up to the Maastricht summit is best understood in terms of a holding action. The British government sought, by its active engagement in the IGC negotiating process, to limit as far as possible the scope of changes deemed largely to be undesirable in advance. This essentially negative agenda was reflected in such UK initiatives as emerged during the negotiation process. As regards the institutional reform of the Community, the strongest British government priority emerged as the inclusion of a concept of subsidiarity in the Treaties. In contrast to the German government's presentation of the idea, the British formulation equated subsidiarity with the limitation of Community powers and, where possible, the renationalization of some areas of competence that had already slipped national control.[33] Similarly, as regards the development of a Common Foreign and Security Policy, the central British negotiating objective was clearly that of preserving the integrity of the Atlantic Alliance as the cornerstone of the European security order. Perhaps the most interesting British initiative in this regard took the form of a joint Anglo-Italian proposal on defence made public in October 1991.[34] In the face of the growing

---

[30] M. Thatcher, *The Downing Street Years* (London, 1993), 760.

[31] *Parliamentary Debates, House of Commons (Hansard), Sixth Series* (hereafter: *H.C. Deb.*), vol. 178, 30/10/1990, 873.   [32] George, *An Awkward Partner*, 236–8.

[33] See J. Peterson, 'Subsidiarity: A Definition to Suit Any Vision', *Parliamentary Affairs* 47/1 (1994), 116–32.

[34] Reprinted in Laursen and Vanhoonacker, *The Intergovernmental Conference*, 413–14.

momentum behind the joint Franco-German initiatives on defence, the Anglo-Italian document represented an attempt, from the British point of view, to introduce a compromise proposal in which 'the development of a European identity in the field of defence [would] be construed in such a way as to reinforce the Atlantic Alliance'.[35]

The nature and balance of the Treaty on European Union, finally agreed at Maastricht in December 1991, has been endlessly debated. The first reactions tended to see the final accord as something of a success for the United Kingdom and, conversely, as something of a disappointment for the German government. A closer examination of the Treaty, placing it in the context of longer term historical processes, would none the less tend to alter—if not to reverse—this balance sheet.

On the one hand, Prime Minister Major was quick to proclaim 'Game, Set and Match for Britain'. The rhetorical flourish notwithstanding, it is relatively easy to portray the result as a short-term negotiating success for the PM. His handling of the actual negotiations, in particular his detailed mastery of his brief, was widely praised.[36] The government secured the removal of any reference to a 'federal vocation' in the Treaties, while also ensuring a double opt-out for the United Kingdom on EMU and on the Social Chapter. More generally, the Treaty's institutional changes were kept within much more limited bounds than the more strongly federalist states would have wished. At the same time, however, these short-term negotiating successes were to a large extent bought at the cost of longer-term United Kingdom influence. By being seen as the major stumbling block to further efforts at integration, as well as excluding itself from key areas of future policy development, the United Kingdom strongly reinforced the existing perceptions of its 'semi-detachment' from the European project.[37]

On the other hand, initial response to the Treaty in Germany tended to be critical of Chancellor Kohl for having 'sold-out the D-mark' against only relatively limited progress on political union.[38] This, however, probably takes too much of a short-term view. While the Maastricht Treaty was modest as far as the realization of a 'federal' agenda was concerned, it was nonetheless a significant step down the road to a closer political union. Significant new powers were granted to the European Parliament. Substantial new areas of competence were accorded to the Community. Albeit on an intergovernmental basis, the mechanisms for both a Common Foreign and Security Policy and greater co-operation in Justice

---

[35] Ibid. 413.

[36] 'Major's 11th-hour Attack Stole the Show', *Guardian*, 12/12/1991.

[37] The UK's longer term isolation was strongly underlined at the time by Ian Davidson. See 'Hollow Victory for Britain as It Launches Two-Tier Europe', *Financial Times*, 12/12/1991.

[38] See 'Germans Nervous at Loss of D-Mark', *Financial Times*, 12/12/1991, and 'Kohl Claims Satisfactory Compromise at Maastricht', *The Times*, 12/12/1991.

and Home Affairs were agreed. Indeed, the overall balance of the Treaty did not greatly depart from the compromise positions put forward in the various joint Franco-German documents discussed above.

However one wishes to read the balance of the agreement reached at Maastricht, it is clear that the Treaty marked the beginning of a process as much as the end of one. Formally, the Treaty put in motion processes concerning the achievement of both EMU and Political Union. As regards the former, a detailed blueprint, including specific dates, was put in place. While less was accomplished as regards the latter, the holding of a new IGC on institutional reform was nonetheless agreed as part of the package. In both cases, the Treaty thus generated ongoing processes which, inescapably, set the agenda for the future negotiations.

The aftermath of the Maastricht negotiations, however, also saw a marked shift in public opinion. Both the negative vote in the June 1992 Danish referendum on the Treaty and the wafer-thin majority in the French ratification referendum three months later highlighted a waning enthusiasm for the European project. Growing German anxieties over the impending loss of the Deutschmark, as well as often acrimonious parliamentary debates over the loss of sovereignty in the UK, fit this more general pattern. In contrast to the Single European Act of 1987 which had generated a positive *élan* for further integration, Maastricht produced a somewhat soured political climate for the ensuing Amsterdam Treaty negotiations.

THE AMSTERDAM TREATY NEGOTIATIONS AND BEYOND

(a) Economic and Monetary Union

The issue of European Economic and Monetary Union, as noted in the Introduction, was not formally part of the negotiations which led to the Amsterdam Treaty in June 1997. This treaty was instead concerned with questions of EU institutional reform. None the less, the issue of EMU did overshadow the prospects of concluding this intergovernmental conference on time. This became especially apparent during the final months of the negotiations.

Parallel to the IGC, two politically sensitive decisions were taken on EMU which aimed to clarify some of the existing Maastricht Treaty provisions.[39] At their December 1996 summit meeting in Dublin, the member states agreed to create a new European Monetary System (EMS II). Operational

[39] Other decisions include the change-over scenario for the single currency, the European currency's name (the 'EURO') and the legal framework of the Euro. See *European Presidency Conclusions*, (Madrid, Dec. 1995, and Amsterdam, June 1997).

since January 1999, its function is to provide an institutional link between those countries participating in monetary union and those not joining the project during the first wave. More controversially, the governments also decided to establish a 'Stability and Growth Pact', which specifies the procedures and the sanctions in the case that a country participating in EMU runs excessive public deficits.[40]

In the autumn of 1995, the German Finance Minister revised the government's earlier proposals for legally binding sanction mechanisms against those countries staying above the agreed deficit limit.[41] The negotiations on this 'Stability Pact' mirrored the earlier Maastricht debates on the relevance of automatic sanctions as a deterrence against unrestrained fiscal policies. As on previous occasions, the debate centred around Franco-German disagreements over the degree of flexibility and political discretion of the proposed rules. By April 1996, Germany had secured French support on the general principles of the plan. In exchange Helmut Kohl gave his own approval to the new EMS II.[42] Although generally sympathetic towards the idea of a new monetary system, Germany had remained sceptical of entering into obligations which would force the European Central Bank to intervene on behalf of other European currencies. Such a policy could potentially undermine the stability of the single currency.

The United Kingdom remained sceptical of the new proposals and tried to avoid being coerced into joining either of them. While supporting the French bargaining position over the 'Stability and Growth Pact', the British government essentially reaffirmed its existing EMU 'opt-out' by insisting that the new fiscal rules should only apply to those states joining the single currency. The Government also insisted that participation in the revised EMS should be voluntary. Both demands were accommodated in the final agreement. On other technical issues, such as the changeover scenario for the euro, the British government sought to retain as much influence as possible, given the project's long-term impact on the British economy.

The election victories of the French Socialists and the Labour Party in the months leading up to the Amsterdam summit of June 1997 did not fundamentally alter the political equation as regards EMU. The French Socialists sought to shift the focus away from the stringent budget deficit rules to the question of unemployment. They also emphasized long-standing French demands for the creation of some form of 'economic

---

[40] *Conclusions of the European Council* (Dublin, Dec. 1996).

[41] 'Waigel schmiedet einen Stabilitätspakt für Europa', *Handelsblatt*, 11–12/11/1995.

[42] 'EU finance ministers limber up for battle of wills', *Financial Times*, 12/4/1996. See also the conclusions of the Economics and Finance Ministers in Verona. 'The Informal Meeting of Finance Ministers', *Agence Europe*, 15–16/4/1996, 6–9.

government' to provide a political counterweight to the autonomy of the European Central Bank. This change of emphasis strained Franco-German relations and potentially endangered the prospects of reaching agreement on the technical aspects of the 'Stability and Growth Pact'. For a few weeks, it even seemed that the final agreement on the Amsterdam Treaty might have to be postponed. Nevertheless, the conflict was ultimately sidestepped by the joint decision to strengthen the employment dimension of the new treaty and to convene a special EU 'employment' summit in the autumn of 1997. In December 1997, the two countries further spearheaded an agreement on the creation of the so-called 'Euro Group', a name chosen to reflect the informal character of the meetings. This body, bringing together the finance ministers of the euro countries, provides a forum for the co-ordination of economic policies amongst EMU participants.

After Labour's election victory in May 1997, Britain supported EMU 'in principle'. This political commitment was reiterated by the publication of the National Changeover Plan for the euro in February 1999.[43] In contrast to its Conservative predecessors, the Labour government's position on monetary union is determined by economic considerations rather than by constitutional principles. This does not in itself increase the probability of British participation in the early years of the single currency's operation. In his October 1997 speech to the House of Commons, Chancellor of the Exchequer Gordon Brown laid down tough conditions for membership.[44] The final decision on membership is to be taken on the basis of the degree of real economic convergence and economic flexibility demonstrated by the EU. The impact of EMU on investment trends, the British financial services industry and the national employment level will also be relevant for the decision.[45] Moreover, the goverment has repeatedly stressed that membership of EMU remains conditional on a positive outcome of a referendum in the United Kingdom.

In May 1998, the EU governments decided to irrevocably fix the exchange rates among the currencies of eleven member states on 1 January 1999 and to introduce a single currency by July 2002. The large membership of EMU reflects the efforts made by all governments to meet the Maastricht Treaty convergence criteria in the set timetable. Greece was excluded on economic grounds. The United Kingdom and Denmark made use of their political opt-outs and were joined by Sweden.

The governments' decision was overshadowed by French insistence on nominating Jean-Claude Trichet as President of the European Central Bank. The majority of countries (including Germany) supported the Dutch candidate and sitting EMI President, Wim Duisenberg. The dispute once

[43] See Tony Blair's address to the House of Commons, *H.C. Deb.*, vol. 326, 23/02/1999, 179–83.
[44] See Brown's speech, *H.C. Deb.*, vol. 299, 27/10/1997, 583–605.   [45] Ibid.

more raised questions about the future political independence of the ECB.[46] Holding the Presidency of the European Council at the time, the British government played a central role in bringing about a compromise. While Duisenberg was formally appointed head of the ECB, he has left open the option to resign early in favour of Trichet. It can be argued that facilitating this compromise marked the high tide of British influence on EMU. That said, the exclusion from the ECB Board and the 'Euro Group' of Finance Ministers demonstrate that the United Kingdom remains sidelined in the EMU process.

The German elections of September 1998 brought a SPD–Green coalition into power which was more sympathetic to French demands for greater economic policy co-ordination and employment policies. This found expression in Franco-German initiatives on European taxation and an attempt to find a common EU response to the international monetary crises of 1998. The United Kingdom greeted these moves with scepticism. The initial months of the government's tenure also saw marked turbulence associated with Oskar Lafontaine's brief stint as Finance Minister (he resigned in March and was succeeded in April 1999 by Hans Eichel, formerly Prime Minister of the state of Hesse). Lafontaine, in particular, was openly critical of the ECB's restrictive monetary policy.[47] Nevertheless, Germany's basic position towards EMU remained consistent after the election. Chancellor Gerhard Schröder made clear that he accepted the EMU provisions negotiated under his predeccessor.

(b) Political Union

The first moves in the negotiating process which ultimately led to the Amsterdam Treaty may be dated from September 1994, with the publication by the CDU/CSU parliamentary party (*Fraktion*) of the controversial 'Reflections on European Policy' discussion paper.[48] Although not an official statement of either government or party policy, the document was none the less widely read as a signal that the German government intended to use the new IGC to secure the advances on Political Union which it had been unable to obtain at Maastricht. The document, authored by Wolfgang Schäuble and Karl Lamers, put forward a 'maximalist' version of the future progress of European integration. On the question of institutional reform, the Schäuble/Lamers paper advocated the need for a new 'quasi-constitutional' arrangement which 'must be oriented to the model of a federal state'. In an equally radical vein, it

---

[46] See 'EU Deal Puts Single Currency to the Test', *Financial Times*, 4/5/1998.
[47] See 'Power Struggle over the Euro', *Financial Times*, 6/12/1998.
[48] CDU/CSU-Fraktion des Deutschen Bundestages, 'Reflections on European Policy', issued on 1 Sept. 1994. An abridged version may be found in T. Salmon and W. Nicholl (eds.), *Building European Union: A documentary history and analysis* (Manchester, 1997), 255–261.

contended that a common European defence must be established as a matter of great urgency, rather than only being created 'in time' as envisaged in the Maastricht Treaty. Logically connected to this acceleration of the integration process, the document further spoke of the emergence of a 'hard core' of states within the European Union. Highly contentiously, it was specified that this 'hard core' group, though open to expansion over time, was likely at the outset to include only Germany, France, and the Benelux countries.

The document unsurprisingly generated considerable controversy. Even within the government, Foreign Minister Klaus Kinkel quickly distanced himself from the concept of a 'hard core' of member states.[49] Further afield, strong criticism came particularly from the Italian and the Spanish governments, unwilling to see their countries relegated to a European second division. Perhaps less predictably, the 'hard core' concept also prompted sharply critical remarks from Prime Minister Major. On the face of it, the paper's emphasis on the emergence of a 'hard core' of states appeared simply to draw the logical conclusions of the British government's own 'opt-outs' agreed at Maastricht. These 'opt-outs' could be seen as pointing to the creation of a European Union of 'variable geometry' in which not all states would participate in all policy areas. At the same time, however, the Schäuble/Lamers paper underlined the possibilities for exclusion or marginalization which this logic of variability might further entail. Speaking in Leiden a week after the paper's publication, Major made clear that any move in the direction of an 'exclusive hard core either of countries or policies' would be strongly opposed by the UK government.[50]

The controversy surrounding the Schäuble/Lamers paper proved to be something of a tempest in a teapot, as its 'maximalist' agenda could not be politically sustained. Already in June 1995, two further CDU/CSU discussion papers set out a more modest agenda concentrated on the second and third pillars of the Union (the CFSP and co-operation in the area of Justice and Home Affairs).[51] The document submitted by Foreign Minister Kinkel to the March 1996 Turin European Council, putting forward 'German Objectives for the Intergovernmental Conference', also struck a more modest chord, stressing that the current IGC must not

[49] 'Kinkel refuse d'avaler le noyau dur de l'Europe', *Libération*, 6/9/1994.

[50] 'Europe: A Future that Works', speech delivered by Prime Minister John Major, Leiden University, 7/9/1994. An abridged version may be found in Salmon and Nicholl (eds.), *Building European Union*, 261–3.

[51] Summarized in European Parliament, Task Force on the 1996 Intergovernmental Conference (hereafter EP Task Force), *White Paper on the 1996 Intergovernmental Conference*, vol. 2: *Summary of the Positions of the Member States of the European Union with a View to the 1996 Intergovernmental Conference*, 45–50. See also 'Le Parti de Helmut Kohl lance de nouvelles propositions sur l'Europe', *Le Monde*, 11–12/6/1995.

be overloaded.[52] Later in the year, Chancellor Kohl similarly evoked the possibility of a 'Maastricht III' Conference. Speaking on the eve of the October 1996 Dublin European Council meeting, the Chancellor appeared to accept that the results of the current round of Treaty revision would fall well below the German government's original objectives.[53]

A similar modesty of ambition also marked the joint Franco-German efforts during the course of the IGC. Chancellor Kohl and President Chirac did indeed maintain previous practice, issuing two joint letters (in December 1995 and December 1996) which sought to set the agenda and sustain the pace of the Treaty revision process.[54] These letters, however, lacked the clear political impetus which had underpinned the joint Kohl–Mitterrand initiatives of the previous round. Franco-German initiatives in the run-up to Amsterdam essentially concentrated on a relatively modest package of reforms, trying to clear up as much of the 'unfinished business' of Maastricht as possible. The two governments' most ambitious proposals came in the area of justice and home affairs. Here, they sought a major expansion of EU competence in order to deal more effectively with growing cross-border problems of crime, as well as an incorporation of the Schengen ('open borders') Treaty into the structures of the EU. Their joint proposals on the CFSP largely reaffirmed previously agreed objectives. The two governments sought to provide for greater majority voting on foreign policy matters, as well as an improvement of the EU's own planning capabilities in the area. The German Government also acquiesced to a French proposal for the appointment of a 'Mr/Ms CFSP', a designated individual who would act as the EU's representative in external affairs. Long-standing demands for the progressive integration of the WEU into the EU were also reiterated. Franco-German proposals on institutional reform were notably modest. Here, the two governments' key proposal centred on the idea of 'flexibility' or 'enhanced co-operation'. An elaborate framework was put forward to allow for an increased recourse to the practice of 'differentiated integration', whereby a limited group of states would be allowed to develop deepened forms of co-operation amongst themselves within the structures of the Union.[55] It was clearly intended to create a mechanism which would prevent an obstructionist member state, like the United Kingdom, from indefinitely

[52] Summarized in EP Task Force, *White Paper*, 39–40. See also 'Bonn Proposes Lean Agenda for IGC', *Financial Times*, 27/3/1996.

[53] 'Paris and Bonn Scale Back EU Reform Plans', *Financial Times*, 5–6/10/1996.

[54] The Chirac–Kohl letter of 6/12/1995 is summarized in EP Task Force, *White Paper*, 87–8. Their joint letter of 9/12/1996 is summarized in *European Report* 2182, 11/12/1996. See also P. Lemaître and H. H. Schlenker, 'The Future of the Franco-German Relationship', *Challenge Europe* 12 (1997), 5.

[55] The two countries put forward a detailed proposal for Treaty amendment. This is reproduced as a supplement to *European Report* 2169, 26/10/1996.

blocking the future progress of the integration process. Yet, the emphasis on a mechanism facilitating *future* change was also a tell-tale sign that the current process was not expected to produce major institutional reforms.

Although the IGC agenda became a relatively modest one, it none the less posed substantial problems for the UK government. The acrimonious Maastricht ratification debate and the narrowness of the Tory majority in the Commons placed Prime Minister Major in a highly vulnerable situation. Domestic and, in particular, intra-party politics appeared to lock the British government into a position from the outset of the negotiations where it could agree no major Treaty reforms. A climate of opinion emerged amongst the other member states that no negotiation with the current UK government was likely to succeed. One must, however, be careful to distinguish rhetoric from reality as regards the extent of UK isolation. Over the course of the IGC, the image grew of a '14 to 1' division within the EU, portraying the UK as resisting the advances uniformly advocated by the fourteen other member states. This was, quite simply, not true. It was rare for the UK to be entirely isolated on any specific issue. Similarly, the UK's formal submission to the IGC, the 'Partnership of Nations' document published in March 1996, can be seen as having struck a moderate tone relative to the constraints under which the Government was operating.[56] There was, however, a fundamental sense in which the UK government was genuinely isolated. For the UK, arguably alone amongst the fifteen member states, the failure to reach a final agreement might reasonably be portrayed as an optimal result. The UK government remained committed to maintaining the status quo, if not actively seeking to reverse it in certain respects.[57] There was, at base, an evident lack of commitment to the process itself.

Given the low probability of reaching an agreement with the sitting Tory government, the negotiators' attention turned at a relatively early stage to the Labour Party. These early soundings, later to be confirmed in practice, produced quite mixed results. There was clearly more 'give' in the Labour position than in that of the Conservative government.[58] Labour

[56] 'A Partnership of Nations: The British Approach to the European Union Intergovernmental Conference 1996', March 1996, Cm. 3181. See also 'Mr. Major's EU Tightrope', *Financial Times*, 13/3/1996.

[57] S. George, 'The Approach of the British Government to the 1996 Intergovernmental Conference of the European Union', *Journal of European Public Policy* 3/1 (1996), 45–62. While George is correct in portraying the UK as fundamentally a 'status quo state', certain proposals made under the Conservative government pertaining to the functioning of the EC legal order did appear to seek an actual reversal of aspects of the integration process. See the 'Memorandum by the United Kingdom on the European Court of Justice', July 1996.

[58] Labour formally set out its policies at the time of the 1995 Party Conference in 'The Future of the European Union: Report on Labour's Position in Preparation for the Intergovernmental Conference 1996'. See also the critical analysis of G. Leicester, 'Europe After Major: Can Labour Make a Difference?', Fabian Society Discussion Paper no. 27 (Sept. 1996).

indicated that it would sign up to the Social Chapter. It similarly indicated that it would accept more majority voting in the Council of
Ministers on selected issues, as well as a quite general extension of the
European Parliament's co-decision powers. On second and third pillar issues,
however, Labour adopted essentially the same line as the Tories. It did
not wish to see the extension of qualified majority voting in the Common Foreign and Security Policy, nor did it wish to see the gradual incorporation of the WEU into the EU at that time. It also insisted that
co-operation in the area of Justice and Home Affairs remain strictly
intergovernmental, further stressing that the UK would not give up its
border controls. Echoing the position of the Tory government, Labour
also expressed deep reservations about the inclusion in the Treaty of
generalized provisions permitting the development of various forms of
'flexibility' or 'enhanced co-operation'.[59] Thus, while a Labour election
victory could be seen as opening up a somewhat wider margin of
manoeuvre, it was apparent from an early stage that a change of government in London would not see a major acceleration of the integration
process.

The June 1997 Treaty of Amsterdam has been seen by most commentators as a very modest document, representing little real progress
on the major issues left outstanding at Maastricht. The modesty of the
document may, in good part, be seen as an accurate reflection of the
modesty of French and German ambitions. Progress was largely made at
Amsterdam in those areas which had already been highlighted in the two
Chirac/Kohl letters discussed above. The Treaty's creation of a 'zone
of freedom, security and justice', including the incorporation of the
Schengen Convention into the structures of the Union, had already been
foreshadowed in earlier joint Franco-German proposals.[60] The reform of
the 'mechanics' of the CFSP, as agreed at Amsterdam, similarly corres-
ponds to previously enunciated Franco-German objectives. The Treaty also
included a general clause permitting the development of forms of
'enhanced co-operation' which follows closely along the lines set out in
earlier Franco-German proposals. Conversely, on more general issues of
institutional reform, where the Franco-German pair had not put forward
much in the way of concrete proposals, little progress was made at the
summit itself. Both the strengths and the weaknesses of the Amsterdam

---

[59] 'Cook set to dash "multi-speed" Europe Hopes', *Financial Times*, 2/12/1996. Labour
confirmed its reservations concerning the introduction of a general 'flexibility' provision into
the Treaties shortly after assuming power. See the statement made by Doug Henderson, Minister
for Europe, to the 5/5/1997 meeting of the IGC Working Group of Personal Representatives
[http://www.fco.gov.uk/texts/1997/may/05/hend 1.txt].

[60] It was, none the less, at German insistence that a national veto was maintained in politically sensitive areas such as asylum, immigration, and visa policies. See 'Enlargement May Test
EU's Treaty', *Financial Times*, 19/6/1997, and 'EU Fails to Decide How Best To Decide', *Guardian*,
19/6/1997.

Treaty reflected, very directly, the extent to which the Franco-German motor had been engaged during the process.

From the British point of view, Amsterdam, like Maastricht, may easily be portrayed as a negotiating success. The newly elected Blair government achieved its major objectives at the summit. Contrary to what the Prime Minister claimed afterwards, however, it was difficult to credit the new government with 'a fresh constructive approach to Europe'.[61] Rather, as in the case of Major at Maastricht, Tony Blair's negotiating successes were essentially negative. While largely successful in blocking unwanted changes, little positive British influence could be detected in the Treaty. Only the inclusion of a (fairly weak) employment chapter could be partially ascribed to UK influence. Beyond this area, the new government succeeded in securing a UK 'opt-out' from the new 'area of freedom, security, and justice', as well as blocking any move at that time to incorporate the WEU into the EU.[62] Strong British pressure also played a crucial role in maintaining national vetoes as regards both the CFSP and the use of the new 'enhanced co-operation' mechanism. Under Blair, as under Major, the UK continued to act primarily as a brake on the integration process, opting out where the brakes could not be effectively applied.

CONCLUSION

Both the Maastricht and the Amsterdam Treaty negotiations have borne out the conventional wisdom that France and Germany, acting in tandem, are the necessary 'motor' of the integration process. Where a strong political impetus emerges from Paris and Bonn, as in the Maastricht process, substantial results can be achieved. Conversely, when the motor fails to engage, as was largely the case during the Amsterdam process, the results tend to be quite modest. Nevertheless, though Franco-German agreement remains a crucial determinant of the progress of European integration, some differences may be detected between the EMU and the Political Union negotiation processes. As regards Political Union, a rough balance may be seen to exist between the two states. The positions put forward, particularly in the joint Kohl–Mitterrand and Kohl–Chirac letters, bear the marks of genuine (if occasionally awkward) compromises between divergent national views of the integration project. Conversely, in the area

---

[61] Statement by Prime Minister Blair on the Amsterdam European Council, in *H.C. Deb.*, vol. 296, 18/6/1997, 313.

[62] The UK government has since substantially changed its position on the inclusion of WEU activities under the rubric of the EU. Following the lead given by the Anglo-French Joint Declaration of 3–4 Dec. 1998, the Cologne European Council of 3–4 June 1999 agreed in principle to the inclusion of specified WEU activities within the EU. This transfer encompasses the so-called 'Petersberg tasks', concerned with peacekeeping and humanitarian intervention.

of EMU, Germany has acted as something a 'hegemon', defining the terms and conditions of the move towards a single currency. Much of the turbulence in the run-up to the Amsterdam summit can be explained in terms of persisting Franco-German disagreements over EMU. Continued French attachment to the creation of an 'economic government' at the European level conflicted sharply with German attempts to build further safeguards against political intervention into the process. Although the SPD–Green coalition has been more sympathetic to French demands, this has not fundamentally altered Germany's position on EMU, especially after the resignation of Oskar Lafontaine as Finance Minister in March 1999.

For those wishing to see an active British engagement in Europe, the 1990s have been marked by a dreary consistency. The election of a Labour government in May 1997 did not mark an immediate change. In sharp contrast to the Single European Act and the 'Single Market Initiative' of the 1980s, British governments did not exercise a major positive influence on either the Maastricht or the Amsterdam Treaties. Rather, their influence has been almost purely negative, blocking change (either alone or in ad hoc coalitions) but seldom if ever initiating it. Coupled with this essentially defensive posture, there has also been a growing propensity to 'opt-out' of new areas of co-operation. Under a Conservative Government, the UK secured opt-outs from the Social Chapter and EMU. The Labour Government, while opting into the Social Chapter, none the less simultaneously opted out of new 'open borders' arrangements.

Finally, the question remains to be posed as to whether these seemingly well-entrenched national positions are likely to change in the foreseeable future. In the case of Germany, there has been some discussion since unification on whether the country's new international position has changed its traditionally strong commitment towards the supranational path of European integration. The recent German demands for a budgetary rebate, as well as the modesty of the agenda it pursued at Amsterdam, seem to indicate such a reassessment of its traditional position. None the less, it appears that unification did not fundamentally alter the perceptions of German political elites towards the EU. In the medium term it has rather reinforced their commitment to the process, reflecting the shared belief that German unity and European integration go hand in hand.[63] The Schröder government has, in this regard, displayed a strong continuity with its predecessor.[64]

---

[63] See G. Hellman, 'The Sirens of Power and German Foreign Policy: Who is Listening?', *German Politics* 6/2 (1997), 29–57; and W. E. Paterson, 'Beyond Semi-Sovereignty: The New Germany in the New Europe', *German Politics* 5/2 (1996), 167–84.

[64] See in particular the speech by Foreign Minister Joschka Fischer to the European Parliament in Strasbourg on 12 January 1999. English text available at http://www.eu-presidency.de/ausland/englisch/03/0302/ 00098/index.htm.

In the case of the UK, there also appears little likelihood of major short-term changes. The Labour government has displayed much greater pro-European instincts than its Conservative predecessors. Yet, though enjoying a very comfortable Commons majority, it does not seem willing to run much ahead of what it deems to be a largely Euro-sceptic and reticent public opinion. In the medium to longer term, however, there are deeper indications of a possible change in the culture of government which may make the United Kingdom a much better 'fit' into the European integration project.[65] Both devolution at home and a more ready acceptance of a logic of interdependence at the international level signal a willingness to adopt a less absolutist notion of parliamentary and national sovereignty.[66] If attitudinal shifts of this sort prove enduring, the UK should be much better placed to deal with the future IGCs that will, inevitably, accompany the envisaged enlargement of the EU. The next stage in the process opens with an institutional reform around 2000.

[65] The poor 'fit' between the existing British state and the EU political system is interestingly discussed in S. Wilks, 'Britain and Europe: Awkward Partner or Awkward State?', *Politics* 16/3 (1996), 159–65.

[66] G. Leicester, 'Europe After Major', 16–18, offers an interesting analysis of the possible connection between domestic devolution and a change of European policy.

BIBLIOGRAPHY

A Partnership of Nations. The British Approach to the European Union Intergovernmental Conference 1996, Cm. 3181 (London: HMSO, 1996).

Adenauer, Konrad, *Erinnerungen, Vol. 2: 1953–1955* (Stuttgart: Deutsche Verlags-Anstalt, 1966).

Agence Europe, 20 Dec. 1990; 23 April 1999.

Aldous, Richard, 'A Family Affair: The Art of Personal Diplomacy', in Richard Aldous and Sabine Lee (eds.), *Harold Macmillan and Britain's World Role* (Basingstoke: Macmillan, 1996), 9–35.

Alexander, David, 'Truer and Fairer: Uninvited Comments on Invited Comments', *The European Accounting Review* 5/3 (1996), 483–493.

—— and Nobes, Christopher, *A European Introduction to Financial Accounting* (Hemel Hempstead: Prentice Hall, 1994).

Allen, David, 'Britain and Western Europe', in Michael Smith, Steve Smith, and Brian White (eds.), *British Foreign Policy: Tradition, Change and Transformation* (London: Unwin Hyman, 1988), 168–92.

—— 'British Foreign Policy and West European Co-operation', in Peter Byrd (ed.), *British Foreign Policy Under Thatcher* (Oxford: Philip Allan/St Martin's Press, 1988), 35–53.

Alting von Geusau, Frans A. M., *De som der delen: Europa voor en na de omwenteling* (Amsterdam: Meulenhoff, 1991).

Altmann, Normen, *Konrad Adenauer im Kalten Krieg: Wahrnehmungen und Politik, 1945–1956* (Mannheim: Palatium Verlag, 1993).

Altvater, Elmar, 'A Contest without Victors: Politics in the Context of the Geo-Economy', *Journal of Area Studies* 7 (1995), 57–67.

Ambrosius, Gerold, *Wirtschaftsraum Europa: Vom Ende der Nationalökonomie* (Frankfurt/M.: Fischer Taschenbuch Verlag, 1996).

Anderson, Jeffrey J., 'Hard Interests, Soft Power and Germany's Changing Role in Europe', in P. Katzenstein (ed.), *Tamed Power: Germany in Europe.* (Ithaca, NY: Cornell University Press, 1997), 80–107.

—— and Goodman, John, 'Mars or Minerva? A United Germany in a Post-Cold War Europe', in R. Keohane, J. Nye, and S. Hoffmann (eds.), *After the Cold War: International Institutions and State Strategies in Europe, 1989–1991* (Cambridge, Mass.: Harvard University Press, 1993), 23–62.

Annan, Noel, *Changing Enemies: The Defeat and Regeneration of Germany* (London: Harper Collins, 1995).

Arenth, Joachim, *'Der Westen tut nichts'. Transatlantische Kooperation während der zweiten Berlin-Krise (1958–1962) im Spiegel neuer amerikanischer Quellen* (Frankfurt/M.: Peter Lang, 1993).

—— 'Die Bewährungsprobe der Special Relationship: Washington und Bonn (1961–1969)', in K. Larres and T. Oppelland (eds.), *Deutschland und die*

USA im 20 Jahrhundert: Geschicte der politischen Beziehungen (Darmstadt: Wissenschaftliche Buchgesellschaft, 1997), 151–77.

Ascherson, Neal, 'Measure by Measure. Blair Plans the Polite Revolution', *The Independent on Sunday*, 4/5/1997, 19.

Ash, Timothy Garton, *In Europe's Name: Germany and the Divided Continent* (London: Jonathan Cape, 1993).

Attali, Jaques, *Verbatim*, vol. 3 (Paris: Fayard, 1995).

Ausland, John C., *Kennedy, Khrushchev, and the Berlin–Cuba Crisis, 1961–64* (Oslo: Scandinavian University Press, 1996).

Avery, Graham, and Cameron, Fraser, *The Enlargement of the European Union* (Sheffield: Sheffield Academic Press, 1998).

Bachmann, Axel, 'Die Beziehungen der DDR zu den angelsächsischen Ländern', in Hans-Joachim Veen and Peter R. Weilemann (eds.), *Die Westpolitik der DDR. Beziehungen der DDR zu ausgewählten westlichen Industrieländern in den 70er und 80er Jahren* (Melle: Verlag Ernst Knoth, 1989), 69–131.

Bachmann, Reinhard, 'Wettbewerbsfähigkeit auf dem Prüfstand: Das britische und das deutsche Wirtschaftsmodell im Vergleich', *Signal*, Newsletter of Anglo German Foundation for the Study of Industrial Society (Autumn 1997), 5–7.

Bahr, Egon, *Zu meiner Zeit* (Munich: Blessing, 1996).

Baker, David, and Seawright, David (eds.), *Britain for and against Europe: British Politics and the Question of European Integration* (Oxford: Oxford University Press, 1998).

Baker, Howard, Nunn, Sam, Scowcroft, Brent, and Frye, Alton, 'Enlarge the European Union before NATO', Letter printed first in *The New York Times*, reprinted in *The International Herald Tribune*, 6/2/1998.

Ball, Stuart J., *The Cold War: An International History, 1947–91* (London: Arnold, 1998).

Balmaceda, Margarita M., 'Ukraine, Russia, and European Security: Thinking Beyond NATO Expansion', *Problems of Post-Communism* 45/1 (1998), 21–9.

Bank of England, *The Hard ECU in Stage 2: Operational Requirements* (London: Bank of England, 1990).

Barclay, David E., and Glaser-Schmidt, Elisabeth (eds.), *Transatlantic Images and Perceptions: Germany and America since 1776* (Cambridge: Cambridge University Press, 1997).

Baring, Arnulf (ed.), *Germany's New Position in Europe: Problems and Perspectives* (Oxford: Berg, 1994).

Bark, Dennis L., and Gress, David R., *A History of West Germany*, vol. 1: *From Shadow to Substance, 1945–1963*, 2nd edn. (Oxford: Blackwell, 1993).

Barrell, Ray (ed.), *Economic Convergence amd Monetary Union in Europe* (London: Sage, 1992).

Bartlett, Christopher J., *'The Special Relationship': A Political History of Anglo-American Relations since 1945* (Harlow: Longman, 1992).

Becker, Bert, *Die DDR und Großbritannien 1945/49 bis 1973. Politische, wirtschaftliche und kulturelle Kontakte im Zeichen der Nichtanerkennungspolitik* (Bochum: Brockmeyer, 1991).

Becker, Peter, 'Der Nutzen der Osterweiterung für die Europäische Union', *Integration* 21/4 (1998), 225–37.

Begg, Iain, 'Introduction: Regulation in the European Union', *Journal of European Public Policy* 3 (1996), 525–35.

Bell, Marion, 'Britain and East Germany: The Politics of Non-Recognition' (unpub. M.Phil. thesis, University of Nottingham, 1977).

Bell, Philip M. H., 'A Historical Cast of Mind: Some Eminent English Historians and Attitudes to Continental Europe in the Middle of the Twentieth Century', *Journal of European Integration History* 2/2 (1996), 5–19.

—— *France and Britain 1940–1994: The Long Separation* (London: Longman, 1997).

Bender, Peter, *Neue Ostpolitik: Vom Mauerbau bis zum Moskauer Vertrag*, 4th edn. (Munich: dtv, 1996).

Bennett, Robert J. (ed.), *Trade Associations in Britain and Germany: Responding to Internationalisation and the EU* (London: Anglo-German Foundation for the Study of Industrial Society, 1997).

—— 'Trade Associations: Britain and Germany Compared', in Robert J. Bennett (ed.), *Trade Associations in Britain and Germany: Responding to Internationalisation and the EU* (London: Anglo-German Foundation for the Study of Industrial Society, 1997), 12–22.

Bertram, Christoph, 'Why NATO Must Enlarge', *NATO Review* 45/2 (1997), 14–16.

Biener, Herbert, 'What is the Future of Mutual Recognition of Financial Statements and Is Comparability Really Necessary?', *The European Accounting Review* 3/2 (1994), 335–42.

Birke, Adolf M., and Heydemann, Günter (eds.), *Britain and East Germany since 1918* (Munich: K. G. Saur, 1992).

Blair, the Rt Hon. Tony, Prime Minister, in *House of Commons, Parliamentary Debates*, 18 June 1997, 313–14; and 16 March 1999, 891–92 and 897.

—— *The Third Way: New Politics for the New Century* (London: Fabian Society, 1998).

Bluth, Christoph, *Britain, Germany, and Western Nuclear Strategy* (Oxford: Clarendon Press, 1995).

Bond, Martyn, Smith, Julie, and Wallace, William (eds.), *Eminent Europeans: Personalities Who Shaped Contemporary Europe* (London: Greycoat, 1996).

Booz, Rüdiger M., *Hallsteinzeit: deutsche Außenpolitik 1955–1972* (Bonn: Bouvier, 1995).

Bortfeldt, Heinrich, 'Die Vereinigten Staaten und die deutsche Einheit', in Klaus Larres and Torsten Oppelland (eds.), *Deutschland und die USA im 20. Jahrhundert. Geschichte der politischen Beziehungen* (Darmstadt: Wissenschaftliche Buchgesellschaft, 1997), 256–73.

Bozo, Frederic, 'A French View', in R. Davy (ed.), *European Détente: A Reappraisal* (London: Sage, 1992), 54–85.

Brands, Maarten C., 'Überforderung durch Machtzunahme. Deutschland als integrierende oder zentrifugale Kraft', *Internationale Politik* 52/2 (Feb. 1997), 34–40.

Brandt, Willy, *My Life in Politics* (London: Hamish Hamilton, 1992).

Brechtefeld, Jörg, 'Europe's Double Transformation Crisis', *International Relations* 13/4 (April 1997), 25–39.

Brochhagen, Ulrich, *Nach Nürnberg: Vergangenheitsbewältigung und Westintegration in der Ära Adenauer* (Hamburg: Junius, 1994).

Brock, Georg, 'Geht von Deutschland eine Bedrohung aus?' *Internationale Politik* 52/2 (Feb. 1997), 23–8.

Bromwich, Michael, and Hopwood, Anthony, 'Some Issues on Accounting Standard Setting: An Introductory Essay', in Michael Bromwich and Anthony Hopwood (eds.), *Accounting Standard Setting: An International Perspective* (London: Pitman, 1983).

Brown, the Rt Hon. Gordon, speech before the British–American Chamber of Commerce, New York, 5 Dec. 1996, British Information Service, New York, Internet Information [http://www. britain-info.org].

—— 'Britain Leading in Europe', speech by the Chancellor of the Exchequer at the Royal Institute of International Affairs, London, 17 July 1997.

Buda, Dirk, *Ostpolitik á la Francaise: Frankreichs Verhältnis zur UdSSR von de Gaulle bis Mitterrand* (Marburg: Verlag Arbeit und Gesellschaft, 1990).

Bullard, Sir Julian, Contribution in Jeremy Noakes *et al.* (eds.), *Britain and Germany in Europe, 1949–1990* (Oxford: Oxford University Press/German Historical Institute, 2000 [forthcoming]).

Buller, Jim, 'Britain as an Awkward Partner: Reassessing Britain's Relations with the EU', *Politics* 15/1 (1995), 33–42.

Bulletin of the European Communities, Supplement 7/1985, 'A People's Europe'.

—— Supplement 3/1992, 'Europe and the challenge of enlargement,' report presented by the Commission to the Lisbon European Council held on 26 and 27 June 1992.

—— Supplement 12/1992, 'Edinburgh European Council: Conclusions of the Presidency'.

—— Supplement 6/1993, 'Copenhagen European Council: Conclusions of the Presidency'.

—— Supplement 5/97, European Commission, 'Agenda 2000: For a stronger and wider Union'.

—— Supplement 2/1998, European Commission, 'Agenda 2000: Financing the European Union'.

—— Supplement 3/1999, 'Berlin European Council, Conclusions of the Presidency'.

Bulletin of the European Union, 12/1994, 'Report from the Council to the Essen European Council on a strategy to prepare for the accession of the associated CCEE,' Annex 4 to 'Essen European Council: Conclusions of the Presidency'.

—— Supplement 6/1994, 'Corfu European Council: Conclusions of the Presidency'.

Bulmer, Simon, 'Britain and Germany in the European Union: British Realism and German Institutionalism?', paper presented to the *Conference of Europeanists*, Chicago, 14–16 March 1996.

—— 'Setting and Influencing the Rules', in D. G. Mayes (ed.), *The Evolution of the Single European Market* (Cheltenham: Edward Elgar, 1997), 30–48.

—— 'Shaping the Rules? The Constitutive Politics of the European Union and German Power', in P. Katzenstein (ed.), *Tamed Power: Germany in Europe* (Ithaca, NY: Cornell University Press, 1997), 49–79.

—— and Paterson, William (eds.), *The Federal Republic of Germany and the European Community* (London: Allen & Unwin, 1987).

—— and —— 'West Germany's Role in Europe: Man-Mountain or Semi-Gulliver?', *Journal of Common Market Studies* 28 (1989), 95–117.

—— and —— 'Germany in the European Union: gentle giant or emergent leader?', *International Affairs*, 72/1 (1996), 9–33.

—— George, Stephen, and Scott, Andrew (eds.), *The United Kingdom and EC Membership Evaluated* (London: Pinter, 1992).

—— Jeffery, Charlie, and Paterson, William E., 'Deutschlands europäische Diplomatie: die Entwicklung des regionalen Milieus', in Werner Weidenfeld (ed.), *Deutsche Europapolitik. Optionen wirksamer Interessenvertretung* (Bonn: Europa Union Verlag, 1998), 11–102.

Burr, William (ed.), *The Berlin Crisis, 1958–1962* [Documents] (Alexandria, Va.: National Security Archive, 1991).

—— 'Avoiding the Slippery Slope: The Eisenhower Administration and Berlin', *Diplomatic History* 18 (1994), 177–205.

Busch, Andreas, 'The Crisis in the EMS', *Government and Opposition* 29 (1994), 80–96.

Butler, Michael, *More than a Continent* (London: Heinemann, 1986).

Byrd, Peter (ed.), *British Foreign Policy Under Thatcher* (Oxford: Philip Allan/St Martin's Press, 1988).

Byrnes, James F., *Speaking Frankly* (London: Heinemann, 1947).

Cairns, David, 'What Is the Future of Mutual Recognition of Financial Statements and Is Comparability Really Necessary?', *The European Accounting Review* 3/2 (1994), 343–52.

Calingaert, Michael, *European Integration Revisited: Progress, Prospects, and U.S. Interests* (Boulder, Colo.: Westview Press, 1996).

Callaghan, James, *Time and Chance* (London: Collins/Fontana, 1988).

Cameron, Fraser, 'Britain and Germany as European Partners, 1949–1989', in Adolf M. Birke and Marie-Louise Recker (eds.), *Upsetting the Balance: German and British Security Interests in the Nineteenth and Twentieth Century* (Munich: K. G. Saur, 1999), 177–87.

Campbell, John, *Edward Heath: A Biography* (London: Jonathan Cape, 1994).

Camps, Miriam, *Britain and the European Community, 1955–63* (Princeton: Princeton University Press, 1964).

Casper, Steven, and Vitols, Sigurt, 'The German Model in the 1990s: Problems and Prospects', *Industry and Innovation* 4/1 (1997), 1–13.

Cassells, Peter, 'Welfare, Security and Economic Performance', in David Foden and Peter Morris (eds.), *The Search for Equity* (London: Lawrence and Wishart in association with ETUI and UNISON, 1998), 114–21.

Castle, Barbara, *The Castle Diaries, 1974–76* (London, Book Club Associates, in association with Weidenfield and Nicholson, 1980).

CDU/CSU Fraktion des Deutschen Bundestages, 'Reflections on European Policy', Sept. 1994.

Cecchini, Paolo, *The European Challenge* (Aldershot: Wildwood House, 1988).

Chan, S., 'In Search of Democratic Peace: Problems and Promises', *Mershon International Studies Review* 41 (1997), 59–91.

Chennels, Lucy, and Griffiths, Rachel, *Taxing Profits in a Changing World* (London: The Institute for Fiscal Studies, 1997).

Childs, David, 'British Labour and Ulbricht's State: The Fight for Recognition', in Adolf M. Birke and Günter Heydemann (eds.), *Britain and East Germany since 1918* (Munich: K. G. Saur, 1992), 95–106.

Cigar, Norman, *Genocide in Bosnia: The Policy of Ethnic Cleansing* (Austin: Texas A&M University Press, 1995).

Close, Paul, *Citizenship, Europe and Change* (Basingstoke: Macmillan, 1995).

Cockfield, Arthur, *The European Union: Creating the Single Market* (Chichester: Chancery Law Publishing, 1994).

European Commission, *Bulletin of the European Communities*, Supplement 7/85 (A Peoples' Europe). (Luxemburg: Office for Official Publications of the European Communities, 1985).

—— *The Fourth Company Accounts Directive of 1978 and The Accounting Systems of the Federal Republic of Germany, France, Italy, The UK, US, and Japan* (Luxemburg: Commission of The European Communities, 1986).

—— *Association agreements with the countries of Central and Eastern Europe*, Communication from the Commission to the Council and Parliament, COM/90/398 final (Brussels, 27 Aug. 1990).

—— *One Market One Money* (Luxemburg: Office for Official Publications of the European Communities, 1990).

—— *Reflection Group's Report*, SN 520/95 (Brussels, 5 Dec. 1995).

—— *Study on alternative strategies for the development of relations in the field of agriculture between the EU and associated countries with a view to future accession of these countries (Agriculture strategy paper)*, 'Fischler report,' CSE (95) 607, Brussels, Dec. 1995.

—— An Examination of The Conformity between The Internation Accounting Standards and The European Accounting Directives (Luxemburg: Commission of The European Communities, 1996).

—— 'Commission Communication to the Council and to the European Parliament, Services of General Interest in Europe', COM (96) 443, final version of 11 Sept. 1996.

—— 'Agenda 2000: for a Stronger and Wider Europe', *Bulletin of the European Union*, Supplement, 5/97 (1997).

—— 'Agenda 2000: Financing the European Union—Commission report on the operation of the own resources system', Supplement 2/98, *Bulletin of the European Union*, Annex 8, Table 5 (1998).

European Communities, *Report of the Committee for the Study of Economic and Monetary Union* (Luxemburg: European Communities, April 1989).

—— Task Force on the 1996 Intergovernmental Conference, *White Paper on the 1996 Intergovernmental Conference: Volume II, Summary of the Positions of the Member States of the European Union with a View to the 1996 Intergovernmental Conference* (Luxemburg: European Parliament, 1996).

Committee for the Study of Economic and Monetary Union, *Report on Economic and Monetary Union in the European Community*, 'Delors report' (Luxemburg, 1989).

Cook, Joanne 'Restructuring Social Rights in the EU. Does a Flexible Employment and Benefits Regime Entrench Exclusion and Inequality?', in Maurice

Roche and Rik van Berkel (eds.), *European Citizenship and Social Exclusion* (Aldershot: Ashgate, 1997), 151–68.

Cook, the Rt Hon. Robin, *The British Presidency: Giving Europe Back to the People*, speech by the Foreign Secretary to the Institute for European Affairs, Dublin, 3 Nov. 1997.

Corbett, Richard, *The Treaty of Maastricht* (Harlow, Essex: Longmans, 1993).

Crockatt, Richard, *The Fifty Year War: The United States and the Soviet Union in World Politics, 1941–1991* (London: Routledge, 1995).

Dahrendorf, Ralf, *On Britain* (London: BBC Books, 1982).

Daintith, Terence C. (ed.), *Implementing EC Law in the United Kingdom: Structures for Indirect Rule* (Chichester: Wiley Chancery Law, 1995).

Danchev, Alex, 'On Specialness,' *International Affairs* 72/4 (1996), 737–50.

Danner, Mark, 'The US and the Yugoslav Catastrophe', *The New York Review of Books*, 20/11/1997.

—— 'America and the Bosnian Genocide', *The New York Review of Books*, 4/12/1997.

—— 'Endgame in Kosovo', *The New York Review of Books*, 6/5/1999.

Davies, Mike, Paterson, Ron, and Wilson, Allister, *UK GAAP Generally Accepted Accounting Practice in the United Kingdom* (London: Macmillan Reference Ltd., 1997).

Davy, Richard, 'Großbritannien und die Deutsche Frage', *Europa-Archiv* 45/4 (1990), 139–44.

Deakin, Simon, 'Contract Law and Inter-firm Co-operation: The Role of Good Faith', *Signal* (Autumn 1997), 3 ff.

Dearing, Sir Ronald, *The Making of Accounting Standards: A consultative document from the DTI. Report of the Review Committee* (London: Department of Trade and Industry, 1989).

Deighton, Anne, *The Impossible Peace: Britain, the Division of Germany, and the Origins of the Cold War, 1945–1947* (Oxford: Clarendon Press, 1990/1993).

—— 'La Grande-Bretagne et la Communauté européenne, 1958–1963', *Histoire, Économie, et Société* 13/1 (1994), 113–30.

—— 'Britain and the Three Interlocking Circles,' in A. Varsori (ed.), *Europe, 1945–1990s: The End of an Era?* (London: Macmillan, 1995), 155–69.

—— (ed.), *Building Postwar Europe: National Decision-Makers and European institutions* (London: Macmillan, 1995).

—— (ed.), *Western European Union 1954–1997: Defence, Security, Integration* (Oxford: European Interdependence Research Unit, 1997).

—— 'The Last Piece of the Jigsaw: Britain and the Creation of Western European Union, 1954', *Contemporary European History* 7/2 (1998), 181–96.

—— and Milward, Alan S. (eds.), *The European Economic Community, 1957–1963: Widening, Deepening, Acceleration* (Bonn: Nomos, 1998).

—— and Piers Ludlow, '"A Conditional Application": British Management of the First Attempt to seek Membership of the EEC, 1961–63', in A. Deighton (ed.), *Building Postwar Europe: national decision-makers and European institutions* (London: Macmillan, 1995), 107–26.

Denton, Geoffrey R., 'Re-Structuring the EC Budget: Implications of the Fontainebleau Agreement', *Journal of Common Market Studies* 23/2 (Dec. 1984), 117–40.

—— *Enlarging the Union: The Intergovernmental Conference of the European Union 1996*, Federal Trust Papers Number Five (London: Federal Trust, 1996).

Diekmann, K., and Reuth, R. G., *Helmut Koht: Ich wollte Deutschlands Einheit*, 3rd edn. (Berlin, 1996).

Dietsch, Ulrich, *Aussenwirtschaftliche Aktivitäten der DDR gegenüber den Mitgliedsländern der Europäischen Gemeinschaft* (Hamburg: Verlag Weltarchiv, 1976).

Dimbleby, David, and Reynolds, David, *An Ocean Apart: The Relationship between Britain and America in the 20th Century* (London: BBC Books/Hodder & Stoughton, 1988).

Dinan, Desmond, *Ever Closer Union? An Introduction to the European Community*, 2nd edn. (Basingstoke: Macmillan, 1999).

Dobler, Wolfgang, 'Britain's Image of Germany', *German Politics* 6/3 (1997), 152–65.

Documents on British Policy Overseas, 3rd ser., vol. 1 (London: The Stationery Office, 1997).

Dodge, Roy, *Foundations of Business Accounting* (London: Chapman & Hall, 1993).

Douglas-Home, Alec (Lord Home of the Hirsel), *The Way the Wind Blows: Memoirs* (London: Collins, 1976).

Duff, Andrew (ed.), *The Treaty of Amsterdam: Text and Commentary* (London: Federal Trust/Sweet & Maxwell, 1997).

Dunbabin, J. P. D. *The Cold War: The Great Powers and their Allies* (London: Longman, 1994).

Dwan, Renata, 'An Uncommon Community: France and the European Defence Community, 1950–1954' (D.Phil. thesis, University of Oxford, 1996).

Dyson, Kenneth, 'West Germany: The Search for a Rationalist Consensus', in Jeremy Richardson (ed.), *Policy Styles in Western Europe* (London: Allen and Unwin, 1982), 17–46.

—— *Elusive Union: The Process of Economic and Monetary Union in Europe* (London: Longmans 1994).

—— and Featherstone, Kevin, 'EMU and Economic Governance in Germany', *German Politics* 5/3 (1996), 337–9.

Ebster-Grosz, Dagmar and Pugh, Derek S., *Anglo-German Business Collaboration: Pitfalls and Potentials* (London: Macmillan, 1996).

Eden, Anthony, *Full Circle* (London: Cassell, 1960).

Edwards, Geoffrey, 'British Attitudes Towards West Germany', *International Relations* 8/4 (Nov. 1982), 2227–41.

—— 'National Approaches to the Arab-Israeli Conflict: The UK', in D. Allen and A. Pijpers (eds.), *European Foreign-Policy Making and the Arab-Israeli Conflict* (Dordrecht: Martinus Nijhoff 1984), 47–59.

Eisenhower, Dwight D., *The White House Years*, vol. 2: *Waging Peace, 1956–1961* (New York, 1965).

Eißel, Dieter, 'Reichtum unter der Steuerschraube?', in Ernst-Ulrich Huster (ed.), *Reichtum* (Frankfurt/M.: Rowohlt, 1997), 127–57.

Eizenstat, Stuart E., 'Farewell Remarks to the EU Committee of the American Chamber of Commerce', 8 Feb. 1996, U.S. Department of State, Internet Information [http://www. state_gov.useu].

Eymelt, Friedrich, *Die Tätigkeit der DDR in den nichtkommunistischen Ländern, V. Grossbritannien* (Bonn: DGfAP, 1970).

Faini, Riccardo, and Portes, Richard (eds.), *European Union Trade with Eastern Europe* (London: Centre for Economic Policy Research, 1995).

Falin, Valentin, *Politische Erinnerungen* (Munich: Droemer, 1993).

Falke, Andreas, 'Veränderte amerikanische Einstellung zur EG. Der Binnenmarkt und die Gatt-Verhandlungen', *Europa-Archiv* 46/6 (1991), 190–200.

Falkner, Gerda, 'European Works Councils and the Maastricht Social Agreement: Towards a New Policy Style?', *Journal of European Public Policy* 3/2 (1996), 192–208.

Fink, Hans-Jürgen, 'Westeuropa: Übrige Westeuropäische Länder. Großbritannien', in H. A. Jacobson *et al.* (eds.), *Drei Jahrzehnte Außenpolitik der DDR. Bestimmungsfaktoren, Instrumente, Aktionsfelder* (Munich: Oldenbourg, 1979), 513–18.

Finlayson, Geoffrey, *Citizen, State, and Social Welfare in Britain 1830–1990* (Oxford: Clarendon Press, 1994).

Foreign and Commonwealth Office, 'Britain in the European Community—The Budget Problem', September 1982, reprinted in Trevor Salmon and Sir William Nicoll (eds.), *Building European Union—A documentary history and analysis* (Manchester: Manchester University Press, 1997).

Forster, Anthony, 'The Ratchet of European Defence: Britain and the Reactivation of Western European Union, 1984–1991', in A. Deighton (ed.), *Western European Union 1954–1997*: Defence, Security, Integration (Oxford: European Interdependance Research Unit, 1997), 29–45.

—— 'Britain and the Negotiation of the Maastricht Treaty: A Critique of Liberal Intergovernmentalism', *Journal of Common Market Studies* 36/3 (1998), 347–68.

Foster, Edward, and Schmidt, Peter, *Anglo-German Relations in Security and Defence: Taking Stock* (London: Royal United Services Institute for Defence Studies, 1997).

Franck, Christian, 'New Ambitions: From the Hague to Paris Summits (1969–1972)', in Roy Pryce (ed.), *The Dynamics of European Union* (London: Croom Helm, 1987), 130–48.

Francke, Klaus, 'Balancing Transatlantic Relations', *NATO Review* 45/5 (1997), 17–21.

Freedman, Judith, 'Defining Taxable Profit in a Changing Accounting Environment', *British Tax Review* 5 (1995), 434–44.

Freedman, Lawrence, and Menon, Anand, 'Conclusion: Defence, States and Integration', in Joylon Howorth and Anand Menon (eds.), *The European Union and National Defence Policy* (London and New York: Routledge, 1997).

Fromm, Hermann, *Deutschland in der öffentlichen Kriegszieldiskussion Großbritanniens 1939–1945* (Frankfurt/M.: Peter Lang, 1982).

Fulbrook, Mary, *Anatomy of a Dictatorship: Inside the GDR, 1949–1989* (Oxford: Oxford University Press, 1995).

Furlong, Paul, and Cox, Andrew (eds.), *The European Union at the Crossroads: Problems in Implementing the Single Market Project* (Boston Lincs.: Earlsgate Press, 1995).

Fursdon, Edward, *The European Defence Community: A History* (London: Macmillan, 1980).

Gaddis, John Lewis, *We Now Know: Rethinking Cold War History* (Oxford: Oxford University Press, 1997).

Gaida, Burton C., *USA-DDR. Politische, kulturelle und wirtschaftliche Beziehungen seit 1974* (Bochum: Brockmeyer, 1989).

Garrett, Geoffrey, 'The Politics of Maastricht', in B. Eichengreen and J. Frieden (eds.), *The Political Economy of European Monetary Unification* (Boulder, Colo.: Westview Press, 1993).

Garthoff, Raymond L., *Détente and Confrontation: American–Soviet Relations from Nixon to Reagan* (Washington, DC: Brookings Institution, 1994).

Gearson, John P. S., *Harold Macmillan and the Berlin Wall Crisis, 1958–62: The Limits of Interests and Force* (Basingstoke: Macmillan, 1998).

Genscher, Hans-Dietrich, 'Dimensions of German Foreign Policy', *Aussenpolitik* 25/4 (1974), 363–74.

—— *Erinnerungen* (Berlin: Siedler, 1995).

George, Stephen, *Britain and European Integration since 1945* (Oxford: Blackwell, 1991).

—— (ed.), *Britain and the European Community: The Politics of Semi-Detachment* (Oxford: Oxford University Press, 1992).

—— 'A Reply to Buller', *Politics* 15 (1995), 43–47.

—— 'The Approach of the British Government to the 1996 Intergovernmental Conference of the European Union', *Journal of European Public Policy* 3/1 (1996), 45–62.

—— *An Awkward Partner: Britain in the European Community*, 3rd edn. (Oxford: Oxford University Press, 1998).

Geyer, Michael H., 'Der Kampf um die nationale Repräsentation. Deutsch-deutsche Sportbeziehungen und die Hallstein-Doktrin', *Vierteljahrshefte für Zeitgeschichte* 44 (1996), 55–86.

Giddens, Anthony, *The Third Way: The Renewal of Social Democracy* (Oxford: Polity Press, 1998).

Gielisch, Dagmar, *Die ehemalige DDR und das Projekt 'Europäischer Binnenmarkt'. Versuch einer Bestandsaufnahme und Analyse ihrer Wirtschaftsbeziehungen zur Europäischen Gemeinschaft* (Münster: Lit, 1992).

Giesbert, Franz-Olivier, *François Mitterrand: Une Vie* (Paris: Seuil, 1996).

Gillingham, John, *Coal, Steel and the Re-Birth of Europe, 1945–1955* (Cambridge: Cambridge University Press, 1991).

Gnesotto, Nicole, 'Lessons of Yugoslavia', *Chaillot Papers* 14 (March 1994), Institute for Security Studies of the Western European Union.

Goetz, Klaus H., 'Integration Policy in a Europeanised State: Germany and the Intergovernmental Conference', *Journal of European Public Policy* 3/1 (1996), 23–44.

Goldberger, Bruce, 'Why Europe Should not Fear the Germans', *German Politics* 2 (1993), 288–310.

Goma, Richard, 'The Social Dimension of the European Union: a New Type of Welfare System?', *Journal of European Public Policy* 3/2 (1996), 209–30.

Gordon, Philip H., *France, Germany, and the Western Alliance* (Boulder, Colo.: Westview Press, 1995).

—— 'Does the WEU Have A Role?', *The Washington Quarterly* 20/1 (Winter 1996), 125–40.

Gough, Ian, 'Social Welfare and Competitiveness', *New Political Economy* 1/2 (1996), 209–32.

Gow, James, *Triumph of the Lack of Will: International Diplomacy and the Yugoslav War* (London: Hurst, 1997).

Grabbe, Heather, and Hughes, Kirsty, *Enlarging the EU Eastwards* (London: Pinter/RIIA, 1998).

Grahl, John, and Teague, Paul, *1992 The Big Market: the Future of the European Community* (London: Lawrence and Wishart, 1990).

—— and —— 'The Crisis of Economic Citizenship in the EU: Lean Production and the German Model' in Michael Roche and Rik van Berkel (eds.), *European Citizenship and Social Exclusion* (Aldershot: Ashgate, 1997), 67–82.

—— and —— 'Is the European Social Model Fragmenting?', *New Political Economy* 2/3 (1997), 405–26.

—— and —— 'The Crisis of Economic Citizenship in the EU: Lean Production and the German Model', in Michael Roche and Rik van Berkel (eds.), *European Citizenship and Social Exclusion*, (Aldershot: Ashgate, 1997), 65–81.

Graml, Hermann, *Die Alliierten und die Teilung Deutschlands. Konflikte und Entscheidungen 1941–1948* (Frankfurt/M.: Fischer Taschenbuch, 1985).

Grant, Charles, *Delors: Inside the House that Jacques Built* (London: Nicholas Brealey, 1994).

Grewe, Wilhelm, *Rückblenden, 1951–76* (Frankfurt: Propyläen, 1979).

Griffiths, Ian, *Creative Accounting: How to Make Your Profits What You Want Them to Do* (London: Sidgwick & Jackson Ltd., 1986).

Grünert, Holle, and Lutz, Burkart, 'East German Labour Market in Transition: Segmentation and Increasing Disparity', *Industrial Relations Journal* 26/1 (1995), 19–31.

Haas, Peter M., 'Introduction: Epistemic Communities and International Policy Co-ordination', *International Organization* 46/1 (1992), 1–36.

Haftendorn, Helga, *Nato and the Nuclear Revolution: A Crisis of Credibility, 1966–1967* (Oxford: Clarendon Press, 1996).

Haller, Axel, 'The Relationship of Financial and Tax Accounting in Germany: A Major Reason for Accounting Disharmony in Europe', *International Journal of Accounting* 27 (1992), 310–23.

—— 'International Accounting Harmonisation. American Hegemony or Mutual Recognition with Benchmarks? Comments and Additional Notes from a German Perspective', *The European Accounting Review* 4/2 (1995), 235–47.

Hampton, Mary N., 'Institutions and Learning: Explaining Incremental German Foreign Policy Innovation', *European Security* 5/4 (Winter 1996), 543–63.

Hanrieder, Wolfram, *Germany, America, Europe: Forty Years of German Foreign Policy* (New Haven: Yale University Press, 1989) (2nd rev. and exp. German edition, Paderborn: Schöningh, 1995).

Harmon, Mark, and Heisenberg, Dorothy, 'Explaining the European Currency Crisis of September 1992', *German Politics and Society* 29 (1993), 19–51.

Harryvan, A. G. and van der Harst, J., *Documents on European Union* (London: Macmillan, 1997).

Hartley, Keith, Uttley, Matthew, and Cox, Andrew, 'European Community Public Procurement Policy: Contract Awards and the Problems of Implementation', in Paul Furlong and Andrew Cox (eds.), *The European Union at the Crossroads*, 161–86.

Haseler, Stephen, *The English Tribe: Identity, Nation and Europe* (Basingstoke: Macmillan, 1996).

Healey, Denis, *The Time of My Life*, paperback edn. (London: Penguin, 1990).

Heath, Edward, *The Course of My Life: My Autobiography* (London: Hodder and Stoughton, 1998).

Heise, Arno, 'Neoliberale Empfehlungen zur Beschäftigungspolitik in Theorie und Praxis: Großbritannien und Deutschland im Vergleich', *WSI-Mitteilungen* 11/1997, 758–70.

Hellman, Gunther, 'The Sirens of Power and German Foreign Policy: Who is Listening?', *German Politics* 6/2 (1997), 29–57.

Hepple, Bob, 'Social Rights in the European Economic Community: A British Perspective', *Comparative Labor Law Journal* 11/4 (1990), 425–40.

—— 'The Implementation of the Community Charter of Fundamental Social Rights', *The Modern Law Review* 53/5 (1990), 643–54.

Her Majesty's Treasury, *An Evolutionary Approach to Economic and Monetary Union* (London: H. M. Treasury, 1989).

Herspring, Dale R., 'After NATO Expansion: The East European Militaries', *Problems of Post-Communism* 45/1 (1998), 10–20.

Herzog, Roman, 'Die Globalisierung der deutschen Außenpolitik ist unvermeidlich,' Rede des Bundespräsidenten beim Festakt zum 40. Jahrestag der Deutschen Gesellschaft für Auswärtige Politik, *Bulletin des Presse- und Informationsamtes der Bundesregierung*, No. 20 (15 March 1995), 161–5.

Heurlin, Bertel (ed.), *Germany in Europe in the Nineties* (Basingstoke: Macmillan, 1996).

Heuser, Beatrice, *NATO, Britain, France and the FRG: Nuclear Strategies and Forces for Europe, 1949–2000* (London: Macmillan, 1997).

—— *Nuclear Mentalities? Strategies and Belief in Britain, France, and the FRG* (New York: St Martin's Press, 1998).

Heydemann, Günther, 'Partner oder Konkurrent? Das britische Deutschlandbild während des Wiedervereinigungsprozesses 1989–1991', in Franz Bosbach (ed.), *Feindbilder* (Cologne: Böhlau, 1992), 201–34.

Hildebrand, Klaus, *No Intervention. Die Pax Britannica und Preußen 1865/66–1868/70. Eine Untersuchung zur englischen Weltpolitik im 19. Jahrhundert* (Munich: Oldenbourg, 1997).

Hill, Christopher, 'The United Kingdom and Germany', in B. Heurlin (ed.), *Germany in Europe in the Nineties* (Basingstoke: Macmillan, 1996), 222–40.

Hinterhoff, Eugen, *Disengagement* (London: Stevens, 1959).

H. M. Treasury, *An Evolutionary Approach to Economic and Monetary Union* (London: HMSO, Nov. 1989).

Hoagland, Jim, 'NATO is in Transition, So Why not Talk about It?', *The International Herald Tribune*, 19/3/1998.

Hoffmann, Jürgen, 'Trade Union reform in Germany: Some Analytical and Critical Remarks Concerning the Current Debate', *Transfer* 1 (1995), 98–113.

Holbrooke, Richard, *To End a War* (New York: Random House, 1998).

Hombach, Bodo, *Aufbruch: Die Politik der neuen Mitte* (Düsseldorf: Econ, 1998).

Horne, Alistair, *Macmillan, 1957–1986*, vol. 2 of the official biography (London: Macmillan, 1989).

Howarth, Marianne, 'KfA Ltd und Berolina Travel Ltd. Die DDR-Präsenz in Großbritannien vor und naeh der diplomatischen Anerkennung', *Deutschland-Archiv* 32/4 (1999), 591–600.

Howe, Geoffrey, 'The Future of the European Community: Britain's Approach to the Negotiations', *International Affairs* 60/2 (Spring 1984), 187–92.

—— Conflict of Loyalty (London: Macmillan, 1994).

Hu, Yau-su, *Europe Under Stress* (London: Butterworth, 1981).

Hughes, Kirsty, *What Role for Britain in the EU? Prospects for the Late 1990s* (London: Friedrich-Ebert-Stiftung, 1996).

Huhne, Christopher, 'Don't throw the baby out . . .', *New Statesman*, 2/1/1998.

Huntington, Samuel, P., 'The Clash of Civilizations?', *Foreign Affairs* 72/3 (1993), 22–49.

—— *The Clash of Civilizations and the Rewriting of World Order* (New York: Simon & Schuster, 1996).

Hurd, Douglas, 'Political Cooperation', *International Affairs* 57/3 (Summer 1981), 383–93.

Hutton, Will, 'The Keynesian Angle' (Debate on Global Free Trade), *New Political Economy* I/1 (1996), 101–6.

Hyde, Filippo, *The German Way: Aspects of Behaviour, Attitudes, and Customs in the German-Speaking World* (Lincolnwood, Ill.: NTC Publishing Group, 1996).

Institute of European Affairs, *IGC Update*, No. 8 (Dublin: Institute of European Affairs, 1997).

Instone, Ralph, 'Realised Profits: Unrealised Consequences', *The Journal of Business Law*, March (1985), 106–14.

Jackson, Ian, 'Co-operation and Constraint: Britain's Influence on American Economic Warfare Policy in CoCom, 1948–1954' (Ph.D. thesis, Queen's University of Belfast, 1997).

Jacobi, Otto, Keller, Berndt, and Müller-Jentsch, Walther, 'Germany: Codetermining the Future?', in Anthony Ferner and Richard Hyman (eds.), *Industrial Relations in the New Europe* (Oxford: Basil Blackwell, 1992), 220–69.

James, Harold, and Stone, Marla (eds.), *When the Wall Came Down: Reactions to German Unification* (London: Routledge, 1992).

Jeffery, Charlie, 'The Länder Strike Back. Structures and Procedures of European Integration Policy-Making in the German Federal System', *University of Leicester Discussion Papers in Federal Studies*, FS94/4 (1994), 1–30.

—— 'A Giant with Feet of Clay? United Germany in the European Union', *University of Birmingham Discussion Papers in German Studies*, IGS95/6 (1995), 1–34.

Jeffery, Charlie, 'Britische Positionen zur Regierungskonferenz 1996—Ein Wandel in Sicht?', in *Maastricht II—Zum Erfolg verurteilt? Herausforderung und Perspektiven der europäischen Integration* (Erfurt: Thüringer Ministerium für Justiz und Europaangelegenheiten, 1996).

Jenkins, Charles, *Paying for an Enlarged European Union* (London: Federal Trust, 1999).

Jenkins, Roy, 'Britain and Europe: Ten Years of Community Membership', *International Affairs* 59/2 (Spring 1983), 147–53.

Jochum, Michael, *Eisenhower und Chruschtschow. Gipfeldiplomatie im Kalten Krieg, 1955–60* (Paderborn: Schöningh, 1996).

Jopp, Mathias, and Schmuck, Otto (eds.), *Die Reform der Europäischen Union: Analysen—Positionen—Dokumente zur Regierungskonferenz 1996/97* (Bonn: Europa Union Verlag, 1996).

—— et al. (eds.), *Integration and Security in Western Europe* (Boulder: Westview Press, 1991).

—— Maurer, Andreas, and Schmuck, Otto (eds.), *Die Europäische Union nach Amsterdam: Analysen und Stellungnahmen zum neuen EU-Vertrag* (Bonn: Europa Union Verlag, 1998).

Josseline, Daphne, *Money politics in the new Europe: Britain, France and the single financial market* (Basingstoke: Macmillan, 1997).

Judah, Tim, *The Serbs: History, Myths, and the Destruction of Yugoslavia* (New Haven, 1997).

—— 'Kosovo's Road to War', *Survival* 41/2 (1999), 5–18.

Judt, Tony, 'New Germany, Old NATO', *New York Review of Books*, 29/5/1997.

Kahl, Martin, 'European Integration, European Security, and the Transformation in Central Europe', *Journal of European Integration* 20/2–3 (1997), 153–86.

Kaiser, Karl, 'Interdependence and Autonomy: Britain and the Federal Republic in their Multinational Environment', in Karl Kaiser and Roger Morgan (eds.), *Britain and West Germany: Changing Societies and the Future of Foreign Policy* (London: Oxford University Press, 1971).

—— and Morgan, Roger (eds.), *Britain and West Germany: Changing Societies and the Future of Foreign Policy* (London: Oxford University Press, 1971).

—— and Roper, John (eds.), *British–German Defence Co-operation: Partners within the Alliance* (London: Jane's, 1988); [German edition: *Die stille Allianz: deutsch-britische Sicherheitskooperation*, Bonn: Deutsche Gesellschaft für Auswärtige Politik, 1987].

Kaiser, Monika, *Machtwechsel von Ulbricht zu Honecker: Funktionsmechanismen der SED-Diktatur in Konfliktsituationen 1962 bis 1972* (Berlin: Akademie Verlag, 1997).

Katzenstein, Peter J., *Policy and Politics in West Germany. The Growth of a Semi-Sovereign State* (Philadelphia: Temple University Press, 1987).

—— 'Germany and Mitteleuropa: An Introduction', in P. Katzenstein (ed.), *Mitteleuropa. Between Europe and Germany* (Oxford: Berghahn, 1997).

—— Tamed Power: Germany in Europe (Ithaca, NY: Cornell University Press, 1997).

Keatinge, Patrick, and Murphy, Anna, 'The European Council's Ad Hoc Committee on Institutional Affairs (1984–85)', in Roy Pryce (ed.), *The Dynamics of European Union* (London: Croom Helm, 1987), 217–37.

Kennedy, Paul, *The Rise and Fall of Great Powers: Economic Change and Military Conflict from 1500 to 2000* (New York: Random House, 1987).

Keohane, Robert O. and Stanley Hoffmann (eds.), *The New European Community: Decision making and Institutional Change* (Oxford: Westview Press, 1991).

Kettenacker, Lothar, *Krieg zur Friedenssicherung. Die Deutschlandplanung der britischen Regierung während des Zweiten Weltkrieges* (Göttingen: Vandenhoeck & Ruprecht, 1989).

Kielinger, Thomas, *Crossroads and Roundabouts: Junctions in German-British Relations* (London/Bonn: Cassels/Bouvier, 1997) [also available in German].

Kiessler, Richard and Elbe, Frank, *Ein runder Tisch mit scharfen Ecken. Der diplomatische Weg zur Wiedervereinigung* (Baden-Baden: Nomos, 1993 [engl. edition: A Round Table with Sharp Corners: the diplomatic path to German unity, Baden-Baden: Nomos, 1996].

Kitzinger, Uwe, *Diplomacy and Persuasion: How Britain Joined the Common Market* (London: Thames and Hudson, 1973).

Klein, Hans, *Es begann im Kaukasus. Der entscheidende Schritt in die Einheit Deutschlands* (Berlin: Ullstein, 1991).

Kohl, Helmut, *Ich wollte Deutschlands Einheit*, ed. Kai Diekmann and Ralph Georg Reuth (Berlin: Propyläen, 1996).

Köhler, Henning, *Adenauer: Eine Politische Biographie* (Frankfurt/M.: Propyläen, 1994).

Kopstein, Jeffrey, *The Politics of Economic Decline in East Germany, 1945–1989* (Chapel Hill: University of North Carolina Press, 1997).

Kosthorst, Daniel, *Brentano und die deutsche Einheit. Die Deutschland- und Ostpolitik des Außenministers im Kabinett Adenauer 1955–1961* (Melle: Knoth, 1993).

Kraus, Elisabeth, *Ministerien für das ganze Deutschland? Der Alliierte Kontrollrat und die Frage gesamtdeutscher Zentralverwaltungen* (Munich: Oldenbourg, 1990).

Krickus, Richard J., 'The Case for Including the Baltics in NATO', *Problems of Post-Communism* 45/1 (1998), 3–8.

Küsters, Hans-Jürgen, 'West Germany's Foreign Policy in Western Europe, 1949–58: The Art of the Possible,' in C. Wurm (ed.), *Western Europe and Germany: The Beginnings of European Integration, 1945–1960* (Oxford: Berg, 1995), 55–85.

—— and Hofmann, Daniel (eds.), *Deutsche Einheit. Sonderedition aus den Akten des Bundeskanzleramtes 1989/90* (Munich: Oldenbourg, 1998).

Kwizinskij, Julij, *Vor dem Sturm. Erinnerungen eines Diplomaten* (Berlin: Siedler, 1993).

La Serre, Françoise de, Leruez, Jacques, and Wallace, Helen (eds.), *French and British foreign policies in transition: the challenge of adjustment* (New York: Berg, 1990).

Labour Party, 'The Future of the European Union: Report on Labour's Position in Preparation for the Intergovernmental Conference 1996' (London: Labour Party, 1995).

—— *The future of the European Union*, Report to the Party Conference on Labour's position in preparation for the Intergovernmental Conference 1996 (London: Labour Party, 1995).

LaFeber, Walter, *America, Russia and the cold war, 1945–1990*, 8th edn. (New York: McGraw-Hill, 1996).

Lamb, Richard, *The Macmillan Years, 1957–1963: The Emerging Truth* (London: John Murray, 1995).

Lamborn, Alan C., *The Price of Power: Risk and Foreign Policies in Britain, France, and Germany* (London: Unwin Hyman, 1991).

Lamont, Norman, *In Office* (London: Little, Brown, 1999).

Lane, Christel, 'Is Germany following the British path? A Comparative analysis of stability and change', *Industrial Relations Journal* 25/3 (1994), 187–98.

—— 'Trade assocations and inter-firm relations in Britain and Germany', in Robert J. Bennett (ed.), *Trade associations in Britain and Germany* (London: Anglo-German Foundation for the Study of Industrial Society, 1997), 23–32.

Larres, Klaus, 'Preserving Law and Order: Britain, the United States and the East German Uprising of 1953', *Twentieth Century British History* 5/3 (1994), 320–50.

—— *Politik der Illusionen: Churchill, Eisenhower und die deutsche Frage, 1945–55* (Göttingen: Vandenhoeck & Ruprecht, 1995).

—— 'Germany and the West: The "Rapallo Factor" in German Foreign Policy from the 1950s to the 1990s', in Klaus Larres and Panikos Panayi (eds.), *The Federal Republic of Germany since 1949: Politics, Society and Economy before and after Unification* (London: Longman, 1996), 278–326.

—— 'Integrating Europe or Ending the Cold War? Churchill's Post-War Foreign Policy,' *Journal of European Integration History* 2/1 (1996), 15–49.

—— 'Eisenhower, Dulles und Adenauer: Bündnis des Vertrauens oder Allianz des Mißtrauens? (1953–61)', in K. Larres and T. Oppelland (eds.), *Deutschland und die USA im 20. Jahrhundert: Geschichte der politischen Beziehungen* (Darmstadt: Wissenschaftliche Buchgesellschaft, 1997), 119–50.

—— and Oppelland, Torsten (eds.), *Deutschland und die USA im 20. Jahrhundert: Geschichte der politischen Beziehungen* (Darmstadt: Wissenschaftliche Buchgesellschaft, 1997).

—— 'Germany in 1989: The Development of a Revolution', in Klaus Larres, *Germany since Unification: The Domestic and External Consequences* (Basingstoke: Macmillan, 1998), 33–59.

—— 'Konrad Adenauer (1874–1967)', in Torsten Oppelland (ed.), *Portraits der deutschen Politik 1949–1969*, Vol. 1 (Darmstadt: Wissenschaftliche Buchgesellschaft, 1999), 13–24.

—— 'Großbritannien und der 17. Juni 1953: 'Die deutsche Frage und das Scheitern von Churchills Entspannungs-politik nach Stalins Tod', in Christoph Kleßmann and Bernd Stöver (eds.), 1953-Krisenjahr des Kalteu Krieges in Europa (Cologne: Böhlau Verlag, 1999), 155–79.

—— 'Torn between Idealism and Egotism: The United States and European Integration, 1945–1990,' *Irish Journal of American Studies* 8 (1999) [forthcoming].

Laursen, Finn, and Vanhoonacker, Sophie (eds.), *The Intergovernmental Conference on Political Union: Institutional Reforms, New Policies and International Identity of the European Community* (Maastricht: European Institute of Public Administration, 1992).

Lawson, Nigel, 'What Sort of European Financial Area?', talk at the Royal Institute of International Affairs in London (25/1/1989).

Leaman, Jeremy, *The Political Economy of West Germany 1945–1985* (London: Macmillan, 1988).

—— 'The Rhetoric and Logic of the *Wende*', *German Politics* 2/1 (1993), 124–35.

—— 'Central Banking and the Crisis of Social Democracy—A Comparative Analysis of British and German Views', *German Politics* 4/3 (1995), 22–48.

—— 'Germany in the Context of Globalisation', *Debatte—Review of Contemporary German Affairs* 5/1 (1997), 91–104.

Lee, Sabine, 'Perception and Reality: Anglo-German Relations during the Berlin Crisis 1958–59', *German History* 13 (1995), 47–69.

—— 'Germany and the First British Application', in A. Deighton and A. S. Milward (eds.), *The European Economic Community, 1957–1963: Widening, Deepening, Acceleration* (Bonn: Nomos, 1999).

Lee Williams, Alan and Lee Williams, Geoffrey, 'NATO's Future in the Balance: Time for a Rethink?', *University Advisory Committee of the Atlantic Council of the United Kingdom* (London, 1995).

Lefebvre, Stephane, and Ben Lombardi, 'Germany and Peace Enforcement: Participating in IFOR', *European Security* 5/4 (Winter 1996), 564–87.

Lehmann, Ines, *Die deutsche Einigung von außen gesehen. Angst, Bedenken und Erwartungen in der ausländischen Presse*, Vol. 1 (Frankfurt/M., 1996).

—— 'Zwangläufige deutsche Dominanz? Über Konstanten britischer Europaperzeptionen', *Tel Aviver Jahrbuch für deutsche Geschichte* 26 (1997), 235–49.

Leicester, Graham, 'Europe After Major: Can Labour Make A Difference?' (London: Fabian Society, 1996).

Leisink, Peter, 'Work and Citizenship in Europe', in Maurice Roche and Rik van Berkel (eds.), *European Citizenship and Social Exclusion* (Aldershot: Ashgate, 1997), 51–66.

Lemaître, P., and Schlenker, H. H., 'The Future of The Franco-German Relationship', *Challenge Europe* 12 (1997).

Lemke, Michael, 'Kampagnen gegen Bonn. Die Systemkrise der DDR und die West-Propaganda der SED, 1960–1963', *Vierteljahrshefte für Zeitgeschichte* 41 (1993), 151–74.

Leupold, Bernd, *'Weder anglophil noch anglophob.' Großbritannien im politischen Denken Konrad Adenauers* (Frankfurt/M.: Peter Lang, 1997).

Libal, Michael, *Limits of Persuasion: Germany and the Yugoslav Crisis, 1991–92* (Westport, Conn.: Praeger, 1997).

Linsel, Knut, *Charles de Gaulle und Deutschland* (Sigmaringen: J. Thorbeke, 1998).

Lipgens, Walter, and Loth, Wilfried (eds.), *Documents on the History of European Integration*, vol. 3: *The Struggle for European Union by Political Parties and Pressure Groups in Western European Countries 1945–1950* (Berlin and New York: de Gruyter, 1988).

Lipgens, Walter, and Loth, Wilfried (eds.), *Documents on the History of European Integration*, vol. 4: *Transnational Organizations of Political Parties and Pressure Groups in the Struggle for European Union, 1945–1950* (Berlin and New York: de Gruyter, 1991).

Lippert, Barbara, and Becker, Peter, 'Bilanz und Zukunft des Strukturierten Dialogs,' *Integration*, 20/2 (1997), 56–71.

—— Hughes, Kirsty, Grabbe, Heather, and Becker, Peter, *Conflict and Co-operation in the Enlarged European Union? British and German Interests* (London: Cassell/RIIA, 1999).

Lord, Christopher, *Britain's Entry into the European Community under the Heath Government of 1970–74* (Aldershot: Dartmouth, 1993).

Loth, Wilfried, 'Franco-German Relations and European Security, 1957–1963,' in A. Deighton and A. S. Milward (eds.), *The European Economic Community, 1957–1963: Widening, Deepening, Acceleration* (Bonn: Nomos, 1999).

Louis, William R., and Bull, Hedley (eds.), *The Special Relationship: Anglo-American Relations since 1945* (Oxford: Oxford University Press, 1986).

Ludlow, N. Piers, *Dealing with Britain: the Six and the First UK Application to the EEC*, (Cambridge: Cambridge University Press, 1997).

—— 'Constancy and Flirtation: Germany, Britain and the EEC, 1956–1972' (paper presented at Exeter University, March 1998).

Lundestad, Geir, *'Empire' by Integration: The United States and European Integration, 1945–1997* (Oxford: Oxford University Press, 1998).

—— *East, West, North, South: Major Developments in International Politics, 1945–1996*, 4th edn. (Oslo: Scandinavian University Press, 1999).

McAdams, A. James, *Germany Divided: From the Wall to Reunification* (Princeton: Princeton University Press, 1993).

McCarthy, Patrick (ed.), *France-Germany, 1983–93: The Struggle to Cooperate* (New York: St Martin's Press, 1993).

McCourt, Patricia, and Radcliffe, George, 'Les Relations Fiscalité-Comptabilité in France: A Model for Europe?', *British Tax Review* 5 (1995), 461–83.

Macmillan, Harold, *Riding the Storm, 1956–59* (London: Macmillan, 1971).

Mählert, Ulrich, *Kleine Geschichte der DDR* (Munich: Beck, 1998).

Majone, Giandomenico, 'The European Community between Social Policy and Social Regulation', *Journal of Common Market Studies* 31/2 (1993), 153–71.

—— (ed.), *Regulating Europe* (London: Routledge, 1996).

Major, John, 'Raise your Eyes, There Is a Land Beyond,' *The Economist*, 25 Sept. 1993.

—— *Europe: A Future that Works*, William and Mary Lecture given at the University, Leiden, 7 Sept. 1994.

—— *The Autobiography* (London: HarperCollins, 1999).

Mandelbaum, Michael, *The Dawn of Peace in Europe* (New York: Twentieth Century Fund Press, 1996).

Marchiewitz, Gilbert, 'Globalisierung, Sozialkonkurrenz und die Notwendigkeit internationaler Zusammenarbeit', *WSI-Mitteilungen* 11/1997, 771–79.

Markovits, Andrei, and Reich, Simon, 'Should Europe Fear the Germans?', *German Politics and Society* 23 (1991), 1–20.

—— and —— 'A Realistic Appraisal? A Rejoinder to Goldberger', *German Politics* 3 (1994), 129–32.

Marquand, David, *The New Reckoning: Capitalism, States and Citizens* (Oxford: Polity Press, 1997).

Marsh, David, 'Reinventing German Capitalism', *German Politics* 5/3 (1996), 395–403.

Martin, Hans-Peter, and Schumann, Harald, *Die Globalisierungsfalle. Der Angriff auf Demokratie und Wohlstand* (Reinbek bei Hamburg: Rowohlt, 1996).

Mauer, Victor, 'Macmillan und die Berlinkrise, 1958–59', *Vierteljahrshefte für Zeitgeschichte* 44 (1996), 229–56.

Maxwell, Robert J., *An Unplayable Hand? BSE, CJD and the British Government* (London: King's Fund, 1997).

Mayer, Hartmut, 'Germany's Role in the Fouchet Negotiations,' *Journal of European Integration History* 2/2 (1996), 39–59.

—— 'Early at the Beach and Claiming Territory? The Evolution of German Ideas on a New European Order,' *International Affairs*, 73/4 (1997), 721–37.

Mayes, David G. (ed.), *The Evolution of the Single European Market* (Cheltenham: Edward Elgar, 1997).

Mazzucelli, Colette, *France and Germany at Maastricht: Politics and Negotiations to Create the European Union* (New York: Garland, 1997).

Meehan, Elizabeth, *Citizenship and the European Community* (London: Sage, 1993).

Meissner, Boris, 'Die deutsch-sowjetischen Beziehungen seit dem Zweiten Weltkrieg', *Osteuropa* (1985), 631–52.

Meny, Yves, and Knapp, Andrew, *Government and Politics in Western Europe: Britain, France, Italy, Germany*, 3rd edn. (Oxford: Oxford University Press, 1998).

Merkl, Peter H. (with a contribution by Gert-Joachim Glaessner), *German Unification in the European Context* (University Park: Pennsylvania State University Press, 1993).

Meyer, Thomas, *Die Transformation der Sozialdemokratie. Eine Partei auf dem Weg ins 21. Jahrhundert* (Bonn: Dietz, 1998).

Miall, Hugh, *Shaping the New Europe*, Chatham House Papers (London: RIIA, 1993).

Mierlo, Hans, Statement, Madrid, 8/7/1997, CNN, Internet Information [http://cnn.com/world].

Minford, Patrick, 'The General Interest Case' (Debate on Global Free Trade), *New Political Economy* I/1 (1996), 97–101.

Misik, Robert, *Die Suche nach dem Blair-Effekt: Schröder, Klima und Genossen zwischen Tradition und Pragmatismus* (Berlin: Aufbau Verlag, 1998).

Mitterrand, François, *De l'Allemagne, De la France* (Paris: Odile Jacob, 1996).

Monti, Mario, *The Single Market and Tomorrow's Europe* (London: Kogan Page, 1997).

Moravcsik, Andrew, 'Negotiating the Single European Act: National Interests and Conventional Statecraft in the European Community', *International Organization* 45/1 (1991), 19–56.

Moravcsik, Andrew, and Kalypso Nicolaïdis, 'Explaining the Treaty of Amsterdam: Interests, Influence, Institutions', *Journal of Common Market Studies* 37/1
(1999), 59–85.

Morgan, Roger, 'Dimensions of West German Foreign Policy', *West European
Politics* 4/2 (May 1981), 87–96.

—— 'The British View', in Edwina Moreton (ed.), *Germany between East and
West* (Cambridge: Cambridge University Press, 1987).

—— 'Brandt and Schmidt: Germany's View of Europe', in Martyn Bond *et al.*
(eds.), *Eminent Europeans: Personalities who shaped contemporary Europe*
(London: Greycoat Press, 1996), 138–61.

—— and Bray, Caroline (eds.), *Partners and Rivals in Western Europe: Britain,
France, and Germany* (London: Gower, 1986).

Müller-Stewens, Günter and Schäfer, Michael, 'The German Market for Corporate Control: Structural Development, Cross-Dorder Activities and Key
Players', in Geoffrey Owen and Ansgar Richter (eds.), *Corporate Restructuring
in Britain and Germany* (London: Anglo-German Foundation, 1997).

Mumford, Michael J., 'United Kingdom', in David Alexander and Simon
Archer (eds.), *European Accounting Guide*, 2nd edn. (Orlando, Fla.: Harcourt
Brace & Company, 1995).

Munro, Colin, 'The Acceptance of a Second German State', in Adolf M. Birke
and Günter Heydemann (eds.), *Britain and East Germany since 1918* (Munich:
K. G. Saur, 1992), 121–30.

Naumann, Gerhard, and Trümpler, Eckhard, *Von Ulbricht zu Honecker:
1970—ein Krisenjahr der DDR* (Berlin: Dietz, 1990).

Neville-Jones, Pauline, 'The Genscher/Colombo Proposals on European
Union', *Common Market Law Review* 20 (1983), 657–99.

Niblett, Robin, 'Disunion: Competing Visions of Integration', *The Washington
Quarterly* 20/1 (1996), 91–108.

Nicholls, Anthony J., *The Bonn Republic: West German Democracy, 1945–1990*
(London: Longman, 1997).

Nicoll, William, 'Tailpiece', *European Business Journal* 7/3 (1995), 63.

Niedhart, Gottfried, Junker, Detlef, and Richter, Michael W. (eds.), *Deutschland
in Europa. Nationale Interessen und internationale Ordnung im 20. Jahrhundert*
(Mannheim: Palatium Verlag, 1997).

Ninkovich, Frank, *Germany and the United States: The Transformation of the
German Question since 1945*, updated edn. (New York: Twayne, 1995).

Noakes, Jeremy *et al.* (eds.), *Britain and Germany in Europe, 1949–1990* (Oxford:
Oxford University Press, 2000) [forthcoming].

Noelle-Neumann, Elisabeth, 'Öffentliche Meinung und Außenpolitik. Die fehlende
Debatte in Deutschland', *Internationale Politik* 50/8 (Aug. 1995), 3–12.

Nugent, Neil, *The Government and Politics of the European Community*, 4th edn.
(Basingstoke: Macmillan, 1999).

Nuttal, Simon, *European Political Cooperation* (Oxford: Oxford University
Press, 1992).

O'Donnell, Rory, 'Modernisation and Social Partnership', in Robin Wilson
(ed.), *New Thinking for New Times* (Belfast: Democratic Dialogue, 1995), 24–33.

Official Journal of the European Communities, 'Europe Agreement establishing
an Association between the European Communities and their Member States

for the one part and the Republic of Poland for the other part', L348 vol. 36, 31 Dec. 1993.

Orde, Anne, *The Eclipse of Great Britain: the United States and British Imperial Decline, 1895–1956* (London: Macmillan, 1996).

Ordelheide, Dieter, and Pfaff Dieter, *European Financial Reporting: Germany* (London: Routledge, 1994).

Organization for Economic Cooperation and Development (OECD), *Progress in Structural Reform* (Paris: OECD, 1990).

—— *Economic Survey—United Kingdom* (Paris: OECD, 1994).

Ostermann, Christian, 'Im Schatten der Bundesrepublik. Die DDR im Kalkül der amerikanischen Deutschlandpolitik (1949–1989/90)', in K. Larres and T. Oppelland (eds.), *Deutschland und die USA* (Darmstadt: WBG, 1997), 230–55.

Ovendale, Richard, *Anglo-American Relations in the Twentieth Century* (Basingstoke: Macmillan, 1998).

Owen, David, *Balkan Odyssey: An Uncompromising Personal Account of the International Peace Efforts Following the Breakup of the Former Yugoslavia* (New York: Harcourt Brace, 1995).

Owen, Sir Geoffrey, 'Lessons for Britain from German Corporate Governance', *Accountancy* (April 1995), 75–6.

Padgett, Stephen (ed.), *Adenauer to Kohl: The Development of the German Chancellorship* (London: Hurst & Company, 1994).

—— 'The Failure of Britain's European Policy: Reactions to German Unification and European Union', *unpublished paper* (1994).

Padoa-Schioppa, Tomasso, *The Road to Monetary Union in Europe: The Emperor, the Kings, and the Genies* (Oxford: Oxford University Press, 1994).

Paterson, William E., 'Gulliver Unbound: The Changing Context of Foreign Policy', in G. Smith *et al.* (eds.), *Developments in German Politics* (London: Macmillan, 1992), 137–52.

—— 'Beyond Semi-Sovereignty: The New Germany in the New Europe', *German Politics* 5/2 (1996), 167–84.

—— and Jeffery, Charlie, 'Großbritannien nach dem Machtwechsel. New Labour, Devolution und Europapolitik', *Konrad-Adenauer-Stiftung Arbeitspapiere* (1997).

Pedersen, Thomas, *Germany, France and the Integration of Europe: A Realist Interpretation* (London and New York: Pinter, 1998).

Peterson, John, 'Subsidiarity: A Definition to Suit Any Vision', *Parliamentary Affairs* 47/1 (1994), 116–32.

Pfaff, Dieter and Schröer, Thomas, 'The Relationship between Financial and Tax Accounting in Germany—the Authoritativeness and Reverse Authoritativeness Principle', *The European Accounting Review* 5, Supplement (1996), 963–79.

Philip Morris Institute, *Is the Single Market Working?* (Brussels: PMI, 1996).

Piepenschneider, Melanie, 'Die Positionen der Mitgliedstaaten und EU-Organe im Überblick. Standpunkte, Spielmaterial und Sprengsätze', in M. Jopp and O. Schmuck (eds.), *Die Reform der Europäischen Union*. Analysen—Positionen —Dokumente zur Regierungskonferenz 1996/97 (Bonn, 1996), 75–100.

Pijpers, Alfred, Regelsberger, Elfriede, and Wessels, Wolfgang (eds.), *European Political Cooperation in the 1980s: A Common Foreign Policy for Western Europe* (Dordrecht: Martinus Nijhoff, 1988).

Pinder, John, *The Building of the European Union*, 3rd edn. (Oxford: Oxford University Press, 1998).

Pixley, Jocelyn, 'Employment and Social Identity. Theoretical Issues', in Maurice Roche and Rik van Berkel (eds.), *European Citizenship and Social Exclusion* (Aldershot: Ashgate, 1997), 119–34.

Plötz, Peter, and Bolz, Klaus, *Westhandel der DDR. Eine vergleichende Betrachtung des Handels mit der Bundesrepublik Deutschland und den übrigen OECD-Länders* (Hamburg: Verlag Weltarchiv, 1987).

Pritzkoleit, Kurt, Das kommandierte Wunder: Deutschlands Weg im 20. Jahrhundert (Vienna and Munich: Deach, 1959).

Pryce, Roy (ed.), *The Dynamics of European Union* (London: Croom Helm, 1987).

Ratzan, Scott C., *The Mad Cow Disease: Health and the Public Good* (London: UCL Press, 1998).

Ray, James L., *Democracy and International Conflict* (Columbia, SC: University of South Carolina Press, 1995).

Rees, G. Wyn, 'Britain and the Western European Union', *European Security* 5/4 (Winter 1996), 529–42.

—— *The Western European Union at the Crossroads: Between Trans-Atlantic Solidarity and European Integration* (Boulder, Colo.: Westview Press, 1998).

Reich, Simon, 'Foreign Direct Investors in the US', *Review of International Political Economy* 3/1 (1996), 27–64.

Reynolds, David, 'A "Special Relationship": America, Britain and the International Order since the Second World War,' *International Affairs* 62/1 (1985/6), 1–20.

Rhodes, Richard, *Deadly Feasts: Tracking the Secrets of a Terrifying New Plague* (London: Simon & Schuster, 1997).

Roberts, Frank, *Dealing with Dictators: the Destruction and Revival of Europe, 1930–70* (London: Weidenfeld & Nicolson, 1991).

Röder, Andreas, 'Staatskunst statt Kriegshandwerk. Probleme der deutschen Vereinigung von 1990 in internationaler Perspektive', *Historisches Jahrbuch* 118 (1998), 227–9.

Rohde, David, *Endgame: The Betrayal and Fall of Srebrenica, Europe's Worst Massacre since World War II* (New York: Farrar, Straus and Giroux, 1997).

Rohe, Karl, Schmidt, Gustav, and Pogge von Strandmann, Hartmut (eds.), *Deutschland, Großbritannien, Europa. Politische Traditionen, Partnerschaft und Rivalität* (Bochum: Brockmeyer, 1992).

Rosenau, James N., 'Pre-theories and Theories of Foreign Policy', in R. Barry Farrell (ed.), *Approaches to Comparative and International Politics* (Evanston, Ill.: Northwestern University Press, 1966).

—— 'Foreign Policy as an Issue Area', in J. N. Rosenau (ed.), *Domestic Sources of Foreign Policy* (New York: The Free Press, 1967), 11–50.

—— 'A Pre-theory Revisited: World politics in an Era of Cascading Interdependence', *International Studies Quarterly* 28 (1984), 245–305.

Ross, George, 'The European Community and Social Policy: Regional Blocs and a Humane Social Order', *Studies in Political Economy* 40/2 (1993), 41–73.

Rothwell, Victor, *Britain and the cold war 1941–1947* (London: Cape, 1982).

Royal Institute for International Affairs (ed.), *British Foreign Policy: Some Relevant Documents (January 1950–April 1955)* (London: RIIA, 1955).

Ruding Committee, *Conclusions and Recommendations of The Committee of Independent Experts on Company Taxation* (Luxemburg: Commission of The European Communities, 1992).

Rudolf, Peter, 'The Future of the United States as a European Power: The Case of NATO Enlargement, *European Security* 5/2 (Summer 1996), 175–195.

Rupieper, Hermann-Josef, 'Die Reaktionen der USA auf die Gründung der DDR', in Elke Scherstjanoi (ed.), *'Provisorium für längstens ein Jahr': Die Gründung der DDR* (Berlin: Akademie Verlag, 1993), 59–66.

Russett, Bruce, *Grasping the Democratic Peace* (Princeton: Princeton University Press, 1993).

Sally, Razeen, 'Ordoliberalism and the Social Market: Classical Political Economy from Germany', *New Political Economy* 1/2 (1996), 233–57.

Salmon, Trevor, and Nicoll, William (eds.), *Building European Union: a documentary history and analysis* (Manchester: Manchester University Press, 1997).

Sanderson, Joe, 'The EU Green Paper on Public Procurement: A Better Way Forward or a Missed Opportunity', *European Business Journal* 10/2 (1998), 64–70.

Sandholtz, Wayne, 'Choosing Union: Monetary Politics and Maastricht', *International Organization* 47/1 (1993), 1–39.

Schäfer, Claus, 'Mit falschen Verteilungs-"Götzen" zu echten Standort-problemen', *WSI-Mitteilungen* 10/1996, 597 ff.

Scharpf, Fritz, 'Economic Integration, Democracy and the Welfare State', *Journal of European Public Policy* 4/1 (1997), 18–36.

Schäuble, Wolfgang, and Lamers, Karl, 'Überlegungen zur Europäischen Politik,' (Bonn: CDU/CSU Fraktion des Deutschen Bundestages, 1 Sept. 1994), reproduced in English as 'Reflections on European Policy,' in Karl Lamers, *A German Agenda for the European Union* (London: Federal Trust and Konrad Adenauer Stiftung, 1994).

Scheel, Walter, 'Aktuelle Probleme der Außenpolitik der Bundesrepublik Deutschland', *Europa-Archiv* 13 (1973), 433–8.

Scherstjanoi, Elke, ' "In 14 Tagen werden Sie vielleicht keinen Staat mehr haben". Vladimir Semenov und der 17. Juni 1953', *Deutschland-Archiv* 31/6 (1998), 907–37.

Schertz, Adrian W., *Die Deutschlandpolitik Kennedys und Johnsons: Unter-schiedliche Ansätze innerhalb der amerikanischen Regierung* (Cologne: Böhlau, 1992).

Schevardnadze, Eduard, *The Future Belongs to Freedom* (London: Sinclair-Stevenson, 1991).

Schirdewan, Karl, *Aufstand gegen Ulbricht. Im Kampf um politische Kurskorrektur, gegen stalinistische, dogmatische Politik* (Berlin: Aufbau Taschenbuch Verlag, 1994).

Schmidt, Gustav (ed.), *Grossbritannien und Europa—Grossbritannien in Europa: Sicherheitsbelange und Wirtschaftsfragen in der britischen Europapolitik nach dem Zweiten Weltkrieg* (Bochum: Brockmeyer, 1989).

Schmidt, Gustav, '"Tying" (West) Germany into the West—But to What? NATO? WEU? The European Community?', in C. Wurm (ed.), *Western Europe and Germany: The Beginnings of European Integration, 1945–1960* (Oxford: Berg, 1995), 137–74.

—— Zwischen Bündnissicherung und priviligierter Partnerschaft: die deutsch-britschen Beziehungen und die Vereinigten Staaten von Amerika, 1955–1963 (Bochum: Brockmeyer, 1995).

Schmidt, Helmut, *Die Deutschen und ihre Nachbarn*, paperback edn. (Berlin: Siedler, 1992).

Schmidt, Klaus-Peter, *Die Europäische Gemeinschaft aus der Sicht der DDR, 1957–1989*, 2nd edn. (Hamburg: Kovac, 1995).

Schmidt, Peter, 'Germany, France and NATO', *Strategic Studies Institute; Strategic Outreach Roundtable Paper and Conference Report* (US Army War College, Oct. 1994).

Schönfelder, Wilhelm and Thiel, Elke, *Ein Markt—Eine Währung. Die Verhandlungen zur Europäischen Wirtschafts- und Währungsunion* (Baden-Baden: Nomos Verlag, 1994).

Schröder, Gerhard, Chancellor of the FRG, Government Policy Statement on the Conclusion of the EU Summit meeting in Berlin and on the NATO operation in Yugoslavia (Bonn, 26 March 1999).

Schröder, Ulrich, 'Corporate Governance in Germany: The Changing Role of the Banks', *German Politics* 5/3 (1996), 356–70.

Schubert, Venanz (ed.), *Deutschland in Europa: Wiedervereinigung und Integration* (St Ottilien: EOS Verlag, 1996).

Schuetze, Walter P., 'What is the future of mutual recognition of financial statements and is comparability really necessary?', *The European Accounting Review* 3/2 (1994), 330–4.

Schulte, Gregory L., 'Bringing Peace to Bosnia: A Basis for the Future?', *NATO Review* 45/2 (1997), 22–6.

Schwartz, Thomas A., 'Victories and Defeats in the Long Twilight Struggle: The United States and Western Europe in the 1960s', in Diane Kunz (ed.), *The Diplomacy of the Crucial Decade: American Foreign Policy in the 1960s* (New York: Columbia University Press, 1994), 115–48.

—— 'The Berlin Crisis and the Cold War', *Diplomatic History* 21 (1997), 139–48.

Schwarz, Hans-Peter, 'Germany's National and European Interests', *Daedalus* 123/2 (1994), 81–106 in Arnulf Baring (ed.), *Germany's New Position in Europe: Problems and Perspectives* (Oxford: Berg, 1994), 107–30.

Seckler, Günter, 'Germany', in David Alexander and Simon Archer (eds.), *European Accounting Guide*, 2nd edn. (Orlando, Fla.: Harcourt Brace and Company, 1995).

Secretary of State for Foreign and Commnwealth Affairs, 'A Partnership of Nations: The British Approach to the European Union Intergovernmental Conference', Cm.3181 (London: HMSO, 1996).

Seidelmann, Reimund, 'Costs, Risks, and Benefits of a Global Military Capability for the European Union', *Defence and Peace Economics* 8 (1997), 123–43.

—— 'NATO's Enlargement as a Policy of Lost Opportunities', *Journal of European Integration* 20/2–3 (1997), 233–46.

Seldon, Anthony (with Lewis Baston), *Major: a political life* (London: Weidenfeld and Nicholson, 1997).

Serre, Françoise de la, 'The Scope of National Adaptation to EPC', in Pijpers, Alfred, Regelsberger, Elfriede, and Wessels, Wolfgang (eds.), *European Political Cooperation, in the 1980s: A Common Foreign Policy for Western Europe* (Dordrecht: Martinus Nijhoff, 1988).

Simonian, Haig, *The Privileged Partnership: Franco-German Relations in the European Community* (Oxford: Clarendon Press, 1985).

Sloan, Stanley, 'Transatlantic relations: Stormy Weather on the Way to Enlargement', *NATO Review* 45/5 (1997), 12–7.

Smith, Geoffrey, *Reagan and Thatcher* (New York: W. W. Norton, 1991).

Smith, Julie, 'The 1975 Referendum', *Journal of European Integration History* 5 (1999), 41–56.

Smyser, W. R., *Germany and America: New Identities, Fateful Rift?* (Boulder, Colo.: Westview Press, 1994).

Solano, Javier, 'Preparing for the Madrid Summit', *NATO Review* 45/2 (1997), 3–6.

Sommer, Theo, 'Europe and the American Connection', *Foreign Affairs* 58/3 (1980), 622–36.

—— 'Britain and the European Community: A German View', *The World Today* (April 1983), 129–36.

Soskice, David, 'German Technology Policy, Innovation and National Institutional Frameworks', *Industry and Innovation* 4/1 (1997), 75–96.

Soutou, Georges-Henri, L'Alliance Incertaine: les rapports politico-strategiques franco-allemands, 1954–1996 (Paris: Fayard, 1996).

—— 'Le General de Gaulle et le Plan Fouchet d'Union Politique Europeenne: un Projet Strategique', in A. Deighton and A. S. Milward (eds.), *The European Economic Community, 1957–1963: Widening, Deepening, Acceleration* (Bonn: Nomos, 1999).

Spanger, Hans-Joachim Spanger, *The GDR in East–West Relations*, Adelphi Papers 240 (London: Brassey's, 1989).

Speidell, Lawrence S., *International Accounting Standards versus U.S. GAAP Should Analysts Care?*, paper presented at the 1997 Annual Conference of the Association for Investment Management and Research, New Orleans, May 1997.

Spence, David, 'Enlargement without Accession: The EC's Response to German Unification', *RIIA Discussion Papers* 35 (1991).

—— 'The European Community and German Unification', in Charlie Jeffery and Roland Sturm (eds.), *Federalism, Unification and European Integration* (London: Frank Cass, 1993), 136–63.

Sperling, James and Kirchner, Emil J. (eds.), *Recasting the European Order: Security Architectures and Economic Co-operation* (Manchester: Manchester University Press, 1997).

—— and —— 'The security architectures and institutional futures of post-1989 Europe', *Journal of European Public Policy* 4/2 (June, 1997), 155–70.

Staritz, Dietrich, *Geschichte der DDR 1949–1990*, expanded edn. (Darmstadt: WGB, 1996).

Steinherr, Alfred (ed.), *Thirty Years of European Monetary Integration: From the Werner Plan to EMU* (London: Longman, 1994).

Steininger, Rolf, 'Germany after 1945: Divided and Integrated or United and Neutral?', *German History* 7 (1989), 5 ff.

—— *The German Question: The Stalin Note of 1952 and the problem of reunification* (New York: Columbia University Press, 1990).

Stelkens, Jochen, 'Machtwechsel in Ost-Berlin. Der Sturz Walter Ulbrichts', *Vierteljahrshefte für Zeitgeschichte* 45 (1997), 503–33.

Stepanovsky, Jiri, 'International Relations in Central and Eastern Europe,' in Forschungsinstitut der Deutschen Gesellschaft für Auswärtige Politik, *Central and Eastern Europe in Transition* (Bonn: DGFAP, 1991), 4–6.

Stephens, Philip, *Politics and the Pound. The Tories, the Economy and Europe* (London: Macmillan, 1996).

Stevenson, Richard W., *The Rise and Fall of Détente, 1953–1984* (Basingstoke: Macmillan, 1985).

Stirk, Peter M. R., *A History of European Integration since 1914* (London: Pinter, 1996).

Storf, Otto, *Business Risks and Opportunities in Eastern Europe and the Soviet Union*, paper for conference of the Centre for European Policy Studies (Brussels, Nov. 1990).

Streeck, Wolfgang, 'More Uncertainties: German Unions Facing 1992', *Industrial Relations* 30/3 (1991), 317–48.

—— 'Citizenship Under Regime Competition: The Case of the European Works Councils', *European Integration on-line Papers* (EIoP) 1/005 (1997) [http://eiop.or.at/eiop/texte/1997–005a.htm, 1–24].

—— 'German Capitalism: Does it Exist? Can it Survive?', *New Political Economy* 2/2 (1997), 237–56.

—— 'Industrial Citizenship under Regime Competition: the Case of the European Works Councils', *Journal of European Public Policy* 4/4 (1997) 643–64.

—— and Schmitter, Philippe C., 'From National Corporatism to Transnational Pluralism: Organized Interests in the Single European Market', *Politics and Society* 19/2 (1991), 133–64.

Stuart, Mark, *Douglas Hurd the Public Servant: an authorised biography* (Edinburgh: Mainstream Publishing, 1998).

Stürmer, Michael, 'Deutschlandpolitik, Ostpolitik and the Western Alliance: German Perspectives on Détente', in Kenneth Dyson (ed.), *European Détente* (London: Pinter, 1986).

Süssmuth, Hans, and Peters, Christoph, 'Die Vereinigung Deutschlands im Spiegel der englischen Tageszeitungen. Eine Momentaufnahme', in Hans Süssmuth (ed.), *Deutschlandbilder* (Baden-Baden: Nomos, 1996).

Talbott, Strobe (ed.), *Khrushchev Remembers*, vol. 2: *The Last Testament* (London: Deutsch, 1974).

Taylor, A. J. P., *The Course of German History*, rev. edn. (New York: Capricorn Books, 1962).

Teltschik, Horst, *329 Tage. Innenansichten der Einigung* (Berlin: Siedler, 1991).

Tew, Brian, 'Onwards to EMU', in Dennis Swann (ed.), *The Single European Market and Beyond: A Study of the Wider Implications of the Single European Act* (London: Routledge, 1992), 193–213.

Thatcher, Margaret, *Britain and Europe*, text of the speech delivered in Bruges by the Prime Minister on 20th September 1988 (London: Conservative Central Office, 1988).

—— *The Downing Street Years* (New York and London: Harper Collins, 1993; pbk. edn. 1995).

—— 'When Powell was Right', *Daily Telegraph*, 23/11/1998.

Thekaekara, Mari Marcel, 'The View from the Ground' (Debate on Global Free Trade), *New Political Economy* 1/1 (1996), 115–8.

Thorell, Per, and Whittington, Geoffrey, 'The Harmonization of Accounting within the EU: Problems, Perspectives and Strategies', *The European Accounting Review* 3/2 (1994), 215–39.

Thygesen, Niels, 'The Delors Report and European Economic and Monetary Union', *International Affairs* 65/4 (1989), 637–52.

Trachtenberg, Marc, *A Constructed Peace: The Making of the European Settlement, 1945–1963* (Princeton: Princeton University Press, 1999).

Trautmann, Günter (ed.), *Die häßlichen Deutschen? Deutschland im Spiegel der westlichen und östlichen Nachbarn* (Darmstadt: Wissenschaftliche Buchgesellschaft, 1990).

Traynor, Ian, and Bates, Stephen, 'Iraq Crisis: Dutch Attack Blair for Siding with US', *The Guardian*, 19/2/1998.

Treverton, Gregory, F., *America, Germany, and the Future of Europe* (Princeton: Princeton University Press, 1992).

Tugendhat, Christopher, *Making Sense of Europe* (Harmondsworth: Pelican Books, 1987).

Turner, Ian D. (ed.), *Reconstruction in Postwar Germany: British Occupation Policy and the Western Zones, 1945–1955* (Oxford: Berg, 1989).

Twine, Fred, *Citizenship and Social Rights: The Interdependence of Self and Society* (London: Sage, 1994).

Unger, Frank, Wehr, Andreas, and Schönwälder, Karen, *New Democrats, New Labour, Neue Sozialdemokraten* (Berlin: Elefanten Press, 1998).

Unwin, Peter, *Hearts, Minds and Interests: Britain's Place in the World* (London: Profile, 1998).

Urban, George R., *Diplomacy and Disillusion at the Court of Margaret Thatcher: An Insider's View* (London: I. B. Tauris, 1996).

Urwin, Derek W., *The Community of Europe: A History of European Integration since 1945*, 2nd edn. (London: Longman, 1995).

Uterwedde, Henrik, 'Le Modèle allemand. Fin ou recommencement?', *Documents. Revue des Questions Allemandes* 3 (1996), 8–14.

Vansittart, Robert, *Black Record: Germans Past and Present* (pamphlet, London, 1941).

Varsori, Antonio (ed.), *Europe, 1945–1990s: The End of an Era?* (London: Macmillan, 1995).

Vernet, Daniel, 'Europäisches Deutschland oder deutsches Europa?', *Internationale Politik* 52/2 (Feb. 1997), 15–22.

Visser, Jelle and van Ruysseveldt, Joris, 'From Pluralism to Where? Industrial Relations in Great Britain', in Joris van Ruysseveldt and Jelle Visser (eds.), *Industrial Relations in Europe: Traditions and Transitions* (London: Sage in association with the Open University of the Netherlands, 1996), 42–81.

Visser, Jelle and van Ruysseveldt, Joris, 'Robust Corporatism, Still? Industrial Relations in Germany', in Joris van Ruysseveldt and Jelle Visser (eds.), *Industrial Relations in Europe: Traditions and Transitions* (London: Sage in association with the Open University of the Netherlands, 1996), 124–74.

Volle, Angelika, 'Deutsch-Britische Beziehungen. Eine Untersuchung des bilateralen Verhältnisses [. . .]' (Bonn: unpub. Ph.D. diss., 1976).

—— *Grossbritannien und der Europäische Einigungsprozess* (Bonn: Europa Union Verlag, 1989).

Wallace, Helen, 'The British Presidency of the EC Council of Ministers: The Opportunity to Persuade', *International Affairs* 62/4 (Autumn 1986), 583–99.

—— 'At Odds with Europe,' *Political Studies* 45/4 (1997), 677–88.

Wallace, William, 'European Defence Cooperation: The Reopening Debate', *Survival*, 26/6 (1984), 251–61.

—— *Britain's Bilateral Links Within Western Europe* (London: RIIA, 1984).

—— 'What Price Independence? Sovereignty and interdependence in British politics', *International Affairs* 62/3 (1986), 367–89.

Wallerstein, Michael, Golden, Miriam, and Lange, Peter, 'Unions, Employers' Associations and Wage-Setting Institutions in Northern and Central Europe 1950–92', *Industrial and Labor Relations Review* 50/3 (1997), 379–98.

Walters, Vernon A., *Die Vereinigung war voraussehbar. Hinter den Kulissen eines entscheidenden Jahres* (Berlin: Siedler, 1994).

Warner, Isabel, 'The Foreign Office View of Macmillan's Visit to Moscow', in *Foreign and Commonwealth Office, Historical Branch, Occasional Papers, No. 7* (London, 1993), 24–5.

Watson, Alan, 'Thatcher and Kohl: Old Rivalries Revisited' in M. Bond, J. Smith, and W. Wallace (eds.), *Eminent Europeans: Personalities Who Shaped Contemporary Europe* (London: Greycoat, 1996), 264–84.

Watt, Donald Cameron, *Britain looks to Germany: British Opinion and Policy towards Germany since 1945* (London: O. Wolff, 1965).

—— 'Anglo-German Relations Today and Tomorrow', in K. Kaiser and R. Morgan (eds.), *Britain and West Germany: Changing Societies and the Future of Foreign Policy* (London: Oxford University Press, 1971), 203–18.

Weale, Albert, 'Environmental Rules and Rule-Making in the European Union', *Journal of European Public Policy* 3 (1996), 594–611.

Webber, Douglas (ed.), *The Franco-German Relationship in the European Union* (London: Routledge, 1999).

Weber, Hajo, 'The German Associations: Structure and Erosion?', in Robert J. Bennett (ed.), *Trade Associations in Britain and Germany*, 46–51.

Weber, Hermann, *Geschichte der DDR*, 2nd edn. (Munich: dtv, 1986).

Weidenfeld, Werner, *Was ändert die Einheit? Deutschlands Standort in Europa* (Gütersloh: Bertelsmann, 1993).

Weise, Christian, 'Der EU-Beitritt ostmitteleuropäischer Staaten: Ökonomische Chancen und Reformbedarf für die EU,' *Integration*, 20/3 (1997), 175–90.

Weiss, Manfred, 'Labour Law and Industrial Relations in Europe 1992: A German Perspective', *Comparative Labor Law Journal* 11/4 (1990), 411–24.

Well, Günther van, 'Die europäische Einigung und die USA', *Europa-Archiv* 46/18 (1991), 527–36.

Wemdon, Bryan, 'British Trade Union Responses to European Integration', *Journal of European Public Policy* 1/2 (1994), 243–61.

Wenger, Andreas, 'Kennedy, Chhruschtschow und das gemeinsame Interesse der Supermächte am Status quo in Europa', in *Vierteljahrshefte für Zeitgeschichte* 46 (1998), 69–99.

Wettig, Gerhard, 'Stalin and German Reunification: Archival Evidence on Soviet Foreign Policy in Spring 1952,' *Historical Journal* 37/2 (1994), 411–9.

—— *Bereitschaft zu Einheit in Freiheit? Die sowjetische Deutschland-Politik 1945–1955* (Munich: Olzog, 1999).

White, Brian, 'Britain and East–West Relations', in Michael Smith, Steve Smith, and Brian White (eds.), *British Foreign Policy: Tradition, Change and Transformation* (London: Unwin Hyman, 1988), 149–67.

Whittingon, Geoffrey, 'Accounting Standard Setting in the UK after 20 Years: A Critique of the Dearing and Solomons Reports', *Accounting and Business Research* 19/75 (1989), 195–205.

—— 'Tax Policy and Accounting Standards', *British Tax Review* 5 (1995), 452–6.

Wilkes, George (ed.), *Britain's Failure to Enter the European Community, 1961–63: The Enlargement Negotiations and Crises in European, Atlantic and Commonwealth Relations* (Ilford, Essex: Frank Cass, 1997).

Wilks, Stephen R. M., 'Regulatory Compliance and Capitalist Diversity in Europe', *Journal of European Public Policy* 3 (1996), 536–59.

Wilks, Stuart, 'Britain and Europe: Awkward Partner or Awkward State?', *Politics* 16/3 (1996), 159–65.

Williams, Alan Lee, and Williams, Geoffrey Lee, 'Nato's Future in the Balance: Time for a Rethink?', *University Advisory Committee of the Atlantic Council of the United Kingdom* (London, 1995).

Williams, Francis, *A Prime Minister Remembers: The Pre-War and Post-War Memoirs of the Rt Hon Earl of Attlee* (London: Heinemann, 1961).

Williamson, David G., *The British in Germany 1918–1931: The Reluctant Occupiers* (Oxford: Berg, 1991).

Willman, Paul, 'Merger Propensity and Merger Outcomes among British Unions, 1986–1995', *Industrial Relations Journal* 27/4 (1996), 331–8.

Wilson, Allister, 'Harmonisation: Is It Now or Never for Europe?', *Accountancy* (Nov. 1994), 98.

Wilson, Harold, *The Labour Government, 1964–70: A Personal Record* (London: Weidenfeld & Nicolson & Michael Joseph, 1971).

Wood, Michael, 'Being a Good European: Britain Leads the EU in Utility Regulation' *New Economy* 5 (1998), 53–7.

Wood, Stephen, *Germany, Europe and the Persistence of Nations: Transformation, interests and identity, 1989–1996* (Aldershot: Ashgate, 1998).

Woodward, Susan L., *Balkan Tragedy: Chaos and Dissolution after the cold war* (Washington, DC: Brookings Institution, 1995).

Woolcock, Stephen, 'Competition between rules' in D. G. Mayes (ed.), *The Evolution of the Single European Market* (Cheltenham: Edward Elgar, 1997), 66–86.

Woolcock, Stephen, Hodges, Michael, and Schreiber, Kristin, *Britain, Germany and 1992: the limits of deregulation* (London: Pinter, 1990).

Woyke, Wichard, 'Außenpolitische Kontinuität—aber auch Veränderungen. Fünf Jahre deutsche Außenpolitik', in Ralf Altenhof and Ekhard Jesse (eds.), *Das wiedervereinigte Deutschland. Zwischenbilanz und Perspektiven* (Munich: Droste Verlag, 1995), 363–421.

Wright, Jonathan C. R., 'The Role of Britain in West German Foreign Policy since 1949', *German Politics* 5/1 (April 1996), 26–42.

Wurm, Clemens (ed.), *Western Europe and Germany: The Beginnings of European Integration, 1945–1960* (Oxford: Berg, 1995).

Wyllie, James H., *European Security in the New Political Environment* (Harlow: Addison Wesley Longman, 1997).

Young, Hugo, *This Blessed Plot: Britain and Europe from Churchill to Blair* (London: Macmillan, 1998).

Young, John W., *Britain and European Unity, 1945–92* (Basingstoke: Macmillan, 1993).

Zelikow, Philip and Rice, Condoleezza, *Germany Unified and Europe Transformed: A Study in Statecraft* (Cambridge, Mass.: Harvard University Press, 1995).

Ziebura, Gilbert, *Die deutsch-französischen Beziehungen 1945–1995. Mythen und Realitäten* (Stuttgart: Neske, 1997).

Ziegler, Philip, *Wilson: The Authorised Life of Lord Wilson of Rievaulx* (London: Weidenfeld and Nicolson, 1993).

Zubok, Vladislav M., 'Khrushchev and the Berlin Crisis (1958–1962)', *Cold War International History Project*, Working Paper No. 6 (1993).

Zwahr, Hartmut, *Ende einer Selbstzerstörung: Leipzig und die Revolution in der DDR* (Göttingen: Vandenhoeck & Ruprecht, 1993).

INDEX